COGNITIVE ASPECTS OF
ELECTRONIC TEXT PROCESSING

COGNITIVE ASPECTS OF
ELECTRONIC TEXT PROCESSING

Herre van Oostendorp
and Sjaak de Mul (Eds.)

Advances in Discourse
Processes
Volume LVIII

Ablex Publishing Corporation
Norwood, New Jersey

Printed in the United States of America

Library of Congress Cataloging-in-Publication Data

Cognitive aspects of electronic text processing / Herre van
    Oostendorp, Sjaak de Mul.
        p.   cm. — (Advances in discourse processes ; v. 58)
    Includes bibliographical references and index.
    ISBN 1-56750-235-0 (cloth). — ISBN 1-56750-236-9 (pbk.)
    1. Text processing (Computer science)   2. Cognition.
    I. Oostendorp, Herre van.   II. Mul, de Sjaak.   III. Series.
QA76.9.T48C64   1996
005—dc20   96-4090
                                                             CIP

Ablex Publishing Corporation
355 Chestnut Street
Norwood, New Jersey 07648

Contents

List of Contributors   vii

Series Preface   ix

1   Introduction: Cognitive Aspects of Electronic
Text Processing   1
    Herre van Oostendorp and Sjaak de Mul

2   Reading, Writing, and Learning in Hypermedia
Environments   7
    Susan R. Goldman

3   Bringing Insights from Reading Research to Research
on Electronic Learning Environments   43
    Donald J. Leu, Jr. and David Reinking

4   Comprehending Electronic Text   77
    Mark G. Gillingham

5   TIMS: A Framework for the Design of Usable
Electronic Text   99
    Andrew Dillon

6   A Dialogue Perspective on Electronic Mail:
Implications for Interface Design   121
    Kerstin Severinson Eklundh

7   The Paper Model for Computer-based Writing   137
    Kerstin Severinson Eklundh, Ann Fatton,
and Staffan Romberger

8   Interface Design and Optimization of Reading
of Continuous Text   161
    Paul Muter

9   Designing Screens for Learning   181
        R. Scott Grabinger and Rionda Osman-Jouchoux

10 What Makes a Good Hypertext?   213
        Cliff McKnight

11 Task and Activity Models in Hypertext Usage   239
        Jean-François Rouet and André Tricot

12 Lessons Learned from Redesigning Hypertext
    User Interfaces   265
        Keith Instone, Barbee Teasley, and Laura Leventhal

13 Technology, Representation, and Cognition:
    The Prefiguring of Knowledge in Cognitive
    Flexibility Hypertexts   287
        Punyashloke Mishra, Rand J. Spiro,
        and Paul J. Feltovich

Author Index   307

Subject Index   317

List of Contributors

Sjaak de Mul
Utrecht University
Department of Psychonomics
Psychological Laboratory
Heidelberglaan 2
3584 CS Utrecht
The Netherlands
email: oostendorp@fsw.ruu.nl

Andrew Dillon
School of Library and Information
    Science
400 East 7th Street
Indiana University
Bloomington, IN 47405
email: adillon@ucs.indiana.edu

Kerstin S. Eklundh
Interaction and Presentation
    Laboratory
Department of Computer Science
Royal Institute of Technology
S-100 44 Stockholm, Sweden
email: kse@nada.kth.se

Ann Fatton
Interaction and Presentation
    Laboratory
Department of Computer Science
Royal Institute of Technology
S-100 44 Stockholm, Sweden
email: kse@nada.kth.se

Paul J. Feltovich
Department of Educational Psychology
210 Education Building
University of Illinois at Urbana-
    Champaign
1310 S. 6th Street
Urbana, IL 61801
email: rspiro@uxl.cso.uiuc.edu

Mark G. Gillingham
Michigan State University
340 Erickson Hall
East Lansing, MI 48824
email: markgill@MSU.edu

Susan R. Goldman
Learning Technology Center
Box 45
Peabody College
Vanderbilt University
Nashville, TN 37203
email: goldmans@ctrvax.vanderbilt.edu

R. Scott Grabinger
Division of Instructional Technology
University of Colorado
Campus Box 106
P.O. Box 173364
Denver, CO 80217-3364
email: sgrabing@carbon.cudenver.edu

Keith Instone
Computer-Human Interaction
    Laboratory
Department of Computer Science
Bowling Green State University
Bowling Green, OH 43403
email: instone@cs.bgsu.edu

Donald J. Leu, Jr.
School of Education
Syracuse University
170 Huntington Hall
Syracuse, NY 13244-2340
email: djleu@suvm.syr.edu

Laura Leventhal
Computer-Human Interaction
    Laboratory
Department of Computer Science
Bowling Green State University
Bowling Green, OH 43403
email: instone@cs.bgsu.edu

Cliff McKnight
Department of Information and Library
    Studies
Loughborough University of Technology
Loughborough, Leicestershire,
    LE11 3TU
United Kingdom
email: c.mcknight@lut.ac.uk

Punyashloke Mishra
Department of Educational Psychology
210 Education Building
University of Illinois at Urbana-
    Champaign
1310 S. 6th Street
Urbana, IL 61801
email: rspiro@uxl.cso.uiuc.edu

Paul Muter
Department of Psychology
University of Toronto
Toronto, Ont.
Canada M5S 1A1
email: muter@psych.toronto.edu

Rionda Osman-Jouchoux
Division of Instructional Technology
University of Colorado
Campus Box 106
P.O. Box 173364
Denver, CO 80217-3364
email: sgrabing@carbon.cudenver.edu

David Reinking
School of Education
Syracuse University
170 Huntington Hall
Syracuse, NY 13244-2340
email: djleu@suvm.syr.edu

Staffan Romberger
Interaction and Presentation
    Laboratory
Department of Computer Science
Royal Institute of Technology
S-100 44 Stockholm, Sweden
email: kse@nada.kth.se

Jean-Francois Rouet
Language and Communications
    Laboratory
Universite de Poitiers
95 Avenue du Recteur Pineau
86022 Poitiers Cedex
France
email: jean-francois.rouet@imag.fr

Rand J. Spiro
Department of Educational Psychology
210 Education Building
University of Illinois at Urbana-
    Champaign
1310 S. 6th Street
Urbana, IL 61801
email: rspiro@uxl.cso.uiuc.edu

Barbee Teasley
Computer-Human Interaction
    Laboratory
Department of Computer Science
Bowling Green State University
Bowling Green, OH 43403
email: instone@cs.bgsu.edu

Andre Tricot
Language and Communications
    Laboratory
Universite de Poitiers
95 Avenue du Recteur Pineau
86022 Poitiers Cedex
France
email: jean-francois.rouet@imag.fr

Herre van Oostendorp
Utrecht University
Department of Psychonomics
Psychological Laboratory
Heidelberglaan 2
3584 CS Utrecht
The Netherlands
email: oostendorp@fsw.ruu.nl

Series Preface

Roy O. Freedle

Series Editor

This series of volumes provides a forum for the cross-fertilization of ideas from a diverse number of disciplines, all of which share a common interest in discourse—be it prose comprehension and recall, dialogue analysis, text grammar construction, computer simulation of natural language, cross cultural comparisons of communicative competence or other related topics. The problems posed by multisentence contexts and the methods required to investigate them, while not always unique to discourse, are still sufficiently distinct as to benefit from the organized model of scientific interaction made possible by this series. Scholars working in the discourse area from the perspective of sociolinguistics, psycholinguistics, ethnomethodology and the sociology of language, educational psychology (e.g., teacher-student interaction), the philosophy of language, computational linguistics, and related subareas are invited to submit manuscripts of monograph or book length to the series editor. Edited collections of original papers resulting from conferences will also be considered.

VOLUMES IN THE SERIES

Vol. I   Discourse Production and Comprehension. Roy O. Freedle (Ed.), 1977.

Vol. II   New Directions in Discourse Processing. Roy O. Freedle (Ed.), 1979.

Vol. III   The Pear Stories, Cognitive, Cultural, and Linguistic Aspects of Narrative Production. Wallace L. Chafe (Ed.), 1980

Vol. IV   Text, Discourse and Process: Toward a Multidisciplinary Science of Texts. Robert de Beaugrande, 1980.

Vol. V   Ethnography and Language in Educational Settings. Judith Green & Cynthia Wallat (Eds.), 1981.

Vol. VI   Latino Language and Communicative Behavior. Richard P. Duran (Ed.), 1981.

Vol. VII   Narrative, Literacy and Face in Interethnic Communication. Ron Scollon & Suzanne Scollon, 1981.

Vol. VIII   Linguistics and the Professions. Robert J. DiPietro (Ed.), 1982.

Vol. IX   Spoken and Written Language: Exploring Orality and Literacy. Deborah Tannen (Ed.), 1982.

Vol. X   Developmental Issues in Discourse. Jonathan Fine & Roy O. Freedle (Eds.), 1983.

Vol. XI   Text Production: Toward a Science of Composition. Robert de Beaugrande, 1984.

Vol. XII   Coherence in Spoken and Written Discourse. Deborah Tannen (Ed.), 1984.

Vol. XIII   The Development of Oral and Written Language in Social Contexts. Anthony D. Pellegrini & Thomas D. Yawkey (Eds.), 1984.

Vol. XIV   What People Say They Do With Words. Jeff Verschueren, 1985.

Vol. XV   Systemic Perspectives on Discourse, Volume 1: Selected Theoretical Papers from the 9th International Systemic Workshop. James D. Benson & William S. Greaves (Eds.), 1985.

Vol. XVI   Systemic Perspectives on Discourse, Volume 2: Selected Applied Papers from the 9th International Systemic Workshop. James D. Benson & William S. Greaves (Eds.), 1985.

Vol. XVII   Structures and Procedures of Implicit Knowledge. Arthur C. Graesser & Leslie F. Clark, 1985.

Vol. XVIII   Contexts of Reading. Carolyn N. Hedley & Anthony N. Baratta (Eds.), 1985.

Vol. XIX   Discourse and Institutional Authority: Medicine, Education, and Law. Sue Fisher & Alexandra Dundas Todd (Eds.), 1986.

Vol. XX   Evidentiality: The Linguistic Coding of Epistemology. Wallace Chafe & Johanna Nichols (Eds.), 1986.

Vol. XXI   The Acquisition of Literacy: Ethnographic Perspectives. Bambi B. Schieffelin & Perry Gilmore (Eds.), 1986.

Vol. XXII   Cognitive and Linguistic Analyses of Test Performance. Roy O. Freedle & Richard P. Duran (Eds.), 1987.

Vol. XXIII   Linguistic Action: Some Empirical-Conceptual Studies. Jef Verschueren (Ed.), 1987.

Vol. XXIV   Text and Epistemology. William Frawley, 1987.

Vol. XXV   Second Language Discourse: A Textbook of Current Research. Jonathan Fine (Ed.), 1988.

Vol. XXVI   Systemic Functional Approaches to Discourse. James D. Benson & William S. Greaves (Eds.), 1988.

Vol. XXVII   Language Development: Learning Language, Learning Culture. Ruqaiya Hasan & James Martin (Eds.), 1989.

Vol. XXVIII   Multiple Perspective Analyses of Classroom Discourse. Judith L. Green & Judith O. Harker (Eds.), 1988.

Vol. XXIX   Linguistics in Context: Connecting Observation and Understanding. Deborah Tannen (Ed.), 1988.

Vol. XXX   Gender and Discourse: The Power of Talk. Alexandra D. Todd & Sue Fisher (Eds.), 1988.

Vol. XXXI   Cross-Cultural Pragmatics: Requests and Apologies. Shoshana Blum-Kulka, Juliane House & Gabriele Kasper (Eds.), 1989.

Vol. XXXII   Collegial Discourse. Allen D. Grimshaw, 1989.

Vol. XXXIII   Task, Talk, and Text in the Operating Room: A Study in Medical Discourse. Catherine Johnson Pettinari, 1988.

Vol. XXXIV   The Presence of Thought. Introspective Accounts of Reading and Writing. Marilyn S. Sternglass, 1988.

Vol. XXXV   Japanese Conversation: Self-Contextualization Through Structure and Interactional Management. Senko Kumiya Maynard, 1989.

Vol. XXXVI   Cognitive Assessment of Language and Math Outcomes. Sue Legg & James Algina (Eds.), 1990.

Vol. XXXVII   Pragmatics, Discourse and Text: Some Systematically Inspired Approaches. Erich H. Steiner and Robert Veltman (Eds.), 1988.

Vol. XXXVIII   Conversational Organization and Its Development. Bruce Dorval (Ed.), 1990.

Vol. XXXIX   Developing Discourse Practice in Adolescence and Adulthood. Richard Beach & Susan Hynds (Eds.), 1990.

Vol. XL   Text and Texture: Patterns of Cohesion. Sally Stoddard, 1991.

Vol. XLI   Conversation Analysis of a Martial Therapy Session: The Pursuit of a Therapeutic Agenda. Jerry Edward Gale, 1991.

Vol. XLII   Medical Discourse and Systemic Frames of Comprehension. Ronald J. Chenail, 1991.

Vol. XLIII   What's Going On Here? Complementary Studies of Professional Talk. Allen Day Grimshaw et al., 1994.

Vol. XLIV   Ambiguous Harmony: Family Talk in America. Hervé Varenne, 1992.

Vol. XLV   American and Japanese Business Discourse: A Comparison of Interactional Styles. Haru Yamada, 1992.

Vol. XLVI   Scientific Discourse: An Analysis of Biomedical Journal Articles' Discussion Sections. Betty Lou DuBois, 1995.

Vol. XLVII   Repetition in Discourse: Interdisciplinary Perspectives, Volume 1. Barbara Johnstone (Ed.), 1994.

Vol. XLVIII   Repetition in Discourse: Interdisciplinary Perspectives, Volume 2. Barbara Johnstone (Ed.), 1994.

Vol. XLIX   Word Choice and Narration in Academic Lectures: An Essay on Artistic Language Use. Barbar Strodt-López, 1993.

Vol. L   Discourse in Society Systemic Functional Perspectives. Peter H. Fries and Michael Gregory (Eds.), 1995.

Vol. LI   How Language Works. Jonathan Fine, 1993.

Vol. LII   Empirical Approaches to Literature and Aesthetics. Roger Kreuz & Mary MacNealy (Eds.), 1995.

Vol. LIII   Naturalistic Text Comprehension. Herre van Oostendorp & Rolf A. Zwaan (Eds.), 1994.

Vol. LIV   Cognition, Empathy, & Interaction: Floor Management of English and Japanese Conversation. Reiko Hayashi, 1995.

Vol. LV   Caged in Our Own Signs: A Book About Semiotics. Kyong Liong Kim, 1996.

Vol. LVI   Literate Apprenticeships: The Emergence of Language in the Preschool Years. Kenneth Reeder, Jon Shapiro, Rita Watson, & Hillel Goelman (Eds.), 1996.

Vol. LVII   Meaning and Form: Systemic Functional Interpretations. Margaret Berry, Christopher Butler, Robin Fawcett, & Guowen Huang (Eds.), 1996.

Vol. LVIII   Cognitive Aspects of Electronic Text Processing. Herre van Oostendorp & Sjaak de Mul (Eds.), 1996.

Vol. LIX   Modeling Discourse Topic: Sequential Relations and Strategies in Expository Text. Dionysis Goutsos, 1996.

Vol. LX   Colloquium: Dilemmas of Academic Discourse. Karen Tracy, 1996.

Vol. LXI   New Foundations for a Science of Texts. Robert de Beaugrande, 1996.

1

Introduction: Cognitive Aspects of Electronic Text Processing

Herre Van Oostendorp
Sjaak de Mul

Utrecht University, The Netherlands

INTRODUCTION

This book is about the cognitive aspects of discourse processing in an electronic environment. These aspects will be encountered and prove to be crucial in almost all of the activities that take place in such an environment: reading, learning and writing, making annotations to electronic text in journals, searching and retrieving text information, reading and navigating in hypertext, and communicating by electronic mail (e-mail).

The type of information considered in this volume is the electronic document, consisting of linear text as well as nonlinear text, such as hypertext. These information sources are used in a variety of applications: e-mail applications, electronic journal browsers, word processors in which reading and composing continuous electronic text is combined, hypertext systems, and so forth. Special attention is given to interface characteristics and interface design for these applications.

AIMS OF THE BOOK

Related to this last-mentioned focus of attention, at least two points of view will be dealt with. First, there is the perspective of cognitive science. Psychological (and linguistic) studies on how people read and learn from printed text provide basic models for electronic text processing. However, it is not clear whether text processing in an electronic environment involves and instigates specific strategies, because of its computer-based and sometimes nonlinear format, as is the case with hypertext.

A second approach stems from the field of cognitive ergonomics and computer science. Reading a text and writing text can be seen as an interaction between a user and a complex device. On the user side, parameters such as training, cognitive abilities, and experience in the domain influence the way people process text information. On the system side, design options may affect the reader's and writer's activities, such as, for instance, screen size, shape and location of text windows, annotation facilities, and search facilities.

A combined discussion of the two approaches in one volume could help in enhancing the study of discourse processing in an electronic environment. The general purpose of this book is to communicate that notions from computer science and cognitive ergonomics (e.g., interface design) can be very useful for researchers working in the field of cognitive psychology, and vice versa, that cognitive models of reading and writing and empirical data of experiments with real subjects can be useful to computer science and cognitive ergonomics. Both approaches meet in this book. Ultimately, it is essential that scholars from different fields join together to understand and fully exploit these new electronic text processing environments, so that understanding and learning are improved. It is the aim of this book to contribute to this dialogue.

CHAPTER OVERVIEW

The first four chapters discuss general aspects of reading and learning of information presented in a hypermedia environment. In hypermedia we see a combination of text, sound, graphics, or dynamic video in one and the same "document."

In the last decade the potential possibilities of hypermedia to present information have been recognized and used in practice. This form of presentation challenges the assumptions of the theory of text comprehension and learning from texts, a topic that is discussed by Goldman in Chapter 2. One main assumption is that learners process verbal information in a linear order. However, hypermedia impose a nonlinear order, which requires new learning strategies from learners and new research perspectives from researchers. The reader's skills at monitoring and evaluation of comprehension become more important than in a conventional text environment. The way in which we assess learning from text is challenged also. Examination of the mental models readers construct could take over the role of the more traditional assessment, such as recall and recognition. Furthermore, Goldman discusses how learners can benefit from the written interaction with others to build their knowledge.

Traditionally, reading is seen as an interactive process between reader and text. This idealized notion of reading now can be realized in electronic learning environments. However, in Chapter 3 Leu and Reinking observe that the design of existing electronic environments learning is seldom based on data and theory. Reading research can suggest useful ideas for guiding work within electronic learning contexts, such as understanding the nature and role of strategic knowledge, and connecting reading and writing on a thoughtful way in order to promote learning.

Gillingham deals with the problem (Chapter 4) that electronic text allows readers several new options for assistance to understanding and learning from text. First, text resources can provide readers with information related to a text, for example, background information. Second, task strategy resources attempt to teach readers strategies to approach a text that may help to increase comprehension, for example, selecting important information to the task, rereading important sections. Third, manipulation of context-specific strategies may enhance comprehension. Computers can be used to provide electronic (con)text encouraging to engage in displayed text information and to comment text written by peers, thereby facilitating learning subject matter.

The reality of electronic text usage is far from ideal, despite the hype around Internet, World Wide Web, electronic journals, hypertext, and so forth. Improvement might be sought in the development of a framework for analyzing reader–documentation interaction, in order to conceptualize human information usage that is needed to examine and evaluate designs for electronic documents. The chapter by Dillon (Chapter 5) offers such a framework. The framework (TIMS) he provides consists of four components: Task, Information, Manipulation, and Standard Reading.

Specific attention is given to the communicative role computers may fulfill. For a growing number of people, e-mail has become an interactive medium of communication, which shares more characteristics with spoken conversation than with traditional communication via letters. However, the design of e-mail systems often does not meet the conditions for successful interactive communication between users. Eklundh (Chapter 6) discusses some important aspects of the interface for e-mail communication from a dialogue perspective. She places emphasis on aspects affecting the interactivity of communication, and how the user can grasp and act on the communicative event.

Much of the discussion and research so far has been devoted to the way users read and learn from screen without discussing in detail how users write and read at the same time. The writing process is constrained by the text that is already produced, and the writer needs to reread it continuously in order to form a representation on which further writing is based (Flower & Hayes, 1981). Therefore, the way the text is presented and made accessible is of central importance for the writer of lengthy texts. Eklundh, Fatton, and Romberger (Chapter 7) present a writing environment that gives a sufficient global view of a document, and supports the writer's spatial memory.

In the next two chapters perceptual factors related to legibility and readability are discussed. A basic problem underlying all electronic text environment usage—hypermedia as well as hypertext— is how to optimize reading via electronic equipment. Muter (Chapter 8) gives a useful overview of the (perceptual) variables relevant to the reading of electronic text, and comments on a number of them, such as color, polarity, variables affecting the perception of flicker, and so forth.

Besides these fundamental perceptual characteristics, designers also should decide on matters such as where status and progress information, navigation buttons, content displays, control buttons, and so on will be located, and use graphic devices such as shading, lines, and boxes to separate one area from another. In this respect two fundamental criteria are reviewed by Grabinger and Osman-Jouchoux (Chapter 9): organization and visual interest. These two constructs provide thumb rules for arranging text elements to create readable and studyable screens.

Four chapters are specifically related to "hypertext." In short, hypertext is an electronic form of text presentation that supports the linking of nodes or chunks of text in any order (more on hypertext can be found in, e.g., McKnight, Dillon & Richardson, 1991). Hypertexts are created to enable people to carry out tasks using the information contained in these systems. The contribution by Mc-Knight (Chapter 10) emphasizes the fact that users, tasks, and texts vary tremendously and that designers of hypertext systems need to understand the interaction of these three aspects to be able to develop usable hypertext applications (Eason, 1984; Gall and Hannafin, 1994; Marchionini and Shneiderman, 1988). Hence he concludes with the view that the design of a hypertext that presents a particular information resource must be user-centered and task-based.

In the study by Rouet and Tricot (Chapter 11), the focus is on task aspects. They state that more attention should be paid to the cognitive analysis of the information processing tasks with which users are confronted. In this chapter several approaches to the analysis of information processing tasks are described, as well as empirical studies that focus on the cognitive processes involved in hypertext usage. Rouet and Tricot suggest that proper hypertext usage requires users to build up a task representation and a task management strategy. Finally, they propose a general framework to represent the task and activities of hypertext users in order to obtain useful insights for the design of more usable hypertexts.

Designing effective and usable hypertext systems is difficult, even when the characteristics of the task, the user, and the text are taken into account. One way to create better hypermedia systems is to use the process of interactive design and redesign. In Chapter 12, Instone, Teasly, and Leventhal illustrate and comment on this method by describing the design process of several user interfaces of hypermedia systems and they demonstrate how empirical evidence was used to redesign the systems.

Mishra, Spiro, and Feltovich (Chapter 13) look at the manner in which hypertext influences both the process and the outcome of cognition. They point out that the structure of hypertext technology is not neutral with regard to its effect on cognition. They discuss briefly the principles of Cognitive Flexibility Theory, and describe more fully the manner in which hypertext systems based on Cognitive Flexibility Theory prefigure representation and cognition and thereby enhance the critical thinking skills in students and the transfer of knowledge.

In the Introduction of this chapter we expressed the wish that the approach of cognitive ergonomics and computer science to the design of electronic text will meet with the approach of cognitive psychology in this book. The overview must have made clear that—at least for the reader—the approaches are brought closer to each other now.

REFERENCES

Eason, K. D. (1984). Towards the experimental study of usability. *Behaviour & information technology, 3*(2), 133–143.

Flower, L. S., & Hayes, J. R. (1981). A cognitive process theory of writing. *College composition and communication, 32,* 365–387.

Gall, J. E., & Hannafin, M. J. (1994). A framework for the study of hypertext. *Instructional science, 22*(3), 207–232.

Marchionini, G., & Shneiderman, B. (1988). Finding facts vs. browsing knowledge in hypertext systems. *Computer, 21*(1), 71–80.

McKnight, C., Dillon, A., & Richardson, J. (1991). *Hypertext in context.* Cambridge: Cambridge University Press.

2

Reading, Writing, and Learning in Hypermedia Environments

Susan R. Goldman

Learning Technology Center, Vanderbilt University

INTRODUCTION

Hypermedia is emerging as an increasingly prevalent form of information presentation. As such it presents interesting challenges to the assumptions and practices that have dominated theories of text comprehension and learning from text. Key among these is the assumption that learners process verbal information in a linear order, at least most of the time. Hypermedia makes it possible to juxtapose text, sound, graphics, and dynamic video all in the same "document." It creates the possibility for multiple entry points and more divergent approaches to reading, understanding, and learning. However, to capitalize on these potential opportunities to learn in flexible information environments, learners must assume more responsibility for structuring and organizing the information (cf., Brown et al., 1993; Lin, 1993; Scardamalia et al., 1989; Scardamalia & Bereiter,

1991). In traditional text, the responsibility for this has been borne largely by authors, researchers as text authors and task designers, and classroom teachers. As well, learners must develop their skills at monitoring their understanding and regulating their reading behavior to a degree far greater than that necessary in linearly presented texts (cf., Baker & Brown, 1984). In short, the essential nonlinearity of hypertext raises new learning issues for learners and researchers of those activities (Foltz, in press; Schnotz, 1994).

A second assumption challenged by hypermedia concerns the way in which we assess learning from text. The ubiquitous recall, or retelling, task does not align well with more authentic reasons for creating and using hypermedia systems (e.g., Cognition and Technology Group at Vanderbilt, 1993a; Goldman, Pellegrino, & Bransford, 1994). The emphasis on different ways to assess learning in the context of hypermedia systems converges with efforts in discourse processing to examine the mental models that readers construct. These models go beyond the construction of a propositional textbase representation and the use of recognition and recall tasks (e.g., Coté, 1994; Schmalhofer & Glavanov, 1986; van Dijk, 1987; van Dijk & Kintsch, 1983). The capabilities of hypermedia systems can provide scaffolds for learners to actively construct representations of their knowledge. Furthermore, readers can show what they know in ways that go far beyond traditional assessments (cf., Scardamalia et al., 1992).

In this chapter it is argued that hypermedia systems can play a transformative role in our thinking and research on text processing and learning. This is illustrated by comparing conceptions of hypermedia learning environments to more traditional ones. The first section of the chapter briefly reviews the historical roots of studying learning from text in linearly constrained environments and the dominant research paradigms. The second section gives a brief historical perspective on hypertext and argues that the multiply linked nature of hypertext systems affords support for learners to more actively and flexibly construct mental representations for the information and thus mitigate against inert knowledge (Cognition and Technology Group at Vanderbilt, 1993b; Whitehead, 1929). The third section considers the kinds of learner skills that become more important in such environments and efforts to scaffold the acquisition of these learning skills. Note that relatively little attention is focused on interface design perspectives; rather, the focus is on the psychological processes involved. In the fourth section, examples are provided of the kinds of learner collaboration and knowledge building activities that hypermedia learning environments afford when learners learn by building the hypermedia environments (e.g., Scardamalia, Bereiter, & Lamon, 1994). Promising research directions are considered throughout the chapter.

COMPREHENSION MODELS FOR LINEAR TEXT

Theories of text comprehension generally assume linearly organized information that readers process sequentially in the presented order, at least initially. For example, sentences of a text are arrayed one after another and usually, readers read the first sentence then the second, and so on. The general linear and sequential order, taking in one sentence after the next, is the default mode of reading a text. Even when readers have the option to read the sentences of a text in a different order (e.g., Goldman & Saul, 1990a), they tend to do an initial "forward-order" read before they look at sentences out of the sequential order. Furthermore, most violations of the sequential order are for purposes of re-examining portions of the text that have been read previously. Skipping ahead in the text tends to be a rare event (e.g., Goldman & Saul, 1990a).

The assumption of linearity has created an advantage for text over nonlinguistic input in terms of developing theories of comprehension and learning. Many years ago, Lashley (1951) noted that the linear order of language was a central feature of the linguistic system that made it different from understanding nonlinguistic input. Although the *input* order of language was linear, meaning was not wholly derived from considering the relationships between adjacent words. Rather, meaning relationships among nonadjacent elements were extremely important. However, these could be constructed from the memory trace of the linearly ordered input, a trace that was shown to have predictable decay rates (e.g., Kintsch, 1974; Sachs, 1967). Linear input constraints do not appear to apply to nonlinguistic input. For example, when attempting to understand a graphical display of information, there may be preferred scanning strategies, but there is no natural or inherent starting point for processing and the visual array is far less suggestive of a linear processing strategy. Individuals may start processing information from any part of the visual array that they wish. Where the eye goes next is probably influenced by many factors, especially a variety of techniques used to focus attention in visual displays. As a consequence, we have more developed theories of the text and aural components of hypermedia systems than of any of the other components.

The linear component of linguistic input made possible relatively precise theories of meaning construction because researchers could be relatively clear about the order in which the words in a sentence or paragraph would become available to the learner. Indeed, certain text genres originated in an oral tradition where constraints on sequentiality were inherent in the delivery mode. Listeners could not comprehend words and sentences that had not yet been uttered, so comprehension was constrained by the order in which the story was told or in which the lecturer presented the information. By stopping the process at different points in time, it was possible to look at emerging representations and how they might change with new input (e.g., Langer, 1986; Sachs, 1967).

A second legacy from the oral tradition is related to the comprehender's primary purpose in listening comprehension: to understand and remember the information presented. Without the luxury of written records, the wisdom of the culture was entrusted to those who could remember and retell it. One thing that made it easier to remember orally presented narrative information was the use of a consistent structure, often repeated cyclically in the text. For example, in the Western tradition, such consistent structures developed that they could be described as a series of episodes where each episode had a fairly consistent syntactic and semantic structure (Prince, 1973). Indeed, a number of rule systems were developed to describe that structure (e.g., Mandler & Johnson, 1977; Rumelhart, 1975; Stein & Glenn, 1979). The semantics of many stories are based on goal-directed action plans and rely on comprehenders' common sense theories of human action (Heider, 1958). When memory for the exact information contained in the orally told story could not be maintained, retellers could rely on their knowledge and intuitive theories of human action to "reconstruct" the story. Similarly, in non-Western cultures, where different cultural capital comprise the knowledge base, memory for Western stories is poorer; and Westerners' memories for stories not conforming to Western conventions is poor in terms of information remembered and organization of the information (e.g., Kintsch & Greene, 1978). Over time distortions from the original conformed to the retellers own knowledge and expectations (cf., Bartlett, 1932). Language learners in a culture, especially children, display an increasing ability to remember more of an aurally presented story in the canonical order as their general language skills and experiential knowledge increase (Goldman, 1982; Mandler & Johnson, 1977; Stein & Glenn, 1979).

Conventions for linearly organizing orally delivered texts were highly functional. The transition to written modes did little to alter the tendency to think linearly about the presentation of linguistic material, perhaps because early writing was pictographic and there were no mechanisms for depicting temporal or causal order other than sequentially ordered pictures (Gleitman & Rozin, 1977). The emergence of an arbitrary symbol system did little to change the linear organization of information, although in different languages the linearity differs. For example, in Hebrew, we read right to left; in English, left to right; and in Chinese, top to bottom starting in the left-most column.

Thus, although hypermedia environments consist of nonlinguistic media, such as graphics and video, the most salient comparisons of learning from hypermedia environments are with theoretical and empirical work on comprehending and learning from text.

Linear Text Processing and Discourse Structures

For some rhetorical genres, the order of information presentation maps onto the underlying logical structure of the text. For example, many narratives relate the events in the temporal order in which they occurred. The temporal ordering often corresponds with and conveys the underlying causal connections among events (cf., Stein & Goldman, 1981; Trabasso & van den Broek, 1985). Narratives are the descendants of oral literacy traditions, so this correspondence between temporal order and underlying order should not be surprising.

Much of the work on text comprehension has focused on narrative understanding. Thus it should be no surprise that theories and research on language comprehension have relied on a sequential processing framework, at least implicitly. Processing studies do indeed provide empirical justification for this stance. Research on eye movements and text inspection patterns indicates that readers of English do systematically proceed through a multisentence text from left to right, starting at the top of the text and moving downward (e.g., Goldman & Saul, 1990a; Just & Carpenter, 1987; Rayner & Sereno, 1994). Other than for purposes of previewing there is little benefit to "jumping ahead" in conventional text. On the contrary, jumping ahead often leads to confusion because the text was written with the assumption that readers would read linearly and *not* jump ahead (Foltz, in press).*

---

*However, note readers who enjoy reading the last chapter first to "see what happens." Many of us regard this as "cheating" in the sense that a reader is *supposed* to read in sequential order. Other readers as well as authors make this assumption.

However, there has been too great an emphasis on the structure of the input rather than on the strategies that comprehenders employ to make sense of text. The emphasis on the structure of the linguistic input rather than on the readers' active processing activities is consistent with a transmission model of learning and a view of the learner as relatively passive (cf., Bransford, Goldman, & Vye, 1991; Brown, 1992; Cognition and Technology Group at Vanderbilt, 1990, 1993a,b). If knowledge could be regarded as encapsulated in text, all the learner would have to do would be to take in the information. If the information were well-organized, the learner would understand and remember more than if the information was poorly organized. Indeed, comprehension studies showed that readers found it easier to remember stories that conformed to a canonical event order than those in which that order was scrambled (e.g., Kintsch, Mandel, & Kozminsky, 1977; Mandler & DeForest, 1979; Stein & Nezworski, 1978).

However, text is structured at a number of levels, and although experiencing the text in its "natural" linear order may be important for learning, it is not sufficient for advanced learning and understanding (Spiro & Jehng, 1990). To understand authentically complex narrative, Spiro and Jehng (1990) argue, there must be ways to approach segments of the narrative from multiple perspectives and to cross-connect to other segments, psychologically if not literally. Revisiting parts of the text is a strategic process, governed by prior knowledge of content, discourse forms and conventions and mediated by processes that evaluate representational coherence (e.g., Goldman & Saul, 1990a; Goldman, Varma, & Coté, 1995). Hypermedia environments should be ideally suited to the cross-connection process.

The cross-connection process should become more important as one deals with texts in which the underlying logical structure departs from the linearly organized surface text. Text genres that function to inform (e.g., articles written for popular magazines and newspapers, essays, text book selections, etc.) have less well-defined and more variable underlying coherence structures than stories (Beck & McKeown, 1989). Despite the underlying structural characteristics, all are traditional text forms and are written to be read in a linear, sequential manner. Accordingly, the linear order of occurrence in many informational texts does not correspond to the underlying logical organization. Rather, the linguistic input must be reorganized to accurately reflect relationships among the concepts, facts, and so forth.

Writers' recognition of the importance of the "reorganization" of presented ideas often is manifested by the inclusion of surface text cues to that underlying organization. These include a variety of rhetorical devices and signals (e.g., Goldman & Saul, 1990a,b; Lorch, 1989; Meyer, 1975) to the appropriate organization of the content. The "appropriate organization" is tied to the knowledge domain in question and to the particular function and theme of the passage. Thus, when reading informational text, the linear organization of the passage can be expected to depart from an "ordering" that more accurately reflects the interrelationships in the passage and their relationship to the knowledge domain. For these reasons, opportunities to explore the text from multiple perspectives and "crisscross" the landscape, are particularly important to advancing and deepening understanding (Spiro & Jehng, 1990; Spiro, Vispoel, Schmitz, Samarapungavan, & Boerger, 1987).*

This is not to say that there are not "standard" organizational genres for informational text. They are not as predictable as story texts and they lack singular organizing mechanisms for relating the different ideas that are presented. For example, causal and temporal mechanisms underlie the global organization of story events (e.g., Goldman & Varnhagen, 1983, 1986; Stein & Glenn, 1979; Stein & Goldman, 1981; Trabasso & van den Broek, 1985; van den Broek, 1990). These two organizing relations may be present in informational text, but there are usually more global organizational schemes that are important for understanding in the content domain.

Consider two types of global organizations for informational passages: description and problem resolution (Anderson & Armbruster, 1984). In a descriptive text several concepts are introduced and each is elaborated on. Often hierarchical relations are present. Figure 2-1 is a schematic of a representative descriptive passage. It is about distance, and we have used it in some of our research (e.g., Goldman & Saul, 1990a,b; Goldman & Varma, 1995; Goldman, Varma, & Coté, 1995). The numbers in the figure refer to sentences in the text. The first sentence introduces and defines a superordinate concept, *Distance.* In the process of further refining the definition, two subtypes, *absolute* and *relative distance,* are introduced. The rest of the passage expands on subtypes of *relative distance.* Each of these is defined and then exemplified or elaborated. In understanding descriptive passages, it is important for readers to rep-

---

*One exception to this is procedural text such as directions. In these texts, the more the information corresponds to the order of execution of the actions, the more well-formed the text.

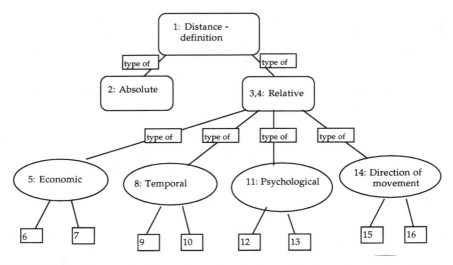

FIGURE 2-1. Schematic of the information structure of a descriptive passage, *Distance*.

resent the kinds of hierarchical, "nonadjacent" relations depicted in Figure 2-1 (e.g., by representing the subtype relationships among the concepts and by attaching the elaborations to the appropriate node in the hierarchical scheme).

A somewhat different but nonetheless ubiquitous global organization is that of problem resolution. In texts of this type, the first section of the text typically describes a problem (often including a number of contributing causes that might be elaborated on). Having defined the problem, the remainder of the passage often consists of proposed solutions and their evaluation (cf., Voss, 1984). In problem resolution passages, there are frequently two or three sentence causal sequences. However, unlike stories, the global organization of the passage does not arise through a single causal chain linking all important passage information. Rather, readers must recognize different alternative solutions and their associated, causally linked antecedents and consequences. Thus, representations formed for problem resolution texts need to include some relatively local cause–effect links as well as a more global representation of the relation of the problem to each proposed resolution, and any relationships across different ways to resolve the problem.

A good bit of the research on processing linear text has been concerned with whether and how readers construct the kinds of logical organizations that have been discussed for descriptive and problem resolution texts. Because there is a great deal of diversity among informational texts (even those with the same underlying, logical structure) there are a number of techniques that are used to alert readers to the underlying organization. Research indicates that inserting graphical and linguistic signals to the organization of the information enhances comprehension of informational texts (e.g., Bransford & Johnson, 1972; Mayer, Dyck, & Cook, 1984; Meyer, 1975; Stark, 1988). Graphical signals include such things as paragraphing, indentation, bold facing and italicizing and headings and subheadings. Linguistic signals include such devices as enumeration markers, phrases that cue the logical or semantic relationship of specific information to the text as a whole (e.g., *in summary, the most important result, on the contrary,* etc.) (see for reviews Beck & McKeown, 1989; Lorch, 1989). An obvious prerequisite to obtaining enhancement effects from the use of these devices is that comprehenders need to know how to interpret them (cf., Goldman & Murray, 1993).

There is also some evidence that cues to the structure of the information are helpful only if readers cannot discern the organizational structure of the information on their own (e.g., Goldman & Durán, 1988; Goldman & Saul, 1990b; McNamara, Kintsch, Songer, & Kintsch, in press). A number of proponents of hypertext suggest that this is one area where the graphic capabilities of hypertext systems would be particularly beneficial: They could be used to provide the reader with the kind of schematic shown in Figure 2-1 and thereby assist the reader in representing the logical organization of the information (e.g., Hammond & Allinson, 1989; Monk, Walsh, & Dix, 1989). As we indicate in the following, these techniques are not always effective but might be more so if readers generated them on their own.

Readers with high prior knowledge in an area might have less need of either linguistic or graphic cues to the organization. Indeed, the bulk of the work on comprehension, learning, and memory has used as subjects individuals whose knowledge in a domain is often at novice or intermediate levels. Spiro and Jehng (1990) argue that for advanced learning in many complex domains, such as medicine, biology, and so forth, sequentially based readings of information fall short because they do not permit the construction of a rich interconnected representation of concepts.

Representation and Task Influences (Purpose)

Implicit in the discussion thus far is that an important goal of reading is the construction of a coherent mental representation of the text; actually, several kinds of mental representations. The textbase (Kintsch et al., 1993; Kintsch & van Dijk, 1978; van Dijk & Kintsch, 1983; van Dijk, 1987) is a relatively encapsulated representation that corresponds very closely to the presented text. The situation (van Dijk & Kintsch, 1983; van Dijk, 1987), or mental model (Johnson-Laird, 1983) reflects the integration of new information from the text with prior knowledge. (Langer, 1986, refers to these as envisionments or text worlds.) Situation or mental model representations often are viewed as reflecting deeper understanding of the information than that reflected in a textbase representation.

Recent research indicates that readers' goals and the tasks they are given impact the nature of the representations that are constructed (e.g., Mannes & Kintsch, 1987; Schmalhofer & Glavanov, 1986). For example, many studies of discourse comprehension have asked readers to recall what they read. Good performance on this task can be achieved from a good textbase representation. However, inference making and application of what was presented to new situations appear to rely on the more integrative situation model representation. These discrepancies in performance speak to the distinction between "rote memorization" of information and what might be called "true learning." True learning involves constructing knowledge that results in "well integrated knowledge with multiple ties to other concepts" that "is more quickly accessed and available for use when needed" (McNamara et al., in press; see also Kintsch et al., 1993).

A number of studies indicate that learning is enhanced when readers engage in processing that forms connections among text elements and prior knowledge in an effort to "explain" the concepts (e.g., Chan, Burtis, Scardamalia, & Bereiter, 1992; Chi, Slotta, & deLeeuw, 1994; Goldman, Coté, & Saul, 1994; Saul, Coté, & Goldman, 1993). This processing may involve providing explanations of the presented information, drawing concept maps, approaching the information from multiple perspectives (Spiro & Jehng, 1990; Spiro et al., 1987), and so forth.

Implications for Hypermedia Learning Environments

The issue of whether nonlinear capabilities will enhance comprehension is addressable only in the context of thinking about the match between the linear input order, some target situation model(s), and the organization of the prior knowledge relevant to the information in the text. If a linear input order matches the "order" of the situation model order, hypertext capabilities will probably afford little facilitation. The greater the disparity between the linear organization and the organization needed to reflect a coherent situation model, the greater the potential for hypertext to facilitate knowledge construction. For example, for stories in which the order of mention matches the temporal and causal organization of events, small effects of the nonlinear capabilities present in hypermedia environments might be expected.* For informational text (except procedures for doing things), larger facilitation effects might be expected.

There are at least two caveats to this overly ambitious claim: First, to the degree that readers have been "raised" on traditional text, facilitative effects of hypertext might be more difficult to discern. Younger readers who are perhaps more attuned to electronic media actually might show greater facilitative effects of hypermedia systems than older, more entrenched readers. Readers may find it easier to read the way they are used to reading rather than learn a new way of reading that exploits the affordances of hypermedia environments. Second, advantages of hypertext may be visible only in more advanced phases of learning in a domain (Spiro & Jehng, 1990). In typical experimental situations, college sophomores or school children usually are at beginning or intermediate levels of learning in a domain. However, a relatively complete, organized knowledge base needs to exist before learners can capitalize on the multiple cross-connections afforded by hypertext. In the next section we consider some of the affordances of hypermedia and empirical data bearing on their impact on memory and learning.

HYPERMEDIA ENVIRONMENTS FOR LEARNING

Hypertext was designed as a nonlinear medium. Its underlying structure of nodes and links intentionally mirrors theories of knowledge representation in humans. As a nonlinear web of linked nodes, the processes associated with traversing the network (search) and retrieving specific information from it are just as complicated as they are when we attempt to address these issues in models of human memory. Indeed, the design issues that best the creator of a hypertext system are myriad and novel when compared to those facing designers of linear media. For example, as discussed earlier, when information is presented linearly the author can make fairly accurate assumptions about the information that the learner has

---

*Vocabulary is an obvious exception to this claim as are stories in which there are intermittent flashbacks or flash forwards.

already been exposed to. When designing a hypertext system, the pattern of nodes and access links must be organized to insure that regardless of the route the learner takes to get to a particular node, the information at that node can be understood sensibly (cf., Foltz, in press).

Where did hypertext come from? Vannevar Bush (1945) is credited with the initial idea of creating a reference system that permitted user-assigned pathways among information. Later, Engelbart (1963) implemented a system that used a database of nonlinear text. His system was actually a shell containing connection capabilities but no information. As information was put into the system, connections were made to other information. Nelson (1988) actually was responsible for coining the term *hypertext*. He used it to refer to text that was accessible in a nonsequential manner. Nelson believed that implementation of hypertext on computer systems actually would redefine how people worked with documents. Thus, hypertext emerged as a new genre of text in which the nonlinear format allowed access to large bodies of information and promoted "rich" learning (Duffy & Knuth, 1990). As the technology made it more feasible to store and access audio, graphic, and video information, hypermedia learning environments emerged.

At first glance it might seem relatively straight forward to test whether people process text differently in hypertext as compared to traditional linear text formats. One approach to this issue uses traditional methods of studying text comprehension (e.g., Beishuizen, Stoutjesdijk, & Zanting, 1995; Foltz, 1993; Gordon, Gustavel, Moore, & Hankey, 1988; Schneiderman, 1987). Researchers ask whether readers understand more and use different strategies to read hypertext as compared to linearly presented material. Most of these studies show few differences in strategy and little advantage for hypertext over linear text. In fact, readers rarely "jump" outside the linear text to access supplementary material, look up definitions of words, and so forth (Hasselbring & Goin, personal communication). There are a number of possible explanations for these mixed results. One class of explanations deals with issues of interface design and familiarity with the capabilities of the system. In essence, users of the system read the text the same way because they don't understand or see the utility of the various functions afforded by the hypertext system (cf., Anderson-Inman, Horney, Chen, & Lewin, 1993). Alternatively, users may try to navigate in the environment, but because of cumbersome interface designs, give up and read the text as if it were in a traditional format.

Another class of explanations concerns the match between task demands and the affordances of hypermedia environments. Many of the initial studies used the same tasks as have been typically used in text processing studies: recall tasks. Adequate recall can be supported by a textbase representation, a representation that frequently can be constructed by sticking pretty faithfully to the sequential input order of the text. If reading for purposes of recalling the information, there may be no particular functional value to exploiting the branching options of hypermedia environments.

More authentic uses of hypertext systems are as on-line information resources. To effectively mine such databases, readers need to rely on more than just text processing strategies. They also need to make decisions about when they need more information, what they need, and how to get it. Effective use of hypermedia environments necessarily involves search and retrieval skills not typically associated with comprehension tasks, especially when learners are given rather nebulous directions such as, "Learn the information for a test on it," or "Read the information so that you understand it." If readers are faced with other tasks, such as question answering or problem solving, and are to process text for the purpose of accomplishing those tasks, it seems quite likely that we would see different processing activities than those we see when they are reading to recall (cf. Britt, Rouet, Georgi, & Perfetti, 1994; Schnotz, 1994). And these activities would be functionally driven by the task requirements. (See Goldman & Durán, 1988, and Guthrie, 1988, for information search models for linear text and Graesser & Franklin, 1990, for models of question answering.) In short, effective use of hypermedia environments as information resources, as opposed to text presentation systems, calls for greater use of comprehension monitoring and self-evaluation than required by typical recall tasks. These issues are considered more explicitly in the next section.

REQUIREMENTS FOR LEARNING IN HYPERMEDIA ENVIRONMENTS

Any medium brings with it a set of processing demands on the user. As Alan Kay (1990) states

> What does a medium ask you to become in order to use it? Print requires a rational reader; television, a passive observer; the telephone, a conversationalist. When structured into learning environments that motivate guided inquiry, hypermedia has the potential to develop more user metacognition than linear media (p. 120).

If the user cannot meet the demands made by the medium, benefits will not be evident. Specifically, to realize the benefits of being able to explore information in multiple ways, individuals must be able to structure and integrate the information in meaningful ways, thereby avoiding the "lost in hyperspace" syndrome (cf., Britt et al., 1994). Whether hypertext facilitates cognitive flexibility by allowing "a topic to be explored in multiple ways using a number of different concepts or themes" (Spiro & Jehng, 1990) will depend on how well readers organize, regulate, manage, and evaluate their knowledge acquisition processes. These metacognitive processes comprise reflective thinking, a cognitive activity critical to engaging in lifelong learning (e.g., Baker, 1985; Baker & Brown, 1984; Barron et al., in press; Brown, Bransford, Ferrara, & Campione, 1983; Brown, Campione, & Day, 1981; Collins, 1996; Lin, 1994).

The very nature of hypermedia supports far more active and constructive reading than has been pursued in many of the extant studies. A few of the functions available to users are: search, browse, connect, and collect. These functions demand metacognitive functioning unlike that demanded in reading from a book. Also, there may be fewer cues than in a linear text to the kinds of connections that might be made. Many of the linguistic and graphical signals discussed earlier convey underlying semantic relationships (e.g., phrases such as *however, as a result, in addition,* and enumeration terms such as *first, second,* etc.), In hypertext environments there is less certainty about the order in which information will be read; hence, there are more constraints on the use of these kinds of signals. However, if the learner can construct multiple links among the information nodes and can do so in different ways, the benefits are likely to be more accessible, flexible learning. The important issues concern the circumstances that promote meaningful link connection, multiple routes through the information, and flexible learning.

Ineffective learning in hypermedia systems has been attributed to the absence of appropriate learning strategies and/or the lack of knowledge or metacognitive skills needed to make meaningful decisions (Merrill, 1980; Rigney, 1978; Schnotz, 1994; Steinberg, 1989; Tennyson & Rothen, 1979). In response, a number of systems were designed that provided external support. For example, graphics, maps, and charts were used to provide external support for understanding the knowledge organization in the system (Hammond & Allinson, 1989; Larkin & Dee-Lucas, 1990; Monk et al., 1989; Steinberg, Baskin, & Matthews, 1985; Steinberg, Baskin, & Hofer, 1986). Others provided on-line explanations of the purposes of specific activities the users were engaged in (Recker & Pirolli, 1992). However, the results of introducing such external supports were not all that encouraging: Performance on immediate task performance tended to improve but students did not maintain or transfer their knowledge very well (Steinberg et al., 1985, 1986; Tennyson, 1980; Tennyson & Rothen, 1979). Indeed, users viewed some of the external supports as adding to cognitive overload rather than reducing it (e.g., Recker & Pirolli, 1992).

Explanations for the disappointing results of providing external supports for learning center on the importance of learners appropriating the supports or generating them on their own in the first place. In fact, the presence of too many external supports actually may discourage learners from generating their own strategies and metacognitive processes for learning (Steinberg, 1989). A decade ago, in reviewing the literature on metamemory research, Brown, Bransford, Ferrara, & Campione (1983; cf., Case, 1978) concluded that unless the learner understood the utility and conditions of use of a particular "learning aid," forced use would temporarily improve performance but spontaneous use would be unaffected. Furthermore, research indicates that self-generated explanations of information in (linear) text are predictive of better memory and problem solving (Bielaczyc, Pirolli, & Brown, 1995; Chan, Burtis, Scardamalia, & Bereiter, 1992; Chi, de Leeuw, Chiu, LaVancher, 1994; Goldman, Coté, & Saul, 1994; Saul, Coté, & Goldman, 1993). There also is some indication that scaffolding reflective activities when working in a hypermedia system is beneficial: Lin (1993) found that providing explicit metacognitive cues to adult users of a hypermedia biology simulation system improved far transfer performance. These cues, in the form of questions, required subjects to attempt to explain, evaluate, and justify their decision processes with respect to their plans, data collection, and conclusions. On the far transfer test, a number of students spontaneously generated questions that prompted the same kinds of reflective activity that they had been exposed to during the intervention. They noted that these questions had been most helpful to them during the intervention.

Hypermedia systems have tremendous potential for assisting learners with constructing their own supports for comprehension and learning. And they open up new opportunities for exploring the strategies learners use to construct meaning. Consider a hypermedia reading environment that could augment traditional text cards with the following tools that could be linked to the whole text or to individual words, sentences, or paragraphs.

1. a notepad that learners could use to jot down important ideas and explanations, including decisions about the sensibleness of a text, evaluations of understanding, and questions stimulated by the information in the text;

2. a graphics tool that permitted learners to draw diagrams of the relationships between concepts;

3. a linking tool that permitted learners to construct links between concepts and ideas in the text, in a way that could later be used as a map of the text;

4. an inquiry tool with which learners could highlight words or phrases whose meaning they were unsure of; and

5. the option to reveal or hide annotations to the text.

The process of creating any of these annotations is the important comprehension activity because they induce active, coherence-building processing of the text. Such an augmented reading system might provide prompting for self-explaining, questioning, and connecting ideas at a level that would support readers engaging in these activities yet would not create cognitive overload.

The annotations themselves would provide useful data collection mechanisms for researchers interested in comprehension strategies. From the standpoint of educational practice, the annotations could provide information about individuals' strengths and weaknesses in general comprehension skills and in specific content domain areas. With augmentations such as these tools, the distinction between a database that is built by the learner and one that is provided by the system designer begins to blur seriously. The system described earlier does not as yet exist (as far as I know). However, some aspects of such a system have been tested (cf., Erickson & Salomon, 1991, and van Oostendorp, in press, for research on annotation and notetaking). For example, Anderson-Inman and colleagues (Anderson-Inman et al., 1993) have created *Electro-Text*, a hypertext system for specific stories that provides the reader with a number of comprehension-enhancing capabilities, including links between story events, self-monitoring comprehension questions specifically indexed to the story, definitions of vocabulary words in context, and so forth. They note that their field trials of this system revealed that not all students appreciated the enhancements, preferring to read the text as a regular book. These results may reflect the importance of considering the interaction of interface design and psychological process issues in the construction of hypermedia learning environments.

The most critical feature of the imagined hypermedia environment sketched in the preceding is the active role that the learner must play. Quite intentionally this imagined hypermedia environment bears a family resemblance to a communal database system that has been under development for approximately eight years: Scardamalia and Bereiter's Computer Supported Intentional Learning Environment (CSILE) (Scardamalia et al., 1989). CSILE is a hypermedia communal database in which learners are expected to construct knowledge actively. In this environment it is possible to learn much about text processing as well as text production.

HYPERMEDIA AS KNOWLEDGE CONSTRUCTION ENVIRONMENTS: THE CASE OF CSILE

A major impetus for the CSILE system were findings from Bereiter and Scardamalia's research on writing (1987). One of the conclusions from that research was that certain kinds of general questions could prompt increased output, writing fluency, and quality. However, a critical obstacle for individuals was lack of knowledge specific to the topic domain about which they were writing. At the same time, it seemed important to enlarge the system beyond the individual, given the importance of social interactions and community in knowledge acquisition, writing, and communication, especially for bootstrapping learning through reflective thinking (e.g., Brown, 1992; Brown et al., 1993; Graves, 1983; Schön, 1983; Vygotsky, 1986). Scardamalia et al. (1989) enlarged the vision of hypertext systems as on-line databases of static information that users browse or query: CSILE is a database environment for knowledge construction. Because it is a communal data base it provides opportunities for the social construction of meaning, reflective thinking, and metacognitive process. As such it presents a new set of challenges for understanding how people comprehend and learn.

The standard CSILE installation has several client machines connected to a file server. The core of CSILE is the communal student-generated database. The database consists of a series of text notes, comments on those notes, graphic notes (e.g., picture, diagram), and links and buttons that interconnect them. In CSILE, students work individually and collaboratively, commenting and building on one another's understanding. Anyone can add a comment to a note, link notes, or attach a graphic note to another note, but only authors can edit or delete notes. Authors are notified when a comment has been made on one of their notes.

From an instructional standpoint, the emphasis is on encouraging students to articulate their theories and questions, to explore and compare different perspectives, and to reflect on their joint understanding. The CSILE environment generally encourages a focus on problems rather than on categories of knowledge. Rather than a taxonomic approach to a new content domain, students are more likely to be faced with process questions, e.g., not "the life support systems needed for a trip to Mars" but "how life support systems function interdependently in the constrained environment of a space vehicle." It is frequently the teacher's role to "seed" discussion questions, point out possible links that could be made, and suggest reference material that might be consulted.

The CSILE environment offers an avenue for communication and collaboration that produces a complex hypermedia database. Each note is a node in an information web and student-generated links tie them together. Students need to navigate in this environment because in addition to adding their own notes to the database, they are responsible for reading the database and commenting on other students' ideas. Both roles encourage reflection and revision in thinking: The process of writing itself leads students to be more thoughtful about their ideas and encourages students to formulate their theories explicitly. Having to review the ideas of others, with the responsibility of commenting on them, leads to critical reading. Responding to comments creates an air of constant modification and review of one's own thinking. Several published reports document the positive effects of using CSILE on reading, writing, and thinking skills (e.g., Scardamalia & Bereiter, 1991; Scardamalia, Bereiter, & Lamon, 1994; Scardamalia et al., 1992).

Bootstrapping Understanding: Two Projects

The CSILE system seems like an ideal method for involving students in their learning and in contentful conversations with their peers. In this section two projects are reported that illustrate the kinds of understandings that can develop in a knowledge-building hyper-media environment.

CSILE in use in an undergraduate class

I teach an undergraduate course on language understanding, and last semester I decided to have students use CSILE in conjunction with the course. They were required to enter their thoughts, ideas, and questions into the CSILE database each week. One of my goals in doing so was to establish a discourse community that would not be limited to the classroom meetings. Students entered a variety of notes but access to computers limited the degree of commenting that they did on each others' notes. Nevertheless, there were some interesting exchanges that were quite revealing of students' understanding of the material they were reading. For example, students were forthcoming about ideas they needed to understand, illustrated in the following:

1. In reference to Reichman's (1985) article on discourse, specifically, p. 163: Reichman writes that "If the interpreter knows what the communicator intends, communication is redundant." Wouldn't this communication simply be complete, rather than redundant since the conversants must understand one another in order for communication to take place in the first place?

2. On page 10, Tannen (1989) says that "one cannot truly understand the meaning of a given utterance without having a broad grasp of conversational coherence: where the utterance came from and where it is headed." Is this the same thing as understanding sarcasm in one's voice versus taking what the person has said literally?

Ideally, students would respond to each others' questions and in so doing build an understanding. One student's response to the second question illustrates this:

3. I think so. I took Tannen's remark to mean that a listener needs to READ BETWEEN THE LINES. Tannen states that it is not enough to merely grasp the "meaning" of the words. The listener also needs to know what it means in the context of their relationship, the situation, and the past and present.

There were also examples of more extended entries that illustrate the kind of self-questioning and reflecting that begins to emerge as students make greater use of CSILE. Consider the following notes written approximately one third of the way into the semester. In each, classic issues in language and psychology are expressed.

In the Tannen article on men and women communicating (which I found very interesting and relatable), I thought the two "worlds" she talked about was a good way to approach the problems that men and women have communicating. The question I asked myself was "Do you think men and women think and communicate differently because of these environments, or do these environments exist because men and women have biologically different ways of thinking and therefore produce these different worlds? I have not come up with my answer yet—it's difficult because their are so many exceptions to consider.

Here we see the discovery of the classic nature–nurture issue and the desire to understand causal mechanisms. A second perplexing issue emerged in the note of another student:

> Tannen's chapter on Repetition reminded me of a quote I heard a long time ago: "Nothing has been said that has not been said before." Particularly, Becker's comment that "At present we have no way of telling the extent to which a sentence like 'I went home' is a result of invention, and the extent to which it is a result of repetition, countless speakers before us having already said it and transmitted it to us in toto. Is grammar something where speakers "produce" constructions, or where they "reach for" them from a pre-established inventory? Think about your own speech. How much of what you say is truly original. Or is anything you say original? Even when I think about personal conversations about my friends, family or a date, if you re-place names do you think you could find almost a carbon copy of your words, sentences, even conversations somewhere in time? Do you all agree or disagree? If you agree, does that put us closer to animals, by limiting our ability to create novel structures in language. Are our limits just much greater than an animal's?

This student has expressed an issue that has been the subject of much linguistic and psychological debate: rule governed versus experiential history as a basis for language production (cf., MacDonald, Perlmutter, & Seidenbert, 1994). Not only does this note indicate good reflective thinking about the material, but she is actively trying to engage her classmates in an extended discussion. The communal database thus creates new discourse genres with which readers are faced: They were writing for each other as audience, not for the instructor. The process appears to have been an opportunity to think deeply about some important ideas. An important research question that emerges with the advent of these kinds of communal communication environments is the applicability in these new environments of readers' comprehension strategies—strategies that have been developed in more traditional oral and written language genres.

There were several pragmatic limitations on the undergraduates' use of CSILE that limited the degree to which deep understanding and interstudent communication patterns emerged. The most important was access to the database for purposes of browsing and commenting on other student's notes. Had students had access from their dorm rooms, I expect more knowledge building would have occurred. Even with limited access students found the process useful because it "made me write down what I was thinking" and "I got to see what other students were thinking." From my point of view as the instructor, the notes and comments were an extremely useful formative assessment technique (Goldman et al., 1994). Many of my in-class discussions were stimulated by the issues students were raising in their notes and comments. CSILE also provide a way for me to more directly respond to students' individual questions and needs in a timely fashion. At the same time the notes and comments were available to all students because CSILE is a public database and everyone has access to all information. This contrasts with the situation that occurs during office hours when you spend perhaps half an hour discussing an issue with one student when the whole class might benefit from the discussion. Thus, the CSILE hypermedia environment afforded many opportunities for students to make their thinking visible. The benefits were limited because students did not access other students' notes frequently enough to engage in knowledge building. Nevertheless, some knowledge building occurred through instructor–student interactions in CSILE.

With greater access over an extended project, one would expect to see more evidence of knowledge building than was observed in the pilot project I conducted. There is some evidence for the accuracy of this expectation in data from middle school students who had been working with CSILE as part of their science research projects.

A grade school science project

Knowledge building and advances in understanding can be assessed by tracing through the content of a linked set of student notes and comments. Another indicator is the organization and reorganization of the database. In CSILE there is the capability to impose various kinds of organizations on a corpus of notes through the creation of buttons linked to groups of notes, in a typical hyper-card fashion. Examples of how students build on one another's comments are provided first. This is followed by an example of how the same set of notes can be linked in multiple ways to organizing frameworks. This design of the interface capabilities in the CSILE database makes it possible to create information networks that allow students to "criss-cross" the landscape (cf. Spiro et al., 1987), and in so doing increase their understanding.

Building on other people's ideas. A class of third and fourth grade students (eight–nine year olds) were doing research on habitats and endangered species (Tiessen & Ward, 1994).* They had

*This work was supported by a grant from the James S. McDonnell Foundation.

already done research on specific endangered species and there was class discussion in which the teacher solicited a variety of reasons that species might be endangered (e.g., habitat destruction, overcollecting, pollution, loss of food source, etc.). However, exactly how each of these reasons caused a species to be or become endangered was not well articulated by the children. The teacher used a series of discussion notes in the CSILE database to encourage children to consider the causal relationships, e.g., *How is loss of food endangering species and what can be done about it?* Discussion notes permit multiple users to enter their thoughts in the same "note" so that when the discussion note is opened all of the notes generated in the discussion are available for inspection. Students entered their ideas and tagged them as reflecting one of several kinds: information, requests for explanations, and solutions. (Other idea types are also possible, i.e., "My Theory" or "New Learning.")

Table 2-1 shows the sequence of notes that were entered in the discussion of the Loss of Food Source factor. The notes illustrate the operation of complex comprehension, production, and metacognitive processing among several of the students. Six different individuals participated in the discussion but they generated 13 notes. The conversation reflected in the notes indicates assertions followed by requests for clarification or further explanation. These questions indicate content monitoring and evaluation processes. One note is particularly interesting as an example of "seeding the database:" Note 4, written by the teacher suggests the idea of a food chain. "Seeding" the database with ideas like these is one of the mechanisms for scaffolding the knowledge building process. Two of the notes reflect monitoring of mechanics, that is, of spelling (11) and sentence construction (13). Thus, the majority of the notes monitored the content of the assertions and arguments being put forth or responded to questions. This is most easily seen in a graphic representation of the interchange, as shown in Figure 2-2.

In Figure 2-2, overlapping note numbers indicate that the same individual is "speaking." Question marks show links that are requests for explanations or information. Two of the six students (1001 and 1005) generated most of the notes.

Student 1005 is a particularly interesting case of a girl who uses the discussion to solidify her understanding. She enters the discussion in response to the seeded question with a qualified statement about food chains (see note 6). In the very note she reflects the need to understand loss of food at a more general level than that of the specific species, "I Need to Understand how all these species are losing their food." Note 8 seeks information from one of the other

TABLE 2.1

An Example of a CSILE Discussion Note on Loss of Food Source as a Factor Contributing to Species Endangerment*

Problem: How is Loss of Food Source Endangering a Species and What Can Be Done About It?

1. *Information:* The San Bruno Elfin butterfly is losing its food. Its food is only one thing which is pacific sonecrop. And when the people go rock or sand quarrying they dig up the rocks or sand and they might put it on the plant. So the Burno Elfin Butterfly is losing its food. (1001)
2. *Information:* The Missoin Blue Butterfly is endanered because non native plants take over areas of the lupine. (the food of the butterfly) (1002)
3. *Please Explain:* I didn't understand San Ja what you ment in your note. (1002)
4. *I Need to Understand:* These butterflies are endangered because their food is disappearing. Are the species they eat also endangered? (1003)
5. *Information:* The California Brown Pelican is losing it's food so it can not eat. And it need's food for it's baby's. And that's why it is in loss of food sors. (1004)
6. *Solution:* It depends on what the species is if the species eats plankton then plankton has to be protected and what plankton eats must be also protected and so on through the food chain.
7. *I Need to Understand:* How all these species are losing their food. (1005)
8. *I Need to Understand:* Dear Mike, why is the Pelican losing its food? (1005)
9. *Please Explain:* Tom I don't know what you don't understand in my note so could you please explain (3). So I can help you. (1001)
10. *Information:* The Pelican loses its food because of overfishing so if it eats fish then for it to have enough food people would have to not fish as much which can put restaunts like th eFish Market out of business so restraunts like the Fish Market will go and fish as much as they can without breaking the law, sometimes the restrauants do break the law and then their is not enough food for the pelican because the fish is endangered and the pelican becomes endangered adn so on through the food chain. (1005)
11. *I Need to Understand:* Mike sources is spelled source instead of sors (1001)
12. *Solution:* If the species eats something that people eat too then restraunts and stores will get kill that same animal and the animal that eats the species will become endangered. So if those restrants and stores sell more other things then their will still be enough for the species that eats the species the restraunts and stores are killing then there is still the species that the restraunts and stores are killing which will become endangeered because of hunting so therefore if the restraunts and stores sell less meat it will have to not hunt as much which will please the carnivores, the vegetarians, the predators and the prey. If the species is such as a butterfly then it's food will probably run low because of introduced species which take more sources and more nutrients because they have evolved into new plants which will take all the nutrients and make not only what the butterfly eats but the butterfly whatever eats the butterfly and etc. etc. all through the food chain. (1005)
13. *I Need to Understand:* Why did you put htat after something what does htat mean? and what do you mean by people eat too then restraunts and stores will get kill that same animal and the animal that eats the species will become endangered. I don't get it why did you write this Paul?. (1006)

*Specific names of students have been changed. Numbers in parentheses are coded to different students. The numbers in the table are not the numbers in the original database. Italicized phrases are the labels students tagged their notes with.

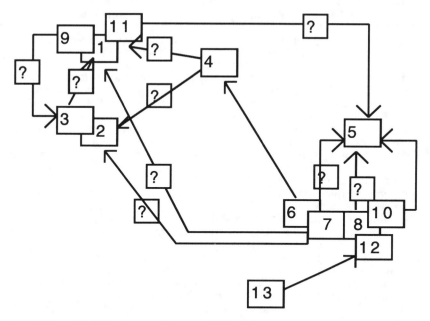

FIGURE 2-2. A trace of the interchange in the CSILE discussion note shown in Table 2-1.

students, but in notes 10 and 12 she elaborates a theory about the animal mentioned in note 5, as well as how this might be a more generalized phenomenon.

This fragment of a communal database illustrates several interesting issues for research on comprehension in electronic hypermedia. First, the children are generating information for authentic audiences in response to questions that are meaningful to them, conditions that should optimize written language production. Interesting research questions concern how students allocate processing resources when generating their notes. For example, it appears from these notes that students are not paying much attention to the mechanical aspects of language production, such as spelling, punctuation, and sentence structure. These features of language are monitored by the other students participating in the written conversation, however. The distribution of attention to content versus structure and how it changes with the kind of note being written (an initial idea vs. one that is to be published as part of a more permanent record of work) are examples of interesting potential research issues.

Second, responding to the notes and ideas of others requires rather sophisticated comprehension monitoring skills. Exactly how students use their own prior knowledge in constructing sufficient meaning to ask questions or comment on the ideas of others seems like a fruitful area in which to pursue research on comprehension and monitoring strategies.

Organizational frames for information and interface design.   A second aspect of the CSILE communal database is the opportunities it provides for information to be organized in multiple ways. The students who participated in the discussion note on loss of food sources had previously entered information about the specific species on which they had been doing research. This information was originally entered for each species according to a list of topics: phylogenetic group, habitat, lifestyle, nutrition, physical characteristics, and reason for endangerment. After everyone had entered their individual information graphics were used to organize the notes. Three different organizations were created. Each one allowed the expression of different organizing principles. The first was a phylogenetic tree that students were to link their notes to in any way they saw fit. The tree (Figure 2-3) captures differences in the biological complexity of the species they had researched. The teacher wanted to introduce another interface that would encourage the students to focus on the importance of relationships between habitat and biological systems. She created a map of their region of the state and asked children to link their notes so that the various species were appropriately distributed over the state. Users could click on an area of the state and access all the species that shared that habitat. The introduction of the map graphic is a good example of how teachers (or other learning facilitators) can "seed" the database with ideas that drive the discussion to deeper levels of understanding. Finally, a thematic organizer was generated. Students constructed a concept map on paper in a whole-class discussion around the central idea "reasons for endangerment." This graphic was the final one to which the students' various notes on their species were linked. The graphic then served as an interface for accessing notes about different species according to the reason for endangerment (Figure 2-4).

Each interface expressed different aspects of the relationships among the species, endangerment and geography. Few of these relationships had been evident from the individual notes. Furthermore, by establishing links among the notes in different ways, students can criss-cross the landscape from multiple perspectives. A potentially interesting empirical question is whether it matters if learners criss-cross a self-generated landscape or a landscape of information generated by others.

There is much to be learned about how students process the

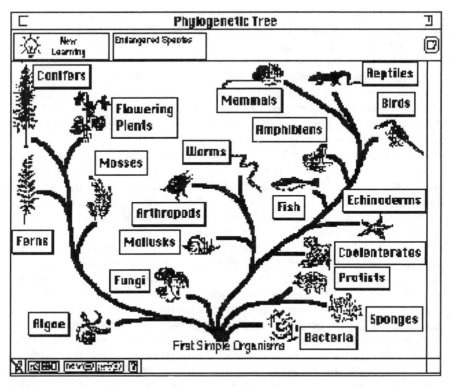

FIGURE 2-3. Phylogenetic tree as an organizer and interface for the endangered species database.

information in communal databases. In fact, CSILE is perhaps one of the most promising hypermedia environments in which to examine knowledge construction processes because the information has not been "pre-organized" for some community or group of learners. CSILE includes provisions for key wording and top-tagging and these can later be used as search heuristics. To what degree they are used in that fashion is an open question. Furthermore, there are interesting issues regarding how users "trace" a line of thinking through the notes, comments, and links, and if the indexing systems are helpful. Fruitful questions to pursue in this hypermedia environment concern the circumstances governing decisions to link notes and to undertake acute reorganizations of the database. Because the information is built by the community, it is the community that increments, revises, and reorganizes the knowledge, thereby providing a window on important learning processes.

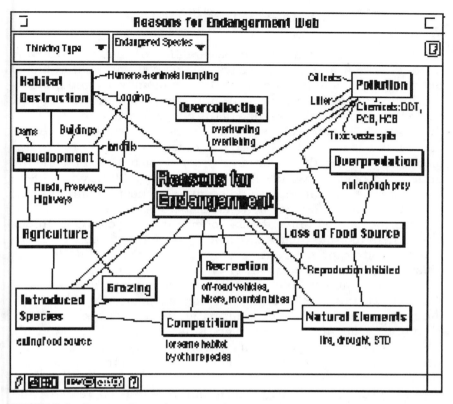

FIGURE 2-4. Reasons for endangerment as an organizer and interface for the endangered species database.

In a communal system, where is the role for understanding comprehension processes at the individual level? Clearly, this is an important focus of research because the knowledge construction process critically depends on the comprehension and monitoring processes of the individuals participating in the community. An additional, potentially interesting issue is the process of reconstructing the path by which understanding was achieved. In oral conversation, it is often difficult to track the development of an argument, position, or body of evidence. The written record present in a hypermedia system such as CSILE provides a way of tracing that development. The trace process itself raises interesting process issues because this is a nontrivial task. The processes whereby conversations and interchanges are reconstructed from traces itself demands interesting comprehension and reasoning strategies.

SUMMARY AND CONCLUSIONS

Hypermedia affords a number of possibilities for enabling authentic reading, writing, and learning activities. However, the multiply linked nature of the medium means that skills of monitoring and evaluating comprehension become more important than in a linear text environment. In the first section of the chapter, major findings from the research on comprehension processes for linear text were discussed. It was noted that text genres differ with respect to the isomorphism between the linear input order of the information and the underlying logical structure. The branching capabilities possible in hypermedia environments would seem to be most helpful in those cases where the difference between the two is greater.

Hypermedia environments also offer a number of opportunities for learners to build their knowledge by benefiting from written interaction with others. Several examples were provided of the kinds of learning that may occur in electronic environments that allow learners to comment upon the work of others, reorganize information, and generally reflect on what they are learning. These environments have a role to play in formative assessment because they encourage students to make their thinking visible (Barron et al., 1995). As well, the hypermedia environment itself is a public performance arena in which learners can demonstrate what they know.

Hypermedia environments move our research on reading and writing into new sets of questions while retaining important links with work on linear text processing. These electronic environments create new demands for reflective thinking on the part of learners and their teachers and thereby have the potential to further truly deep understanding.

ACKNOWLEDGMENTS

Discussions with a number of colleagues have helped shape the ideas in this chapter, most notably: Brigid Barron, John Bransford, Nathalie Coté, Ted Hasselbring, Mary Lamon, Xiadong Lin, James Pellegrino, Elizabeth Saul, Marlene Scardamalia, Sashank Varma, and Nancy Vye. Thanks to Herre Van Oostendorp for helpful comments on an earlier draft of this chapter.

REFERENCES

Anderson, T. H., & Armbruster, B. B. (1984). Content area textbooks. In R. C. Anderson, J. Osborn, & R. J. Tierney (Eds.), *Learning to read in American schools: Basal readers and content texts.* Hillsdale, NJ: Erlbaum.

Anderson-Inman, L. Horney, M. A., Chen, D., & Lewin, L. (1993). *Hypertext literacy: Observations from the ElectroText Project.* Paper presented at the American Educational Research Association, Atlanta, GA.

Baker, L. (1985). How do we know when we don't understand? Standards for evaluating text comprehension. In D. L. Forrest-Pressley, G. E. MacKinnon, & T. Gary Waller (Eds.), *Metacognition, cognition, and human performance* (pp. 155–205). Orlando, FL: Academic Press.

Baker, L., & Brown, A. L. (1984). Cognitive monitoring in reading. In J. Flood (Ed.), *Understanding reading comprehension: Cognition, language, and the structure of prose* (pp. 21–44). Newark, DE: International Reading Association.

Barron, B., Vye, N. J., Zech, L., Schwartz, D., Bransford, J. D., Goldman, S. R., Pellegrino, J., Morris, J., Garrison, S., & Kantor, R. (1995). Creating contexts for community based problem solving: The Jasper challenge series. In C. Hedley, P. Antonacci, & M. Rabinowitz (Eds.), *Thinking and literacy: The mind at work* (pp. 47–71). Hillsdale, NJ: Erlbaum.

Bartlett, F. C. (1932). *Remembering: A study in experimental and social psychology.* Cambridge, England: Cambridge University Press.

Beck, I. L., & McKeown, M. G. (1989). Expository text for young readers: The issue of coherence. In L. B. Resnick (Ed.), *Knowing, learning, and instruction: Essays in honor of Robert Glaser* (pp. 47–66). Hillsdale, NJ: Erlbaum.

Beishuizen, J., Stoutjesdijk, E., & Zanting, A. (1994). *Study strategies and outcomes in a linear or non linear hypertext environment.* Paper submitted for presentation at the European Research on Learning and Instruction.

Bereiter, C., & Scardamalia, M. (1987). *The psychology of written composition.* Hillsdale, NJ: Erlbaum.

Bielaczyc, K., Pirolli, P., & Brown, A. L. (1995). Training in self-explanation and self-regulation strategies: Investigating the effects of knowledge acquisition activities on problem solving. *Cognition and Instruction, 13,* 221–252.

Bransford, J. D., Goldman, S. R., & Vye, N. J. (1991). Making a difference in peoples' abilities to think: Reflections on a decade of work and some hopes for the future. In L. Okagaki & R. J. Sternberg (Eds.), *Directors of development: Influences on children* (pp. 147–180). Hillsdale, NJ: Erlbaum.

Bransford, J. D., & Johnson, M. K. (1972). Contextual prerequisite for understanding: Some investigations of comprehension and recall. *Journal of Verbal Learning and Verbal Behavior, 11*, 717–726.

Britt, M. A., Rouet, J-F., Georgi, M. C., & Perfetti, C. A. (1994). Learning from history texts: From causal analysis to argument analysis. In G. Leinhardt, I. L. Beck, & C. Stainton (Eds.), *Teaching and learning in history* (pp. 47–84). Hillsdale, NJ: Erlbaum.

Brown, A. L. (1992). Design experiments: Theoretical and methodological challenges in creating complex interventions in classroom settings. *Journal of Learning Sciences, 2*, 141–178.

Brown, A. L., Ash, D., Rutherford, M., Nakagawa, K., Gordon, A., & Campione, J. C. (1993). Distributed expertise in the classroom. In G. Salomon (Eds.), *Distributed cognitions* (pp. 188–228). New York: Cambridge University Press.

Brown, A. L., Bransford, J. D., Ferrara, R. A., & Campione, J. C. (1983). Learning, remembering, and understanding. In J. H. Flavell & E. M. Markman (Eds.), *Handbook of child psychology: Vol. 3. Cognitive development*. New York: Wiley.

Brown, A. L., Campione, J. C., & Day, J. D. (1981). Learning to learn: On training students to learn from texts. *Educational Researcher, 10*, 14–21.

Bush, V. (1945). As we may think. *Atlantic Monthly, 176*(1), 101–108.

Case, R. (1978). Implications of a developmental psychology for the design of effective instruction. In A. M. Lesgold, J. W. Pellegrino, S. D. Fokkema, & R. Glaser (Eds.), *Cognitive psychology and instruction* (pp. 441–463). New York: Plenum Press.

Chan, C. K. K., Burtis, P. J., Scardamalia, M., & Bereiter, C. (1992). Constructive activity in learning from text. *American Educational Research Journal, 29*, 97–118.

Chi, M. T. H., deLeeuw, N., Chiu, M., & LaVancher, C. (1994). Eliciting self-explanations improves understanding. *Cognitive Science, 18*, 439–477.

Chi, M. T. H., Slotta, J. D., & deLeeuw, N. (1994). From things to processes: A theory of conceptual change for learning science concepts. *Learning and Instruction, 4*, 27–43.

Cognition and Technology Group at Vanderbilt. (1990). Anchored instruction and its relationship to situated cognition, *Educational Researcher, 19*(6), 2–10.

Cognition and Technology Group at Vanderbilt. (1993a). Integrated media: Toward a theoretical framework for utilizing their potential. *Journal of Special Education Technology, 12*, 71–85.

Cognition and Technology Group at Vanderbilt. (1993b). Toward integrated curricula: Possibilities from anchored instruction. In M. Rabinowitz (Ed.), *Cognitive science foundations of instruction* (pp. 33–55). Hillsdale, NJ: Erlbaum.

Collins, A. (1996). Design issues for learning environments. In S. Vosniadou, E. De Corte, R. Glaser, & H. Mandl (Eds.), *International perspectives*

on the psychological foundations of technology-based learning environ-
ments (pp. 347–362). Hillsdale, NJ: Erlbaum.

Coté, N. (1994, November). *Overcoming the inert knowledge problem in*
learning from expository text. Paper presented at the annual meeting
of the Mid-South Educational Research Association, Nashville, TN.

Duffy, T. M., & Knuth, R. A. (1990). Hypermedia and instruction: Where is
the match? In D. H. Jonassen & H. Mandl (Eds.), *Designing hyper-*
media for learning (pp. 199–225). New York: Springer-Verlag.

Englebart, D. C. (1963). A conceptual framework for the augmentation of
man's intellect. In *Vistas in information handling, Vol. 1.* London: Spar-
tan.

Erickson, T., & Salomon, G. (1991). Designing a desktop information system: Observations and issues. *CHI'91 Conference Proceedings* (pp. 49–
54). NY: Addison-Wesley.

Foltz, P. W. (in press). Comprehension, coherence and strategies in hypertext
and linear text. In J. F. Rouet, J. J. Levonen, A. P. Dillon, & R. J. Spiro
(Eds.), *Hypertext and cognition.* Hillsdale, NJ: Lawrence Erlbaum.

Foltz, P. W. (1993). *Readers' comprehension and strategies in linear text and*
hypertext. (Tech. Rep. #93-01). Boulder, CO: University of Colorado,
Institute of Cognitive Science.

Gleitman, L. R., & Rozin, P. (1977). The structure and acquisition of reading
I: Relations between orthographies and the structure of language. In
A. S. Reber & D. L. Scarborough (Eds.), *Toward a psychology of read-*
ing. Hillsdale, NJ: Erlbaum.

Goldman, S. R. (1982). Knowledge systems for realistic goals. *Discourse*
Processes, 5, 279–303.

Goldman, S. R., Coté, N., & Saul, E. U. (1994, January). *Children's strate-*
gies for making sense of informational text. Paper presented at the
Fifth Annual Winter Text Conference, Jackson Hole, WY.

Goldman, S. R., & Durán, R. P. (1988). Answering questions from ocean-
ography texts: Learner, task and text characteristics. *Discourse Pro-*
cesses, 11, 373–412.

Goldman, S. R., & Murray, J. (1993). Knowledge of connectors as cohesion
devices in text: A comparative study of native English and ESL speak-
ers. *Journal of Educational Psychology, 84,* 504–519.

Goldman, S. R., Pellegrino, J. W., & Bransford, J. D. (1994). Assessing
programs that invite thinking. In E. L. Baker & H. F. O'Neill, Jr. (Eds.),
Technology assessment in education and training (pp. 199–230). Hillsdale, NJ: Lawrence Erlbaum.

Goldman, S. R., & Saul, E. U. (1990a). Flexibility in text processing: A
strategy competition model. *Learning and Individual Differences, 2,*
181–219.

Goldman, S. R., & Saul, E. U. (1990b). *Paragraphing and task effects on*
reading strategies. Paper presented at the meetings of the Psychonomics Society, New Orleans, LA.

Goldman, S. R., & Varma, S. (1995). CAPping the construction-integration model of discourse comprehension. In C. Weaver, S. Mannes, & C. Fletcher (Eds.), *Discourse comprehension: Models of processing revisited* (pp. 337–358). Hillsdale, NJ: Erlbaum.

Goldman, S. R., Varma, S., & Coté, N. (1995). Extending capacity constrained construction integration: Toward "smarter" and flexible models of text comprehension. In B. K. Britton & A. C. Graesser (Eds.), *Models of text comprehension* (pp. 73–113). Hillsdale, NJ: Erlbaum.

Goldman, S. R., & Varnhagen, C. K. (1983). Comprehension of stories with no-obstacle and obstacle endings. *Child Development, 54,* 980–992.

Goldman, S. R., & Varnhagen, C. K. (1986). Memory for embedded and sequential story structures. *Journal of Memory and Language, 25,* 401–418.

Gordon, S., Gustavel, J., Moore, J., & Hankey, J. (1988). The effects of hypertext on reader knowledge representation. In *Proceedings of the 32nd Annual Meeting of the Human Factors Society* (pp. 296–300).

Graesser, A. C., & Franklin, S. P. (1990). QUEST: A cognitive model of question answering. *Discourse Processes, 13,* 279–303.

Graves, D. H. (1983). *Writing: Teachers and children at work.* Exeter, NH: Heinemann Educational Books.

Guthrie, J. T. (1988). Locating information in documents: Examination of a cognitive model. *Reading Research Quarterly, 23,* 178–199.

Hammond, N., & Allinson, L. (1989). Extending hypertext for learning: An investigation of access and guidance tools. In *Proceedings of Hypertext 2,* York, UK.

Heider, F. (1958). *The psychology of interpersonal relations.* New York: Wiley.

Johnson-Laird, P. N. (1983). *Mental models.* Cambridge, MA: Harvard University Press.

Just, M. A., & Carpenter, P. A. (1987). *The psychology of reading and language comprehension.* Boston: Allyn and Bacon, Inc.

Kintsch, W. (1974). *The representation of meaning in memory.* Hillsdale, NJ: Erlbaum.

Kintsch, W., Britton, B. K., Fletcher, C. R., Kintsch, E., Mannes, S. M., & Nathan, M. J. (1993). A comprehension-based approach to learning and understanding. In D. L. Medin (Ed.), *The psychology of learning and motivation: Advances in research and theory* (Vol. 30, pp. 165–214). New York: Academic Press.

Kintsch, W., & Greene, E. (1978). The role of culture specific schemata in the comprehension and recall of stories. *Discourse Processes, 1,* 1–15.

Kintsch, W., Mandel, T. S., & Kozminsky, E. (1977). Summarizing scrambled stories. *Memory and Cognition, 5,* 547–552.

Kintsch, W., & van Dijk, T. A. (1978). Toward a model of text comprehension and production. *Psychology Review, 85,* 363–394.

Langer, J. A. (1986). *Children reading and writing: Structure and strategies.* Norwood, NJ: Ablex.

Larkin, J. H., & Dee-Lucas, D. (1990). *Review strategies and content inte-*

gration with traditional text and hypertext. Paper presented at the National Science Foundation Teaching and Learning Meeting. Washington, DC.

Lashley, K. S. (1951). The problem of serial order in behavior. In L. A. Jeffress (Eds.), *Cerebral mechanisms in behavior* (pp. 112–136). New York: Wiley.

Lin, X. D. (1993). *Far Transfer Problem-Solving In A Non-Linear Computer Environment: The Role of Self-Regulated Learning Processes.* Unpublished dissertation, Purdue University, W. Lafayette, IN.

Lin, X. D. (1994). *Technology for reflective thinking: Why and how.* Unpublished manuscript.

Lorch, Jr., R. F. (1989). Text signaling devices and their effects on reading and memory processes. *Educational Psychology Review* (Vol. 1, pp. 209–234). New York: Plenum.

MacDonald, M. C., Perlmutter, N. J., & Seidenberg, M. S. (1994). Lexical nature of syntactic ambiguity resolution. *Psychological Review, 101,* 676–703.

Mandler, J. M., & DeForest, M. (1979). Is there more than one way to recall a story? *Child Development, 50,* 886–889.

Mandler, J. M., & Johnson, N. J. (1977). Remembrance of things parsed: Story structure and recall. *Cognitive Psychology, 9,* 111–151.

Mannes, S. M., & Kintsch, W. (1987). Knowledge organization and text organization. *Cognition and Instruction, 4,* 91–115.

Mayer, R. E., Dyck, J. L., & Cook, L. K. (1984). Techniques that help readers build mental models from scientific text: Definitions pretraining and signaling. *Journal of Educational Psychology, 76,* 1089–1105.

McNamara, D. S., Kintsch, E., Songer, N. B., & Kintsch, W. (in press). Are good texts always better? Interactions of text coherence, background knowledge, and levels of understanding in learning from text. *Cognition and Instruction.*

Merrill, D. M. (1980). Learner control in computer-based learning. *Computers & Education, 4,* 77–95.

Meyer, B. J. F. (1975). *The organization of prose and its effects on memory.* Amsterdam: North-Holland.

Monk, A. F., Walsh, P., & Dix, A. J. (1989). A comparison of hypertext, scrolling, and folding as mechanisms for program browsing. In D. M. J. & R. Winder (Eds.), *People and computers IV* (pp. 421–435). Cambridge: Cambridge University Press.

Nelson, T. (1988). Managing immense storage. *Byte, 13,* 225–238.

Prince, G. (1973). *A grammar for stories.* The Hague: Mouton.

Rayner, K., & Sereno, S. C. (1994). Eye movements in reading: Psycholinguistic studies. In M. A. Gernsbacher (Ed.), *Handbook of psycholinguistics.* San Diego: Academic Press.

Recker, M. M., & Pirolli, P. (1992). Student strategies for learning programming from a computational environment. In *Proceedings on the International Conference on Intelligent Tutoring Systems,* Montreal, Canada.

Reichman, R. (1985). *Getting computers to talk like you and me: Discourse context, focus, and semantics (an ATN model)* (pp. 3–19). Cambridge, MA: The MIT Press.

Rigney, J. W. (1978). Learning strategies: A theoretical perspective. In H. F. O'Neill, Jr. (Ed.), *Learning strategies* (pp. 165–205).

Rumelhart, D. E. (1975). Notes on a schema for stories. In D. Bobrow & A. Collins (Eds.), *Representation and understanding: Studies in cognitive science.* New York: Academic Press.

Sachs, J. S. (1967). Recognition memory for syntactic and semantic aspects of connected discourse. *Perception & Psychophysics, 2,* 437–442.

Saul, E. U., Coté, N., & Goldman, S. R. (1993, April). *Students' strategies for making text make sense.* Paper presented at the annual meeting of the American Educational Research Association, Atlanta, GA.

Scardamalia, M., & Bereiter, C. (1991). Higher levels of agency for children in knowledge building: A challenge for the design of new knowledge media. *The Journal of the Learning Sciences, 1,* 37–68.

Scardamalia, M., Bereiter, C., Brett, C., Burtis, P. J., Calhoun, C., & Smith Lea, N. (1992). Educational applications of a networked communal database. *Interactive Learning Environments, 2,* 45–71.

Scardamalia, M., Bereiter, C., McLean, R. S., Swallow, J., & Woodruff, E. (1989). Computer-supported intentional learning environments. *Journal of Educational Computing Research, 5,* 51–68.

Scardamalia, M., Bereiter, C., & Lamon, M. (1994). Bringing the classroom into World War III. In K. McGilly (Ed.), *Classroom lessons: Integrating cognitive theory and classroom practice* (pp. 201–228). Cambridge, MA: MIT Press/Bradford Books.

Schmalhofer, F., & Glavanov, D. (1986). Three components of understanding a programmer's manual: Verbatim, propositional, and situational representations. *Journal of Memory and Language, 25,* 279–294.

Schneiderman, B. (1987). User interface design for the Hyperties electronic encyclopedia. In *Proceedings of ACM Hypertext '87* (pp. 189–194). Chapel Hill, NC: ACM.

Schnotz, W. (1994). Strategy-specific information access in knowledge acquisition from hypertext. In L. Resnick, R. Säljö, & C. Pontecorvo (Eds.), *Discourse, tools, and reasoning: Situated cognition and technologically supported environments.* Heidelberg, New York: Springer.

Schön, D. A. (1983). *The reflective practioner.* New York: Basic Books.

Spiro, R. J., & Jehng, J. C. (1990). Cognitive flexibility and hypertext: Theory and technology for the nonlinear and multidimensional traversal of complex subject matter. In D. Nix and R. J. Spiro (Eds.), *Cognition, education, and multimedia: Exploring ideas in high technology* (pp. 163–205). Hillsdale, NJ: Erlbaum.

Spiro, R. J., Vispoel, W. L. Schmitz, J., Samarapungavan, A., & Boerger, A. (1987). Knowledge acquisition for application: Cognitive flexibility and transfer in complex content domains. In B. C. Britton & S. Glynn

(Eds.), *Executive control processes in reading* (pp. 177–199). Hillsdale, NJ: Erlbaum.

Stark, H. A. (1988). What do paragraph markings do? *Discourse Processes, 11*, 275–303.

Stein, N. L., & Glenn, C. F. (1979). An analysis of story comprehension in elementary school children. In R. Freedle (Ed.), *Multidisciplinary approaches to discourse processing*. Norwood, NJ: Ablex.

Stein, N. L., & Goldman, S. R. (1981). Children's knowledge about social situations: From causes to consequences. In S. Asher, & J. Gottman (Eds.), *The development of children's friendships* (pp. 297–321). New York: Cambridge University Press.

Stein, N. L., & Nezworski, T. (1978). The effects of organization and instructional set on story memory. *Discourse Processes, 1*, 177–193.

Steinberg, E. R. (1989). Cognition and learner control: A literature review, 1977–1988. *Journal of Computer-Based Instruction, 16*(4), 117–121.

Steinberg, E. R., Baskin, A. B., & Hofer, E. (1986). Organizational/memory tools: A technique for improving problem-solving skills. *Journal of Educational Computing Research, 2*(2), 169–187.

Steinberg, E. R., Baskin, A. B., & Matthews, T. D. (1985). Computer-presented organizational memory aids as instruction for solving pico-Fomi problems. *Journal of Computer-Based Instruction, 12*(2), 44–49.

Tannen, D. (1989). *Talking voices: Repetition, dialogue, and imagery in conversational discourse*. Cambridge: Cambridge University Press.

Tennyson, R. D. (1980). Instructional control strategies and content structure as design variables in concept acquisition using computer-assisted instruction. *Journal of Educational Psychology, 72*(4), 525–532.

Tennyson, R. D., & Rothen, W. (1979). Management of computer-based instruction: Design of an adaptive control strategy. *Journal of Computer-Based Instruction, 5*(3), 63–71.

Tiessen, E., & Ward, D. (1994). *(Re)modeled uses of multimedia and hypermedia in education*. Paper presented at ED-MEDIA'94, annual meeting of the Association for the Advancement of Computing in Education. Vancouver, British Columbia.

Trabasso, T., & van den Broek, P. (1985). Causal thinking and the representation of narrative events. *Journal of Memory and Language, 24*, 612–630.

van den Broek, P. W. (1990). The causal inference marker: Towards a process model of inference generation in text comprehension. In D. A. Balota, G. B. Flores d'Arcais, & K. Rayner (Eds.), *Comprehension processes in reading* (pp. 423–445). Hillsdale, NJ: Erlbaum.

van Dijk, T. (1987). Episodic models of discourse processing. In R. Horowitz & S. J. Samuels (Eds.), *Comprehending oral and written language* (pp. 161–196). San Diego: Academic Press.

van Dijk, T., & Kintsch, W. (1983). *Strategies of discourse comprehension.* New York: Academic Press.

van Oostendorp, H. (in press). Studying and annotating electronic text. In J. F. Rouet & J. Levonen (Eds.), *Hypertext and cognition.* Hillsdale, NJ: Erlbaum.

Voss, J. F. (1984). On learning and learning from text. In H. Mandl, N. L. Stein, & T. Trabasso (Eds.), *Learning and comprehension of text* (pp. 193–212). Hillsdale, NJ: Erlbaum.

Vygotsky, L. (1986). *Thought and language.* Cambridge, MA: The MIT Press.

Whitehead, A. N. (1929). *The aims of education & other essays.* New York: Macmillan.

3

Bringing Insights from Reading Research to Research on Electronic Learning Environments

Donald J. Leu, Jr.

Syracuse University

David Reinking

University of Georgia and the National Reading Research Center

INTRODUCTION

Since Rumelhart (1976) first proposed an interactive model of text processing, it has become nearly axiomatic in the reading community to describe reading as an interactive process (e.g., Hittleman, 1988; Kim & Goetz, 1994; May, 1986). Rumelhart's model portrayed the nature of reading comprehension as an internal interaction *within* the mind of the reader; multiple, parallel processing, knowledge sources simultaneously interacted with one another, sharing information about a text until one interpretation was determined to best represent meaning. Since this early work by Rumelhart, however, the internal interaction that takes place during reading gradually has come to be redefined as an external interaction. Today, the concept of reading as an interactive process frequently is used to described what takes place *between* a reader and a text; readers are thought to interact with a text as they construct meaning and achieve comprehension (Tierney & Pearson, 1983; Tierney & Shanahan, 1991). Current interpretations of reading as an interactive process often give the impression that both text and reader contribute equally to a dynamic, interactive relationship.

Unfortunately, viewing reading as an interaction between reader and text is an idealized and somewhat metaphorical interpretation of this process. As Reinking (1992) has pointed out, the notion that readers and texts interact is not completely accurate since an interaction implies that at least two elements actively engage one another. During reading, readers are the only active participants; traditional texts, of course, remain static.

Electronic learning environments, however, provide an opportunity to operationalize this idealized notion of a dynamic, reciprocal interaction between readers and texts. We use the term "electronic learning environments" to refer to environments where text carries at least a portion of the information within an interactive electronic medium. Electronic learning environments include what are commonly referred to as hypertext (Bolter, 1991), hypermedia (Marchionni, 1988), or multimedia (Schank, 1994). Within electronic learning environments, readers actively manipulate the nature of the information they encounter as they navigate through flexibly structured resources in an attempt to construct meaning. Recent examples of what we refer to as electronic learning environments include many locations on the World Wide Web and the increasing number of CD-ROM programs used at school and at home to promote learning.

Many electronic learning environments actively respond to readers who seek information from multiple media sources. Hillinger (1992), noting this interactive potential, refers to electronic learning environments as "responsive text" since they can respond to the unique needs of a reader seeking to construct meaning. An electronic learning environment, for example, might pronounce a word for a young student struggling with decoding, provide an explanation for a difficult concept unfamiliar to a user, animate a complex process to illustrate causes and consequences, provide a video segment to demonstrate a procedural routine, or display written responses by other users about their learning experiences. Consistent with Rumelhart's early model, comprehending printed material in electronic learning environments involves an internal interaction *within* the mind of the reader as different knowledge sources share information about the meaning that is constructed. However, comprehending printed material in electronic learning environments also brings into play a dynamic, external interaction *between* a reader who may seek additional information and an electronic learning environment responding to these requests. As a result, the previously metaphorical interactions between readers and texts now become real.

Although the potential of electronic learning environments for assisting students has been discussed often (e.g., Balathy, 1990; Blanchard, 1990; Van Dyke Parunak, 1991b), virtually every leading scholar in this area has bemoaned the limited empirical research and theory that could produce better understanding of these environments; there is far more intuitive speculation in this area than there is systematic research and theory development (Alexander, Kulikowich & Jetton, 1994; Spiro & Jehng, 1990). As a result, the design of electronic learning environments is nearly always based on intuition and hunch rather than data and theory. It is likely this weakness has limited the ability of current designs to support students' learning.

Recently, intriguing theoretical perspectives about learning in these dynamic environments have begun to emerge (Bolter, 1991; Scardamalia & Bereiter, 1991; Spiro, Feltovich, Jacobson, & Coulson, 1992). These will be helpful in creating more focused, theoretically driven research agendas. Although these focused perspectives are useful, we believe it is also important to draw from lines of research in diverse disciplines, including reading, in order to develop questions that can contribute to broader theoretical frameworks that might be missed with a narrower view.

It is ironic that we suggest that work in reading research might be useful to identify promising research issues within electronic learning environments whereas, at the same time, we argue that the central construct in much of this research, the dynamic interaction between reader and text, is often misinterpreted. Yet, this is exactly what we propose. We assume that electronic learning environments, where interactions between readers and texts occur literally, will make many insights about interactions discovered from reading research even more salient. We recognize, however, that the utility of these insights will be modified by several factors, such as the differences between internal and external interactive processes, the more numerous symbol systems available to an electronic medium using multiple media to convey information, the important differences between reading comprehension and learning, and the different attributions individuals assign to traditional texts and electronic learning environments. Nevertheless, we believe that insights from reading research may provide a useful initial agenda for pursuing research on learning within the much more dynamic, responsive, and truly interactive electronic environments that are now possible.

The purpose of this chapter is to discuss how several insights from reading research, central to understanding the more limited interactions between readers and texts, can apply to electronic learning environments. We believe each may be useful to inform our understanding of the more powerful interactions that take place within responsive, electronic learning environments. Six insights from reading research are especially important to consider.

1. It is more important to study interactive processes than products;
2. In order to understand interactive processes, one must understand the role of prior knowledge.
3. In order to understand interactive processes, one must understand the role of strategic knowledge.
4. In order to understand interactive processes, one must understand the role of interest and other motivational factors.
5. Interactive processing is supported when reading and writing are connected.
6. Research and software design are both enhanced when they are grounded in classroom contexts.

We believe studying each of these areas within electronic learning environments will inform the development of broader, theoretical frameworks to guide further research. At the same time, the data gathered from exploring these areas should provide useful insights into software design that maximally supports students' learning. In fact, we will argue that more consistent and profound outcomes in electronic learning environments have yet to be realized because important insights in each of these areas have yet to be considered in the design of current software.

As we discuss each issue, we will review related work occurring in both reading research and research on electronic learning environments. Throughout the discussion, we hope it will become clear how our backgrounds in reading research have guided our explorations into this area. Although some might argue this limits our perspective on these fundamental issues, we believe our backgrounds provide a special lens with which to look at electronic learning environments. As scholars from other fields also contribute their own special perspectives to these issues, our understanding of learning within electronic environments will benefit. Ultimately, it is essential that scholars from diverse fields join together to understand and exploit fully these new contexts so that teaching and learning are improved. We hope to contribute to this dialogue.

IT IS MORE IMPORTANT TO STUDY INTERACTIVE PROCESSES THAN PRODUCTS

A central aspect of studying interactions in reading research has been to concentrate on the process rather than the product. *Product outcomes generally have been useful only as they inform us about the nature of the reading process.* Given our backgrounds in this area, it appears fundamental to us that research on electronic learning environments begins to focus on interactive processes as much as on the products of learning. By looking carefully at the interactions between students and electronic learning environments we will be able to develop better explanations for how outcomes are achieved in these environments, something that is fundamental for both theory development and the design of more supportive learning environments.

Research on reading during the 1970s and early 1980s focused on reading processes, largely from a cognitive perspective. Research into the reading process established the central psychological reality for many important cognitive constructs that continue to influence theory and practice today. Schema-theoretic research, for example, explored the nature of our mental representations for concepts (Anderson & Pearson, 1984) and procedural scripts (Schank & Abelson, 1977) as well as the construction of mental models (Collins, Brown, & Larkin, 1980) and situation models (van Dijk & Kintsch, 1983). Miscue research was a direct outgrowth of linguistic and cognitive theory and provided insights into the expectations readers generated during reading (Leu, 1982). In addition, research into the nature and role of discourse knowledge contributed important insights into the consequences of text structure for comprehension (Armbruster, 1984; Meyer, 1975). Finally, important work on inferential processes allowed us to understand the active contributions readers make to the meaning they assign to text (Trabasso, 1981). When combined with other work, such as the development of automaticity theory (Samuels & Eisenberg, 1981), these early lines of research provided us with powerful insights about the nature of the reading process. In an important way, they also have informed more recent, socially grounded research into the nature of reading development that also tends to focus on process issues (Newman, Griffin, & Cole, 1989).

The emphasis on process issues in reading stands in dramatic contrast to what we find in the research on electronic learning environments, where the emphasis often appears to be on learning outcomes. It is clear to us that outcome-based research is important to demonstrate the ability of electronic learning environments to assist learning, especially given the limited nature of compelling and consistent research results on this issue (e.g., McGrath, 1992; Schare, Dunn, Clark, Soled, & Gilman, 1991; van der Berg & Watt, 1991). Clearly, a stronger case needs to be made for the efficacy of electronic learning environments. However, one of the reasons more consistent results have not been obtained is that the design of these studies has not yet been informed by systematic research about the processes associated with interactive learning environments. Process research would do much to help us understand optimal support structures for learning. For example, which types of dynamic, information support do students gravitate toward as they attempt to create meaning within electronic learning environments? Which informational support structures yield increases in learning? Do students with different levels of prior knowledge benefit from different types of informational support structures? When text is present, do students with different levels of reading achievement benefit from different types of information? Which types of media sources best support certain types of learning? Answers to these and other process questions will inform the development of more supportive electronic learning environments and lead to more consistent and compelling data on their efficacy.

Although some studies have explored process issues in relation to static physical features such as screen size or text layout (e.g., De Bruijn, de Mul, & Van Oostendorp, 1992; Dillon, 1994), we find relatively little work on interactions with dynamic features such as those described in the preceding paragraph. This gap is surprising given the importance of defining more supportive electronic learning environments. It is also surprising given the ease with which these data may be obtained with the aid of a computer. Research on internal reading processes always has been limited by the lack of observable process data. With the exception of miscue research, which looks at observable oral reading errors, process research in reading requires manipulating different contexts in order to obtain indirectly patterns that are not readily visible. In studying electronic learning environments, however, it is relatively easy to determine much of the on-line processing by directly observing the overt interactions students have with the learning environment. Providing learners with carefully selected choices in an electronic learning environment and then recording their choices provides unobtrusive opportunities to monitor covert processes.

Some of the work we have conducted in electronic learning environments has been guided by a concern for process issues, often in combination with learning outcomes. For example, one of us (Reinking, Pickle, & Tao, in press), explored the effects of inserted questions on the reading comprehension process of college students. Readers were required to review relevant portions of a text when a question was answered incorrectly. When readers failed to answer an inserted question correctly, they spent more time reviewing the paragraphs necessary to answer inserted questions, but only if they knew that they would receive the same question following review as opposed to a different question. In addition, when students knew that a different question would follow their review of each paragraph they performed better on inferential questions than literal questions on a post-reading test. Studies such as this can provide useful information about the nature of comprehension processing within electronic learning environments and the types of supportive structures that are useful to students. Such studies also provide information about how information can be presented electronically to effect changes in students' learning and study strategies. By analyzing the effects of manipulations in electronic environments we can acquire a more systematic picture of learning processes. Such information is crucial to designing more supportive electronic learning environments for students.

One of us (Leu, Gallo, & Hillinger, 1995) has taken a slightly different approach to understanding process issues by observing patterns of on-screen choices made by students. In this study, a chapter from a sixth-grade social studies textbook was converted into a hypermedia environment in order to evaluate interaction patterns by students who varied in reading achievement level. The study also compared comprehension in the two different information environments. Results indicated higher levels of recall among students in the hypermedia condition when compared to the traditional textbook version of the passage. Most important, though, process data indicated that students differentially exploited supportive features depending on their reading achievement level. Low achieving readers more frequently used a "close-up" feature. The "close-up" feature assisted with acquiring central ideas by providing additional graphical information and interactive animations. Average and high ability readers more frequently used a "check-up" feature. The "check-up" feature allowed students to monitor comprehension by interacting with graphical elements to evaluate their understanding of text segments. In essence, weaker readers attempted to construct meaning, whereas better readers attempted to evaluate the meaning they had constructed. These different patterns of processing by reading achievement level suggest that electronic learning environments need to account systematically for the learning needs and strategies of different types of students. It seems clear from this work that research should explore additional differences between subjects that may influence the ways in which they exploit information presented in electronic learning environments.

An increasingly important issue, for example, concerns the populations that have been used as subjects in studies of electronic learning environments. As Alexander, Kulikowich, and Jetton (1994) point out, these studies most often use high school or college students. When younger subjects are used, it is often to study writing processes (e.g., Turner & Dipinto, 1992) or to foster cooperative learning strategies (e.g., Signer, 1992). If this pattern continues, we run the risk of developing theoretical frameworks that ignore developmental differences in how students interact with electronic learning environments, specifically the types of information they find most useful to learning. In addition, we may erroneously propose software solutions for younger students based on data from older students, who process information differently.

There are other ways, of course, to generate process data during learning with electronic environments. Work by Scardamalia and Bereiter (1991), for example, takes a somewhat different approach but provides us with important insights about the use of student-generated questions to guide students in building knowledge structures. Other work by Spiro and his colleagues is beginning to test cognitive flexibility theory that deals with learning content in ill-structured domains of knowledge, such as medial diagnoses. Jacobson and Spiro (1993), for example, found greater transfer of knowledge within a complex knowledge domain when college students read information in hypertext. On the other hand, students receiving information in a more conventional environment performed higher on measures of factual knowledge.

All of this work is important to developing greater insight into students' actual learning processes as they interact with electronic learning environments. We believe process issues such as these will become even more important to define optimal designs of computer interfaces as electronic learning environments rapidly include additional interactive, nonprint based information (video, speech, animations, simulations, and graphics). We also believe that careful observation of student interaction patterns is essential if we are to develop greater insight into the nature of these processes. Finally, we believe it is essential to begin exploring these issues in relation to differences in a wide variety of subject characteristics. It is only after accomplishing these goals that we will be able to develop more useful and comprehensive theoretical perspectives and more supportive structures for learning.

UNDERSTANDING THE ROLE OF PRIOR KNOWLEDGE DURING INTERACTIVE PROCESSES

Prior knowledge has been explored extensively as a variable accounting for the comprehension of traditional texts. Prior knowledge has a powerful effect on both the quantity and quality of learning that takes place during reading, producing robust effects that include: increasing interest and recall of information (Alexander, Kulikowich, & Jetton, 1994), increasing the types and quality of self-generated questions (Scardamalia & Bereiter, 1991), and determining the interpretation of ambiguous passages (Bransford & Johnson, 1973). Also, it is clear that the effects of prior knowledge increase as students move through the educational system (Alexander, Kulikowich, & Jetton, 1994) and as the informational density of a passage increases (Tyler & Voss, 1982); prior knowledge effects are most pronounced among older students and when information density is greatest.

Electronic learning environments provide two characteristics that may be especially useful in helping learners overcome a lack of prior knowledge in complex and informationally dense texts: the ability to respond to students' information needs based on their unique differences in prior knowledge and the ability to present information through multiple media. By responding to students' information needs, electronic learning environments achieve a dynamic and responsive quality not possible in static texts and may be able to compensate for the effects of differences in prior knowledge. This potential increases when information can be presented in a variety of different media; students unable to acquire the information through one medium may be able to acquire it through alternative media. Thus, it is important to understand the extent to which electronic learning environments can assist individuals who have little prior knowledge about a topic.

Hillinger and Leu (1994) recently evaluated the ability of a hypermedia environment to overcome limitations of prior knowledge about a complex and informationally dense topic. They created a hypermedia version of a training manual for the repair and maintenance of a CT7-9 turboprop engine and evaluated learning among high and low prior knowledge subjects. High prior knowledge subjects were members of an air force propulsion unit responsible for the repair of F-16 jet fighter planes and familiar with high performance engine systems. Low prior knowledge subjects were university students unfamiliar with high performance engine systems. In this study, the low prior knowledge subjects achieved the same level of learning with the hypermedia environment as the more knowledgeable service personnel, a finding seldom reported in the literature on the comprehension of conventional printed texts. This finding held for both specific, targeted information defined in the learning task before treatment as well as for general, nontargeted information unrelated to the learning task. It also was sustained when covariate analysis controlled for differences in the amount of education between the two populations.

This study also evaluated interactions between levels of prior knowledge and whether the route through the hypermedia environment was controlled by the system or by the user. In the system-control condition, users proceeded through the hypermedia environment in a linear fashion by following a system-controlled guide. This guide assisted learners in accomplishing a series of objectives central to the learning task that was given to all participants. Figure 3-1 illustrates one screen from the system-control condition, showing the nature of this guide as a participant attempted to accomplish the second objective ("Identify the components of the hot section"). Here, the participant has selected the "do it" button in order to "zoom in" on the core section of the engine, the location where the hot section components can be found. He has also opened the text window as directed by the guide and is reading the information about the core section module. During the third objective, the guide will show the participant how to take apart the core section and find

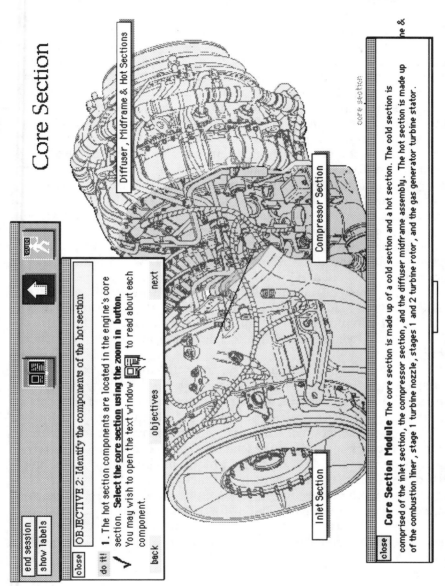

Core Section

Diffuser, Midframe & Hot Sections

Compressor Section

Inlet Section

---

end session

show labels

close | OBJECTIVE 2: Identify the components of the hot section

do it! | 1. The hot section components are located in the engine's core section. **Select the core section using the zoom in button.** You may wish to open the text window ▣ to read about each component.

back | objectives | next

---

core section

close | **Core Section Module** The core section is made up of a cold section and a hot section. The cold section is comprised of the inlet section, the compressor section, and the diffuser midframe assembly. The hot section is made up of the combustion liner, stage 1 turbine nozzle, stages 1 and 2 turbine rotor, and the gas generator turbine stator.

FIGURE 3-1. A view of one screen in the system-control condition showing the nature of the learning guide.

53

each of the hot section components that lie within. As this is done, video, text, and animations will be available to explain the function of each hot section component.

In the user-control condition, subjects were free to explore the hypermedia environment on their own, looking at any area they wished in any sequence they desired. In both conditions, the same types of support structures were available. By using elements of the tool bar at the top of the screen, subjects could view animations illustrating different aspects of jet propulsion theory, watch videos of each part being assembled and disassembled, take the main sections apart on the screen or put them back together, read text explaining essential information about a part, or move in for a closer view of any part. Figure 3-2 shows one screen from the user control condition, including a text segment explaining the function of the combustion liner (one component of the hot section) and a video segment showing how a combustion liner is removed.

The results of this study indicated an interaction between the type of control and level of prior knowledge. Low prior knowledge subjects, asked to learn specific, targeted information, performed best under system control. Higher prior knowledge subjects, asked to learn specific, targeted information, did best under user control. For learning general, nontargeted information, the nature of the control system did not affect learning outcomes for either group.

This study illustrates some of the special characteristics of electronic learning environments that need to be explored in relation to the role of prior knowledge; system control or user control, for example, is not an issue during the reading of a conventional, printed text. The nature of control only becomes important for the rich and complex information structures that are possible in electronic learning environments. There are other unique insights about learning within electronic environments that also would be revealed by thoughtful explorations into the role of prior knowledge. For example, does prior knowledge assist or interfere with the acquisition of knowledge in ill-structured domains where multiple knowledge representations are possible? One might argue that prior knowledge would allow a more multiple-faceted understanding of meaning. On the other hand, it could be argued that prior knowledge might narrow a reader's interpretation and interfere with learning. Work on this issue from the perspective of cognitive flexibility theory (Spiro, Feltovich, Jacobson, & Coulson, 1992) would be helpful for understanding learning in these unique types of domains.

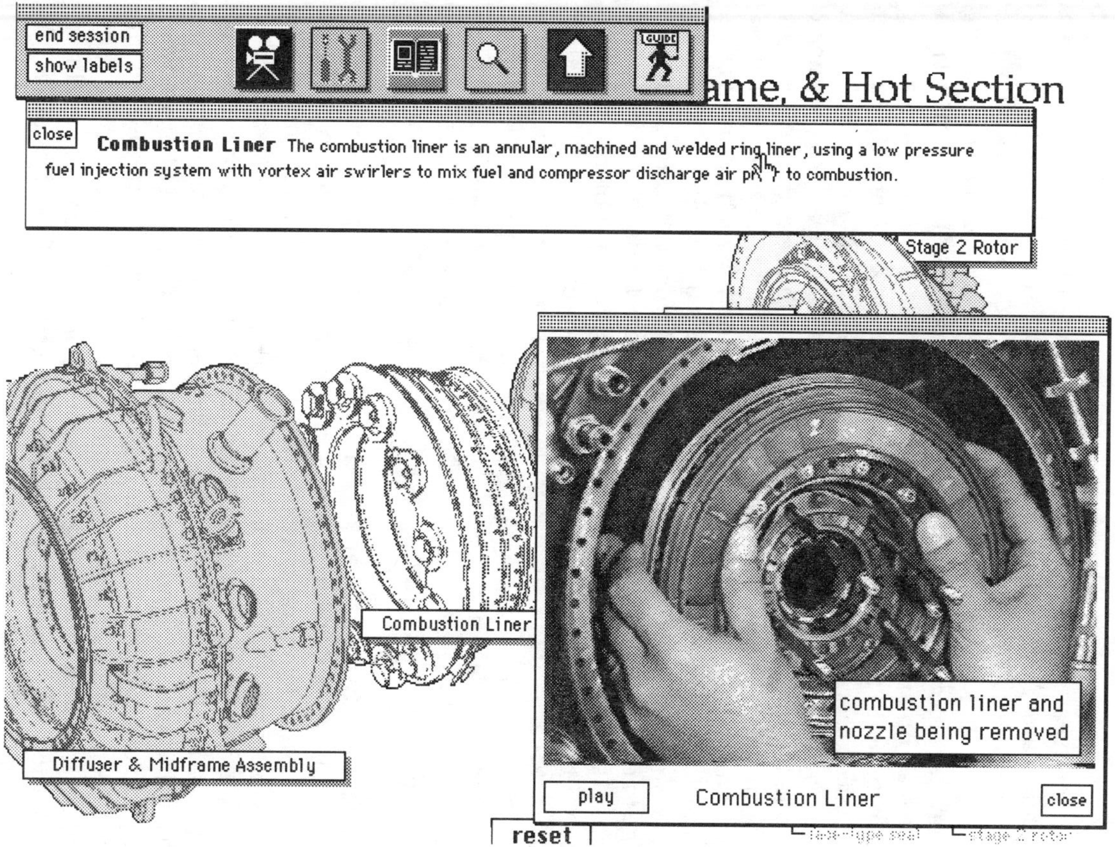
end session
show labels
GUIDE
ame, & Hot Section
close
Combustion Liner The combustion liner is an annular, machined and welded ring liner, using a low pressure fuel injection system with vortex air swirlers to mix fuel and compressor discharge air p to combustion.
Stage 2 Rotor
Combustion Liner
Diffuser & Midframe Assembly
combustion liner and
nozzle being removed
play
Combustion Liner
close
reset

FIGURE 3-2. A view of one screen in the user-control condition showing the nature of different information resources available to the learner.

UNDERSTANDING THE ROLE
OF STRATEGIC KNOWLEDGE

Another area central to any understanding of interactions between students and electronic learning environments is the role of strategic knowledge. Work in reading over the past several decades has demonstrated the importance of strategic knowledge to reading comprehension (Brown, 1980; Paris, Wasik, & Turner, 1991). It comes as no surprise, therefore, that studies in electronic learning environments are also focusing on this important issue (Beeman et al., 1987; Bernstein, 1991; Trumbull, Gay, & Mazur, 1992; Van Dyke Parunak, 1991b). It is quickly becoming clear that strategic knowledge may be even more important within electronic learning environments than within traditional, static texts because electronic environments require more decisions about which sources of information to explore in order to accomplish a learning goal.

As we review the literature, we find most work on strategic knowledge in electronic learning environments has focused on what Bernstein (1991) has referred to as the "navigational problem," the difficulties inherent in navigating through interconnected information nodes. Clearly, this macro level focus on strategic knowledge is important given the unique navigational challenges presented by nonlinear information structures. This work will yield important information about the most appropriate types of interfaces to reduce the strategic knowledge demands of users and support learning processes.

There are two other areas related to strategic processing, however, that we believe are equally important to consider in research on electronic learning environments. First, although many studies focus on navigational and interface issues, we can locate no studies that address strategic decisions at the word, sentence, or paragraph levels when learning information presented in a nonlinear structure. Nor can we find studies examining relationships between these micro-level decisions and graphic-, video-, or audio-based information. Strategic processing at microlevels has been more thoroughly explored in reading comprehension studies using traditional, static texts (Brown, 1980; Garner et al., 1991; Jetton et al., 1992; Paris, Wasik, & Turner, 1991). There are many useful insights that might be drawn from these studies. It is important, however, not to assume that micro-level strategic processes are identical in both traditional texts and electronic learning environments. There are, of course, different sources of information in electronic learning environments. Thus, strategic processing may be different when electronic environments contain audio, animated graphics, and video, especially when all of these information sources appear in combination with written prose. Moreover, from the perspective of limited attention models (e.g., Samuels & Eisenberg, 1981), it is likely that conscious decisions about strategic processing at the macro level, an area where there are greater demands within electronic learning environments, may alter strategic processing at the micro level. Given the importance of micro-level strategic processing from studies of reading comprehension and the unique characteristics of electronic learning environments, studies of micro-level strategic processing may yield important insights for both theory development and software design.

Second, given the importance of strategic processing in most electronic learning environments, we are surprised how often this type of knowledge goes uncontrolled in experimental studies. Often it is assumed that all subjects are equally adept at exercising the strategic knowledge demands of software used in the experiment. Infrequently, a short training session and preassessment measure are used to assure that subjects are familiar with the strategic knowledge demands in the study. In these cases, unfortunately, the training and preassessment measures are seldom thoroughly described and are almost never related to theoretical work on strategic processing, which might clearly identify the different types of strategic knowledge required to exploit the information structure. As a result, the majority of studies seldom ensure that subjects are familiar with the strategic knowledge demands for the learning task. This problem is especially acute when studies compare learning in electronic and traditional text environments or between different types of electronic learning environments. It is important for such studies to demonstrate that participants are equally familiar with the strategic knowledge for their learning context so that differences in outcomes are not explained by strategic knowledge differences.

Work by Paris and his colleagues (Paris, Lipson, & Wixson, 1983; Paris, Wasik, & Turner, 1991) might be useful for planning training and assessment of strategic knowledge before data are collected. Paris has shown that at least three types of strategic knowledge are important during text processing: declarative knowledge ("knowing that"), procedural knowledge ("knowing how"), and conditional knowledge ("knowing when"). Studies of learning in electronic environments might begin to evaluate participants in relation to these different types of strategic knowledge before treatment. The distinctions Paris draws between different types of strategic knowledge may also be useful to study both the macro- and micro-level strategic knowledge necessary for effective learning in electronic environments.

UNDERSTANDING INTEREST AND OTHER MOTIVATIONAL FACTORS

Interest and other motivational factors have long been recognized as central to both reading comprehension (Thorndike, 1917) and, more recently, to learning in electronic environments (Dillon, 1991). Here we will make four suggestions that might guide future studies investigating motivational factors in electronic learning environments.

First, cognitive theories of learning in electronic environments and, consequently, research based on them, will be enhanced if interest and other motivational factors are placed in a more central position and considered more systematically. In reading research, it is clear that interest and other motivational factors are intertwined with all aspects of comprehension and learning. For example, a number of scholars have begun to focus on connections between strategic knowledge and interest (Borkowski, Carr, & Rellinger, 1990; El-Hindi, 1994; Paris, Wasik, & Turner, 1991), attempting to uncover the reciprocal relation they believe to exist between these two elements of reading comprehension. Others have found close connections between interest and process issues (Schiefele, 1991), and between interest and prior knowledge issues (Alexander, Kulikowich, & Schulze, in press). Interest and motivation are also focal issues for the new National Center on Reading Research (Alvermann & Guthrie, 1993), a group who has used the term "engagement" as a more descriptive and encompassing construct. This focus is beginning to yield important results in theory development, research, and practice.

We believe that a more systematic focus on interest and other motivational factors will yield similar gains for work on electronic learning environments. In our review of this issue, we have found a tendency for studies in electronic learning environments to use limited measures of interest, often just one or two items presented in a Likert scale. These measures were nearly always administered before or after interacting with the learning environment. Seldom was interest measured during a student's interaction with the environment. We believe that more complex measures and more on-line assessment will help to develop a richer, more comprehensive understanding of this important factor.

Second, as we consider the nature of interest and other motivational elements in electronic learning environments, it may be useful to consider the construct of locus of control. Locus of control has been a useful construct in the field of reading, both for explaining differences in achievement outcomes as well as providing important insight into process issues (Hiebert, Winograd, & Danner, 1984; Johnston & Winograd, 1985; Short & Ryan, 1984; Winograd, Witte, & Smith, 1986). The term locus of control has been used to frame learners' attributions for outcomes on cognitive tasks. Learners who attribute outcomes to internal factors, such as effort and ability, are thought to be characterized by internal locus of control. Learners who attribute outcomes to external factors, such as luck or the difficulty of the task, are thought to be characterized by external locus of control. Internal locus of control is associated with higher achievement in reading comprehension, whereas external locus of control is associated with lower achievement (Hiebert, Winograd, & Danner, 1984; Wagner, Spratt, Gal, & Paris, 1989).

Some work has begun to study the role of locus of control in electronic learning environments (Gray, 1989). Given the utility of this construct in explaining learning with traditional texts, it might also be a fruitful variable to study more extensively in electronic learning environments. This is true especially since these environments, because of their potential to support learning, might make it possible over time for students to change external attributions for success (the software environment) into internal attributions (their ability).

Third, as we consider interest and other motivational elements in electronic learning environments, it may be useful also to recognize an important conclusion reached by Alexander, Kulikowich, & Jetton (1994). These authors note that it is important to consider Hidi's (1990) distinction between situational interest and individual interest. Situational interest is specific to the learning situation and transitory; often it is measured after a learning experience. Individual interest is a result of an individual's long-term experiences with a topic or domain and more permanent; often it is measured before the learning experience. It is possible, for example, that individual interest in electronic learning environments actually may impede the acquisition of knowledge (Garner & Gillingham, 1992; Wade & Adams, 1990), especially when students have had extensive experiences with electronic games (Schick & Miller, 1992). Students who come to an electronic learning environment expecting to encounter a game may be less interested in exploring an electronic informational structure to acquire important knowledge. Studies that include measures of interest and motivation need to disentangle these two types of interest if we are to develop a clearer understanding of how interest and motivation interact with electronic learning environments.

Finally, work on issues of interest and motivation should not be separated from work on other issues. Indeed, is only within the context of other issues that we can develop a realistic understanding about the contributions interest and motivation make to learning. A study by Dillon (1991) shows how this is likely to be the case where data emerged by looking at the connections between prior knowledge, process issues, strategic issues, and interest issues. The findings of this study indicated that subjects with more prior knowledge and interest for a topic had more knowledge about the discourse structure of the information environment and that this, in turn, led to more comprehension when reading a hypertext document. In addition, subjects with more prior knowledge also were able to navigate strategically through the hypertext document more effectively and used sections of interest more strategically, both of which facilitated comprehension. We believe that such studies provide important support for the need to study these issues in combination, not in isolation.

CONNECTING READING AND WRITING

Reading research has consistently demonstrated that students learn more when reading and writing are connected (Shanahan, 1990; Stotsky, 1983). There is a long and consistent line of work indicating that combining reading and writing experiences is important for reasons that are cognitive, pragmatic, and social.

Cognitively, it is clear that combining reading and writing experiences results in children who learn to both read and write better (Stotsky, 1983). Because both reading and writing rely on related processes, one activity enhances the other (Shanahan, 1990; Tierney & Shanahan, 1991). This relationship can be exploited effectively in the classroom to simultaneously support cognitive development in both areas. In addition, reading and writing, when integrated strategically into classroom experiences, can be a powerful means to increase students' cognitive ability to analyze and think critically about information. Separately, both reading and writing may be used to develop critical thinking skills but when combined, they serve to reinforce each other and produce even greater benefits than if they are used alone (Tierney and Shanahan, 1991). This is especially important since critical thinking skills have been increasingly recognized as an important requirement of citizens who wish to participate fully in an economically and interdependent world (Kirsch & Jungeblut, 1986; Langer, Applebee, Mulis, & Foertsch, 1990; National Commission on Excellence in Education, 1983; Ravitch, 1985; The Secretary's Commission on Achieving Necessary Skills, 1991).

Pragmatically, combining reading and writing experiences also is efficient, a quality whose significance should not be underestimated for busy classroom teachers facing increasing demands on instructional time as political units mandate new curricular areas. In addition to increasing learning, linking reading and writing experiences can result in a more efficient use of limited instructional time. This pragmatic aspect of connecting reading and writing often is viewed by teachers as more important than any other (Shanahan, 1990).

Combining reading and writing experiences also says something important to learners about the nature of literacy. Literacy fundamentally is a social and communicative act (Daniels, 1991): readers attempt to understand the meanings assigned by writers and writers attempt to anticipate the meanings assigned by readers (Tierney & Shanahan, 1991). Viewing literacy as a social phenomenon is something that is well known to proficient readers and writers. Failing to integrate reading and writing increases the chance that literacy learners will miss this fundamental aspect of literacy. As a result, they may be less likely to use literacy in their own lives or to use it less effectively when they do read and write.

Taken together, combining reading and writing creates a powerful context as literacy learners simultaneously develop important academic skills, sharpen their ability to think critically about important issues, meet the increasing content area requirements demanded by our society, and acquire insight about literacy as a social and communicative act. Research investigating electronic learning environments needs to focus more attention on simultaneously integrating electronic learning experiences with writing experiences. This is not to say that studies of written composition in electronic contexts are lacking. Clearly, this is an active area for research (Reinking & Bridwell-Bowles, 1991). Nor is it to suggest that the potential of e-mail communication for learning has not been investigated. Clearly, this area is also receiving a great deal of research attention suggesting that communication experiences in writing can support students' learning (Myers, 1993). It is, however, to suggest that we do not yet know much about the ways in which writing experiences *within* a content-focused, electronic learning environment might support learning. Reading research would suggest that this might be a very powerful way in which to assist students and provide important opportunities for critical thinking.

Recently, Leu (1994) conducted an exploratory study into the potential of connecting reading and writing experiences within an electronic learning environment. Reading and writing experiences were presented to fourth grade students within an electronic environment based on a work of children's literature. Several design features were included in the electronic learning environment developed for the study, including a reader response journal, a classroom bulletin board, and an e-mail system.

Reader response journals often are used by teachers to connect reading and writing in classrooms (Nathan & Temple, 1991). As students read a work of literature, they are encouraged to enter their thoughts and reactions to what they are reading in their journal. This activity allows students to draw insights useful to their cognitive development and to engage in opportunities to think critically about the information they are reading. To support students' responses in their journals, this investigation included a set of potential writing ideas that students could access during their reading of the story. At each location in the passage, students selecting this support option would be presented with a list of writing ideas appropriate for that location. Figure 3-3 illustrates one student's entry in her reader response journal in response to a writing prompt.

The electronic learning environment also created communication opportunities between students so they might perceive reading and writing as social processes. When students view reading and writing as social process they, in turn, are more likely to acquire the cognitive and analytic abilities that are central to literacy proficiency (Shanahan, 1990). To accomplish these purposes, the environment included two types of support features: a classroom bulletin board and an e-mail system.

After students had made an entry in their reader response journal, they could keep it to themselves. In addition, however, they could also send it to the classroom bulletin board to be read by others. In so doing, recursive chains of reading–writing connections were developed as students posted a sequence of responses related to the initial item. An example of one entry in a bulletin board location can be seen in Figure 3-4.

The electronic bulletin board encouraged social interaction through reading and writing, as did an e-mail system that allowed students to send messages to one another about their reading experiences or other personal interests. After writing an entry in their response journal, students could send this message to other students in the

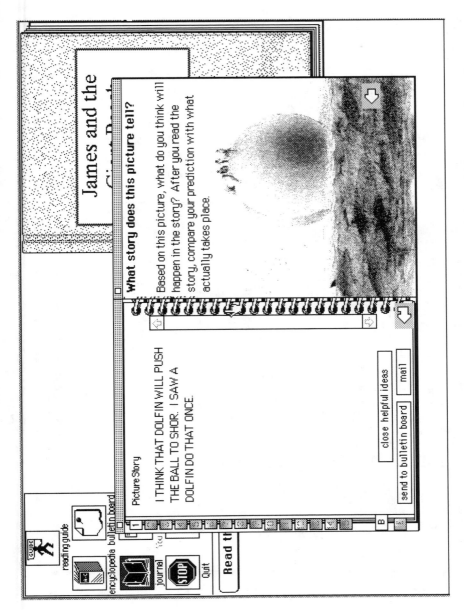

FIGURE 3-3. A view of a screen illustrating one student's entry in her reader response journal.

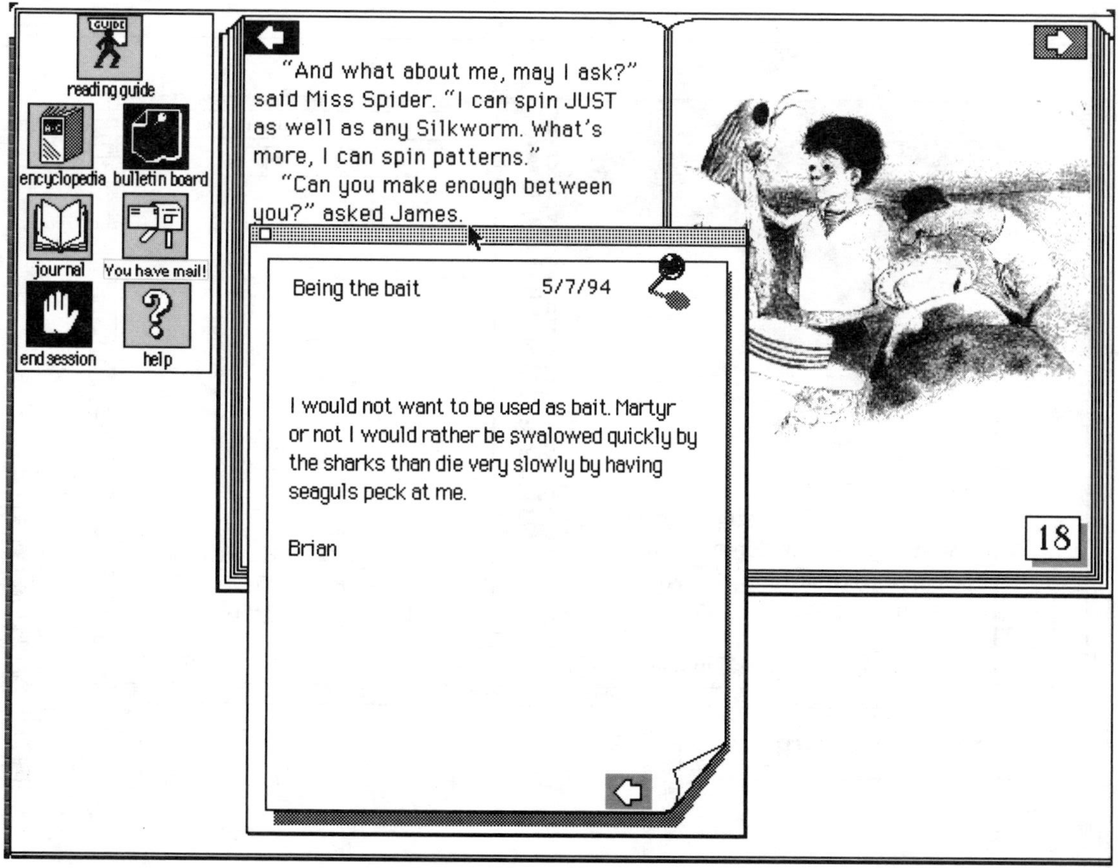

FIGURE 3-4. An example of a bulletin board entry.

64

class by selecting a button labeled "mail" (see Figure 3-3). Students received messages in their individual "mailbox." Sending messages via e-mail proved to be the most frequently used activity that connected reading and writing. It substantially increased the amount of reading and writing that occurred in this class as each message often led to additional opportunities to read and write. Moreover, written responses to the story that were sent via e-mail typically were deeper and more complex than other types of responses. Each of these patterns confirm the instructional utility of connecting reading and writing with electronic learning environments.

The study also yielded an unexpected, but important, result: Electronic writing experiences provided opportunities for communication between students who did not normally communicate in class. While observing students at the computer, it became clear that communication about the story often took place between boys and girls, whereas such mixed-gender communication was infrequent during regular classroom interactions. Additional communication took place between several exceptional students who were "mainstreamed" into the classroom and other students, something that happened less frequently outside of the electronic learning environment. It appears that when writing takes place within electronic learning environments the potential for socially mediated responses to information increases, especially between students who do not often interact with one another.

This exploratory study suggests that writing experiences within an electronic learning environment might support learning in various ways: by increasing the amount of reading and writing; by encouraging deeper, more reflective response; and by increasing communication between students who might not normally communicate. These tentative findings point to the need for further studies to investigate ways in which reading and writing connections might enhance learning within electronic environments.

EXPLORING THE ADVANTAGES OF RESEARCH AND SOFTWARE DESIGN GROUNDED WITHIN CLASSROOM CONTEXTS

It is important to also recognize that interactive processes transcend relationships between readers and texts or between users and electronic learning environments. Research in reading has recently focused on the classroom interactions between teachers and students as they negotiate meaning in texts. This has been one aspect of the current emphasis on grounding research more systematically in classroom contexts. Another has been a move to see teachers as colleagues in classroom research who have a unique perspective from which to view the complexity of teaching and learning (Allen, Buchanan, Edelsky, & Norton, 1992). Interactions that are more broadly conceived, such as these, have something important to contribute to research on the use of electronic learning environments and to research on the design of instructional software.

It is important to ground research on electronic learning environments within classroom contexts because of a frustrating paradox—at the same time that computers have become more widely available in schools, there is little evidence that they have been widely integrated across the curriculum (cf., Anderson, 1993; Becker, 1990; U.S. Congress, Office of Technology Assessment, 1995; Martinez & Mead, 1988; Reinking & Bridwell-Bowles, 1991). The ratio of students to computers in precollege instruction in the United States has increased from 1 to 30 in 1988 (U.S. Congress, Office of Technology Assessment, 1994) to 1 to 16 in 1993 (Anderson, 1993) and the number of computers available in classrooms increases by about 10% each year. Despite this increase, a recent study (Goodson, 1991) indicates that fewer than 15% of all teachers actually use computers in their teaching. Computer technology is becoming more widely available but it is not becoming fully appropriated by teachers and integrated into classroom learning experiences (Newman, 1991).

This conclusion is also supported by Becker (1993), who reports that although 40% of math and science teachers use some computer software in their classes, only three percent of computer-using math teachers engaged students in the use of graphing programs on more than five occasions and only 1% of computer-using science teachers used computer programs that connected with lab equipment on more than five occasions. It seems clear that teachers are not sufficiently appropriating technology and integrating these experiences into their classrooms, despite the increasing availability of that technology. This paradox suggests a need for research that helps us understand how computers can be fully integrated into classroom instruction.

However, why is it important to seek ways to support more rapid technology integration by teachers? One reason is that technology use appears to profoundly change the way that teachers teach. Technology use appears to foster the development of more student-centered classrooms (Collins, 1990), to increase collaboration among students on learning tasks (Schiengold & Hadley, 1990), and to cause teachers to have higher expectations for students (Schiengold & Hadley, 1990). All of these changes improve the nature of classroom learning environments (The Secretary's Commission on Achieving Necessary Skills [SCANS], 1991).

Yet, just introducing technology designed to positively change classroom practice is not enough. There are also several economic considerations. Anderson (1993) estimates that more than $1 billion per year is spent on hardware and software by schools in the United States. Spending this amount on technology seems to require that we use it wisely to ensure a return on investment. Minimal, sporadic, and isolated use of technology belies the potential for technology to reform education.

One way to make technology more cost effective is to reduce training costs by designing software to fit more precisely the needs of classroom stakeholders. One study (SRI, 1991), has estimated the annual cost of training teachers to use technology to be approximately $900 per teacher or about $4 billion per year. However, this figure is based on current software designs that too often are intimidating to teachers or unrelated to their needs. If software were designed to fit more precisely the needs of classroom teachers, it is likely these costs could be substantially reduced.

We believe that technology use will change dramatically, even among teachers who have been most reluctant to integrate it into their classrooms, when two things happen: (1) more systematic research takes place on the use of electronic learning environments that is grounded within classroom contexts; and (2) electronic learning environments are designed in classroom contexts, not technology labs, in order to be more consistent with teachers' instructional needs.

Recently, Reinking and Pickle (1993) have suggested that "formative experiments" (Newman, 1991) be conducted to understand better how to integrate classroom learning with electronic learning environments. This approach uses both qualitative and quantitative methods to study the effects of changes made within the classroom in how electronic learning environments are used. "In a formative experiment, the researcher sets a pedagogical goal and finds out what it takes in terms of materials, organization, or changes in the technology to reach the goal" (Newman, 1991, p. 10). Such an approach is quite promising. It will allow us greater insight into the effects of changes grounded in the reality of classroom contexts.

It is also possible that such an approach to research could be employed usefully to develop electronic learning environments that meet teachers' instructional needs more appropriately than electronic learning environments designed by technical experts unfamiliar with the reality of classroom life. Currently, teachers are not routinely part of software design teams. Occasionally, electronic learning environments are piloted in schools but only after basic design decisions have been made. Traditionally, it has been expensive to make major changes in design because flexible and powerful authoring tools have not been available. As a result, modifications to software are quite limited and piloting experiences are more often used to assist marketing decisions than for formative development. With the advent of recent authoring tools, however, it is easier to change the design of software and to try out several approaches before making final decisions. The availability of these authoring tools should make it possible to engage in formative approaches to software such that students and teachers can be at the center of design decisions.

By taking a formative approach, electronic learning environments can be designed that are informed by the instructional needs of teachers and the learning needs of students. Formative approaches should enable us to shape classroom learning in ways that take advantage of electronic learning environments and to shape electronic learning environments to maximize learning. Both outcomes are important if we want technology to be both available and used in schools to support learning.

SUMMARY AND CONCLUSIONS

In this chapter we have identified issues we believe may help focus current theoretical perspectives, current lines of research, and current software designs within electronic learning environments. We come to this task from our backgrounds in reading research where the metaphor of an interaction between readers and texts has guided research during the past 25 years. Recognizing that this metaphor is not completely accurate for reading traditional texts, we believe, nevertheless, that the major patterns of this work have something important to say to work in electronic learning environments where more dynamic, responsive, and truly interactive patterns characterize the learning process.

We believe that reading research suggests several useful ideas for guiding work within electronic learning contexts: studying interactive processes as much as products, understanding the role of prior knowledge during interactive processes, understanding the role of strategic knowledge, understanding the role of interest and other motivational elements, exploring the potential for learning when reading and writing experiences are connected, and exploring the advantages of research and software design grounded within classroom contexts. As we put these areas forward for consideration by a wider community, we recognize that our insights are governed, and undoubtedly limited, by our backgrounds in reading research; we do not mean to suggest that these are the only issues that are important. We are convinced, however, that research aimed at understanding electronic learning environments will be limited unless we take advantage of the insights from each of the disciplines that find this environment an important context in which to study learning.

REFERENCES

Allen, J., Buchanan, J., Edelsky, C., & Norton, G. (1992). Teachers as "they" at NRC: An invitation to enter the dialogue on the ethics of collaborative and non-collaborative classroom research. In C. K. Kinzer, & D. J. Leu, Jr. (Eds.), *Literacy research, theory, and practice: Views from many perspectives.* Forty-first Yearbook of the National Reading Conference (pp. 357–365). Chicago: National Reading Conference.

Alexander, P. A., Kulikowich, J. M., & Jetton, T. L. (1994). The role of subject-matter knowledge and interest in the processing of linear and non-linear texts. *Review of Educational Research, 64*(2), 210–252.

Alexander, P. A., Kulikowich, J. M., & Schulze, S. K. (in press). How subject matter knowledge affects recall and interest. *American Educational Research Journal.*

Alvermann, D. E., & Guthrie, J. T. (1993). *Themes and directions of the National Reading Research Center. Perspectives in Reading Research No. 1.* Athens, GA: NRRC.

Anderson, R. E. (1993). The technology infrastructure of U.S. schools. *Communications of the ACM, 36*(5), 72.

Anderson, R. C., & Pearson, P. D. (1984). A schema-theoretic view of basic processes in reading. In P. D. Pearson, R. Barr, M. L. Kamil, & P. Mosenthal (Eds.), *Handbook of reading research: Volume I* (pp. 255–292). New York: Longman.

Armbruster, B. B. (1984). The problem of inconsiderate text. In G. Duffy, L. Roehler, & J. Mason (Eds.), *Comprehension instruction: Perspectives and suggestions* (p. 203). New York: Longman.

Balathy, E. (1990). Hypertext, hypermedia, and metacognition: Research and instructional implications for disabled readers. *Journal of Reading, Writing, and Learning Disabilities International, 6*(2), 183–202.

Becker, H. J. (1990). Computer use in the United States schools: An initial report of the U.S. participation in the IEA computers in education survey. Paper presented at the American Educational Research Association, Boston, MA.

Becker, H. J. (1993). Teaching with and about computers in secondary schools. *Communications of the ACM, 36*(5), 70.

Beeman, W. O., Anderson, K. T., Bader, G., Larkin, J., McClard, A. P., McQuillan, P., & Shields, M. (1987). Hypertext and pluralism: From lineal to non-lineal thinking. In *HyperTEXT '87 Proceedings* (pp. 57–86). Chapel Hill, NC: Association for Computing Services.

Bernstein, M. (1991). The navigation problem reconsidered. In E. Berk, & J. Devlin (Eds.), *Hypertext/hypermedia handbook* (pp. 285–298). New York: McGraw-Hill.

Blanchard, J. (1990). Hypermedia: Hypertext—implications for reading education. *Computers in the Schools, 6*, 23–30.

Bolter, J. D. (1991). *Writing space: The computer, hypertext, and the history of writing.* Hillsdale, NJ: Erlbaum.

Borkowski, J. C., Carr, M., & Rellinger, E. (1990). Self-regulated cognition: Interdependence of metacognition, attributions, and self-esteem. In B. F. Jones, & L. Idol (Eds.), *Dimensions of thinking and cognitive instruction* (pp. 53–92). Hillsdale, NJ: Erlbaum.

Bransford, J. D., & Johnson, M. K. (1973). Consideration of some problems of comprehension. In W. Chase (Ed.), *Visual information processing.* New York: Academic Press.

Brown, A. L. (1980). Metacognitive development and reading. In R. J. Spiro, B. C. Bruce, & W. F. Brewer (Eds.), *Theoretical issues in reading comprehension.* Hillsdale, NJ: Erlbaum.

Collins, A. (1990). The role of computer technology. In K. Sheingold, & M. Tucker (Eds.), *Restructuring for learning with technology.* New York: Bank Street College of Education and the National Center on Education and the Economy.

Collins, A., Brown, J. S., & Larkin, K. M. (1980). Inference in text understanding. In R. J. Spiro, B. C. Bruce, & W. F. Brewer (Eds.), *Theoretical issues in reading comprehension* (pp. 385–410). Hillsdale, NJ: Erlbaum.

Daniels, H. A. (1991). Young writers and readers reach out: Developing a sense of audience. In T. Shanahan (Ed.), *Reading and writing together: New perspectives for the classroom.* Norwood, MA: Christopher-Gordon.

De Bruijn, D., de Mul, S., & Van Oostendorp, H. (1992). The influence of screen size and text layout on the study of text. *Behavior and Information Technology, 11*, 71–78.

Dillon, A. (1994). *Designing usable electronic text.* London: Tailor and Francis.

Dillon, A. (1991). Readers' models of text structure: The case of academic articles. *International Journal of Man-Machine Studies, 35*, 913–925.

El-Hindi, A. (1994). Supporting college learners: Relations between meta-cognition, reading and writing proficiency, and locus of control. Unpublished doctoral dissertation, Syracuse University.

Garner, R., Alexander, P. A., Gillingham, M. G., Kulikowich, J. M., & Brown, R. (1991). Interest and learning from text. *American Educational Research Journal, 28,* 643–659.

Garner, R., & Gillingham, M. G. (1992). Topic knowledge, cognitive interest, and text recall: A microanalysis. *Journal of Experimental Education, 59,* 310–319.

Goodson, B. (1991). *Teachers and technology: Staff development for tomorrow's schools.* Alexandria, VA: National School Boards Association.

Gray, S. H. (1989). The effect of locus of control and sequence control on computerized information retrieval and retention. *Journal of Educational Computing Research, 5,* 459–471.

Hidi, S. (1990). Interest and its contribution as a mental resource for learning. *Review of Education Research, 60,* 549–571.

Hiebert, E. H., Winograd, P. N., & Danner, F. W. (1984). Children's attributions for failure and success in different aspects of reading. *Journal of Educational Psychology, 76*(6), 1139–1148.

Hillinger, M. L. (1992). Computer speech and responsive text. *Reading and Writing: An Interdisciplinary Journal, 4,* 219–229.

Hillinger, M. L., & Leu, D. J. (1994). Guiding instruction in hypermedia. *Proceedings of the Human Factors and Ergonomics Society's 38th Annual Meeting,* 266–270.

Hittleman, D. R. (1988). *Developmental reading, K–8.* Columbus, OH: Merrill.

Jacobson, M. J., & Spiro, R. J. (1993). *Hypertext learning environments, cognitive flexibility, and the transfer of complex knowledge: An empirical investigation.* (Report No. CSR-TR-573). Urbana, IL: Illinois University, Center for the Study of Reading. (ERIC Document Reproduction Service No. ED 355 508).

Jetton, T. L., Alexander, P. A., & White, S. H. (1992, December). *Motivating from without: The effects of including personally involving information in content-area texts.* Paper presented at the annual meeting of the National Reading Conference.

Johnston, P. H., & Winograd, P. N. (1985). Passive failure in reading. *Educational Psychologist, 17*(4), 279–301.

Kim, Y. H., & Goetz, E. T. (1994). Context effects on word recognition and reading comprehension of poor and good readers: A test of the interactive-compensatory hypothesis. *Reading Research Quarterly, 29*(2), 179–187.

Kirsch, I., & Jungeblut, A. (1986). *Literacy: Profiles of America's young adults.* Princeton, NJ: Educational Testing Service.

Langer, J. A., Applebee, A. N., Mulis, I. V. S., & Foertsch, M. A. (1990). *Learning to read in our nation's schools: Instruction and achievement in 1988 at grades 4, 8, and 12.* Princeton, NJ: Educational Testing Service.

Leu, D. J., Jr. (1982). Oral reading error analysis: A critical review of research and application. *Reading Research Quarterly, 17,* 420–437.

Leu, D. J., Jr. (1994). Designing hypermedia to connect reading and writing through children's literature. *Proceedings of the National Educational Computing Conference,* 44–55.

Leu, D. J., Jr., Gallo, M. J., & Hillinger, M. (1995). Reading comprehension in hypermedia environments: Reconsidering considerate text in dynamic, electronic environments. Manuscript in preparation.

Leu, D. J., Jr., & Kinzer, C. K. (1995). *Effective reading instruction, K–8.* New York: Macmillan.

Marchionni, G. (1988). Hypermedia and learning: Freedom and chaos. *Educational Technology, 29*(11), 9–12.

Martinez, M. E., & Mead, N. A. (1988). Computer competence: The first national assessment (Research Report No. 17-CC-01). Princeton, NJ: Educational Testing Service.

May, F. B. (1986). *Reading as communication: An interactive approach.* Columbus, OH: Merrill.

McGrath, D. (1992). Hypertext, CAI, paper, or program control: Do learners benefit from choices? *Journal of Research on Computing in Education, 24,* 513–532.

Meyer, B. J. F. (1975). *The organization of prose and its effects on memory.* Amsterdam: North-Holland.

Myers, J. (1993). Constructing community and intertextuality in electronic mail. In D. J. Leu & C. K. Kinzer (Eds.), *Examining central issues in literacy research, theory, and practice* (pp. 251–262). Chicago: National Reading Conference.

National Commission on Excellence in Education. (1983). *A nation at risk: The imperative for educational reform.* Washington, DC: U.S. Department of Education.

Nathan, R., & Temple, C. (1991). Classroom environments for reading and writing together. In T. Shanahan (Ed.), *Reading and writing together: New perspectives for the classroom.* Norwood, MA: Christopher-Gordon.

Newman, D. (1991). Opportunities for research on the organizational impact of school computers. *Educational Researcher, 19*(3), 8–13.

Newman, D., Griffin, P., & Cole, M. (1989). *The construction zone.* Cambridge: Cambridge University Press.

Paris, S. G., Lipson, M. Y., & Wixson, K. K. (1983). Becoming a strategic reader. *Contemporary Educational Psychology, 8,* 293–316.

Paris, S. G., Wasik, B. A., & Turner, J. C. (1991). The development of strategic readers. In P. D. Pearson, R. Barr, M. Kamil, & P. Mosenthal (Eds.), *Handbook of reading research* (pp. 609–640). New York: Longman.

Ravitch, D. (1985). *The schools we deserve: Reflections on the educational crises of our times.* New York: Basic Books.

Reinking, D. (1992). Differences between electronic and printed texts: An agenda for research. *Journal of Educational Multimedia and Hyper-media, 1,* 11–24.

Reinking, D., & Bridwell-Bowles, L. (1991). Computers in reading and writing. In R. Barr, M. L. Kamil, P. B. Mosenthal, & P. D. Pearson (Eds.), *Handbook of Reading Research, Volume II* (pp. 310–340). New York: Longman.

Reinking, D., & Pickle, J. M. (1993). Using a formative experiment to study how computers affect reading and writing in classrooms. In D. J. Leu, & C. K. Kinzer (Eds.), *Examining central issues in literacy research, theory, and practice.* The 42nd Yearbook of the National Reading Conference (pp. 263–270). Chicago, IL: National Reading Conference.

Reinking, D., Pickle, J. M., & Tao, L. (in press). The effects of questions inserted in electronic texts. University of Georgia, University of Maryland & National Reading Research Center.

Rumelhart, D. (1976). Toward an interactive model of reading (Report No. 56). La Jolla, CA: University of California, San Diego, Center for Information Processing.

Samuels, S. J., & Eisenberg, P. (1981). A framework for understanding the reading process. In F. J. Pirozzolo, M. C. Wittrock (Eds.), *Neuropsychological and cognitive processes in reading.* New York: Academic Press.

Scardamalia, M., & Bereiter, C. (1991). Higher levels of agency for children in knowledge building: A challenge for the design of new knowledge media. *The Journal of the Learning Sciences, 1*(1), 37–68.

Shanahan, T. (1990). Reading and writing together: What does it really mean? In T. Shanahan (Ed.), *Reading and writing together: New perspectives for the classroom.* Norwood, MA: Christopher-Gordon.

Schank, R. C. (1994). Active learning through hypermedia. *Multimedia, 1*(1), 69–78.

Schank, R. C., & Abelson, R. P. (1977). *Scripts, plans, goals, and understanding.* Hillsdale, NJ: Erlbaum.

Schare, B. L., Dunn, S. C., Clark, H. M., Soled, S. W., & Gilman, B. R. (1991). The effects of interactive video on cognitive achievement and attitude toward learning. *Journal of Nursing Education, 30,* 109–113.

Sheingold, K., & Hadley, M. (1990). *Accomplished teachers: Integrating computers into classroom practice.* New York: Bank Street College of Education, Center for Technology in Education.

Schiefele, U. (1991). Interest, learning, and motivation. *Educational Psychologist, 26,* 229–323.

Schick, J. E., & Miller, R. M. (1992, April). *Learner control in a hypertext environment with linguistic-minority students.* Paper presented at the Annual Meeting of the American Educational Research Association, Atlanta, GA.

Short, E. J., & Ryan, E. R. (1984). Metacognitive differences between skills and less skilled readers: Remediating deficits through story grammar and attribution training. *Journal of Educational Psychology, 76*(2), 224–235.

Signer, B. R. (1992). A model of cooperative learning with intergroup competition and findings when applied to an interactive reading program. *Journal of Research in Computing in Education, 25,* 141–158.

Spiro, R. J., Feltovich, P. J., Jacobson, M. J., & Coulson, R. L. (1992). Cognitive flexibility, constructivism, and hypertext: Random access instruction for advanced knowledge acquisition in ill-structured domains. In T. M. Duffy, & D. H. Jonassen (Eds.), *Constructivism and the technology of instruction: A conversation* (pp. 57–75). Hillsdale, NJ: Erlbaum.

Spiro, R. J., & Jehng, J. (1990). Cognitive flexibility and hypertext: Theory and technology for the nonlinear and multidimensional traversal of complex subject matter. In D. Nix, & R. Spiro (Eds.), *Cognition, education, and multimedia* (pp. 163–205). Hillsdale, NJ: Erlbaum.

SRI, Inc. (1991). *The Eisenhower mathematics and science education program: An enabling resource for reform.* Summary Report. Washington, DC: U.S. Department of Education.

Stotsky, S. (1983). Research on reading/writing relationships: A synthesis and suggested directions. *Language Arts, 60,* 627–643.

The Secretary's Commission on Achieving Necessary Skills (SCANS). (1991). *What work requires of schools: A SCANS report for America 2000.* Washington, DC: U.S. Department of Labor.

Tierney, R. J., & Pearson, P. D. (1983). Toward a composing model of reading. *Language Arts, 60,* 568–580.

Tierney, R. J., & Shanahan, T. (1991). Research on the reading-writing relationship: Interactions, transactions, and outcomes. In R. Barr, M. L. Kamil, P. Mosenthal, & P. D. Pearson (Eds.), *Handbook of reading research: Volume II* (pp. 246–280). New York: Longman.

Thorndike, E. L. (1917). Reading and reasoning. A study of mistakes in paragraph reading. *Journal of Educational Psychology, 8,* 323–332.

Trabasso, T. (1981). On the making of inferences during reading and their assessment. In J. Guthrie (Ed.), *Comprehension and teaching.* Newark, DE: International Reading Association.

Trumbull, D., Gay, G., & Mazur, J. (1992). Students' actual and perceived use of navigational and guidance tool in a hypermedia program. *Journal of Research on Computing in Education, 24,* 315–328.

Turner, S. V., & Dipinto, V. M. (1992). Students as hypermedia authors: Themes emerging from a qualitative study. *Journal of Research on Computing in Education, 25,* 187–198.

Tyler, S., & Voss, J. F. (1982). Attitude and knowledge effects in prose processing. *Journal of Verbal Learning and Verbal Behavior, 4,* 331–351.

U.S. Congress, Office of Technology Assessment (1995). *Teachers and technology: Making the connection.* Washington, DC: U.S. Government Printing Office.

van der Berg, S., & Watt, J. H. (1991). Effects on educational setting on student responses to structured hypertext. *Journal of Computer-based Instruction, 18,* 118–124.

van Dijk, T. A., & Kintsch, W. (1983). *Strategies of discourse comprehension.* New York: Academic Press.

Van Dyke Parunak, H. (1991b). Toward industrial strength hypermedia. In E. Berk, & J. Devlin (Eds.), *Hypertext/hypermedia handbook* (pp. 381–398). New York: McGraw Hill.

Wade, S. E., & Adams, R. B. (1990). Effects of importance and interest on recall of biographical text. *Journal of Reading Behavior, 4,* 331–351.

Wagner, D. A., Spratt, J. E., Gal, I., & Paris, S. G. (1989). Reading and believing: Beliefs, attributions, and reading achievement in Moroccan school children. *Journal of Educational Psychology, 81*(3), 283–293.

Winograd, P., Witte, R., & Smith, L. (1986). Measuring attributions for reading: A comparison of direct and indirect locus and stability scores. In J. Niles, & R. Lalik (Eds.), *Solving problems in literacy: Learner, teachers, and researchers* (pp. 387–394) Rochester, NY: National Reading Conference.

4

Comprehending Electronic Text

Mark G. Gillingham

Michigan State University
East Lansing, MI

INTRODUCTION

The purpose of this chapter is to critique educational uses of electronic-expository text where the goal is to assist the reader (often a novice) to understand and learn from text. Unlike conventional paper-based text, electronic text allows readers new options for assistance. It has been suggested that computers could increase the comprehension of expository text by offering text resources (Lachman, 1989; Reinking & Schreiner, 1985; Steinberg, 1977; Tobias, 1987) or strategy instruction (Gillingham, Garner, Guthrie, & Sawyer, 1989; Salomon, Globerson, & Guterman, 1989). Text resources provide readers with information related to a text (e.g., background information, vocabulary) or a companion text that is similar in meaning. Strategy instruction attempts to teach readers a way to approach a text (e.g., stopping to summarize) that may help to increase comprehension. As yet there is no agreed upon computer-based method of helping readers comprehend expository text. In this chapter, I will present several approaches to using electronic-text resources that have been used in attempts to enhance comprehension through manipulations of *text, task,* and *context.*

READING WITH ELECTRONIC TEXT

I will limit my discussion of electronic texts to those that attempt to improve, study, or measure reading comprehension of expository text. These electronic texts use a computer-based viewer to provide a screen or window view of new or existing expository text. Through the computer-based viewer, readers have access to one or more resources in addition to the text itself. If electronic texts are worth using, they must offer value above their paper-based counterparts. In addition, they must help readers learn how to read for comprehension. Just presenting text in old ways is not enough to serve the needs of a technologically savvy world (Steinberg, 1984).

Previously, I have argued that much of computer-based instruction uses expository text and that those of us who place text on computers should heed what the research has said about comprehending expository text (Gillingham, 1988). In this argument, special attention was paid to three characteristics of text: structure, considerateness, and prior knowledge requirements. More recently these ideas have been echoed and expanded by Martindale (1993). Expository text is itself structured in specific ways that may help readers understand what they are reading, but electronic texts, unlike paper-based text, can also be programmed to help readers comprehend by tapping appropriate schemas (e.g., revealing the structure of the text or tapping appropriate prior knowledge). Martindale (1993) explains

> Schemas of how text is structured are an important part of literacy. For students to become as proficient at using (electronic texts) as at using printed texts, they need to have schemas for how text is structured in (electronic texts). Thus, one of the most important tasks to be undertaken is to develop structures for organizing information in (electronic texts) (p. 110).

Martindale (1993) argues that these structures must be consistent and generally known—borrowed from paper texts. The fact is that most readers do not know the structure of a text or take advantage of it if they do (Garner, 1987). The real value added to electronic texts must be structural signals for readers and prompting of strategy use. In an important review of children's use (and nonuse) of reading strategies, Garner (1990) writes about the double jeopardy of using reading strategies. The first jeopardy is that they require much from the learner. Reading strategies require a goal, they must be intentionally invoked, they require effort, and they work differentially on different tasks. The second jeopardy is that strategies require active engagement of a text that can be hindered in a number of ways: poor comprehension monitoring, low expectations of success, weak knowledge of text, rejection by student of a given task, and over reliance of primitive strategies (e.g., rehearsal). The task of reading is not simple and therefore creating useful electronic texts will not be easy. The following section will describe selected electronic text resources that have been used to attempt to improve comprehension of exposition.

RESOURCES FOR COMPREHENSION

In this section, I will outline a progression of studies that incorporated one or more reading resources meant to increase the comprehension of electronic text. Studies will be presented that represent resources for text, task, and context strategies. Text resources are reading aids that act directly on a particular text. Text resources represented among these studies are definitions of low frequency words, main idea support, reduction of text difficulty, and accessing prior knowledge. Representative task strategy resources are strategies for answering a synthesis question and creating a summary. Finally, context-specific strategies for reading electronic texts are represented by an exam, sharing with peers, and public reports.

Text Resources

Electronic texts can offer a reader a variety of resources that attempt to assist by adding to or changing the text itself. Glossaries may help readers get passed difficult words. Alternative versions of the text may help readers with different vocabularies comprehend a text. Changes in a text may give a teacher or computer program information on the reading ability of a reader. Also, text changes may help a reader understand the structure of a text or help him or her access known and relevant information. The next sections describes attempts to offer text resources for low-frequency vocabulary, readability, maze, text structure, and prior knowledge.

Low-frequency vocabulary

Low frequency vocabulary are words that appear infrequently in a lexicon and, therefore, would not be as familiar to readers as higher frequency words. Therefore, offering readers definitions of these words in the context of expository text would appear to be a good reading resource. However, Feldman and Fish (1991) found that even though (high-school aged) readers would access this definitional resource, it did not improve their comprehension of short 300-word expository texts compared to a matched control group that did not have access to the definitions. Importantly, Feldman and Fish (1991) observed that definitions were accessed more often for more difficult exposition. This is confusing since one would suppose that the mere exposure to the text required to access definitions would increase comprehension regardless of whether the vocabulary was necessary to understand the text. A problem with research of this type is that we cannot tell why a reader chooses a resource. A given resource may be chosen to solve an apparent problem, because a reader was curious about it, or simply because it exists and can be selected. In addition, we often only know that a resource was selected but not about any cognitive processing that may have occurred. One way to estimate if any processing has occurred is to measure relative time spent on resources. This is what Lachman (1989) did.

In a thoughtful study of electronic expository text with a low-frequency vocabulary resource, Lachman (1989) reviewed the Kintsch and van Dijk (van Dijk & Kintsch, 1983) test comprehension model and tested it in a clever way. Briefly, in the Kintsch and van Dijk model, a reader actively creates a macrostructure from micropropositions read and acted upon by macrostrategies. What is created is a textbase in the reader's mind that is a combination of the extant text and prior knowledge in the form of facts, procedures, contexts, and strategies. Lachman reasoned that readers could be assisted to read for macropropositions (the main ideas) by embedding definitions of words that were essential for the main ideas. He carefully identified a set of words that were essential to the macrostructure of a long 3300-word psychology text and words that were essential only to the microstructure (e.g., intrasentential meaning). This design differed from the Feldman and Fish (1991) design in the length of text (3300 words vs. only 300 words in the Feldman & Fish study) and by virtue of a specific test of two types of vocabulary: important or not important to the main idea. Lachman showed that college-aged readers would use vocabulary resources (86 percent) and, more important, would choose to concentrate (spend more time) on the resources that proved to be relevant to the final test. Lachman primed readers to relevant macrostructure definitions by giving them a mid-text test of the macrostructure. The readers who received the mid-text test increased their reading time of macro-structure definitions that were relevant to the test by 36 percent and decreased their reading time of microstructure definitions that were irrelevant to the test by 18 percent. A control group that did not receive the mid-text test continued to request microstructure- and macrostructure-relevant vocabulary about equally.

Text comprehension researchers must be careful to attend to relevant information. Feldman and Fish (1991) attended to low-frequency vocabulary, but the connection between reading these vocabulary and comprehending the expository text was not made. Vocabulary is only one of the factors that combined to help readers make meaning of text and may not be the most important. Because Lachman (1989) differentiated vocabulary that was relevant to the macrostructure of the text from that which was relevant to the mi-crostructure and tested comprehension of the macrostructure we were able to determine that reading relevant information increases macrostructure comprehension. All resources are not equally im-portant to the comprehension task at hand. These studies suggest that electronic-text resources should help readers decide which of the available resources are most important to their reading goal and help direct readers to those resources.

Readability

Readable writing occurs between a writer and a reader. The writer uses certain conventions that the reader expects (or can easily learn to expect). The conventions include cohesive devices and redundancy at the syntactic, semantic, and discourse levels, all of which make it easier for a reader to access strategies and other knowledge and bring it to bear on the text being read. One promising resource of electronic texts was a more readable alternative text at the touch of a button. Unfortunately, creating more readable text is very difficult.

In a pair of studies, Reinking (Reinking, 1988; Reinking & Schrein-er, 1985) manipulated the readability ("easier, less technical ver-sion") of short expository texts by having teachers rewrite them for less able readers. Even though care was taken to ensure that "eas-ier" passage had fewer difficult words and shorter sentences as the formulae require and conveyed the meaning of the original pas-sages, creating passages that are easier to comprehend based on readability formulas is not easy to do (Armbruster & Anderson, 1984). Readability formulas fail in at least two ways: They are theo-retically weak—contradicting much of current knowledge about reading and they are poorly implemented—violating necessary assumptions (Bertram & Rubin, 1988). Reading comprehension has much to do with aspects of texts and readers that readability formulae do not measure (cf., Irwin, 1990; Muth, 1989; Yuill & Oakhill, 1991). For instance, text structure (Garner, Alexander, Slater, Hare, Smith, & Reis, 1986), prior knowledge of content (Afflerbach, 1990; Alexander, Kulikowich, & Jetton, 1994; Anderson & Davison, 1988) and passage topic interest (Anderson & Davison, 1988; Garner & Gillingham, 1991; Hidi & Baird, 1988; Renninger, Hidi, & Krapp, 1992) are at least as important to comprehension as word frequency and sentence length.

An alternative method of manipulating reading ease, concentrating on text structure, was tried by Gillingham and Garner (1992). The original texts were modified to be easier to read using the method of Armbruster and Anderson (1981, 1984). This method combines attention to text structure and vocabulary to create "considerate" texts. Creating texts that were considerate of the reader was a three-step process: First, difficult words were defined in context; second, implicit cohesive ties were made explicit; and third, modifications were made to increase cohesion within and between sentences. Unfortunately, as with Reinking's technique, there were not significant ease-of-reading advantages for less able readers. Clearly, more can be learned about making texts easier to read. In addition to these methods, it seems appropriate to include readers' prior knowledge and interest variables in future attempts to increase readability (Anderson & Davison, 1988).

Cloze and maze

Comprehending a text has been thought to be a matter of understanding some or all of the "levels" of a passage: The vocabulary resources of an electronic text are word-level resources, whereas summary statements are paragraph- or section-level resources. A variation of providing word-level resources is the cloze. Cloze correlates well with a variety of indices of reading ability, but is used mostly for assessing reading ability. Cloze is a reading task where some words are left out of a passage to be inferred by the reader. Better readers make better inferences more quickly than poorer readers (Horning, 1993). Computers can make the creation of cloze passages easier by automatically deleting every fifth word (the usual cloze form) of a text passage (Gillingham & Waynant, 1989). This is a technique used by some instructional learning systems (ILS) to place novice readers into computer-based lessons (Clarinina, 1992) based on cloze results.

Reading is more than just inferring words within text passages, however (Horning, 1993). In an attempt to expand the capability of cloze and computer-based reading, Gillingham and Garner (1992) created an application (*MacReader*, Figure 4-1) that presented word, sentence, and paragraph cloze. Following the rules of a special type of cloze called maze, which incorporates multiple choices for missing words, (Guthrie, 1973), we created mazes for whole sentences and paragraphs. It was thought that sentence- and paragraph-level mazes would more closely approximate higher level reading and comprehension. Two general models of reading comprehension could be tested. The skill model claims that there is a strict hierarchy in reading skills where words must be known before sentences can be understood and, likewise, sentences must be understood before paragraphs and other larger chunks of text. The comprehension model claims that reading is more than a hierarchy of skills and that strategic readers might comprehend larger chunks of text without completely understanding its vocabulary.

MacReader offers an innovation that is similar to Goldman's (Goldman & Saul, 1990) *Select The Text* application. Whereas *Select The Text* masks text near sentence boundaries that is not being read, *MacReader* selects an intact sentence to be read and measures the elapsed time that sentence is on the screen. In addition, *MacReader* preserves more paragraph information than does *Select The Text* by using a substitute type face that codes information for ascenders, descenders, case, word breaks, and sentence punctuation (Figure 4-1a). Either of these research tools could be the basis of a more extensive computer-based text environment.

MacReader allowed us to test both the skill and comprehension models of reading. Generally, readers in grades 7, 9, and 11 followed the skill model where word-level skills preceded sentence-level skills, which in turn, preceded paragraph-level skills. For seventh grade readers who did not follow the model ($n = 20$ of 78 total), 18 fit the alternative comprehension model—they were proficient at the paragraph level (Figure 4-1c) without showing proficiency at one or both of the word or sentence levels (Figure 4-1a,b). In addition, the maze proved to be more sensitive to reading comprehension ability as measured by readers' ability to write a summary than either grade in school or standard reading score (for grades 9 and 11). Applications like *Select the Text* and *MacReader* could be combined with text resources to narrow the range of resources offered by electronic text applications to those most likely to be of assistance to the reader, thus reducing the chance that readers would spend time and energy on less relevant information and strategies.

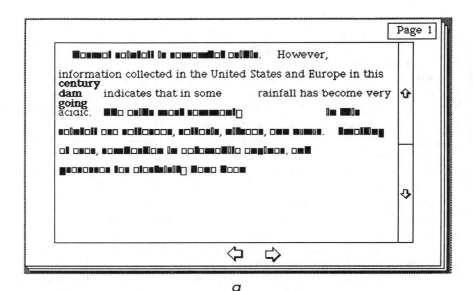

a

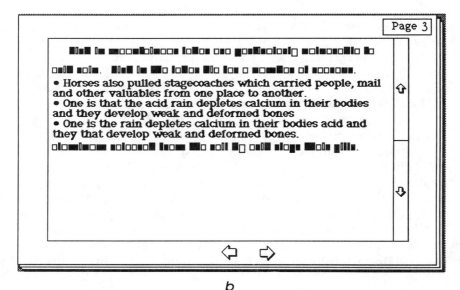

b

Choose the best heading for the paragraph.

> • Sulfurous, sulfuric, nitrous, and nitric acids are common in rainfall.
>
> • Human industry can cause rainfall to become very acidic.
>
> • Foreshocks may be very strong or very feeble and hardly felt.

c

FIGURE 4-1. *MacReader* provides a means to calculate sentence-reading times and to time the accuracy of word-, sentence-, and paragraph-level mazes. *a.* An example of a word-level maze where the reader is to choose from the words ("century," "dam," or "going") to fit into the sentence. At this point in the text depicted in the Figure, the reader has already read the first sentence and has proceeded to the second sentence in which the first of two word-level mazes is shown. In this case, "century" fits best. Of the two foils, "dam" is of the same syntactic type (noun), but is incorrect semantically and "going" is incorrect syntactically (verb) and semantically. *b.* An example of a sentence-level maze where the reader is to choose from the sentences to fit into the paragraph. At the point in the text depicted in the Figure, the reader has already read the first sentence and proceeded to the second sentence, which offers a choice from among three sentences to complete the sentence-level maze. The best choice reads: "One is that the acid rain depletes calcium in their bodies and they develop weak and deformed bones." One foil is syntactically correct, but incorrect semantically ("Horses also pulled stagecoaches which carried people, mail and other valuables from one place to another") and the other choice is syntactically incorrect, but made of the same words (scrambled) as the correct choice ("One is the rain depletes calcium in their bodies acid and they that develop weak and deformed bones"). *c.* An example of a paragraph-level maze where the reader is to choose the best heading (summary statement) of a just read paragraph. The two foils in this case are either too specific ("Sulfurous, sulfuric, nitrous and nitric acids are common in rainfall") or off topic ("Foreshocks may be very strong or very feeble and hardly felt").

Text structure

Reading a novel text of any kind poses problems for the reader, but readers comprehend better when they understand the structure of a text. The structure of a text is different for various types of text. For instance, well written expository texts can be expected to have topic sentences that anticipate subordinate sentences (super-ordination) on the same topic (topical relatedness) that make use of various lexical and graphical ties (cohesion) (Garner et al., 1986; Garner, 1987; Garner & Gillingham, 1987; Gillingham, 1988; Irwin, 1990; Lorch, 1989; Taylor & Samuels, 1983). Electronic texts have incorporated resources that have attempted to address various aspects of text structure. For instance, providing superordinate information regarding a topic (Gillingham et al., 1989; Lachman, 1989) or creating alternative versions of the text that adhere to strict rules of textual considerateness (Gillingham et al., 1989). More could be done using electronic texts to explicitly signal, map, and explain the structure of specific texts.

Prior knowledge

An electronic text might aid a reader by reminding him or her of knowledge already held in long-term store including facts (e.g., Stephen Hawking is a renowned cosmologist), strategies (e.g., to find information on Hawking's bet, scan the text for magazine titles), and beliefs (e.g., I believe I will be assessed on the main ideas of the text rather than isolated detail). Few studies have explored prior knowledge-enhancing resources of electronic texts. In one study of electronic-text resources, we (Gillingham et al., 1989) included two forms of prior knowledge resources: superordinate background information and three nontext-specific reading strategies—rereading important information, distinguishing unimportant from important information, and backtracking to the text from the answer frame. Background information had no measurable effect on the outcome measure, but strategic reading behavior, and task strategies, had significant effects. Perhaps as in Feldman and Fish (1991) where low-frequency vocabulary did not help increase comprehension, background information is not specific enough to increase readers' measured comprehension. In our study, task strategies, which focused on ways of reading rather than on what was read, helped increase readers' comprehension. In the next section, I will provide examples of task strategies that have been incorporated into electronic texts.

Task Strategy Resources

A task strategy resource is a prompt to use a reading strategy that could apply to the current text or other texts (e.g., rereading an important or difficult section, selecting important and excluding unimportant information to the task). Task strategies are not totally independent of a specific text, but unlike text resources, task-strategy resources are related to the task of reading the text for a specific purpose (e.g., general comprehension, search for specific information, big ideas) rather than manipulating the text itself. There are a variety of task-strategy resources that electronic texts might provide and that could improve comprehension of exposition. A few of these strategies have been included in studies of electronic text. Lachman (1989) demonstrated that undergraduate psychology students are able to spontaneously adjust their reading task strategy when given specific information about the goal of their reading. Reasoning that most readers in college courses read to be successful on a test, two variants of test placement were used in the study. For one group, a test of main ideas was placed midway through the 30-screen text. For the other group, the test was only given at the end of the text. For those students who received the mid-text test, relevant macrostructure vocabulary was studied longer (perhaps more carefully) when they pertained to ideas thought to be relevant to the test, which covered text macrostructure. Microstructure vocabulary that did not pertain to the test was given even less time than before the mid-text test. For competent adult readers then, we could expect that informing them about the nature of the reading goal in some context-relevant manner (e.g., a test) would improve their strategic reader behavior. Even if less competent or younger readers had reading strategies like the adults it is uncertain whether they would be informed by a task such as mid-text test.

In Gillingham et al. (1989), we studied task resources—rereading, selecting important from unimportant propositions, and returning to the text to check an answer. Thirty fifth-graders were assigned to no resource, resources available, or resources prescribed conditions. Two texts were used from a biology textbook that were rated to be equally familiar and interesting. Unlike Lachman's study of experienced readers, our study looked at novice fifth grade readers, who did not use task strategies as proficiently. Most readers did not spontaneously use available resources even though a variety of resources and information were provided including examples of using the task strategy, a sample of the synthesis question goal task, and access to the question at all times. Each of these examples attempted to give the reader enough information prior to reading that she could concentrate on a specific task during reading—to answer the question. However, for the group that was prescribed task strategy resources and for others from the resources available group who chose them spontaneously, performance on the synthesis question was significantly better. Comparing the effect of task and text resources one finds that task strategies added significantly to a prediction of the score on the synthesis questions ($R^2 = .89$, $F(3,8) = 21.80$, $p < .001$), whereas text resources (definitions and background information) did not.

Unlike the college-aged readers in Lachman's study, few fifth grade children in our study spontaneously recognized the situation, which in this case was one where they would be gathering information necessary to answer a synthesis question. Since the question was available at all times during reading, we can look toward poor or unenacted strategies as the main reason for poor performance. For most novice readers, electronic texts must do more than simply inform them of the reading goal. In our study, fifth grade children had to be shown the strategies and asked to perform them before a significant increase in reading comprehension occurred. Creators of electronic text must find ways to teach task strategies and remind readers to use them during their text processing.

Task strategies for inconsiderate electronic texts

We have seen in Lachman (1989) that adult readers can act strategically when given the limited choice of whether or not to choose a potentially valuable vocabulary resource and that fifth grade children are mostly overwhelmed by several text and task resources to help them answer a known synthesis question (Gillingham et al., 1989). However, even adults can become strategically confused when the electronic text is inconsiderate.

In a study of adults' comprehension in a hypertextual environment (Gillingham, 1993), a nonlinear text about Stephen Hawking was constructed from a variety of sources. The nodes of the text had the strict structure of a three-level binary tree (Jonassen, 1986) where the lowest level was a five-paragraph text used previously (Garner, Alexander, Gillingham, Kulikowich, & Brown, 1991). This binary structure aided the study of node traversal when readers were answering three two-part synthesis questions from the text. As in the study of children answering synthesis questions, adults were allowed to view any or all of the three questions before reading or at any time during reading. In fact, they were encouraged to do so. Complete answers to each question required traversal of the text in specific ways, but most answers could be found at deeper levels.

The adult readers did not do well on this task: 37 percent of the readers scored zero and only 23 percent received over half of the points allowed. Those who did poorly on the questions could not adequately form a strategy or could not operate the hypermedium well enough to traverse the nonlinear text. Those who could form a strategy were rewarded with higher scores; yet most readers formed simplistic strategies that looked only at surface features and missed important information deeper in the text. It seemed that adults were not adept at reading this hypertext, but several factors could have been the root cause: The adults may have been computer novices, poor readers generally, or uncomfortable in what they perceived as a test-like setting.

In settings where the content or structure of electronic texts are unfamiliar there is a particular burden on the text designers. As Martindale (1993) pointed out, the structure of the electronic text must be made explicit. In addition, readers need a few strategies (e.g., how and where to reinspect to find main ideas) that they will not only use, but use wisely enough to reach their reading goal.

Context Strategy Resource

As we know, knowledge of text structure and reading strategies is often insufficient for meaningful comprehension of expository text (Garner, 1987, 1990). Not only does one read for a purpose, but in a context. Recall that in Lachman's (1989) study, students who were given a mid-text test on the macropropositions of the text increased their accessing of macrostructure vocabulary and decreased their accesses of microstructure vocabulary. The context of reading for a test affected their reading behavior. Computers and electronic texts can and do exist in various social contexts where workstations are networked or groups of students work together on an electronic text. It is obvious that computers are necessary in these contexts, but there is much to be learned about how they can be most benefi-cial.

In an attempt to learn what roles computer technology might play in collaborative learning and working situations, Gay and Grosz-Ngate (1994) connected three small groups of designers together with a special network that allowed multiple-media communication (written text, audio, and video). Each group of designers worked on different aspects of the same project—to create a working model of motorized windmill from Lego blocks. Although this study does not show how traditional electronic texts are read, it does demonstrate as-yet untried resources that might be used in reading environ-ments. In the complex yet realistic context, several types of knowl-edge might be important for success: knowledge of general design, specific Lego building, communications, and intra- and intergroup dynamics. These various knowledge sources were supported by the multimedia system as Gay and Grosz-Ngate point out

As students work on a project supported by multimedia, they can bring the knowledge developed in different disciplines to bear on their problem. Because multimedia by definition involves knowledge represented in different forms (e.g., graphics, film clips, video, spoken and written text), it can help convey knowledge that is not easily conveyed verbally. Hence, it can augment the acquisition of tacit knowledge that is part and parcel of socialization into a community of practice and provide students with the opportunity to learn in context (p. 421).

The multimedia hypertext available to the designers constituted a database of information about task instructions, design, and specific and background information about the materials (e.g., batteries and generators). The data from this exploratory research show that designers relied on hypertext for early guidance and direction and again after initial design attempts. The designers saw the text as an important resource and sought it for information that was relevant to their tasks. The notion of reading electronic texts in the context of larger assignments and projects is very relevant to the issues of reader engagement—that is, effort and motivation.

Reading is a difficult activity in which a reader must be motivated to expend large amounts of energy. For many readers, this expenditure of energy is more likely to happen in a social context where authentic conversations related to the task occur (Brown, Collins, & Duguid, 1989; Rogoff & Lave, 1984). To determine what changes in reading behavior might occur in a social reading context, I created an electronic text for a cohort of graduate students in a preservice teacher program (see Figure 4-2 for sample pages from "Elementary School Music and Art," which was a module of a larger course). Students were asked to read the original electronic text, expand this text with their own expository text that required integration of information, and read text written by their peers to identify common elements or topics that could be linked together using hypertextual links. Because of the constraints on data collection, only assigned activities and casual observations could be collected. These data were encouraging. Students were highly engaged over a period of time, enthusiastically read their peers' work, engaged peers in conversations about what they had read, and made sensible connections from peers writing to their own.

Figure 4-2a is an example of one of the pages from the course module "Elementary School Music and Art." This page acts as a place holder for links to student-generated topics about integrating music and art into other elementary subject matter. The specific task was to read a case about a teacher named Betsy who was to

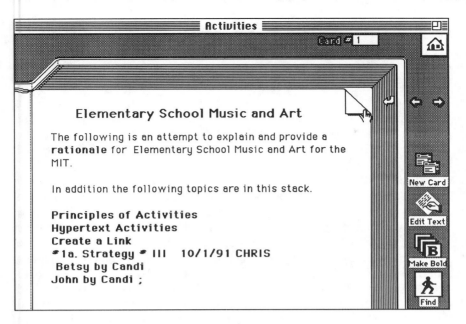

2a

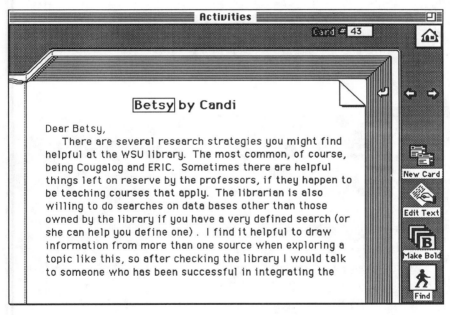

2b

FIGURE 4-2a & b. In this assignment, preservice teachers read two cases about elementary teachers (Betsy and John), who were contemplating the integration of arts content into their curricula. Words and phrases in **bold** are hot links to related material. Each of the lines after the one that begins "In addition . . ." are links to student-written solutions to the problems of Betsy or John. *b.* This screen represents the first page of Candi's solution to Betsy's problem regarding integration of arts in her elementary classroom. In the right column of the screen are several navigation and editing buttons. The "Make Bold" button allows readers to make hot-link connections between pages based on words or phrases.

appear before her school board to argue for integration of subject matter in elementary school. Students in the course were to offer strategies for Betsy to complete her task. Figure 4-2b shows the first page of a letter to Betsy that suggests various strategies that she could use. This page is linked from the page in Figure 4-2a by the words in bold: "Betsy by Candi."

Adults might be engaged in an activity to spend considerable energy on reading for meaning, but will younger children? When children work in groups to create a report, they are charged with reading each others' work through several rounds of editing. To encourage this type of reading for editing, I created a template for a multimedia science report called *HyperReport* (see Figure 4-3). Children aged eight to ten spent several weeks on a project that culminated in a series of oral and written reports to various audiences. The main evidence for engaged reading for comprehension was the ability of a child to ask meaningful questions of the author. In this context, both authors and readers learned to expect text to make sense and, eventually, demanded that it did. Readers asked questions of the text and authors went back to their written words to edit them.

Creating HyperReports is an example of how electronic text within a computer-based environment can facilitate learning subject-

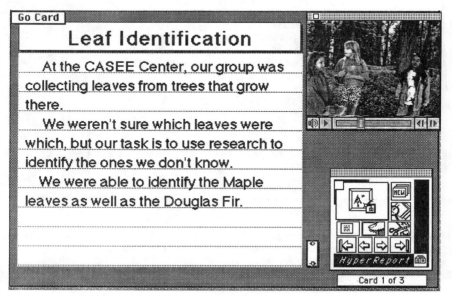

a

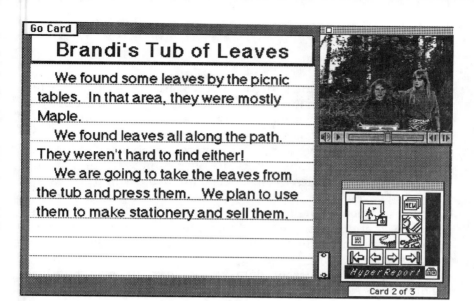

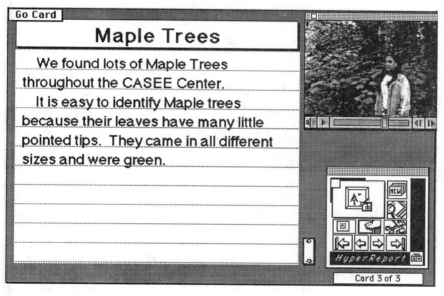

FIGURE 4-3a, b & c. This *HyperReport* on the topic of tree leaves was created by a team of three girls in a combined third and fourth grade classroom who took two short trips to a nearby forest (CASEE Center) to collect physical and video specimens of tree leaves. Members of their class had access to this report among their other informational books. *HyperReports* allow writers to create a title and text for each page. Each page can be annotated with a still picture or digitized movie. Readers can access pages sequentially or by title when using the "Go Card" pull down menu in the upper left-hand corner or the page, which lists all pages in the report. Readers can also view and review pictures or movies. Both authors and readers have access to a movable palette of buttons (lower left corner of the page) that control navigation, editing, and pictures. *b.* Page two of the "Tree Leaves" report: "Brandi's Tub of Leaves." *c.* Page three of the "Tree Leaves" report: "Maple Trees."

matter (e.g., science) and general language arts knowledge. The text and movies depicted in Figure 4-3 represent only part of the study of language arts in which students were engaged. During planning and resource-gathering stages, students used a variety of computer-based technologies including text editors, databases, and e-mail. During the production stage students used cameras, scanners, and multimedia technologies to edit their movies and still pictures. For the Tree Leaves HyperReport, each member of the group created one page and acted as editors for their peers. Figure 4-3a, has a title field (Leaf Identification), text field, and a movie area that were designed and produced by the student. Similarly, Figures 4-3b,c follow this style. During presentations of their work, students split tasks of reporting processes, data, results, next steps, and answering questions from the audience. Students held group meetings after a presentation to determine what if anything should be changed in their HyperReport or presentation.

DISCUSSION

Electronic text holds great promise for conveying expository text to readers and, perhaps, helping them become more competent. I have given examples of electronic texts, which have resources that fall into three categories: text, task, and context. In this final section, I will review these categories and make suggestions for other ways in which electronic texts might help readers.

The most attention has been paid to resources that work with a text in some manner (vocabulary, readability, cloze, text structure, and prior knowledge). Each of these resources seems to have some practical use, but selecting the right combination of them confuses researchers, designers, and readers alike. Applications such as *Select the Text* and *MacReader* could be used to narrow the range of resources offered by electronic text applications to those most likely to be of assistance to the reader. Pursuing more research on text-based resources seems necessary, but it is not clear what the payoff will be. At least some of the effort placed on text resources has been to make them better or "smarter," we might use our resources better by helping electronic-text environments make readers smarter (Scardamalia, Bereiter, McLean, Swallow, Woodruff, 1989).

Task strategy resources concentrate on the purpose for reading and the strategies one might invoke to reach a goal. Lachman (1989) demonstrated that good readers, who have a repertoire of strategies (e.g., read the important information more carefully) and can identify a goal (e.g., read for a test on the main ideas) can make good use of a resources that fits this purpose. Less experienced readers may need help with the goal and strategies to meet that goal (Garner et al., 1986). Simply providing appropriate strategies is not enough if readers do not know when or how to use them (Gillingham et al., 1989). In this case, electronic texts must know enough about the reader to become more active informers, coaches, and teachers (Alexander et al., 1994) or direct readers to human resources—perhaps their peers. Peers can help provide rich and complex environments that are important for learning subject matter from exposition.

As Lachman (1989) discovered, conveying the context in which readers will read an electronic text is sometimes enough to invoke complex reading strategies in competent readers. For novice readers (perhaps most readers), more will need to be done to enrich or take advantage of a reading context. Computers can be used to provide electronic texts for groups of readers (e.g., Arts Activities) and to direct readers to actively engage the original text and text written by their peers. The examples of adults (Arts Activities) and children (HyperReports) that I have described are only pointers to the possibilities that new forms of electronic text might have. Writing and reading of electronic text can be more spontaneous and vital than its paper-based counterpart because electronic text is not limited to the same boundaries. It is yet to be determined if environments for electronic texts can assist readers in moving through the complex task of understanding and learning from text.

REFERENCES

Afflerbach, P. P. (1990). The influence of prior knowledge on expert readers' main idea construction strategies. *Reading Research Quarterly, 25,* 31–46.

Alexander, P. A., Kulikowich, J. M., & Jetton, T. L. (1994). The role of subject-matter knowledge and interest in the processing of linear and nonlinear texts. *Review of Educational Research, 64,* 201–252.

Anderson, R. A., & Davison, A. (1988). Conceptual and empirical bases of readability formulas. In A. Davison, & G. M. Green (Eds.), *Linguistic complexity and text comprehension: Readability issues reconsidered* (pp. 23–53). Hillsdale, NJ: Erlbaum.

Armbruster, B. B., & Anderson, T. H. (1981). *Content area textbooks* (Rdg. Ed. Rep. No. 23), Urbana, IL: University of Illinois, Center for the Study of Reading.

Armbruster, B. B., & Anderson, T. H. (1984). *Producing "considerate" expository text: Or easy reading is damned hard writing* (Rdg. Ed. Rep.

No. 46). Urbana, IL: University of Illinois, Center for the Study of Reading.

Bertram, B., & Rubin, A. (1988). Readability formulas: Matching tools and task. In A. Davison, & G. M. Green (Eds.), *Linguistic complexity and text comprehension: Readability issues reconsidered* (pp. 5–22). Hillsdale, NJ: Erlbaum.

Brown, J. S., Collins, A., & Duguid, P. (1989). Situated cognition and the culture of learning. *Educational Researcher, 18*(1), 32–42.

Clarinina, R. B. (1992). Prescriptions in reading computer-assisted instruction: Reading versus writing. *Journal of Computer-Based Instruction, 19,* 58–63.

Feldman, S. C., & Fish, M. C. (1991). Use of computer-mediated reading supports to enhance reading comprehension of high school students. *Journal of Educational Computing Research, 7,* 25–36.

Garner, R. (1987). *Metacognition and reading comprehension.* Norwood, NJ: Ablex.

Garner, R. (1990). Children's use of strategies in reading. In D. F. Bjorklund (Ed.), *Children's strategies: Contemporary views of cognitive development* (pp. 245–268). Hillsdale, NJ: Erlbaum.

Garner, R., Alexander, P. A., Gillingham, M. G., Kulikowich, J. M., & Brown, R. (1991). Interest and learning from text. *American Educational Research Journal, 28,* 643–659.

Garner, R., & Gillingham, M. G. (1987). Students' knowledge of text structure. *Journal of Reading Behavior, 19,* 247–259.

Garner, R., & Gillingham, M. G. (1991). Topic knowledge, cognitive interest, and text recall: A microanalysis. *The Journal of Experimental Education, 59,* 310–319.

Garner, R., Alexander, P. A., Slater, W., Hare, V. C., Smith, T., & Reis, R. (1986). Children's knowledge of structural properties of expository text. *Journal of Educational Psychology, 78,* 411–416.

Gay, G., & Grosz-Ngate, M. (1994). Collaborative design in a networked multimedia environment: Emerging communication patterns. *Journal of Research on Computing in Education, 26,* 418–432.

Gillingham, M. G. (1988). Text in computer-based instruction: What the research says. *Journal of Computer-Based Instruction, 15,* 1–6.

Gillingham, M. G. (1993). Effects of question complexity and reader strategies on adults' hypertext comprehension. *Journal of Research on Computing in Education, 26,* 1–15.

Gillingham, M. G., & Garner, R. (1992). Readers' Comprehension of Mazes Embedded in Expository Texts. *Journal of Educational Research, 85,* 234–241.

Gillingham, M. G., Garner, R., Guthrie, J. T., & Sawyer, R. (1989). Children's control of computer-based reading assistance in answering synthesis questions. *Computers in Human Behavior, 5,* 61–75.

Gillingham, M. G., & Waynant, P. (1989). Assessing reading skills and comprehension of expository text with sample computer methods. *Journal, 19*, 31–36.

Goldman, S. R., & Saul, E. U. (1990). Applications for tracking reading behavior on the Macintosh. *Behavior Research Methods, Instruments, & Computers, 22*, 526–532.

Guthrie, J. T. (1973). Reading comprehension and syntactic responses in good and poor readers. *Journal of Educational Psychology, 65*, 294–299.

Hidi, S., & Baird, W. (1988). Strategies for increasing text-based interest and students' recall of expository texts. *Reading Research Quarterly, 23*, 465–483.

Horning, A. S. (1993). *The psycholinguistics of readable writing: A multidisciplinary exploration.* Norwood, NJ: Ablex.

Irwin, J. (1990). *Reading and the middle school student: Strategies to enhance literacy.* Boston: Allyn & Bacon.

Jonassen, D. H. (1986). Hypertext principles for text and courseware design. *Educational Psychologist, 21*, 269–292.

Lachman, R. (1989). Comprehension aids for on-line reading of expository text. *Human Factors, 31*, 1–15.

Lorch, R. F., Jr. (1989). Text-signaling devices and their effects on reading and memory processes. *Educational Psychology Review, 1*, 209–234.

Martindale, M. J. (1993). Mental models and text schemas: Why computer based tutorials should be considered a communication medium. *Journal of Computer-Based Instruction, 20*, 107–112.

Muth, K. D. (Ed.) (1989). *Children's comprehension of text: Research into practice.* Newark, DE: International Reading Association.

Pearson, P. D., & Johnson, D. D. (1978). *Teaching Reading Comprehension.* New York: Holt, Rinehart and Winston.

Reinking, D. (1988). Computer-mediated text and comprehension differences: The role of reading time, reader preference, and estimation of learning. *Reading Research Quarterly, 23*, 484–498.

Reinking, D., & Schreiner, R. (1985). The effects of computer-mediated text on measures of reading comprehension and reading behavior. *Reading Research Quarterly, 20*, 536–552.

Renninger, K. A., Hidi, S., & Krapp, A. (Eds.) (1992). *The role of interest in learning and development.* Hillsdale, NJ: Erlbaum.

Rogoff, B., & Lave, J. (Eds.) (1984). *Everyday cognition: Its development in social context.* Cambridge, MA: Harvard University Press.

Rubin, A., & Bruce, B. (1990). Alternate realizations of purpose in computer-supported writing. *Theory Into Practice, 24*, 256–263.

Salomon, G., Globerson, T., & Guterman, E. (1989). The computer as a zone of proximal development: Internalizing reading-related metacognition from a Reading Partner. *Journal of Educational Psychology, 85*, 1–15.

Scardamalia, M., Bereiter, C., McLean, R. S., Swallow, J., & Woodruff,

E. (1989). Computer-supported intentional learning environments. *Journal of Educational Computing Research, 5,* 51–68.

Steinberg, E. R. (1977). Review of student control in computer-assisted instruction. *Journal of Computer-Based Instruction, 3,* 84–90.

Steinberg, E. R. (1984). *Teaching computers to teach.* Hillsdale, NJ: Erlbaum.

Taylor, B. M., & Samuels, S. J. (1983). Children's use of text structure in the recall of expository material. *American Educational Research Journal, 20,* 517–528.

Tobias, S. (1987). Mandatory text review and interaction with student characteristics. *Journal of Educational Psychology, 79,* 154–161.

van Dijk, T. A., & Kintsch, W. (1983). *Strategies of discourse comprehension.* New York: Academic Press.

Yuill, N., & Oakhill, J. (1991). *Children's problems in text comprehension: An experimental investigation.* New York: Cambridge University Press.

5

TIMS: A Framework For The Design Of Usable Electronic Text

Andrew Dillon

School of Library and Information Science, Indiana University

INTRODUCTION

Despite the claims and the promises, the hype and the visions, the reality of electronic text is far less impressive than the rhetoric that surrounds it. Internet, World Wide Webs, MOSAIC, e-journals, word processors, and of course, hypertext are all pushed forward as examples of this triumph of technology, this liberation of the human reader and writer, this future of unlimited information for everyone. Yet, for all this, as has been outlined in detail elsewhere (see, e.g., Dillon, 1994), the typical reader of an electronic information source likely will suffer loss of orientation, lower reading speeds, and possibly greater fatigue than the typical reader of a paper document for few demonstrable benefits.

Why is this and how can cognitive scientists help overcome these fundamental human engineering problems in technological artifacts? In the present chapter I will seek to answer these questions through the presentation of a framework for analyzing reader–document interaction that has been developed over the last five years through my work with colleagues at the HUSAT Research Institute in the United Kingdom and SLIS at Indiana University in the United

States. This framework, referred to as TIMS (for Task, Information, Manipulation, and Standard Reading), is an attempt at conceptualizing human information usage in a form suitable for considering and evaluating design options for electronic documents. In use it can also support interpretation of findings on reading electronic text and help generate testable hypotheses of human performance with a system. It has been developed from, and subsequently tested and refined on, real artifact design scenarios.

READING ELECTRONIC TEXT: SOME
BASIC HUMAN FACTORS

It is essential when addressing issues of human reading in electronic environments that we ground ourselves in the empirical findings rather than the fantasy of the information revolution. Contrary to the populist image of novice users navigating effortlessly through cyberspace in pursuit of interlinked masses of relevant information, experimental work to date has demonstrated differences between the electronic and paper media in reading at the psychomotor, perceptual, and cognitive levels. Put simply, these differences are both process and outcome based and have largely debunked the notion of hypertext or hypermedia as a liberating technology. Dillon (1992) outlined empirical evidence indicating differences in speed, accuracy, comprehension, fatigue, preference, navigation, and manipulation between paper and electronic media. Without delving deeply into a literature that has been reviewed in detail in the previously mentioned paper, suffice it to say that at best, reliable and valid evidence for the advantages of hypertext only emerge in limited task domains and when the technology has been adequately and iteratively designed in a user-centered fashion. In short, most documented initial (theory-based) attempts at improving on paper have failed and improvements have only been gained through evaluation and redesign (empiricism) (see, e.g., Landauer et al., 1993).

In recognizing this, the intention is not to downplay or reject the potential value of these new tools but to advocate a move beyond the exaggerated and unsubstantiated claims that were the hallmark of the recent (last decade) upsurge of interest in electronic text processing to a more enlightened view of reading and general information usage on the part of humans. The technological determinism remains, often in a cunningly disguised form (see, e.g., most of the educational literature on hypermedia) and proponents keep telling us how wonderful is the new medium without reference to the empirical data that contradict them. Technocracy aside, however, cognitive scientists (a collective term in which I include most social and behavioral scientists working in this domain) are now in a position to shape this technology, armed not only with the strong empirical evidence, but also with an informed sense of what is accomplishable with good design practice.

USER-CENTERED ARTIFACT DESIGN

By good design practice is meant a user-centered approach to artifact creation that can be characterized as iterative, evolving through repeated prototyping and evaluation cycles, with the intention of developing an application that is usable as well as functional. Of necessity, such design practice needs to identify target users and their requirements at the earliest stages, perform detailed task analyses and demonstrate an awareness of all the stakeholders in the new technology. Furthermore, such practice takes as axiomatic the contextual determinism of usability and makes explicit the user, task, and environmental variables impacting a technology's exploitation in both the design and testing of the artifact. This issue has been dealt with repeatedly in the literature on HCI (Human-Computer Interaction) and will not be rehashed further here (see, e.g., Eason, 1988; McKnight et al., 1991; and Shackel, 1991). However, for present purposes it is worth making explicit the meaning of usability that in this case draws on Shackel (1991) in defining it as the artifact's capability, in human functional terms, to be used easily, effectively, and satisfactorily by specific users, performing specific tasks, in specific environments.

The essence of this definition is that it avoids two of the most common problems associated with the usability concept. First, it explicitly places usability at the level of the interaction between users, performing tasks in certain environments, and the artifact. This takes it beyond the typical features-based definitions common in the field, for example, where usability is equated with the presence of menus and a mouse, or conformance with certain standards (as embodied in most style guidelines). Clearly, a moment's reflection in the light of the preceding definition will make it clear why such an index of usability is meaningless.

Second, it operationalizes, and thereby provides us with a means of evaluating, an artifact's usability. The HCI field is rife with what may be termed semantic rephrasing as opposed to definitions of usability, for example, usability equals "user-friendliness," "ease of use," and so forth. Such nondefinitions skirt the issue and provide little if any guidance to those attempting an evaluation or seeking to develop a prototype.

Applied socio-cognitive science practice in this domain is criticized frequently for its putative lack of coherence as a body of knowledge, the poor generalizability of findings, and most commonly, its evaluative rather than predictive nature. (See Chapanis, 1988 for a discussion of these issues in general ergonomics work). Most ergonomists or cognitive scientists involved in the design of artifacts could provide numerous examples of being brought into the design and development process only as an evaluator of a near complete design, often only to identify problems that are both too costly to correct at a late stage and that they believe they could have identified and predicted much earlier if only they had been consulted. An essential tension exists, however, between the nature of our knowledge in the social sciences and our desire to influence design (in large part an engineering discipline) earlier, since the absence of applicable theoretical models of human task performance in realistic domains and the real power of our evaluative skills suggests to engineers and software designers that our knowledge is best applied after theirs, not concurrently and certainly never before.

In advocating a contextually determined view of usability it can be seen that establishing the context of use is an essential first step in usable product development and thereby pushes the cognitive scientist to the very earliest stages of design, the conceptualization stage, to perform user, task, and environmental analyses. In recent years, there has been a growing acceptance in principle, if not so much in practice, of designing in user-centered rather than product-centered manner and considering these user issues at the very onset of the design process.

Although a user-centered approach (properly executed and coupled with the sophisticated prototyping tools currently emerging) makes the development of usable technology more likely, it remains a nonoptimum process that can prove extremely expensive in terms of time and resources. The quality of the original prototype always is dictated by the accuracy or validity of the designer's conceptualization of the intended users and their tasks. (The term designer is here used in the singular for convenience, although in practice much design is a team effort and often is performed by people who would not necessarily describe themselves as "designers.") In the domain of information usage, such conceptualizations often are very weak. The user is seen as "an information processing being with five modalities" (see, e.g., Norman, 1986) and sometimes stringent design laws are laid down on totally spurious interpretations of experimental psychological research, for example, the argument that cognitive psychology "proves" that menus on a computer should never exceed 7 ± 2 items (see, e.g., Dyer & Morris, 1991). The decisions taken at this point, however, are likely to have major ramifications for the product. A primary task for cognitive science, therefore, is the improvement of such articulations of basic science so that better first designs can be developed.

THE NATURE OF THEORY AND DESIGN

A distinction shall be drawn here between theory *in* design and theory *for* design. In the former, it is proposed that the artifacts we create are embodiments of a designer's views of the users and the work they perform. The artifact is thus a conjecture on the designer's part and like all conjectures, is, through the course of its development and its life, open to refutation (either formally in a usability evaluation or practically through real-world rejection of the product). This perspective can prove useful in understanding the nature of the design process and the means by which social scientists may study and influence it. (This perspective is discussed in detail in Dillon, 1994; Carroll & Campbell, 1989).

The latter issue, theory for design, is one that concerns many cognitive scientists interested in the design of more humanly acceptable technologies. It is the search for some form of representation of cognitive science knowledge and concepts that can be utilized by designers in their efforts. In one sense the theory *in* design must subsume the theory *for* design as part of its own *raison détre,* but this is not necessarily the case since the latter would exist even if the former is considered incorrect or inappropriate as a conceptualization. The present chapter is concerned primarily with theory *for* design, but has been influenced in that work by an acceptance of the theory *in* design perspective.

The most relevant disciplines to provide theories for reading and information usage are arguably cognitive psychology, educational psychology, and information science. Indeed, from its outset, psychology viewed reading as an almost perfect experimental task and one whose explanation would represent a triumph for the discipline (Huey, 1908). Educational psychology has a primary interest in the design of artifacts to enhance learning, much of which involves the learner interacting with a document or related information source.

Information science is concerned with the storage and retrieval of all information types, although has often had little to say about the human use of that information once accessed. Despite the concerns, we are not in a position to transfer models and theories easily from any of these disciplines to the design community concerned with developing electronic document systems. Even where practitioners in each of these disciplines become designers themselves, their ability to draw on their native fields in creating an artifact is necessarily limited and at best, weakly articulated.

This should not be taken as a criticism of any discipline. Cognitive psychology, for example does not exist to predict and explain human performance with interactive technology and to accuse it of irrelevance to design would be to assume it ever claimed such human activities as part of its remit (although design might be a logical application domain). Landauer (1995), has called for a reassessment of the value of cognitive psychology in design, but his point seems to be addressed at social scientists and designers who place too much value in the role of this discipline. Landauer's critique is not intended, as some have suggested, to be an attack on the discipline itself, like Kline's (1988) detailed criticism of most contemporary psychology, but a call for a more appropriate use of relevant methods. What such disciplines do offer, however, are perspectives, certain tools and techniques that we might draw on. However, the transfer of technology from one domain (e.g., laboratory studies of word recognition) to another (e.g., the specification of dialogue terms in a software application) is rather more complex than might be imagined (and certainly was envisaged in the early work on HCI), but this should not lead us to dismissal of the providing discipline. We ought to be aware that what we glean from academic disciplines is likely to take a very different shape when utilized in design contexts. In developing such bridging representations, it is inappropriate to apply criteria we use in the academic laboratory, since many of them (e.g., sociological or psychological accuracy, statistical significance, and unambiguous explication) are less likely to hold sway in the design community that seems to be more concerned with usefulness, option constraining, and informing designers what to do.

Models of reading proposed in these contributing disciplines are not directly usable in design, since they are both limited in range of tasks covered and proposed at a level that seems inappropriate to the design world. (See e.g., some of the classic cognitive science work on reading text such as Just & Carpenter, 1980, and consider what design constraints such findings suggest.) This has left the

HCI community to engage in a strongly empirical approach to uncovering aspects of reading electronic text that are important. (See e.g., the program of research undertaken on proofreading from VDUs at IBM by Gould et al., 1987a.) Yet even such an approach remains far from the norm. All too often, theoretical perspectives are drawn on after the fact to rationalize a design perspective (see, e.g., Cunningham et al., 1993 on the contructivist embrace of the Intermedia system) or worse, weak or flawed empiricism is assumed sufficient.

In developing TIMS, an explicit representation was sought of the issues that emerged repeatedly in design contexts involving a variety of hypertext and other electronic documents. These included academic journals, software manuals, process handbooks, and research project archives. The intention of the framework is to provide those developing electronic text to conceptualize the human cognitive, perceptual, and psychomotor factors demonstrably influencing the usability of the created artifact. These factors were derived from several years of experimental investigations of human information usage from an ergonomics perspective. However, the framework is architecture-independent and is neither intended nor articulated as a model of human cognition but as a design framework to support more adequately the articulation of the pertinent human factors in design. TIMS is predicated on the following assumptions of human information usage.

1. Humans read and use information in a goal-directed manner to "satisfice" the demands of their tasks.
2. Humans form models of the structure of, and relationship between, information units.
3. Human information usage consists in part of physical manipulation of information sources.
4. Human reading at the level of word and sentence perception is bounded in part by the established laws of cognitive psychology.
5. Human information usage occurs in contexts that enable the user to apply multiple sources of knowledge to the problem in hand.

These predicates will become clearer as the chapter proceeds. In form TIMS is a qualitative framework and is proposed for use as an advanced organizer for design, as a guide for heuristic and expert usability evaluation, and as a means of generating scientific conjectures about the usability of any electronic text. More on these intentions will be presented later, although full details are provided in Dillon (1994). In the following section, a brief overview of the framework is presented.

THE TIMS FRAMEWORK

The framework is intended to be an approximate representation of the human cognition and behaviors central to the interaction between reader and document. It consists of four interactive elements that reflect the primary components of the reading situation at different phases in any context. They are

1. a Task Model (T) that deals with the reader's needs and uses for the material;
2. an Information Model (I) that provides a model of the information space;
3. a set of manipulation skills and facilities (M) that support physical use of the material; and
4. a Standard Reading Processor (S) that represents the cognitive and perceptual processing involved in reading words and sentences.

These are all interrelated components reflecting the cognitive, perceptual, and psychomotor aspects of reading. Reading, or more generally, human information usage thus is conceptualized not as a matter of scanning words on a page alone (as in some narrow psychological models of reading) or acquiring and applying a representational model of the text's structure, but a product of both these activities in conjunction with manipulating the document or information space and defining and achieving goals and forming strategies for their attainment (all within a certain context). Therefore, for example, a reader recognizes an information need, formulates a method of resolving this need, perceptually and cognitively samples the document or information space by appropriately applying her model of its structure, manipulates it physically as required, and then perceives (in the experimental psychological sense) words on text until the necessary information is obtained. Obviously this is a very simple picture of the reading process; other more complex scenarios are possible, such as the revision of one's reading goal in the light of new information or modifying one's initial information models to take account of new details, and so forth. Each of these elements is described in more detail in the following section.

The Task Model (T)

The reading task is the crucial factor in understanding text use and a parsimonious basis upon which electronic text design can be investigated. Readers interact with texts purposively, to obtain information, to be entertained, to learn, and so on. To do this they must decide what it is they want to get out of the text, determine how they will tackle it (e.g., browse or read start to finish, follow a link or ignore it for now, etc.). Furthermore, during the task they must review their progress and, if necessary, revise the task.

This notion of intentionality in reading gives rise to the idea of planning in the reader's mind. It seems from evidence collected by the author (Dillon, 1994) that such planning is relatively gross, taking the form of such intentions as "go to the index, look for a relevant item, and enter the text to locate the answer to my query," or "to find out what statistical tests were used go to the results section and look for a specific description." However, plans can be much vaguer than these two examples, which probably represent highly specified plans of interaction with the text. Reading an academic article to comprehend the full contents seems to be much less specifiable; the reader is more likely to formulate a plan such as "read it from the start to the finish, skip any irrelevant or trivial bits, and if it gets too difficult jump on or leave it." Furthermore, such a plan may be modified as the reading task develops, for example, the reader may decide that she needs to reread a section several times, or may decide that she can comprehend it only by not reading it all. In this sense planning becomes more situated (see, e.g., Suchman, 1988), where the reader's plans are shaped by the context of the ongoing action and are not fully specifiable in advance.

The Information Model (I)

Readers possess (from experience), acquire (while using), and utilize a representation of the document's structure that may be termed a mental model of the text or information space. Such models allow readers to identify likely locations for information within the document, to predict the typical contents of a document, to know the level of detail likely to be found and to appreciate the similarities between documents, and so on. Indeed, several years of experimental work suggest this must be the case (see also van Dijk and Kintsch, 1983).

The present author follows Brewer's (1987) distinction here between "global" and "instantiated" schemata with regard to such models. In the present context a global schema consists of a representation of how a typical text type is organized, for example, a newspaper is made up of a series of articles covering a range of topics grouped into sections on politics, sport, finance, and so on. These structural representations are general and exist independently of any specific document (although, of course, they only emerge over time after frequent interactions with many documents). An instantiated schema consists of an embodiment of the generic schema based on exposure to a specific text, for example, noting that the particular article one is reading has a very short introduction or there is a diagram of statistical results on the bottom of a left-hand page. In other words, when a reader interacts with a text, the original structural model of the text type becomes fleshed out with specific details of the particular text being read.

This distinction will be referred to here more simply as the difference between a model (generic) and a map (specific). In these terms readers can be said to form mental maps of particular texts as they use them; models help them in this but are not themselves essential for map formation (i.e., it is assumed that a reader can form a detailed map of a document without having been exposed to similar types of text before). In this way, frequent map formation with a document type can be seen as supporting model formation of that document type's generic structure.

In use, the information model helps the reader to organize the text's contents by fitting it into a meaningful structure and thus guards partly against navigational difficulties by providing context, that is, it supports the formation of a mental map of the information space. Thus what is initially a model becomes, with use, a map of a specific text. Where no model exists in advance, it is hypothesized that a map can be formed directly (although it may require more effort on the part of the reader, an empirical issue to be investigated). Similarly, where repeated map formation suggests regularities for a text type, then it is hypothesized that a model for that type may be formed. The point at which a model becomes a map (and the opposite case just outlined) is difficult to quantify and probably not pertinent to present needs but offers a potentially interesting research problem to pursue.

Manipulation Skills and Facilities (M)

Most documents are more than one page or screen in length and thus the reader must be able to physically manipulate the text. With paper, such skills are usually acquired early in life and are largely transferable from one text form to another. If you can manipulate a paperback novel you will have few difficulties with a textbook and so forth, although there are obvious exceptions in the paper domain and the ability to easily manipulate broadsheet newspapers in confined spaces is a specific skill that is relatively unique to that text form.

On the other hand, the manipulations available with paper are limited in terms of what you can do with the text. Most readers can use their fingers to keep pages of interest available while searching elsewhere in the document or flicking through pages of text at just the right speed to scan for a particular section, but beyond these actions, manipulation of documents becomes difficult. When one then considers manipulation of multiple documents these limitations are exacerbated.

Large electronic texts are awkward to manipulate by means of scrolling or paging alone, but the advent of hypertext with its associated "point and click" facilities and graphical user interface qualities has eased this, at least in terms of speed. Yet, the immediacy or intimacy of interaction with electronic text is less than with paper by virtue of the microprocessor interface between reader and information on screens. Furthermore, the lack of standards in current electronic information systems means that acquiring the skills to manipulate documents on one system will not necessarily be of any use for manipulating texts on another. Obviously, electronic text systems afford sophisticated manipulations such as searching that can prove particularly useful for certain tasks and render otherwise daunting tasks (such as locating thematically linked quotations from the bible) now manageable in minutes rather than days. Yet electronic search facilities are far from a guarantee of accurate performance.

The various advantages and disadvantages of manipulation facilities on screens have been discussed in the literature (see Dillon, 1994). Ultimately, the goal is to design transparent manipulation facilities that free the reader's processing capacity for task completion. Slow or awkward manipulations are certain to prove disruptive to the reading process. The framework raises these issues as essential parts of the reading process and therefore important ones for designers to consider in the development of electronic text.

Standard Reading Processor (S)

The final element of the framework is the standard reading processor. It is the element that perceives the document and performs out the activities most typically described as "reading" in the psychological literature (e.g., Just & Carpenter, 1980). Thus eye movements, fixations, letter–word recognition, and other perceptual, linguistic, and (low-level) perceptual and cognitive functions involved in extracting meaning from the textual image are properly located at this level.

Originally, I had termed this component "serial" rather than "standard," since I sought to emphasize the experimental evidence that generally reading occurs in a serial fashion and to counter some of the mythical claims of technocrats that hypertext liberated readers from the constraints of serial reading (see, e.g., Nielsen, 1995). However, this is likely to cause more confusion than the prefix "standard," which seeks to convey a sense both of typicality in execution and of the level of reading analysis found in standard psychological investigations. At the level addressed here, information extraction from a document relies on the reader processing letters, words, and sentences in a form that might be considered explicable in the standard psychological literature.

Decades of psychological investigation have been spent looking at the question of how humans read, and some of the conclusions drawn from this work have been important in understanding the persistent speed deficits noticed in proofreading from screens (Gould et al., 1987b). Present emphasis dictates that the findings on eye movements, reading speeds, letter and word recognition, and so forth are considered sound and offer a physical ergonomic requirement on the standard of image quality required to at least match that of paper.

So far, the basic components of the framework have been described. The TIMS framework should not be considered the equivalent of a cognitive model of reading such as described in van Dijk and Kintsch (1983) or Garnham (1987), but a framework intended to reflect the human aspects of performance during the reading process. The elements are those human factors that seem pertinent to electronic text design. A schematic representation of the framework is presented in Figure 5-1. As shown, the elements are all related and collectively framed within the context in which the activity occurs, that may range from a single document in an office environment, to a digital library in a public cluster and can be established by contemporary user-centered design methods e.g. Shackel, (1991).

In practice, it is not hypothesized that interelement interactions occur in isolated units. Meaningful engagement with a document is more likely to result in multiple rapid interactions between these various elements. For example, a scenario can be envisaged where, reading an academic article for comprehension, the task model interacts with the information model to identify the best plan for achieving completion. This could involve several T $\longrightarrow$ I and I $\longrightarrow$ T interactions before deciding perhaps to serially read the text from

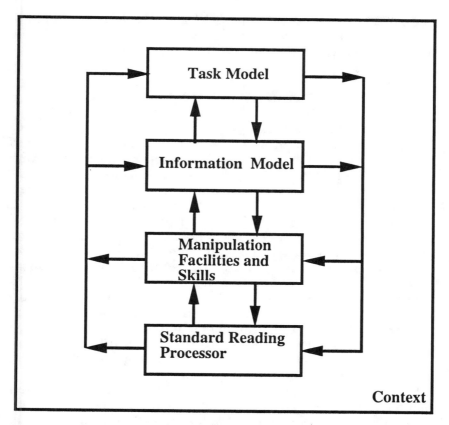

FIGURE 5-1. The TIMS framework.

start to finish. If this plan is accepted then manipulation facilities come into play and standard reading commences. The M ——⟶ S interaction and S ——⟶ M interaction may occur iteratively (with occasional S ——⟶ I interactions as distinguishing features are noted) until the last page is reached, at which point attention passes back ultimately to the T for the reader to consider what to do next.

Also, the speed and the iterative nature of the interaction between these elements is likely to be such that it is difficult to demonstrate empirically the direction of the information flow. In many instances, it would be virtually impossible to prove that information went from M to I rather than the other way and so forth. However, this does not preclude examination of these elements and their interactions in an attempt to understand better the process of reading from a human factors perspective. The elements reflect the major components of reading that emerged as important from several years of studies (described collectively in Dillon, 1994) and are intended as a broad representation of what occurs ergonomically during the reading process.

VERBAL PROTOCOLS AND THE TIMS ELEMENTS

In order to validate the elements making up the TIMS perspective of information usage, a series of verbal protocol analyses of readers interacting with both electronic and nonelectronic documents were performed. The main intention of this test was to see if the elements did indeed emerge in readers' protocols and, more important, if readers articulated thoughts and activities that went beyond the elements described and thus would need to be included in the framework.

The general scenario for the elicitation of these protocols involved readers performing an information search task on a text describing the making of wine. Full details of the study are presented in Dillon (1994), but in the present chapter several extracts from the protocol of one reader, operating on a HyperCard version of the document are presented. The intention here is to demonstrate that the elements proposed in the TIMS framework are manifest in readers' protocols and provide a parsimonious account of reader activity (cognitively and behaviorally) for design purposes. In the first instance, the reader's opening interactions with the HyperCard stack are described.

This segment represented one successful task of two and a half minutes duration. What is interesting for present purposes is the intentions and reactions present in the verbal comments. First, the reader articulates his strategy, the means he has formulated for tackling the task. This is to go to the index and check if terms mentioned in the question are present. Two things are worth noting here. First, the strategy for tackling the task (an obvious T activity in TIMS) is not a clearcut plan but a first pass at narrowing the task space in the hope that by making some progress, a further stage may suggest itself. As Suchman (1988) eloquently pointed out, the idea that users of interactive technologies formulate complete task plans in advance is erroneous, and real activity is much more situated, that is, governed by context.

The second point to note is that in immediately going to the Index and subsequently to the Contents section, the reader indicates knowledge of the layout of the stack and the information such parts of the document might afford. From the TIMS perspective this is a pure I activity.

The remaining first minute of the protocol demonstrates the user's

QUESTION 1
What two subjective impressions are typically used in describing taste?

Time	Comment	Action
0.00	"OK, to the index to see if any of these terms in the question appear in the index"	Hits Index button to get to Index section
0.03–0.024		Reading Index
0.025		Goes back to Contents and reads these
0.35	"I'll have a look in . . . probably section 2, "The Making of Wine' . . . "	Still reading contents, deciding which option to follow
0.58	"I'll go to 'sweetness' because that's the only term in the Contents list that really . . . refers to taste . . . "	During this speech phase, he selects the sweetness button and starts to read that section of the document
1.13	"OK—I seem to have found the answer here . . . "	Continues to read this section
2.05	"Well, part of the answer anyway. . . ."	Writes down "sweetness" on answer sheet.
2.12		Returns to Contents and reads it
2.15	"I'll go into 'Body'. . . "	Selects the body button and begins reading the text that appears
2.26	" . . . which appears to be the other subjective impression"	
2.30		Writes down answer and reads question

standard reading of the contents list (S activity) and the formulation of an appropriate tactic for making progress (T activity), which in this case is the selection of the likely section in the document based on its relationship to the key term the reader has identified in the question.

In the second minute much S activity is manifest as the reader reads through the selected text searching for the answer. Interestingly, he finds part of the answer and thinks it provides the complete information at first but soon realizes this is not the case and further work is required. Obviously, S activity quickly transferred to T, possibly interchangeably (and for present purposes, unimportantly) before determining that a return to the Contents might be appropriate (manifestation of I) and formulating the next stage of progress (T activity). A further period of S activity leads the reader to successful task completion.

In the next section we see the rapid solution to an information task that is rendered possible by the use of the technological facilities. Here, the reader immediately formulates a strategy for handling the task, that is, given the explicit nature of the question, a search term can be formulated that is likely to provide an immediate answer. This is effective T activity. Interestingly, what happens in this case throws some light on a minor flaw in the HyperCard interface. The "Search Again?" window controlling the Find command appears on screen in such a place as to obscure the found term in the text. The reader engages in S activity for a while before moving the window and locating the highlighted term (M activity). A short S stage follows and the reader has found the answer.

Such tight coupling between user and technology can emerge quickly. Given his success with the search facility this reader defaults to using it immediately and by question 5 in his 12-question session he is employing it very effectively.

Apart from the swiftness of the interaction, the reader also makes a passing reference to his sense of having seen this subject tackled "somewhere" in the document (I manifestation). In a sense, then, this is almost a complete linear cycle through the elements (T $\longrightarrow$ I $\longrightarrow$ M $\longrightarrow$ S sequence leading to answer).

For present purposes the protocols will not be examined further. What is being emphasized here is the extent to which the framework provided by TIMS offers a useful summary of the type of activities that readers perform in utilizing an artifact of this nature. A given that it may well do so, what use is intended for such a framework in design.

QUESTION 2
"What term describes wines with an alcohol content of greater than 15%?"

Time	Comment	Action
2.50	"I'll do a search on this one."	Uses Find command and enters "15%" as search item
3.03		OK button on find screen clicked to initiate search
3.28	"The window is lying over the text I'm trying to read. . . . ."	"Search again?" prompt is on screen, user inputs "No"
3.35	"Now I can see it."	"15%" is highlighted, user reads text surrounding it
3.59	"I seem to have found the answer to this. . . ."	Writes down answer

QUESTION 3
What wine is made with rotten grapes?

Time	Comment	Action
7.15	"OK, question 5."	Goes to Contents and reads question
7.25	"I think I'll do a search on this because I have seen it somewhere and I think a search will bring it up. . . ."	
7.42		Selects "Find" command and inputs "rotten," OK on search is clicked at 7.53
7.55	"Yes . . . I've found it."	Reads text and writes down answer

TIMS AS THEORY FOR DESIGN

As a theory of the reading process *for* design purposes, TIMS is not intended to meet stringent cognitive criteria. Indeed, as expressed initially, it is a cognitive architecture-independent representation of human information usage. However, it is posited that several distinct applications of TIMS could prove advantageous to the design world.

In the first instance, the framework is useful as a guiding principle or type of advance organizer of information that gives the designer an orientation toward design enabling the application of relevant knowledge to bear on the problem. Thus, when faced with a design problem requiring electronic documents, the designer could conceptualize the intended readers–users in TIMS terms and thereby guide or inform their prototyping activities.

Second, by parsing the issues into elements, the framework facilitates identification of the important ones to address. This framework suggest four major issues to consider in any information context: the user's task and their perception of it; the information model they possess, must acquire or is provided by the artifact; the manipulation facilities they require or are provided; and the actual "eye-on-text" aspects involved. All are ultimately important, although depending on the task and the size of the information space, some may be more important than others (e.g., for very short texts of one screen or less, manipulation facilities and information models might be less important than visual ergonomics, although task contingencies must be considered here before such a conclusion could be reached).

In the third instance, the framework provides a means for ensuring that all issues relevant to the design of electronic text are considered. It is not enough that research or analysis is carried out on text navi-gation (I issue) and developers ignore image quality or input devices (and vice versa). A good electronic text system will address all issues (indeed it is almost a definition of a good electronic text that it does so).

The preceding applications consider the uses at the first stages of system development. In this sense the term designer encompasses any cognitive scientists seeking to influence the specification of an application. However, the framework also has relevance to later stages of the design process such as evaluation. In such a situation the framework user could assess a system in terms of the four elements and identify potential weaknesses in a design. This would be a typical use for expert evaluation, perhaps the most common evaluation technique in HCI. This form of use has been most commonly made of the framework by the present author.

Outside of the specific life cycle of a product, the framework has potential uses by human factors researchers (or professionals less interested in specific design problems) in that it could be used as a basis for studying reader behaviour and performance. The framework is intended to be a synopsis of the relevant issues in the reading process as identified in the earlier studies. Therefore, it should offer ergonomists or psychologists interested in reader–system interaction a means of interpreting the ever-expanding literature in a reader-relevant light. This is a point worth emphasizing since the transfer of tools and knowledge to users outside of the domain of development has proved a failure in much HCI work.

Certainly an immediate application is to enhance our critical awareness of the claims and findings in the literature on HCI. For example, it is not untypical to hear statements to the effect that "hypertext is better than paper" or "reading from paper is faster than reading from screens" TIMS suggests caution in interpreting such statements. If human information usage involves all elements in the framework then the only worthwhile statements are those that in-clude these. Thus, the statement "hypertext is better than paper" is, according to the TIMS perspective, virtually useless since it fails to mention crucial aspects such as the tasks for which it is better, the nature of the information models required by readers to make it better or worse, the manipulation facilities involved, or the image quality of the screen that effects the standard reading processes of the reader. We know all these variables are crucial since we have over 15 years of research investigating them and trying to untangle their varying effects.

Thus, TIMS suggests statements about reading, to be of value, need to be complete and make explicit each of the elements in its claim. Thus, a more useful statement would be

> For reading lengthy texts for comprehension, for which readers have a well developed information model, on a scrolling window, mouse-based system, screens of more than 40 lines are better than those of 20 lines, though both are worse than good quality paper.

Notice that the truth content of the statement is not what is at issue here. It is the completion of the statement that is important. Incomplete statements (ones not making reference to all elements of the TIMS framework) are too vague to test, since there are unlimited sources of variance that could exist under the general headings "hypertext," "paper," or "is better than." A complete statement might be wrong, but at least it should be immediately testable or refutable given the existing body of empirical data the field has amassed.

CONCLUSION

The cognitive aspects of electronic text processing still are poorly understood and the onus is on cognitive scientists interested in real-world applications to find a suitable means of bridging the scientific and design communities. For the present author, there are two primary motivations for pursuing this task.

First, in the absence of the sound knowledge of humans and their abilities, preferences and weaknesses, the information revolution will be dictated by the growing technocracy, those infatuated with machines more than people. Even if one views with a cynical eye the claims that the information revolution is a turning point in civilization akin to the last great industrial revolution, there is no doubt that this technology is shifting society on several levels. As scientists of the human, it is our responsibility to be involved in such events.

Second, and perhaps less emotive, it is enriching to attempt impacting real-world problems with science. If nothing more, it offers the sternest test of our work and our approach, and to the present author's mind at least, it is hugely enjoyable.

REFERENCES

Brewer, W. (1987). Schemas versus mental models in human memory. In I. P. Morris (Ed.), *Modeling Cognition* (pp. 188–197). London: Wiley.

Carroll, J., & Campbell, R. (1989). Artifacts as psychological theories: the case of HCI. *Behaviour and Information Technology, 8*(4), 247–256.

Chapanis, A. (1988). Some generalizations about generalizations. *Human Factors, 30*(3), 253–268.

Cunningham, D., Duffy, T., & Knuth, R. (1993). The textbook of the future, In C. McKnight, A. Dillon, & J. Richardson (Ed.), (pp. 19–50). *Hypertext: a psychological perspective.* London: Ellis Horwood.

Dillon, A. (1992). Reading from paper versus screens: a critical review of the empirical literature. *Ergonomics: 3rd Special Issue on Cognitive Ergonomics, 35*(10), 1297–1326.

Dillon, A. (1994). *Designing usable electronic text: ergonomic aspects of human information usage.* London: Taylor and Francis.

Dyer, H., & Morris, A. (1991). *Human aspects of library automation.* Aldershot, U.K: Gower Press.

Eason, K. (1988). *Information technology and organisational change.* London: Taylor and Francis.

Garnham, A. (1987). *Mental models as representations of text and discourse.* Chichester: Ellis Horwood.

Gould, J. D., Alfaro, L., Barnes, V., Finn, R., Grischkowsky, N., & Minuto, A. (1987a). Reading is slower from CRT displays than from paper: attempts to isolate a single variable explanation. *Human Factors, 29*(3), 269–299.

Gould, J. D., Alfaro, L., Finn, R., Haupt, B., & Minuto, A. (1987b). Reading from CRT displays can be as fast as reading from paper. *Human Factors, 29*(5), 497–517.

Huey, E. (1908). *The psychology and pedagogy of reading.* New York: Macmillan.

Just, M. A., & Carpenter, P. (1980). A theory of reading: from eye movements to comprehension. *Psychological Review, 87*(4), 329–354.

Kline, P. (1988). *Psychology exposed, or the emperor's new clothes.* London: Routledge.

Landauer, T. (1995). *The trouble with computers: usefulness, usability and productivity.* Cambridge: MIT Press.

Landauer, T., Egan, D., Remde, J., Lesk, M., Lochbaum, C., & Ketchum (1993). Enhancing the usability of text through computer delivery and formative evaluation: The superbook project. In C. McKnight, A. Dillon, & J. Richardson (Eds.), (pp. 71–136). *Hypertext: a psychological perspective.* London: Ellis Horwood.

McKnight, C., Dillon, A., & Richardson, J. (1991). *Hypertext in context.* Cambridge: Cambridge University Press.

Nielsen, J. (1995). *Hypertext and multimedia: The internet and beyond.* New York: Academic Press.

Norman, D. (1986). Cognitive engineering. In D. Norman, and S. Draper (Eds.) *User centered system design* (pp. 31–61). Hillsdale, NJ.

Shackel, B. (1991). Usability—context, framework, definition, design and evaluation. In B. Shackel, & S. Richardson (Eds.), *Human factors for informatics usability* (pp. 21–37). Cambridge: Cambridge University Press.

Suchman, L. (1988). *Plans and situated action.* Cambridge: Cambridge University Press.

van Dijk, T., & Kintsch, W. (1983). *Strategies of discourse comprehension.* London: Academic Press.

6

A Dialogue Perspective on Electronic Mail: Implications for Interface Design

Kerstin Severinson Eklundh

Royal Institute of Technology, Stockholm, Sweden

INTRODUCTION

The use of computers for communication has spread rapidly in the last decade, and new network communities are forming continuously. As a result of this, the computer medium has begun to serve a wider range of communicative purposes. This holds particularly for electronic mail (e-mail), one of the oldest and most well-established forms of computer-mediated communication.

In relation to the widespread use of this medium, however, there has been little research on the effects of the system interface for successful communication. In this chapter, I will examine the role of the e-mail interface from the perspective of allowing a dialogue between users. This is motivated by the fact that more and more users enter a mail system frequently and exchange many messages each day. For such users, e-mail potentially is an interactive medium of communication, resembling and replacing spoken conversations rather than the traditional exchange of written letters (cf., Severinson Eklundh, 1986, 1994).

PERSPECTIVES ON THE USE OF E-MAIL SYSTEMS

An influential line of study of the use of computer-mediated communication systems is characterized by an information processing
perspective. In this view, the user is seen as a consumer of information with a certain search goal. Typical issues have concerned how
the user can orient himself in the incoming information, how to find
the information sought for in a maximally efficient way, and how to
avoid information overflow (see, e.g., Hiltz & Turoff, 1985). This
perspective is often embedded in a tradition of research focusing on
how the use of the computer medium affects the efficiency of organizations (Kerr & Hiltz, 1982; Sproull & Kiesler, 1991).

Another line of research on mail systems, which has placed the
interface in the focus of study, regards electronic communication as
a task managed by an active user who may be simultaneously engaged in other, parallel tasks. The key issues concern how the system should be designed in order to match the user's goals. This view
departs from the tradition of cognitive science, and characterizes
the field of user-centered design of user interfaces (cf., Norman &
Draper, 1986). A number of empirical studies have examined the
use of e-mail from this point of view, attempting to reach conclusions regarding desirable properties of mail systems (see, e.g., Akin
& Rao, 1985; Hjalmarsson et al., 1989).

Research within this tradition has usually not analyzed how the
design of the mail system relates to the conditions for successful
interactive communication between users. This includes, for example, issues such as how users manage to take turns in a dialogue,
how they may perceive the communicative situation and successfully act upon each other's contributions. Surprisingly often in
research on e-mail systems, a mail task is treated as any other task
performed by a single user.

In this chapter, I shall explore the consequences of a *dialogue
perspective* when considering the interface of mail systems. This
implies that the user is recognized as one of several parties who are
active in a communicative exchange, and where each participant
alternates between the roles of sender and receiver. The use of the
term "dialogue" also means that participants act within a shared
context, and with the assumption that the exchange will—at least
ideally—lead to a state of mutual understanding.

Within this perspective, I will discuss some important aspects of
the interface for e-mail communication. This includes examining
how the e-mail system allows for an interactive dialogue between
two parties, both of whom may initiate communication and pursue

communicative goals. Emphasis will be placed on aspects affecting the interactivity of communication, and how the user can grasp and act on the communicative context.

BASIC PROPERTIES OF E-MAIL

Electronic mail normally is used for asynchronous communication, that is, the sender and the receiver communicate at different times, each one reading and writing locally on her own computer screen. Often this is judged as an advantage, since each one of the participants communicates when he or she has the time.

In the typical case, communication is initiated when the sender issues a Send command. The system then prompts the user for receivers and subject, and presents a window or an area for typing the message. When the text has been entered, a command is given for mailing the message.

The next time the receiver enters the system, he or she will find that there is a new message to read. When the receiver issues a Reply command, the new message created automatically gets the same Subject line as the original message, and its sender becomes the new receiver. Technically, dialogue sequences are created in e-mail as a result of this linking between messages and their replies.

Most electronic mail systems keep a personal "mailbox" for every user, that is, a file or database that contains the messages that this user has received and sent. The messages are normally left in the mailbox until the user deletes them. Apart from functions for reading and writing new messages, mail systems offer varying degrees of support for the management of mail tasks, such as storing and retrieving messages, keeping electronic addresses, organizing incoming mail in separate files or folders, and so on.

THE EMERGENCE OF DIALOGUES ON E-MAIL

Although e-mail is a written medium, several factors may contribute to the emergence of an interactive dialogue between users. This exchange of e-mail messages may in some respects be compared to spoken conversation.

First, e-mail is *fast* compared to other forms of written communication. The rapidity of communication is considered by many users to be the prime advantage of the medium (Schaefermeyer & Sewell,

1988). It can take only minutes or even seconds to compose and send a message, and the receiver may read the message and send a response within minutes. Therefore the medium allows for a unique interactivity compared to other asynchronous media.

In Severinson Eklundh (1986), a study was presented of e-mail communication within the Swedish conference system COM, used for professional information exchange between academics in the Stockholm area. The purpose of the study was to investigate the structure of computer-mediated dialogues in a corpus of naturally occurring data, as compared to conversation via spoken media. The study also included interviews and a survey with users on their perception of the computer medium.

Some data from this study may be used as an illustration of the potential rapidity of e-mail communication. Among the 450 complete dialogues (1133 messages) that were subjected to analysis, 62% were terminated within the same or the next day. The users who participated in the study overwhelmingly responded immediately on reading a message. The speed of composition during this process could be observed on the time between the reception of a message and the sending of a response: 49% of the responses were completed and sent away within two minutes from the reception of the message, and 95% within an hour. The corpus contained mostly short, informal messages; the mean length of a message was only 5.2 lines.

Several researchers have examined the similarities between computer-based communication and spoken conversation. Most of them have focused on synchronous, terminal-to-terminal communication, describing it as a kind of "computer talk" (Murray, 1991; Wilkins, 1991). In Severinson Eklundh (1986), the messages collected from the COM system were analyzed with respect to the character of the emerging discourse. In spite of the asynchronous nature of the medium, the dialogues displayed a range of features typical of spoken conversation. Messages contained many instances of interjections and informal expressions, whereas greetings and salutations were hardly ever used. Responses were regularly written in a way that required access to a previously established context, for example, one would use anaphoric pronouns or elliptical expressions when referring to elements introduced in the previous discourse, rather than repeating or rephrasing those elements as in traditional letter communication.

The results of a survey and interviews included in the COM study indicated that the conversational character of the communication was not an absolute quality of the medium, but was partly a result of the participants' strategies of using of the system. For example, many users reported that they would regularly review previous messages in a dialogue in order to grasp the discourse context while reading. Many users pointed out that the design of the COM system actually encouraged this strategy, and thereby the emergence of context-dependent messages, by supporting links to the previous and the next message in a conversational thread and making it easy for users to retrieve these links. We will return to this issue in a later section.

THE INTERFACE OF THE MAIL SYSTEM

In mail systems as in other computer applications, there are several different interface paradigms (see, e.g., Dix et al., 1993; Jones, Bock, & Brassard, 1990). Older systems are often command-based, that is, they require that the user memorizes commands for reading, writing, and sending messages. An example is the classical Unix mail system. Once the user has read through the list of new messages, these are not shown again unless the user issues a command, specifying which messages should be displayed.

More recent systems on personal computers often use menus in combination with a graphical presentation. A list of messages is displayed continuously in a window, in which the user can point and click with a pointing device to select a message. Individual messages are read in their own windows, and several windows can be open at the same time. Some systems allow for direct-manipulation (cf., Shneiderman, 1987), in the sense that messages can be "dragged" from one place on the screen and "dropped" in another place.

This family of interfaces gives the user a more direct, visual access to the current messages. A graphical presentation also makes it possible to support the user's spatial memory by using the location of an element as a retrieval cue. The user might, for example, get support for dragging a copy of an important message to a reserved corner of the screen as a reminder to deal with it later.

Jones, Bock, & Brassard (1990) conducted interviews with e-mail users in their natural work setting, focusing on their perceptions of how the mail system supported their needs. Although the systems used represented different interface paradigms (command line, menu, and direct manipulation systems), the results consistently pointed to four variables affecting usability: visual navigation, organization, integration, and customization.

Visual navigation embodied the need for simultaneous access to several different views of the mail environment. For example, users frequently needed to switch to view a list of the current messages as they were reading a message. *Organization* referred to the need for tools for structuring incoming mail as it grew large in volume. Both of these aspects are related to the need for a global perspective of the task (cf., Severinson Eklundh, Fatton, & Romberger, Chapter 7). *Integration* as a usability issue referred to the need to switch effortlessly between mail and other computer-mediated tasks, and *customization* embodied the user's desires to shape the environment according to her special needs, for example, by setting defaults or suppressing system messages.

At least with regard to the first three of these aspects, it was found that direct-manipulation systems offered more support than command-line systems. For example, they allow users to organize messages by pointing, clicking, and dragging objects rather than by using memorized commands referring to message numbers.

In each interface paradigm, however, one can discuss aspects that affect usability. *Directness* can be expected to be a general, contributing factor in the sense introduced by Hutchins, Hollan, & Norman (1986). This includes a close fit between the user's goals and the operations required to operate the system, both in a semantic and an articulatory sense. In order to understand the nature of this mapping, it is essential to study both the kinds of activities users engage in, and the aspects of the interface that they consider most important in supporting these activities.

In the rest of this chapter, I will focus on the problems occurring during actual communication in e-mail, and try to illustrate how aspects of the interface may affect those problems. This discussion is not intended to be exhaustive, but rather to illustrate that a dialogue perspective is both a fruitful and necessary complement to other approaches when considering the interface of mail systems.

INTERFACE ASPECTS OF THE E-MAIL DIALOGUE

Electronic mail has been characterized as a "lean" medium, in contrast to "richer" media, such as face-to-face communication. This means, among other things, that communication is restricted to one channel, and that there is no possibility of immediate feedback (a review of the literature on media richness is given in Zack, 1993). In spite of these general constraints compared to spoken modalities, it seems clear that the conditions under which the medium is used, and the nature of the resulting communication, are affected both by the specific properties of the mail system and by the participants' patterns of using the system. In the following sections, I will discuss some of these interrelationships in more detail.

Grasping the Communicative Situation

While communicating in e-mail, it is often difficult for users to get a grasp of the current situation and the ongoing discourse. One reason is that the parties are not present simultaneously, focusing on a shared external context as in a face-to-face encounter (Goffman, 1972). Instead, several interchanges may be open at the same time, each one with its own relative time scale. The mail system interface often is not very helpful for obtaining a clear picture of the current situation, in terms of which dialogues are going on and who are the participants. This may add to the inherent ambiguities of the medium, and cause the user to forget or ignore ongoing exchanges (cf., Sproull & Kiesler, 1991, p. 40).

A standard way of showing the situation is to display a list of available messages. In modern mail systems, the user can move between this view and views of individual messages in a mode that supports parallel tasks (cf., Jones, Bock, & Brassard, 1990). However, this presentation is usually insensitive to the structure of the ongoing discourse in terms of distinct dialogues with their specific participants and context. When a user needs to review a recent dialogue in its entirety, the relevant messages have to be searched for individually, and the thread of discourse reconstructed in a manual way.

In order to enforce a concept of dialogue, the system should give support for displaying the entire ongoing thread, that is, presenting a discourse history to each message. Different solutions have been proposed to this problem. Cockburn and Thimbleby (1993) presented an e-mail system that assigns a dialogue structure to a sequence of messages on the basis of heuristic rules involving only the sender, the receiver and the time of sending the message. Using a graphical picture of the structure, the user can "navigate" between the messages within a conversational thread in order to perceive a whole piece of coherent discourse.

Users' sense of conversation also can be reinforced by simpler means. The COM system, which was text-based and menu-driven (Palme, 1984), used the Reply links between messages to trace conversational threads. Special commands could be used during both writing and reading a message, to retrieve the previous message in the thread, or to view all the comments written on a specified message. A survey reported in Severinson Eklundh (1986) showed that this facility was used frequently and that it helped users obtain a sense of the current discourse context.

Some systems do not even store messages sent by the user, but include only the messages received in the list of current messages. In this case there is no basis for a concept of a coherent dialogue in the system, since a complete thread cannot be reconstructed. Other systems let the user set an option of storing these messages. Generally, it can be expected that the need for access to previous communication is dependent on the user's tasks. For users who use mail mainly for unidirectional communication, for example, to receive directions for their work, it may be less important to save complete dialogues than for users who use the medium for genuinely interactive communication, such as discussing or coordinating collaborative tasks (cf., the diverse uses of e-mail found by Mackay, 1989).

In most mail system interfaces, the interlocutors themselves are represented only by their names or electronic addresses. To increase the sense of who are the communicating parties, more varied representations may be considered. Recent work by researchers of CSCW (computer-supported collaborative work) has attempted to increase the "social awareness" by emphasizing visually who are the participants, for example, by displaying face icons for the users within a work group (Marmolin & Sundblad, 1993). In order to initiate communication within the group, the user activates the relevant icons or assembles them in a private "meeting room." However, this type of presentation is limited to groups with a moderate number of participants.

Generally, e-mail communication would be sensed as more direct if the addresses of participants were easier to access (Pliskin, 1989). Many mail users go through large archives of old messages just to find an electronic address stored with an old message, and perhaps copy it or use the "Reply" command in order not to have to type the address again.

Turn-taking and Interactivity

An important class of problems in e-mail concern the turn-taking mechanisms, that is, how the participants in a communicative exchange alternate between the roles of sender and receiver. In e-mail, there is no "conversational floor" to be allocated to one party at a time as in spoken conversation. Instead, users can initiate interaction at any time independently of the receiver being present, and continue writing without restrictions from other participants.

The way that turn-taking operates in e-mail means that it is less interactive than spoken media. The communication is delayed, and participants cannot interrupt each other. In addition, there are no physical, nonverbal cues that allow feedback and help interlocutors interpret the ongoing discourse. Altogether, this means that the participants cannot continuously affect and shape the course of the dialogue as in a face-to-face conversation, which in turn places restrictions on the kinds of discourse allowed by the medium.

Zack (1993) characterizes the turn-taking in e-mail as *alternating* as opposed to genuinely interactive, and theorizes about the conditions for discourse in different media

> In contrast to FTF (fact-to-face communication), EM (e-mail) tends to enforce strict turn-taking. Lacking the capability for interrupting at a fine grain, communicating simultaneously, employing multiple paralinguistic cues, or engaging in instantaneous feedback, it may be inappropriate in circumstances where high-level repair might be required to build mutual understanding (p. 16).

On the basis of a field study in an organizational setting, Zack found that e-mail was suited mainly for communication within an already established context, whereas actively building a shared context between participants is usually dependent on face-to-face communication.

In spite of these characteristics of the computer medium, it is clear that the actual interactivity experienced by users is affected both by system features and by users' strategies. For example: Does the user enter the system several times a day to receive and respond to new messages directly, or perhaps once a week, answering to all waiting messages in a single batch? Does the system allow the user to reply to a message directly upon reading it? Clearly, system features and strategies of use are interlinked, jointly giving rise to a form of communication that may be close and interactive as a conversation, or detached and transactional as a formal administrative task.

Mail systems may support turn-taking in different ways, causing distinct structural patterns in the resulting communication. For example, several types of Reply command may be used to respond to a message within a given discourse context, all creating a new message with the same Subject line. These options have different pragmatic implications. In one kind of reply, the answer goes only to the writer of the original message, whereas another type sends the answer to all recipients of the original message. The more explicitly these alternatives are marked in the interface, and the more natural they are perceived by the user, the more easily the user can respond to an initiative and create a new part of a coherent thread, perceived as such by the receiver.

Partly this is a matter of readability of mail messages. Since reading and responding to mail messages are fast processes, users can be expected to scan the incoming message quickly with respect to sender, subject, and other receivers before replying. When viewing an individual message, however, often it is difficult to identify the relevant information in the header, which may lead to serious mistakes. For example, one may forget to check who were the receivers of the message, and involuntarily send the reply to a whole group of people. This could be avoided if the system could be set to highlight certain information or to suppress other, less relevant information in the header. If a mistake already has occurred, on the other hand, an option to delete the message or change its receivers during the course of delivery would be a form of "repair" suitable to the demands of the medium.

Perhaps the most important aspect influencing turn-taking and interactivity is if it is possible to start writing a response directly upon reading a message. This depends partly on the user's work situation, but also on general features of the computer environment, such as whether the user is working directly on the host machine or has to download information to his own computer at one single occasion to save time or money. In a cognitive sense, the directness of responding is also affected by the extent to which the user must make complex selections or fill in form-based information before typing a message.

Advanced systems have been proposed that impose additional structure on an e-mail dialogue by restricting the format of messages. For example, templates may be offered for different discourse types, such as directives, calls for meetings, and so forth, which regulate turn-taking more profoundly. Such features enable the construction of rules for automatically sorting or filtering messages (Malone et al., 1987). Although these systems are designed to support users' organization of mail tasks, it is an open question whether they may also have side effects, implying a cognitive burden on the sender (Cockburn & Thimbleby, 1993) or an obstacle to the sense of interactivity.

The Lack of Feedback

An inherent property of e-mail (and asynchronous communication generally) is the lack of immediate feedback during a dialogue. Since communication is delayed, a message normally does not lead to any immediate reaction from a receiver. Moreover, it is usually not considered worthwhile to send a message containing only a feedback move, acknowledging or evaluating previous contributions (Severinson Eklundh, 1986). Therefore, a minimal information exchange in e-mail often is strictly two-part, lacking the final feedback move that often terminates a spoken interaction. This lack of feedback may cause uncertainty with regard to the state of a dialogue, in particular whether a dialogue is terminated or not.

Although most mail systems do not provide any help with this problem, the system interface may diminish the feedback problem to a certain extent. Some mail systems give an automatic confirmation of the addressee's reception of a message, or let the user select this as an option. Others, such as COM, print the time of reception in the header of a message when it is reviewed. The survey conducted in the study of e-mail communication in COM (Severinson Eklundh, 1986), showed that almost half of the subjects (49%) reported that they would often or very often check if a message had been received by reviewing it. For example, this would be done when no answer had appeared after a certain time since sending the message. The high checking rate may be seen as an indication that the reduced feedback in e-mail causes situations of uncertainty concerning the state of a dialogue. These situations would be less frequent if systems offered more and simpler ways to acknowledge reception of a message.

Creating and Maintaining a Discourse Context

One of the most pertinent problems while communicating via computer is to preserve the context through a dialogue. The contributions are usually separated in time by hours or days, and several threads may run in parallel with each other, which makes the problem of perceiving the discourse context different from and greater than in spoken conversation.

Virtually all mail systems provide a rudimentary mechanism for preserving a context through the Subject line. Whenever the user issues a Reply command, a template is created for the new message with the same Subject as the previous message. In order to interpret a new response as part of a dialogue, the reader has to scan the incoming message with respect to the sender as well as the Subject line.

In many cases, however, the Subject line is not sufficient to evoke a discourse context for a busy e-mail user. Therefore, other mechanisms are needed to help maintain the context. If the system has explicit support for dialogue context, this will usually be straightforward. For example, the system might display the entire conversational thread preceding a current message as an option (cf., Cockburn & Thimbleby, 1993).

Many mail systems allow users to preserve context simply by inserting a copy of the previous message into a current response. As a rhetorical device this is often called "quoting." This solution has the advantage of being portable across systems, and is used widely, especially in technically oriented e-mail communities. It can be seen as a means of making communication more efficient for the sender, enabling him or her to give a context for a response without paraphrasing the message responded to. However, it is also associated with potential problems for the receiver, related to the readability of the response and to the increased amount of information transmitted.

In Severinson Eklundh and Macdonald (1994) the habits and attitudes toward quoting as a response strategy were surveyed in a large group of heavy e-mail users, recruited among readers of Usenet newsgroups. The results showed that quoting was a frequently used strategy to give a reminder of the context of a message. However, most users used it selectively in order not to burden the reader with excessive repetition of content. The tendency to quote a message depended on several factors such as the receiver, the length, and the nature of the message being responded to.

Interestingly, quoting was perceived by a majority of the users to increase the sense of conversation in the computer medium. This seemed to be related to the fact that it allows the sender to start typing the response immediately, without paraphrasing the content of the message responded to. Also, most users reported that they often used a text editor to intersperse quoted topics and answers, which gives a sense of dialogue to the edited response.

In view of the widespread use of quoting, it is of interest how the interface may support it, and thereby encourage or discourage the user from including parts of an earlier message. In the Usenet study, it turned out that 62% of the users included an earlier message by means of a command in their mail system, whereas 15% used a system that included the message by default. The latter means that the user must deliberately delete the included message in order not to quote. The results showed that the users of this type of mail system actually used quoting twice as often as the other users.

As many as 27% of the users reported that they included the message manually, by "cutting and pasting." Evidently, there were social conventions in favor of quoting on the network, which caused many users to quote in spite of the lack of support for it in their system.

In the study of dialogues on the COM system (Severinson Eklundh, 1986), there were no instances of quoting in the data collected. This can be explained partly by the fact that the system did not give explicit support for it, but instead provided facilities for tracking the context of a dialogue. Another reason probably was that most users communicated only with other COM users, and there was no external pressure or convention to use quoting.

The various ways that a system can support or discourage users from quoting are perhaps best illustrated by giving two contrasting examples. In Unix mail, a command-based mail system, there is a command for including the whole message. The message being written can then be viewed only by issuing another command, and edited by explicitly invoking a text editor, temporarily leaving the mail system. This means that it is a tedious, multistep process to include a message, view the result, and invoke a text editor if it is necessary to select parts of the included message that should be deleted.

A contrasting example is Eudora, a modern mail system for Apple Macintosh with a graphical interface. When the user issues a Reply command, the previous message is inserted automatically, and simultaneously selected (i.e., marked in inverse video). This means that only one keystroke is necessary to confirm the quoting (a click with the mouse) and continue writing or editing the response. Likewise, however, a single keystroke is needed to remove the inserted message from the response (by touching any key on the keyboard, i.e., starting to write the response directly). This solution can be seen as an ingenious way of giving equal support to two different user strategies, not giving favor to one over the other.

CONCLUSIONS

This chapter has discussed some of the conditions for a successful dialogue between users of e-mail. Although e-mail is a "lean" medium compared to face-to-face conversation, the exchange of electronic messages may have conversational properties, partly as an effect of the rapidity of the medium. For users who are regularly connected to a mail system, this implies a unique potential of inter-activity compared to other written media.

We have shown examples of how factors of the interface, on the one hand, and the participants' strategies of use, on the other hand, interact to shape the basic conditions for a dialogue in e-mail. By paying attention to the design of interface, one may increase the bandwidth of the medium at least in a virtual sense, increasing users' engagement in a dialogue. In particular, the interface affects fundamental aspects of a dialogue such as users' sense of interac-tivity and their grasp of the conversational context.

There is a potential conflict in electronic mail between users' needs in a dialogue, on the one hand, and the need for efficient information transfer, on the other hand. The latter is associated with a strive for economy in message handling, which generally may be opposed to a concern for social aspects of communication (Lea, 1991; Severinson Eklundh, 1986). To a certain extent, the choice between these different perspectives may influence both user strat-egies and interface design. For example, interactivity in an e-mail dialogue requires continuous on-line connection and easy-to-use turn-taking mechanisms, whereas a strict emphasis on efficiency may favor a more batch-oriented communication, reading and writ-ing messages off-line to save time or money.

Among the design issues raised within a dialogue perspective of e-mail, there is a reason to place particular significance in the way the system presents the communicative situation to the user. This includes not only access to a graphical view of the current mes-sages, but also an emphasis on the structure of communication in terms of distinct, ongoing, or terminated dialogue threads. Further-more, users need to have easy access to the current discourse con-text while reading a particular message. If these aspects are badly presented in the interface, it may lead to an weaker perception of the ongoing communicative event, and a reduced responsibility and commitment. For example, if users have to put down significant work in order to view and respond to current messages, or if they get no support for retrieving the discourse context of a recently received message, messages will more easily be ignored, misunderstood, or forgotten.

Some of the issues discussed here are still poorly understood, partly because there is a lack of qualitative analyses of users' per-ceptions of e-mail communication. An important issue that has not been dealt with here concerns how factors in the use situation, such as overload, may affect the users' sense of the communicative context and their commitment in a dialogue. These factors merit more attention, as network communication increases in many organizations, and larger groups of professionals work under the demands of communication by e-mail.

REFERENCES

Akin, O., & Rao, D. R. (1985). Efficient computer-user interface in electronic mail systems. *International Journal of Man-Machine Studies, 22*(6), 589–611.

Cockburn, A., & Thimbleby, H. (1993). Reducing user effort in collaboration support. *Proceedings of the 1993 International Workshop on Intelligent User Interfaces* (pp. 215–218).

Dix, A., Finlay, J., Abowd, G., & Beale, R. (1993). *Human-computer interaction.* Englewood Cliffs, NJ: Prentice-Hall.

Goffman, E. (1972). *Encounters: two studies in the sociology of interaction.* Aylesbury, Bucks: Penguin University Books.

Hiltz, S. R., & Turoff, M. (1985). Structuring computer-mediated communication systems to avoid information overload. *Communications of the ACM, 28*(7), 680–689.

Hjalmarsson, A., Oestreicher, L., & Waern, Y. (1989). Human factors in electronic mail system design. *Behaviour and Information Technology, 8*(6), 461–474.

Hutchins, E. L., Hollan, J. D., & Norman, D. A. (1986). Direct manipulation interfaces. In Norman, D. A., & Draper, S. W. (Eds.), *User centered system design.* Hillsdale, Erlbaum.

Jones, S., Bock, G., & Brassard, A. (1990). Using electronic mail—themes across three user interface paradigms. *ACM SIGCHI Bulletin, 21*(3), 45–48.

Kerr, E. B., & Hiltz, S. R. (1982). *Computer-mediated communication systems: status and evaluation.* New York: Academic Press.

Lea, M. (1991). Rationalist assumptions in cross-media comparisons of computer-mediated communication. *Behaviour and Information Technology, 10*(2), 153–172.

Mackay, W. (1989). Diversity in the use of electronic mail: A preliminary inquiry. *ACM Transactions on Office Information Systems, 6*(4), 380–397.

Malone, T. W., Grant, K. R., Lai, K. -Y., Rao, R., & Rosenblitt, D. (1987). Semistructured messages are surprisingly useful for computer-supported coordination. *ACM Transactions on Office Information Systems, 5*(2), 115–131.

Marmolin, H., & Sundblad, Y. (1993). Sharing knowledge in a distributed environment for collaboration. Working Paper COMIC/KTH-4-1, Department of Computing Science, Royal Institute of Technology, Stockholm.

Murray, D. (1991). *Conversation for action. The computer terminal as a medium of communication.* Amsterdam/Philadelphia: John Benjamins Publishing Company.

Norman, D. A., & Draper, S. W. (Eds.) (1986). *User centered system design.* Hillsdale, Erlbaum.

Palme, J. (1984). COM/PortaCOM Conference system: Design goals and principles. *Proceedings of IFIP INTERACT'84: Human Computer Interaction* (pp. 931–932).

Pliskin, N. (1989). Interacting with electronic mail can be a dream or a nightmare: a user's point of view. *Interacting with Computers, 1*(3), 259–272.

Schaefermeyer, M. J., & Sewell, E. H., Jr. (1988). Communicating by electronic mail. *American Behavioral Scientist, 32*(2), 112–123.

Severinson Eklundh, K. (1986). *Dialogue processes in computer-mediated communication: A study of letters in the COM system.* Linköping Studies in Arts and Science 6, University of Linköping.

Severinson Eklundh, K., & Macdonald, C. (1994). The use of quoting to preserve context in electronic mail dialogues. *IEEE Transactions on Professional Communication, 37*(4), 197–202.

Severinson Eklundh, K. (1994). Electronic mail as a medium for dialogue. In L. van Waes, E. Woudstra, & P. van den Hoven (Eds.), *Functional communication quality (Utrecht studies in language and communication).* Amsterdam/Atlanta: Rodopi Publishers.

Schneiderman, B. (1987). *Designing the user interface: Strategies for effective human-computer interaction.* New York: Addison-Wesley.

Sproull, L., & Kiesler, S. (1991). *Connections: New ways of working in the networked organization.* Cambridge, MA: MIT Press.

Wilkins, H. (1991). Computer talk. *Written Communication, 8*(1), 56–78.

Zack, M. H. (1993). Interactivity and communication mode choice in ongoing management groups. *Information Systems Research, 4*(3), 207–239.

7

The Paper Model for Computer-Based Writing

Kerstin Severinson Eklundh
Ann Fatton
Staffan Romberger

Royal Institute of Technology, Stockholm, Sweden

THE WRITING ENVIRONMENT AND THE WRITER'S PERSPECTIVE OF THE TEXT

Much of the research on computers and writing has been devoted to the possible impact of word processing on the processes and products of writing, without discussing in detail the properties of the computer as a writing tool. Recent efforts in the field, however, have shown that the design of the writing environment may have crucial effects on the writing process (see, e.g., Britton & Glynn, 1989; Hansen & Haas, 1988; Lansman, Smith, & Weber, 1993; Neuwirth & Kaufer, 1989; Sharples, 1992). This includes both the way that the text is presented in the human–computer interface, and how the writer can manipulate the text, both locally and globally.

The cognitive model of writing presented by Flower and Hayes (1981) describes writing as a problem-solving activity, involving a complex interplay of the subprocesses of planning, text generation, and reviewing. These subprocesses are "orchestrated" by the writer in a way suitable to the demands of the rhetorical situation. In this model, *the text written so far* is one of the key factors constraining the writer's choices. The writer needs to reread continuously what has been written, both on a local and global basis, to form a representation of the gist of the text and proceed with further planning and writing (Flower et al., 1986). An adequate conception of the written text is not achieved automatically, but depends on the writer's skill and development as well as factors of the writing medium.

During the composition of a lengthy document, the way that the text is presented and accessible to the writer is therefore of central importance. It has emerged that the use of word processors may cause substantial problems for writers when reading and evaluating long documents on the screen, because of the *lack of a global perspective* of the text (Severinson Eklundh, 1992a; Severinson Eklundh & Sjöholm, 1991). The word processor often is used on a small screen, showing a very limited part of the text at a time. Moreover, when the user makes revisions or changes position in the text, the location of the text varies in relation to the screen window. These factors appear to contribute to the lack of an adequate "sense of the text" when writing with a computer (Hansen & Haas, 1988). Most writers need several paper printouts to compensate for the lack of a global perspective (Severinson Eklundh & Sjöholm, 1991).

Studies of the effects of word processing on the organization of the writing process appear to confirm that writers have a predominantly local perspective. In particular, it has been shown that the revisions made with word processors are more often local and affect the surface level of the text compared to writing with pen and paper (Card, Robert, & Keenan, 1984; Lutz, 1987; van Waes, 1993). A recent experimental study, involving writers in a university setting, showed that when the screen size increased, revisions were made on a higher level, and further away from the point of inscription (van Waes, 1991, 1993). In other words, extending the view of the text on the screen directly affected the range of writers' actions.

The advantages of increased view of the text are not exclusive to writing. The use of a larger screen has been shown to yield shorter learning times when reading lengthy texts (de Bruijn, de Mul, & van Oostendorp, 1992). A suggested explanation is that a larger context of the text facilitates the integration of the information units in the text and thereby aids comprehension.

To overcome the problem of a global perspective of the text in word processors, it is crucial that alternative models for text presentation are studied and evaluated. In the following sections, we will describe a model for computer-based writing based on the metaphor of paper pages. The purpose is to provide a writing environment that both gives a sufficient global view of a document, and supports the writer's spatial memory. The model has been implemented in a program, called *Paper,* which will be described in some detail. We will then report the results of a case study of writers using this environment, and discuss how the paper model may be developed further in order to support the writer in developing an adequate sense of the text.

PAPER AS A MODEL FOR TEXT PRESENTATION

When writing or reading on paper, we make constant use of the spatial arrangement of the text to remind ourselves of its inherent structure. This holds in a local as well as a global sense. By a quick visual inspection of a book in our hands, and by flipping the pages for a few seconds, we get a preliminary feel for the size, structure, and content of the text material. Not only are we guided by those physical cues when approaching a new document, they also enable us to remember the text by its appearance and spatial arrangement (Lovelace & Southall, 1983; Rothkopf, 1971).

Handling a text on separate pages of paper also has many other advantages during reading as well as writing. We can for instance order the pages in several different ways, spread them out to be able to look at several pages simultaneously, and use different kinds of pages for different purposes. These aspects have no direct counterpart in a scroll-window presentation of a document.

In a writing program based on the paper model, the user writes the text on simulated paper pages. When the current page is filled with text, a new blank page appears. Like paper sheets on a desktop, the pages can be spread out on the screen to yield an overview of the text.

The following aspects are central in the paper metaphor, and should be part of a program implementing it.

1. *Overview.* The user should be able to view the whole document in order to get a global perspective of the text. This includes the possibility to spread out the pages on the screen, making it possible to see several pages simultaneously, either consecutive pages or pages from different parts of the text. Similarly, the possibilities of gathering pages and moving them by direct manipulation help the writer to organize the desk and thereby keep a better overview of a specific part of a text.

2. *Spatial orientation.* As far as possible, the position of the text on the page should remain constant during the editing of the text. This is expected to support the writer's spatial memory, making it possible to remember where on the page a certain part of the text appears as an aid to memory and orientation in the document. Similarly, the position of a certain page on the screen should be kept constant as long as the user does not change it.

3. *Continuity in the writing process.* The user should be able to write a continuous text without interruption when switching to a new page.

4. *Local and global context.* During both composing and editing, the writer needs adequate support for perceiving the context of the current passage. Whereas a *global context* can be supported by overview facilities helping the writer to get a global sense of the text, a *local context* of a few consecutive pages or passages is also needed to support the writer's ongoing activity, for example, when checking the coherence and consistency of the text.

Although keeping some of the advantages of paper, it is crucial that the use of a paper-based model of writing should not imply abandoning the important benefits of word processors. This poses a challenge when implementing the model in a writing environment. Later, we will discuss some aspects where the paper metaphor may come into conflict with other interface requirements.

THE PAPER PROGRAM

In order to explore the applicability of the paper model to writing, an experimental writing system, Paper, has been constructed. The program was written in the Smalltalk language, and is intended to be used on a graphical workstation with a large screen. The version of the program to be described below runs on Apple Macintosh computer with a 21-in. screen.

Functionality and Interface: General Description

In Paper the user writes on "paper sheets," implemented as rectangular windows. All the sheets in one document have the same size. When a page is full, a new page automatically appears on which the user can go on writing without interruption in the writing process. The individual pages of a text can be moved around the desktop by pointing at them and dragging them to the desired position. When many pages fill the screen, commands for navigating, spreading out pages, and piling can be used. These help the user keep track of and organise the pages, and also support a global perspective of the text.

The Paper interface follows, to a great extent, the Macintosh Human Interface Guidelines (1992). The following classes of functions are supported in Paper, each one corresponding to a menu in the menu bar

1. file management functions (opening and closing files, etc.), in the **File** menu;
2. functions for writing and editing text, in the **Edit** and **Style** menus;
3. "navigating" functions in order to move around among the pages and to switch between them, in the **Go** menu;
4. overview functions, including functions for spreading out and piling pages, in the **Overview** menu;
5. search functions under the **Find** menu.

Writing and Editing on "Sheets of Paper"

When the user starts Paper, a blank untitled sheet is available for writing. This page is then the active page. To make a page active the user just clicks on it. Each page in Paper is labeled with the name of the document to which the page belongs and a page number showing the relative order of the pages within the document (for more details, see the section on page numbering).

The user can now either start writing a new text or open an older document to work with. When the page is full, so that the word just written does not fit on the page, a new page of the same size automatically appears to the right of the full page, enabling the user to see the first and the second pages simultaneously on the screen and providing him or her with a local context to write the second page (see Figure 7-1). If there is already a page at the position where the new one is to appear, then the new page will be slightly displaced to the right and downward. Hence, two pages are never placed exactly on top of each other.

When several pages have been written, each new one appearing to the right of the old one, the right edge of the screen eventually will be reached. The current page will then automatically be moved to

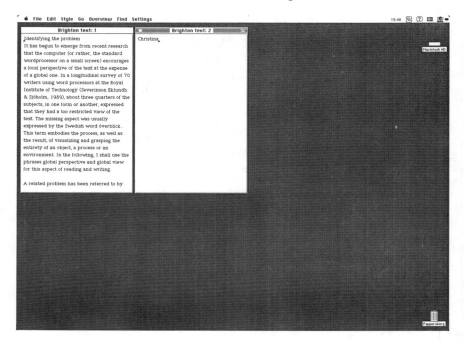

FIGURE 7-1. When the current page is full, a new page automatically created to the right of the previous one, and writing continues on this page.

the left to give room for the new page. In this way, a new, active page will always appear to the right of the previous one (see Figure 7-2).

A new page can also be created explicitly (by using one of the commands **New page after this** or **New page at the end**) to be placed either after the current page or at the end of the text.

Insertion of text on a full page is one of the most problematic operations in the paper-based writing model, since the pages have a fixed size. As mentioned earlier, a goal has been that the program should keep the location of the text in relation to the page constant as far as possible to support the writer's spatial memory. The currently chosen solution to the problem therefore is as follows: When a small insertion is made, for example, if only a spelling error is corrected, usually it will fit into the free space of the line, causing only a minor adjustment of the existing text. However, when a larger insertion is made, for which there is not enough room on the page, the page is split into two pages at the place of the insertion, and writing continues on the first of the two pages. The new page, containing the part of the text following the place of insertion, is placed

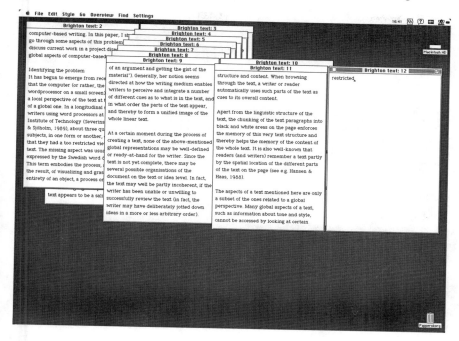

FIGURE 7-2. Screen configuration when the current page has repeatedly been moved because the right edge of the screen has been reached.

to the right of the previous page, and the user can continue to write the inserted text without interruption (see Figure 7-3).

Whenever the user wishes, the text can be compressed by using a command (**Compress text**) that deletes all the white areas arising from page splits. When this is done, pages are renumbered (see the section on page numbering). In this way, the position of the text on the pages actually may be altered, but only on the user's explicit request.

The user can choose among three page sizes, small (note size), medium, and large (approximately A4). This solution has been found to be simple and robust compared to a previous version, in which the user selected the page size by direct manipulation, using a "rubberband rectangle." When a document is opened, the pages have a size according to the value set in the **Settings** menu. It is also possible to change the page size of a document that is already open.

The basic text editing operations (**Copy, Cut, Paste, Find**) are available and work in the standard Macintosh way. Each page of the

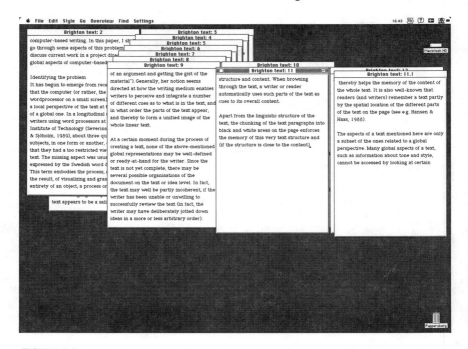

FIGURE 7-3. A document after the insertion of text that makes the page overflow. In the configuration shown in Figure 7-2, the phrase (*if the structure is close to the content*) has been inserted on page 11 after the phrase *this very text structure and.*

text has its own cursor and text selection, but the user can only write on the active page and only the selection of the active page is affected by editing operations. By clicking on another page, the user can go on writing at the same position as when he or she worked with that page earlier, since the cursor remains in the same position when the page is not active. Any selection will also remain unchanged while writing on another page.

Keeping Track of the Pages on the Screen

When there are many pages spread over the desk, overlapping each other, the user will need support for orientation and navigation among the pages. The most straightforward need is to reach a certain page hidden by others or just to find the next or the previous page. By using the commands in the **Go** menu, the user can easily flip the pages forwards or backwards. To "go" to a certain page (specified by page number) means that this page becomes the active one and appears on top of the others.

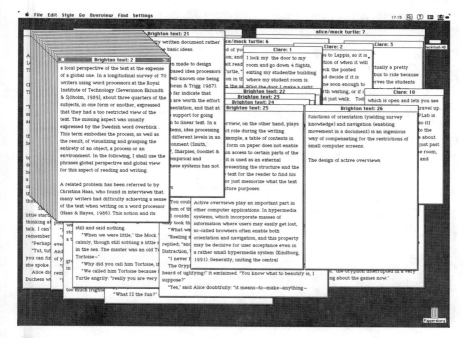

FIGURE 7-4. Screen configuration when the pages 2–20 of the document *Brighton text* have been stacked.

Another way to keep track of the pages is to organize them on the screen and to clean up the desk from time to time. This is also a way of getting a global perspective of a relevant part of the text or the whole text. Rearrangement can of course be done manually by moving pages one by one, for example, placing all the pages of the first chapter of the text in the lower right corner of the screen. But one can also use the **Stack text** command, either on all the pages of the text or on a subset of pages. The pages in the interval referred to by the command will then be repositioned to form a neat stack (see Figure 7-4). The position of the stack is determined from the position of the document's first page when executing the command. When repeatedly using the commands **Go to previous page** and **Go to next page,** the user gets a similar feeling as when flipping through the pages of a book.

Gaining an Overview of the Text

With the commands in the overview menu, the user can spread out the pages neatly in several different ways. Pages can be spread out

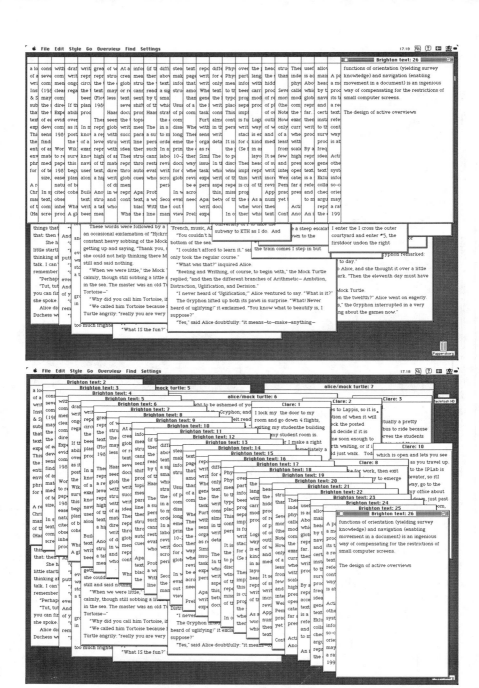

FIGURE 7-5a,b. Two ways of spreading out the pages of a document on the desktop.

over the whole desk, edge to edge if they fit completely, or partly overlapping if there is not enough room, overlapping vertically or horizontally (see Figure 7-5). They can also be spread out in a restricted area of the desk, defined by a rubberband rectangle drawn by the user. Finally, they can be ordered along the diagonal of the screen, a presentation that has the advantage of making all pages visible at any time.

To obtain a local context for the active page, the commands **Next page beside this** and **Previous page beside this** can be used. The active page will then remain active, surrounded by the previous and the next page, respectively.

Page Numbering

Finding a consistent page numbering system was not a trivial problem, since new pages can be created within the document in several different ways. The system adopted in Paper is the following.

A page number in the system consists of a *main page number* possibly followed by a sequence of *subpage numbers* separated by dots. The page number for a new page to be inserted between two consecutive pages, p and q, has the same beginning as the page number of p, and is one unit greater in the first subpage number that makes it fit between p and q. That is also the last subpage number. The following table illustrates the principles.

Current Page	Following Page	New Page, After Current Page
5	7	**6**
5	6	**5.1**
5	5.2	**5.1**
5	5.1	**5.0.1**
5.1	6	**5.2**

EVALUATION OF THE PAPER MODEL

As a preliminary assessment of the usability of the paper model, a case study was carried out with four users, each participating in two writing tasks. These studies were designed to provide a formative evaluation, as a step in developing the Paper program.

The Tasks

Four subjects were asked to write two different texts in Paper. The subjects were all academics, with long experience of both writing and computers. All of them had previously used a word processor on the Macintosh.

The studies included two different writing tasks. The first one was an open-ended task, inviting to a narrative structure: "The holiday of my dreams." The second one was argumentative: "Advantages and disadvantages of an information society." We expected that both of these tasks were difficult enough to put the basic writing environment in Paper on a test, but that the second one would be significantly more demanding with regard to the need for knowledge-forming activity, that it therefore would invite to more reviewing and revising, and require a greater amount of overview of the text.

Methods

The subjects participated in three sessions each, one for the first task and two for the second. It was decided to divide the second task into two sessions, both in order for the writers to achieve longer texts, and to be able to observe a situation where overview is particularly important: to resume writing after a long pause. For the last-mentioned reason, the sessions were also spread out over several weeks.

Both tasks had an approximate time limit. The first one was to take about one and a half hour and the second two hours (one hour in each session).

Two subjects started with the narrative task and the other two with the argumentative one. At the beginning of the first session, the basic functionality and menu options of Paper were explained to the subject. The subjects were told that the experimenter would be present during the sessions and that they could ask her questions if needed. They were also encouraged to comment on any problems occurring.

The experimenter made notes of the spontaneous comments made by the users as well as of problems occurring during the sessions. The sessions were videotaped, both as a backup for situations when no notes could be taken owing to the subject requesting help, and in order be able to reconstruct the screen disposition at various moments during the sessions.

Results

A general result of the case studies was that Paper was experienced as a useful writing environment. Comments made by all subjects indicated that they found the program easy to understand and to learn, and that the overview facilities were particularly appreciated. Some subjects expressed personal feelings about the specific way of writing in the paper model, for example: "It's inviting with some empty pages; it makes you want to write" or "It feels good to be able to see that one has filled that many pages with text—I can put them aside and feel satisfied with myself."

As expected, some differences were noticed in the use of Paper depending on the type of task. In the "holiday" task, the subjects wrote the text in a more linear way, from the beginning to the end, without looking back regularly at other parts of the text. New pages appearing automatically did not disturb the subjects who were able to go on writing without interruption (see the next section). Since these texts were also shorter (seven medium-sized pages on the average) the need for overview was not especially pronounced.

In the second, argumentative task, the users moved more often back and forth to review and revise the text. This is compatible with the results of a recent study of writers using word processors (Severinson Eklundh, 1994), in which tasks requiring knowledge-forming or structuring activity were composed in a less linear way than a reporting task. In the present study, the texts written in the second task were also longer, 12 pages on average. It is therefore not surprising that the overview facilities in Paper were of greater use to the subjects in this task.

The pages themselves were also used in a somewhat more elaborated way in the argumentative task. Some subjects used different pages for different purposes; for example, some pages for making notes or writing an outline, and others for writing running text. One subject expressed a great relief about not having to scroll the text up and down all the time to be able to see the outline she had written. She was used to writing an outline at the beginning of her text when working in a scroll window. Now she was able to keep the outline on a separate page that was located in the left upper corner of the screen, continuously available as a reference.

The possibility to see several pages at the same time, either consecutive pages or pages from different parts of the text, was appreciated by all the subjects. It helped them, for example, to check the consistency between different arguments and keep the language homogeneous through the text. Requiring a good overview both globally and locally, these activities are poorly supported by word processors with a scroll window.

In both tasks, the subjects used Paper mainly in a direct-manipulative way. This means that they preferred clicking on and dragging pages "manually" to using commands for organizing pages in most situations (i.e., to navigate between pages, to clean up the screen, etc.). There are several possible reasons for this preference. The subjects were new to the system, and the texts written contained a moderate number of pages. Considering the concreteness and simplicity of the paper model, it is easier from a cognitive point of view to click and drag pages than to learn a repertoire of commands. The only organizing commands that were used regularly by two of the subjects were the **Spread pages** commands.

We did not observe any general strategy at the time of resumption of writing at the beginning of the second session of the argumentative task. Typically, the subjects would just click on some of the pages to read them before starting to write. One subject used the **Spread pages** command; another one used **Go to next page** a couple of times to review the text.

Interface Problems Encountered

Although the experiences of using Paper were mainly positive, some problems with the interface appeared during the writing sessions. Most of these problems were related to parts of the paper model that are controversial and difficult to implement, in spite of the concrete character of the model.

Page breaks

The insertion of text on a full page is a problematic operation in the paper model, and this was confirmed during the user studies. The subjects felt that the page breaks were "not sensitive enough" and sometimes commented on unwanted consequences of it. For example, replacing a word with a longer one would in some cases have the negative effect of causing a page break. One subject reported that sometimes he avoided making certain changes for this reason.

Blank areas and the compress command

Even though the subjects knew that blank areas on the pages could appear during the writing process and that one could compress the text to get rid of them, they were sometimes confused because of these blank areas.

The main problem is that, although Paper is a page-oriented writing system, the page breaks are not as stable and easy to control as on paper (although the interface may suggest the contrary). In particular, the **Compress** command may suddenly change all the page breaks, and the effect of this can be devastating, especially if the writer has (as most of the subjects did) used some pages for an outline and does not want this outline to be concatenated with the running text. As a result, some of the subjects felt frustrated before they had learned how to handle the pages in this respect.

The subjects also had difficulties getting used to the difference between a blank area resulting from a page break and a succession of return characters. These areas are both white, but the latter consists of characters that can be edited and removed, whereas the first one is a truly empty area, which can only be used for writing text.

It emerged during the sessions that too many blank areas are disturbing for the writer. A subject expressed it in this way: "To keep the location of the text on the pages is important, but the relation of the text to the rest of the text is important too, perhaps even more important." Here we obviously have a conflict between two different aspects of the model: the support for the user's spatial memory on the one hand, and the access to a sufficient local context on the other hand.

Closing the pages of a document

It was confusing for the subjects that one could not click in the closing box at the upper left corner of the window in order to close a single page. Instead, this operation led to the whole document being closed. This is a conflict between the users' view of a Macintosh window, and their view of a document as a sequence of pages belonging together. As a result of this problem, a change has been made in the program so that a menu command must be used to close the pages of a document.

CONCLUSIONS: PLANS FOR FURTHER WORK WITH THE PAPER MODEL

The case study showed that continued work is needed with regard to the paper model. On the one hand, a number of improvements and additions to the Paper program were suggested by the study, some of which are straightforward and others more sophisticated.

On the other hand, some aspects of the model itself should be investigated further, both theoretically and empirically.

The Spatial Position of the Text Relative to the Page

Nearly all the problems arising during the writing sessions were associated with the static property of the text on the page, and various interface aspects related to it (page breaks, blank areas, and the **Compress** command). Clearly, this aspect of the model needs further investigation. Nevertheless, there are two straightforward improvements of the functionality in Paper that address some of the problems encountered.

1. improving the visual difference between blank areas resulting from page breaks, on the one hand, and a series of return characters inserted by the writer, on the other hand; and
2. including a command for inserting concrete ("hard") page breaks, enabling the writer to separate pages that should not be treated as belonging to the running text.

Generally, the user should be able to use pages for special purposes, not only to write running text. We could observe how the subjects spontaneously did so, although the program did not offer specific support for it.

As a continuation of the analysis of the paper model, we are investigating alternative page break strategies that allow text to "flow" between pages in certain situations. The idea is to maintain a satisfying local context (i.e., a text that has not been divided into too many parts) while allowing changes only to have local repercussions; that is, never affect other parts of the text than the active page and the following one. This kind of compromise has been shown to minimize the total area of blanks, but still there are some problems to be solved regarding the functionality supporting such a feature.

Overview Facilities

It was quite obvious that the overview facilities—the most basic aspect of the paper model—were appreciated and taken advantage of by the writers. Therefore, it is important to continue the development of overview functionality in the Paper program. Since the size of the screen is a very restrictive factor, however, different types of overview may have to be used compared to paper presentation.

Generally, one may distinguish between two separate kinds of overview, both of which contribute to the global perspective of a text. *Physical overview* encompasses the user's ability to view and perceive the entire text with all its parts, as it is presented on a writing medium (the screen or a paper page). On a computer with a WYSIWYG ("What you see is what you get") interface, usually there is a fairly good physical overview in a local sense, but a bad one globally. One obvious way of improving the physical overview is to increase the screen size; another one is to print out the text on a high quality printer.

A second form of overview is *logical,* that is, it gives a representation of the conceptual elements of the text and (sometimes) the relationships between them. The simplest example is a table of contents in a book. On a computer, logical overviews may be created in "idea processors" yielding a graphical structure of the ideas underlying the text; or in the outline mode of some word processors, which also enable the writer to choose the level of detail to view the text. Recent case studies have shown that such features may support writer's high level planning and facilitate orientation in a lengthy document (Severinson Eklundh, 1992b).

The basic idea of the paper model relies on a physical overview similar to the one given on paper pages. To compensate for the restricted screen space, however, one may consider adding elements to increase the logical overview. The extent to which this can be done without removing the basic advantages of the metaphor is an open question. This will depend, among other things, on whether the addition of such features creates mismatches in the user's application of the paper metaphor to his or her task (cf., Carroll, Mack, & Kellogg, 1988).

So far, the following types of additional overview functionality have been discussed, the first ones being the most natural ones.

1.   saving room on the screen: This could be done with extended functions for organizing (stacking) the pages, for instance by "magnetic reducing piles." This refers to a location on the desk where the user could place pages, just by dragging and "dropping" them there. The pages could be arranged in any order, and even belong to different documents. The size of the pages would be reduced automatically in the pile and extended when the page is taken out

of it. In addition, functions for reducing the size of the pages of part of a document would be helpful, such as zooming in and zooming out facilities.

2. visualizing the current pages in an optimum way by using, for instance, a fisheye perspective: This means that the active page and its neighboring pages are larger and shown in more detail, whereas distant pages are smaller. This would also have the effect of saving screen space.

3. giving pages distinct visual appearances, such as different colors, titles, and shapes to reflect different documents, page types, and so forth.

4. adding "logical structures" to the pages that would help the user to get a better overview of special parts of the document. An example of a logical structure would be the possibility to define different relations between pages. When the user performs an operation (i.e., formatting) on one page, the other pages in the relation would be "updated" in a similar way. Notice that this notion of page relation could coexist with the possibility of having different *types* of pages in the same document. For instance, the user could define each chapter of the document to consist of a special "type" of pages (this is a way of giving different names to different parts of the same document, and pages of the same type should be consecutive) and define a relation called "first page" that would include all the first pages of the different chapters. This would be a helpful tool to format the first pages (title, chapter number, etc.) in a consistent way.

Toward a More Direct-Manipulative Paper Program

It was notable that the subjects used Paper in a direct-manipulative way. The concreteness of the paper model clearly invites to a direct, manual handling of pages as a basic mode of action. The question of how to improve this directness further therefore should be focused in the continued development of the program. Of course, this does not exclude an improved support for the automatic organization of pages. It can be expected that such support will be more relevant as longer texts are written and the user's experience of the program increases.

The following are possible ways of achieving increased directness in Paper.

1. Creating more direct ways of navigating between pages, for instance by clicking on a special part of the page to activate the next page or to have icons (e.g., arrows left and right) to go to the previous and the next page, respectively. One could even see the pages of one document as associated with links that could be followed and changed.

2. To use double-click (or other direct-manipulative ways) to open a pile or to put a page back on its place in the pile would also make the use of Paper more direct, and also facilitate organizing the desktop. One could also imagine using some "magnetism" to put back a page in a pile: Drag a page and release it on a pile and the page would automatically be put in its correct place in the pile.

3. The possibility to select several pages, for example, by shift-clicking, would enable the user to make operations on several pages simultaneously. This might not necessarily include sequentially ordered pages, but even pages from different documents or including different relations or types.

Like the overview facilities discussed earlier, some of the features proposed earlier would imply a step away from the "true" paper metaphor. One might object that features improving directness should follow the paper metaphor more closely. An example of such a feature would be the use of a touchscreen to move the pages. However, directness can be seen as a more general aspect of interaction that involves minimizing the distance between the user's goals and intentions, on the one hand, and the variables that have to be manipulated in the system to achieve this goal, on the other hand (Hutchins, Hollan, & Norman, 1986). This can be achieved both with and without the use of a metaphor. What is perceived as direct for the user, and the role of the metaphor in this, are partly empirical questions. The experiences from the use of Paper so far, however, indicate that some features of the kind suggested earlier could complement the present functionality without disturbing users' conception of the paper model.

Using the Paper Metaphor in Support for Planning, Reviewing, and Cooperation

The experiences from the case study showed that the central parts of the paper metaphor, that is, support for spatial orientation and overview, are relevant in several ways throughout the writing process. This suggests that the paper metaphor could be used in constructing specific support for various writing activities. Such functionality could be designed to address some well known limitations in current writing systems.

For example, some subjects created special pages for note taking, and kept them visible on a reserved area of the screen during writing. The immediate, visual access to these notes was clearly useful during planning of the writing task. This leads to the question if the paper metaphor could be used in special aids for planning, such as creating, organizing, and storing notes representing ideas.

Word processors generally do not give a sufficient support for planning, especially on a high conceptual level of the writing task. Writers who use word processors have been shown to plan less than writers who work with pen and paper, and their planning concerned lower-lever aspects of the text (Haas, 1989). These results can be related to the observation, discussed earlier, that word processors offer a local perspective of the text, encouraging writers to think and revise within the current sentence or paragraph rather than attending to global concerns even at early stages of writing.

Advanced computer aids for planning have been proposed, which are based on a hypertext representation of the writer's ideas (see e.g., Halasz, Moran, & Trigg, 1987). These systems often rely on the user memorizing intricate mechanisms for linking text nodes and retrieving text from logical relations, which may lead to a significant complexity even in medium-sized tasks. We believe that the simple and natural way of writing notes on separate pages, and using their spatial orientation on the desktop as a memory aid, would complement such planning aids significantly and make them even more useful for overview purposes.

Another important area of writing support concerns automatic reviewing and proofreading. Current tools, such as spell checkers and grammar checkers, are usually considered as applications where the computer performs the bulk of the work, and the writer simply checks or confirms the result. Moreover, the system usually offers only a local view of the text when the writer is to decide whether to adopt or reject changes proposed by the system. We argue that proofreading and revising support should be combined with direct support for the user's own reviewing, particularly a "physical overview" of the kind provided in the paper model. There are many situations when a writer simultaneously needs access to an overview of the text and support for searching or proofreading in the same part of the text. For example, one might need to highlight all occurrences of a word in a chapter to determine if this word occurs too frequently or should be replaced with another word. Such tasks can never be completely automated, but should be solved in cooperation between the user and the computer.

Finally, we suggest that the paper model could be of interest as a basis for a collaborative writing system. A central problem in designing support for collaborating writers concerns the level at which writers' activities should be coordinated. This, in turn, depends on the roles of different contributors in the authoring process (see, e.g., Baecker et al., 1993; Sharples, 1993). Because of its simplicity and robustness, the paper metaphor seems suitable as a general basis for supporting the exchange and coordination of text material between individuals in a work group. This idea rests on the assumption that the page (the size of which can be determined by users) defines an appropriate unit for cooperation in many situations, whereas issues below the page—such as decisions involving the formulation of sentences—are best attended to by individual writers until a late stage in the production of a document. We are presently designing a collaborative version of Paper to be used in case studies of cooperating writers.

In conclusion, we believe that support for overview and spatial orientation of text pages are essential elements in a user-friendly writing system. The experiences of the Paper program so far support the hypothesis that these aspects contribute to a global perspective of the text, which in turn can be expected to facilitate writers' high level planning and contribute to the coherence of the written product. Although there are still many problems to be solved, the paper model has the potential to provide both of these important ingredients, addressing needs arising in different tasks and during various stages of writing.

REFERENCES

Baecker, R. M., Nastos, D., Posner, I., & Mawby, K. L. (1993). The user-centered iterative design of collaborative writing software. In *Proceedings from INTERCHI'93: Human Factors in Computing Systems*. New York: ACM Press, 399–405.

Britton, B. K., & Glynn, S. M. (ed.) (1989). *Computer writing environments: theory, research, and design*. Hillsdale, NJ: Erlbaum.

Card, S. K., Robert, J. M., & Keenan, L. N. (1984). On-line composition of text. *INTERACT'84*. Imperial College, London: IFIP, 231–236.

Carroll, J. M., Mack, R. L., & Kellogg, W. A. (1988). Interface metaphors and user interface design. In Helander, M. (ed.), *Handbook of hu-*

man-computer interaction, Amsterdam, The Netherlands: Elsevier Science Publishers B.V.

de Bruijn, D., de Mul, S., & van Oostendorp, H. (1992). The influence of screen size and text layout on the study of text. *Behaviour & Information Technology, 11*(2), 71–78.

Flower, L. S., & Hayes, J. R. (1981). A cognitive process theory of writing. *College composition and Communication, 32*, 365–387.

Flower, L., Hayes, J. R., Carey, L., Schriver, K., & Stratman, J. (1986). Detection, diagnosis, and the strategies of revision. *College Composition and Communication, 37*(1), 16–55.

Haas, C. (1989). How the writing medium shapes the writing process: Effects of word processing on planning. *Research in the Teaching of English, 23*(2), 181–207.

Halasz, F. G., Moran, T. P., & Trigg, R. H. (1987). NoteCards in a nutshell. In *Proceedings from the CHI + GI Conference (Human Factors in Computing Systems and Graphics Interface)*. (pp. 45–52). New York: ACM Press.

Hansen, J., & Haas, C. (1988). Reading and writing with computers: A framework for explaining differences in performance. *Communications of the ACM, 31*(9), 1080–1089.

Hutchins, E. L., Hollan, J. D., & Norman, D. A. (1986). Direct manipulation interfaces. In Norman, D. A. & Draper, S. W. (eds.), *User centered system design* (pp. 87–124). Hillsdale, NJ: Erlbaum.

Lansman, M., Smith, J. B., & Weber, I. (1993). Using **The Writing Environment** to study writers' strategies. *Computers and Composition, 10*(2), 71–92.

Lovelace, E. A., & Southall, S. D. (1983). Memory for words in prose and their locations on the page. *Memory & Cognition, 11*(5), 429–434.

Lutz, J. A. (1987). A study of professional and experienced writers revising and editing at the computer and with pen and paper. *Research in the Teaching of English, 21*(4), 398–421.

Macintosh Human Interface Guidelines. (1992). Reading, MA: Addison-Wesley.

Neuwirth, C. M., & Kaufer, D. S. (1989). The role of external representations in the writing process: Implications for the design of hypertext-based writing tools. In *Hypertext '89 Proceedings*. New York: ACM, 319–341.

Rothkopf, E. Z. (1971). Incidental memory for location of information in text. *Journal of Verbal Learning and Verbal Behavior, 10*, 608–613.

Severinson Eklundh, K. (1992a). Problems in achieving a global perspective of the text in computer-based writing. *Instructional Science, 21*, 73–84. Also in Sharples (ed.), 1992.

Severinson Eklundh, K. (1992b). The use of "idea processors" for studying structural aspects of text production. In A-C. Lindeberg, N. E. Enkvist, and K. Wikberg (eds.), *Nordic research on text and discourse: NORDTEXT symposium 1990*, Åbo Academy Press, Åbo, 271–287.

Severinson Eklundh, K. (1994). Linear and non-linear strategies in computer-based writing. *Computers and Composition, 11*(3), 203–216.

Severinson Eklundh, K., & Sjöholm, C. (1991). Writing with a computer. A longitudinal survey of writers of technical documents. *International Journal of Man-Machine Studies, 35,* 723–749.

Sharples, M. (ed.) (1992). *Computers and writing: Issues and implementations.* Dordrecht, The Netherlands: Kluwer Academic Publishers.

Sharples, M. (ed.) (1993). *Computer supported collaborative writing.* London: Springer-Verlag.

van Waes, L. (1991). *De computer en het schrijfproces. De invloed van de tekstverwerker op het pauze—en revisiegedrag van schrijvers.* WMW-publikatie 6, Universiteit Twente, Holland.

van Waes, L. (1993). The computer and the writing process. The influence of the word processor on the pausing and revision behavior of writers. *ICTL papers,* UFSIA—University of Antwerp, Belgium.

8

Interface Design and Optimization of Reading of Continuous Text*

Paul Muter

University of Toronto

Reading is the means by which the world does a large part of its work. . . .
The slightest improvement either in the page or in the method of reading
means a great service to the human race (Huey, 1908).

INTRODUCTION

At present, we do not know how to optimize reading via electronic
equipment. In this chapter, some considerations that may help us
do this in the future will be raised, and some of the relevant evidence and theories that do exist will be cited and briefly highlighted.

*Dept. of Psychology University of Toronto, Toronto, Ont. Canada, M5S 3G3,
muter@psych.utoronto.ca

The focus of this chapter is on reading of continuous text, whether in linear form or hypertext form, and with or without the presence of graphics or other types of information.

Paradoxically, computer technology may lead to an increase in the use of text and an increase in literacy, because we are in a window of time in which it is easy and efficient to produce, store, manipulate, and transmit computerized text files, and comparatively difficult to process graphics, sound, or video. The amount of reading of text from electronic displays is increasing substantially every year.

Computerized presentation of text has some clear advantages over paper media (Egan, Remde, Gomez, Landauer, Eberhardt, & Lochbaum, 1989; Yankelovich, 1985), such as ease of searching for information, ease of updating, capability of presenting other media simultaneously, dynamic text presentation (see the following), inexpensive customizability, interactivity, and connectivity.

In past research on optimization of reading, the main two dependent variables have been reading time and comprehension, as measured by recall, questionnaires, or error detection. Some other dependent measures of interest are effective reading rate: reading speed times percent correct on a comprehension test (Jackson & McClelland, 1979), to avoid problems associated with tradeoffs between speed and comprehension; rereading time; and size of saccades, and saccades per unit time (Kolers, Duchnicky, & Ferguson, 1981).

The issue of visual fatigue will not be emphasized in the present paper, but following are some of the dependent measures that have been used.

- accommodation (speed, range, resting focus, fluctuations);
- pupil diameter;
- critical flicker frequency (frequency at which flicker is just perceptible) (Harwood & Foley, 1987);
- blink rate;
- acuity;
- contrast threshold;
- saccade speed;
- fixation duration;
- lacrimation (Yaginuma, Yamada, & Nagai, 1990);
- subjective reports.

PAPER VERSUS CATHODE RAY TUBES (CRT)

Much of the published research on optimization of reading has been done with paper media. Research on reading from paper media has yielded the following results (Frenckner, 1990).

- Upper case print, italics, and right justification by inserting blanks result in slower reading.
- Black characters on a white background produces faster reading than the reverse, and most readers prefer it.
- There is no effect of margins, serifs, or typefaces in general, within reasonable limits.
- Effects of type size, line length, and interline spacing interact.

Bever, Jandreau, Burwell, Kaplan, and Zaenen (1990) found that comprehension was facilitated by adding spaces between major phrases, as determined by a simple automatic parser.

It is unknown to what extent findings from paper media can be extended to electronic media. Certainly at least some of the results do not generalize. For example, Wright and Lickorish (1988) found that color cues were effective as location aids for paper texts but not for computerized texts (although in the former case the backgrounds were colored and in the latter case the text itself). Prominent researchers in the field have expressed the opinion that it is risky to generalize from research on paper to electronic media (e.g., Kolers, Duchnicky, & Ferguson, 1981).

Muter, Latrémouille, Treurniet, and Beam (1982) compared speed and comprehension in reading from a videotex terminal and a book. Results over two hours of reading indicated that, although extended reading from videotex was feasible, it was 28% slower than reading from paper. There was no significant difference in comprehension. Several other researchers also have found decreased efficiency from CRTs of the 1980s (e.g., Gould & Grischkowsky, 1984; Wilkinson & Robinshaw, 1987), some with reading and some with proofreading. Proofreading and reading share some component processes, but other processes are unique to each skill.

Dillon (1992) complained of the "great disparity in procedures" in studies demonstrating slower reading with CRTs than with paper, but this disparity could be interpreted as a virtue: Seeking "robustness in variation" can be a useful strategy in the face of complex interactions (see Interactions).

There are many typical differences between book and computer reading that conceivably could account for the observed slower reading from computer screens of the 1980s (adapted from Muter & Maurutto, 1991).

- resolution
- edge sharpness
- character shape
- intercharacter spacing
- stroke width of characters
- distance between the reading material and the reader
- angle of the reading material
- actual size of characters
- visual angle of characters
- characters per line
- lines per page
- words per page
- interline spacing
- margins
- chromaticity
- polarity (light characters on a dark background vs. the reverse)
- contrast ratio between characters and background
- intermittent versus continuous light
- emissive versus reflected light
- stability (potential flicker, jitter, shimmer, or swim; Stewart, 1979)
- interference from reflections
- absence versus presence of incidental location cues
- aspect ratio
- curvature of screen
- distortion in corners
- system response time
- method for text advancement
- posture of the reader
- readers' familiarity with the medium

It is quite clear that no single variable accounts for the obtained differences in performance between CRTs and paper. Several of the described variables, including resolution, interline spacing, polarity, and edge sharpness, contribute to the effect (Gould, Alfaro, Barnes, Finn, Grischkowsky, & Minuto, 1987; Kruk & Muter, 1984; Muter & Maurutto, 1991). With a more modern system, including a large, higher resolution screen with dark characters on a light background, reading from a computer can be as efficient as reading from a book (Muter & Maurutto, 1991).

Of course, the efficiency of books notwithstanding, electronic text presentation should not simply mimic a book. The strengths and potential of computerized presentation should be pursued and exploited.

SELECTED INDEPENDENT VARIABLES

It is beyond the scope of the present chapter to comprehensively review the empirical evidence and theory on the effects of all of the independent variables that might affect reading via computers. (For reviews, see Dillon, 1992; Frenckner, 1990; and Mills & Weldon, 1988.) In this section, I will present brief comments on a number of independent variables, and more extensive treatment of one variable, color. In my opinion, the worst sins in the computerized presentation of text are committed with the use of color.

Of course, some of the following variables are inextricably intertwined, and some of them interact with each other.

Color

Many disadvantages and potential problems with the use of color in text presentation have been pointed out (Rubin, 1988; Shneiderman, 1987).

- Color displays in effect have lower resolution because three phosphors are required at each point.
- Edges created by color alone are difficult to resolve.
- Approximately 8 percent of males are at least partly color blind, and deficiencies in color vision are sometimes amplified with CRTs because red phosphors have a sharply peaked spectrum.
- The use of color sometimes results in a contrast ratio that is so low that performance is impaired; for example, the author's name is almost illegible on the cover of Rubin (1988).
- The tendency to overuse color (the "fruit salad" approach) can clutter up the screen and create confusion.

- Color displays are not universally available, and are "more costly, heavier, less reliable, hotter, and larger" than mono-chrome displays (Schneiderman, 1987, p. 342).
- Different colors, especially highly saturated ones at opposite ends of the spectrum, sometimes appear to be in different depth planes because of chromatic aberration or color ste-reoscopy, and this can be fatiguing.
- It is difficult to generalize from experiments on the use of color with computers, because different products, for exam-ple, with different phosphors, produce different colors, and phosphors degrade with age. In many experiments purport-edly on color, brightness and contrast are uncontrolled.

In addition

- Misconvergence, produced when the red-green-blue elec-tron guns are imperfectly aligned, can disrupt perception (Travis, 1990).
- Some colors have expected meanings that may contradict the intended meaning. For example, in some nuclear power plants, red denotes on and green denotes off (Bailey, 1982).
- Color perception is affected by context: simultaneous color contrast (e.g., a surrounding blue induces a change toward yellow), and color adaptation effects (Jameson & Hurvich, 1964; Laar & Flavell, 1988).
- Small blue objects (<0.25 degrees of visual angle) are diffi-cult to see (small field tritanopia; Williams, MacLeod, & Hay-hoe, 1981).

Many factors affect the ability to distinguish colors (Silverstein, 1987), including

- wavelength separation;
- color purity;
- brightness;
- stimulus size;
- brightness adaptation level;
- number of colors;
- background (light versus dark);
- stimulus location (central versus peripheral);
- type of discrimination (relative versus absolute); and
- individual differences (e.g., age).

Of course, people often prefer color, and color can be useful to emphasize format, to highlight, to categorize, and to improve aesthetics (Nes, 1986; Rubin, 1988). Color can also aid in visual search (Smith, 1962). To maximize discriminability of colors, evidence suggests that differences in hue and lightness should be maximized and differences in saturation should be minimized (Laar & Flavell, 1988).

Polarity

Evidence suggests (Radl, 1983) that a large majority of users prefer positive polarity (dark characters on a light background). In theory, positive polarity reduces optical distortion, and increases visual acuity, contrast sensitivity, speed of accommodation, and depth of field (Bauer & Cavonius, 1983). It also decreases the problem of interfering reflections of external light (Bauer, 1987). However, the effects of polarity are controversial (Pawlak, 1986; Taylor & Rupp, 1987). A definite disadvantage of positive polarity is an increase in the risk of perceived flicker, although this problem can be overcome with a sufficiently high refresh rate.

Variables Affecting Perception of Flicker

The probability of perceiving flicker increases (Nylen & Bergqvist, 1987; Pawlak, 1986)

- with increasing luminance (e.g., with dark characters on a light background);
- as phosphor persistence time decreases;
- if the screen is seen peripherally;
- if the user is talking (vibrations are transmitted from the vocal cords to the eye);
- with line jitter;
- with the size of the screen; and
- with temporal contrast.

Pixel Attributes

Two goals in display design were suggested by Murch and Beaton (1987). (1) The adjacent raster line (or pixel) requirement: the raster lines or pixels should be imperceptible at typical viewing distances; for example, characters should appear to be continuously constructed. (2) The alternate raster line (or pixel) requirement: an alternating on-off pattern of adjacent rasterlines or pixels should be perceptible at typical viewing distances.

Resolution

One measure of resolution is the resolution: addressability ratio, which is the width of pixels divided by the peak-to-peak distance between pixels (Harpster, Freivalds, Shulman, & Liebowitz, 1989). Harpster et al. found that a high ratio resulted in better visual search performance.

Interline Spacing

The evidence of Wilkins and Nimmo-Smith (1987) suggests that increasing spacing between lines and proportionately decreasing horizontal spacing between letters may improve the clarity and comfort of text without affecting the density of the text. Close interline spacing may impair reading because of vertical masking, and because return sweeps are more difficult (Kruk & Muter, 1984). Evidence of Lunn and Banks (1986) suggests that interline spacing should be variable to prevent fatigue resulting from adaptation to spatial frequency.

Words per Screen

With respect to words per screen, Muter, Latrémouille, Treurniet, and Beam (1982) suggested that reading speed tends to decrease as words per page decreases. Findings consistent with this idea have been reported several times (Creed, Dennis, & Newstead, 1988; de Bruijn, de Mul, & van Oostendorp, 1992; Reisel & Schneiderman, 1987).

Screen Size

There is both theory (Lansdale, 1988) and data (de Bruijn, de Mul, & van Oostendorp, 1992; Dillon, Richardson, & McKnight, 1990) to support the idea that large screens enhance the processing of text, perhaps partly because the number of words per screen can be larger (see the preceding).

Multiple Windows

An experiment on reading of lengthy texts indicated that, after practice with the system, a multiwindow display helped readers to relocate information (Tombaugh, Lickorish, & Wright, 1987).

Scrolling versus Paging

Paging is apparently superior to scrolling in terms of both performance and user preference (Kolers, Duchnicky, & Ferguson, 1981; Schwarz, Beldie, & Pastoor, 1983). One advantage of paging is that incidental memory for location within a page (Rothkopf, 1971) may facilitate processing.

Distance

Within reasonable limits, the distance between the reader and the reading material has no effect on perceptual span (Morrison & Rayner, 1981) or reading efficiency (Kruk & Muter, 1984). With increasing distance, retinal image size decreases linearly, but so does retinal eccentricity (distance of the image from the fovea), and these two effects offset each other exactly. Acuity is a decreasing linear function of eccentricity (Anstis, 1974).

Size of Characters

Within reasonable limits, size of the characters has no effect on proofreading speed (Gould & Grischkowsky, 1986). The probable reason is analogous to the reason that distance has no effect (see the preceding).

Proportional Spacing

Variable letter width (proportional spacing) led to faster reading of lists of isolated words (Beldie, Pastoor, & Schwartz, 1983).

Indentation

Huey (1908) recommended three-space indentation of every other line to facilitate return sweeps, but to my knowledge this idea has never been tested directly.

Hyphenation

Reading is slower if words are divided (hyphenated) at the ends of lines (Nas, 1988).

Highlighting

Techniques for highlighting include (Nes, 1986; Schneiderman, 1987; Tullis, 1988)

- underlining;
- enclosing in a box;
- pointing with an arrow;
- adding asterisks;
- reversing polarity;
- flashing: on-off, fluctuating brightness, or normal and reverse video;
- varying size;
- varying font;
- boldface;
- varying brightness; and
- adding color or audio.

The evidence on highlighting suggests that sometimes it helps and sometimes it has a negative effect (Fisher & Tan, 1989). A key variable seems to be highlighting validity: The percentage of time that a target, as opposed to a distracter, is highlighted.

Case

Searching for words is faster with uppercase characters, but reading of continuous text is slower (Vartabedian, 1971), perhaps because interline masking is greater with uppercase (Nes, 1986). In addition, lowercase enhances reading efficiency because word shape is helpful in word recognition (Rudnicky & Kolers, 1984).

Integration

Ideally, reading from a computer should be integrated easily with other tasks such as decision making, annotating (including unofficial comments), and report writing (Erickson & Salomon, 1991; Wright & Lickorish, 1984). Van Oostendorp (in press) found that performance in annotating text was as good in several computer conditions as in a paper and pencil condition.

Access Devices

The following are some potential enhancements of conventional text that can mimic hypertext and enable selective access, and that may affect efficiency of reading (Jones, 1987).

- parenthetical remarks;
- footnotes;
- appendices;
- tables;
- figures;
- verbal references; for example, "see Section. . ." or "see Smith. . .";
- indices;
- tables of contents;
- section headings; and
- topic sentences of paragraphs.

DYNAMIC TEXT PRESENTATION

Up to this point in the present chapter, it has been assumed that presentation of text is static. In dynamic text presentation, an attempt is made to optimize reading by utilizing some of the special capabilities of the computer. Two methods of dynamic text presentation that have been tested are rapid serial visual presentation (RSVP) and the Times Square format.

RSVP

With RSVP, text is presented at a fixed location on the screen, one word at a time or a few words at a time. Several researchers have demonstrated that readers can perform approximately as efficiently with RSVP as with normal page-format reading (e.g., Juola, Ward, & McNamara, 1982). Several potential uses of RSVP are

- when display space is limited;
- scanning and skimming, which constitute a high proportion of cognitive processing of text;
- reading by users with impaired peripheral vision, for example, retinitis pigmentosa (Williamson, Muter, & Kruk, 1986);
- studying cognitive processes;

- with certain kinds of poor readers, who perform better, after practice, with RSVP than with regular page format (Juola, Haugh, Trast, Ferraro, & Liebhaber, 1987); and
- as an efficient way to present continuous text in general, when optimal parameters are established, because there is no need to expend cognitive capacity on controlling eye movements.

The optimal conditions for RSVP seem to be the following (Juola, Haugh, Trast, Ferraro, & Liebhaber, 1987)

- about 12 characters per window on average;
- two or three words per window;
- idea-unit segmentation; and
- 250–500 msec blank window between sentences.

Giving the user control over RSVP presentation, e.g., over regressions and rate of presentation, sometimes has adverse effects on performance (Chen and Chan, 1990; Muter, Kruk, Buttigieg, & Kang, 1988). However, of course, under many circumstances, people will prefer to have this control.

Times Square Format

Kang & Muter (1989) found that smooth (pixel-by-pixel) horizontal scrolling with a small window (Times Square format) produced performance at least as good as RSVP, contrary to earlier studies that did not use pixel-by-pixel scrolling. In addition, subjects preferred the Times Square format, which is often used in electronic billboards.

INTERACTIONS

A major difficulty in research in text presentation, whether static or dynamic, is that the various independent variables often interact, sometimes in extremely complex ways: The effect of one variable depends on the level of other variables. For example, this has been a problem with respect to typographic variables such as type size, line length, and interline spacing (Frenckner, 1990). The following are some possible approaches for handling the problem of intractable high order interactions.

- Perform a huge number of factorial experiments. (This is not usually practical.)
- Sample randomly from a large range of several factors.
- Reconstrue the problem: "What is sometimes required is not more data or more refined data but a different conception of the problem" (Shepard, 1987, p. 1318).
- Seek "robustness in variation": Try to find evidence for a principle in many relevant settings (Landauer, 1988).
- Prune the alternative space; that is, somehow reduce the number of possibilities under consideration.
- Use an algorithm such as Simplex (Nelder & Mead, 1965) to determine which values of several independent variables to experimentally test next in order to maximize a dependent variable such as reading rate.
- Use a "kitchen sink" approach for practical problems (Muter & Maurutto, 1991): Throw into a single condition every feature that might have a beneficial effect, based on theory or data, and compare it to a control condition.

INDIVIDUAL DIFFERENCES

A second source of problems is individual differences. The use of computers entails huge individual differences, but it also permits extensive individualization (Rich, 1983). It is particularly important to take individual differences into account in human–computer interaction, for several reasons (Bailey, 1982; Egan, 1988).

- As time passes, the group of computer users becomes more and more heterogeneous.
- Individual differences tend to account for more of the variance in performance than do differences in system design or training.
- If individual differences are taken into account in the design of systems, more people can use them.
- It is now known, to some extent, how to accommodate individual differences (see the following).

The effects of age are an important source of individual differences in reading. For example, the following visual functions decline with age (Czaja, 1988).

- acuity, both static and dynamic (for moving objects);
- dark adaptation;
- perception of targets of low contrast;
- peripheral vision;
- accommodation;
- color perception; and
- iconic memory.

Various ways of accommodating user differences have been developed.

- Allow user to personalize system (Bournique & Treu, 1985).
- Develop robust interfaces (Egan & Gomez, 1985): Assay user differences; isolate the source of variation; then redesign to accommodate differences among users.
- Develop user prototypes: Product two or more interfaces, one for each type of user (Morris, 1987), based on: user's self-classification; the answers to a few questions; or dynamic user modeling (user may change).

CONCLUDING COMMENTS

Despite the large number of published experiments on reading continuous text from computers, to my knowledge no circumstances have been found in which reading in normal subjects is more efficient, with respect to speed and comprehension, than from a book. Perhaps performance superior to that achieved with the book has not been demonstrated because the new techniques of presentation require that the user have extended practice, and the experiments in the literature last no more than several hours per reader. Bigger experiments with dozens or even hundreds of hours of testing per subject may be necessary.

A more economical strategy is suggested by some work by Coleman and Kim (1961). They found that several formats, in particular a center-justified format with one word per line, had a positive effect on the processing of tachistoscopically presented text, but no effect or a negative effect on reading, probably because of entrenched habits. With extended practice, the effect might emerge in reading. If it could be established that tachistoscopic studies like this are good predictors of results of reading studies with extensive practice, then studies using tachistoscopic presentation—or analogous studies using computers to flash stimuli—could be used as short-cuts to determine which presentation techniques optimize performance in reading.

On the other hand, perhaps the reason that no computer condition superior to a book has been found is that the bottleneck is in the central processing in the human brain, rather than in the input channels. Carver (1982) found that the optimal rate of reading and listening tended to be constant under a wide range of conditions. It is possible, although unlikely in my opinion, that tinkering with modes of presentation will do little or no good past a certain point, a point that has been reached by the technology of the book. The book has evolved over several centuries to its present highly efficient form. Of course, the evolution of the human brain has not kept pace with the evolution of technology. However, perhaps coordinated developments in computer technology and cognitive science can pave the way toward more efficient reading, and therefore toward the facilitation of work and problem solving in many areas of endeavor.*

REFERENCES

Anstis, S. M. (1974). A chart demonstrating variations in acuity with retinal position. *Vision Research, 14*, 589–592.

Bailey, R. W. (1982). *Human performance engineering.* Englewood Cliffs, NJ: Prentice-Hall.

Bauer, D. (1987). Improving the VDU workplace by introducing a physiologically optimized bright-background screen with dark characters: advantages and requirements. In B. Knave, & P. G. Wideback (Eds.), *Work with display units 86.* Amsterdam: North-Holland.

Bauer, D., & Cavonius, C. R. (1983). Improving the legibility of visual display units through contrast reversal. In E. Grandjean, & E. Vigliani (Eds.), *Ergonomic aspects of visual display terminals.* London: Taylor & Francis.

Beldie, I. P., Pastoor, S., & Schwarz, E. (1983). Fixed versus variable letter width for televised text. *Human Factors, 25*, 273–277.

Bever, T. G., Jandreau, S., Burwell, R., Kaplan, R., & Zaenen, A. (1990). Spacing printed text to isolate major phrases improves readability. *Visible Language, 25*, 75–87.

---

*I thank Valerie Temple for general assistance, and Boyd Blackburn, Pavel Muresan, Oren Satov, and Herre van Oostendorp for helpful comments.

Bournique, R., & Treu, S. (1985). Specification and generation of variable, personalized graphical interfaces. *International Journal of Man-Machine Studies, 22*, 663–684.

Carver, R. P. (1982). Optimal rate of reading prose. *Reading Research Quarterly, 18*, 56–88.

Chen, H., & Chan, K. (1990). Reading computer-displayed moving text with and without self-control over the display rate. *Behaviour & Information Technology, 9*, 467–477.

Coleman, E. B., & Kim, I. (1961). Comparison of several styles of typography in English. *Journal of Applied Psychology, 45*, 262–267.

Creed, A., Dennis, I., & Newstead, S. (1988). Effects of display format on proof-reading with VDUs. *Behaviour & Information Technology, 7*, 467–478.

Czaja, S. J. (1988). Microcomputers and the elderly. In M. Helander (Ed.), *Handbook of human-computer interaction*. Amsterdam: Elsevier.

de Bruijn, D., de Mul, S., & van Oostendorp, H. (1992). The influence of screen size and text layout on the study of text. *Behaviour & Information Technology, 11*, 71–78.

Dillon, A. (1992). Reading from paper versus screens: a critical review of the empirical literature. *Ergonomics, 35*, 1297–1326.

Dillon, A., Richardson, J., & McKnight, C. (1990). The effect of display size and paragraph splitting on reading lengthy text from screens. *Behaviour & Information Technology, 9*, 215–227.

Egan, D. E. (1988). Individual differences in human-computer interaction. In M. Helander (Ed.), *Handbook of human-computer interaction*. Amsterdam: Elsevier.

Egan, D. E., & Gomez, L. M. (1985). Assaying, isolating and accommodating individual differences in learning a complex skill. In R. Dillon (Ed.), *Individual differences in cognition*. New York: Academic Press.

Egan, D. E., Remde, J. R., Gomez, L. M., Landauer, T. K., Eberhardt, J., & Lochbaum, C. C. (1989). Formative design-evaluation of SuperBook. *ACM Transactions on Information Systems, 7*, 30–57.

Erickson, T., & Salomon, G. (1991). Designing a desktop information system: Observations and issues. *Human factors in computing systems: CHI'91*, New York: ACM.

Fisher, D. L., & Tan, K. C. (1989). Visual displays: The highlighting paradox. *Human Factors, 31*, 17–30.

Frenckner, K. (1990). Legibility of continuous text on computer screens—a guide to the literature (TRITA-NA-P9010). Stockholm: Royal Institute of Technology.

Gould, J. D., Alfaro, L., Barnes, V., Finn, R., Grischkowsky, N., & Minuto, A. (1987). Reading is slower from CRT displays than from paper: attempts to isolate a single-variable explanation. *Human Factors, 29*, 269–299.

Gould, J. D., & Grischkowsky, N. (1984). Doing the same work with hard copy and with cathode-ray tube (CRT) computer terminals. *Human Factors, 26,* 323–337.

Gould, J. D., & Grischkowsky, N. (1986). Does visual angle of a line of characters affect reading speed? *Human Factors, 28,* 165–173.

Harpster, J. L., Freivalds, A., Shulman, G. L., & Liebowitz, H. W. (1989). Visual performance on CRT screens and hard-copy displays. *Human Factors, 31,* 247–257.

Harwood, K., & Foley, P. (1987). Temporal resolution: An insight into the video display terminal (VDT) "problem." *Human Factors, 29,* 447–452.

Huey, E. B. (1908/68). *The psychology and pedagogy of reading.* Massachusetts: MIT Press.

Jackson, M. D., & McClelland, J. L. (1979). Processing determinants of reading speed. *Journal of Verbal Learning and Verbal Behavior, 108,* 151–181.

Jameson, D., & Hurvich, L. M. (1964). Theory of brightness and color contrast in human vision. *Vision Research, 4,* 135–154.

Jones, W. P. (1987). How do we distinguish the hyper from the hype in non-linear text? In H.-J. Bullinger, & B. Shackel (Eds.), *Human-computer interaction—INTERACT '87.* Amsterdam: Elsevier.

Juola, J. F., Haugh, D., Trast, S., Ferraro, F. R., & Liebhaber, M. (1987). Reading with and without eye movements. In J. K. O'Regan, & A. Levy-Schoen (Eds.), *Eye movements: From physiology to cognition.* Amsterdam: Elsevier.

Juola, J. F., Ward, N. J., & McNamara, T. (1982). Visual search and reading of rapid serial presentations of letter strings, words, and text. *Journal of Experimental Psychology: General, 111,* 208–227.

Kang, T. J., & Muter, P. (1989). Reading dynamically displayed text. *Behaviour & Information Technology, 8,* 33–42.

Kolers, P. A., Duchnicky, R. L., & Ferguson, D. C. (1981). Eye movement measurement of readability of CRT displays. *Human Factors, 23,* 517–527.

Kruk, R. S., & Muter, P. (1984). Reading of continuous text on video screens. *Human Factors, 26,* 339–345.

Laar, D. V., & Flavell, R. (1988). Towards the construction of a maximally-contrasting set of colors. In D. M. Jones, & R. Winder (Eds.), *People and computers IV.* Cambridge: Cambridge University Press.

Landauer, T. K. (1988). Research methods in human-computer interaction. In M. Helander (Ed.), *Handbook of human-computer interaction.* Amsterdam: Elsevier.

Lansdale, M. W. (1988). The psychology of personal information management. *Applied Ergonomics, 19,* 55–66.

Lunn, R., & Banks, W. P. (1986). Visual fatigue and spatial frequency adaptation to video displays of text. *Human Factors, 28,* 457–464.

Mills, C. B., & Weldon, L. J. (1988). Reading text from computer screens. *ACM Computing Surveys, 19,* 329–358.

Morris, A. (1987). Expert systems. In D. Diaper, & R. Winder (Eds.), *People and computers III.* Cambridge: Cambridge University Press.

Morrison, R. E., & Rayner, K. (1981). Saccade size in reading depends upon character spaces and not visual angle. *Perception & Psychophysics, 30,* 395–396.

Murch, G. M., & Beaton, R. J. (1987). Matching display characteristics to human visual capacity. In B. Knave, & P. G. Wideback (Eds.), *Work with display units 86.* Amsterdam: North-Holland.

Muter, P., Kruk, R., Buttigieg, M. A., & Kang, T. J. (1988). Reader-controlled computerized presentation of text. *Human Factors, 30,* 473–486.

Muter, P., Latrémouille, S. A., Treurniet, W. C., & Beam, P. (1982). Extended reading of continuous text on television screens. *Human Factors, 24,* 501–508.

Muter, P., & Maurutto, P. (1991). Reading and skimming from computer screens and books: The paperless office revisited? *Behaviour & Information Technology, 10,* 257–266.

Nas, G. L. J. (1988). The effect on reading speed of word divisions at the end of a line. In G. C. van der Veer, & G. Mulder (Eds.), *Human-computer interaction: Psychonomic aspects.* Berlin: Springer-Verlag.

Nelder, J. A., & Mead, R. (1965). A SIMPLEX method for function minimization. *Computer Journal, 7,* 308–313.

Nes, F. L. van (1986). Space, colour and typography on visual display terminals. *Behaviour & Information Technology, 5,* 99–118.

Nylen, P., & Bergqvist, U. (1987). Visual phenomena and their relation to top luminance, phosphor persistence time and contrast polarity. In B. Knave, & P. G. Wideback (Eds.), *Work with display units 86.* Amsterdam: North-Holland.

Pawlak, V. (1986). Ergonomic aspects of image polarity. *Behaviour & Information Technology, 5,* 335–348.

Radl, G. W. (1983). Experimental investigations for optimal presentation mode and colours of symbols on the CRT screen. In E. Grandjean, & E. Vigliani (Eds.), *Ergonomic aspects of visual display terminals.* London: Taylor & Francis.

Reisel, J. F., & Schneiderman, B. (1987). Is bigger better? The effects of display size on program reading. In G. Salvendy, S. L. Sauter, & J. J. Hurrell, Jr. (Eds.), *Social, ergonomic and stress aspects of work with computers.* Amsterdam: Elsevier.

Rich, E. (1983). Users are individuals: individualizing user models. *International Journal of Man-Machine Studies, 18,* 199–214.

Rothkopf, E. Z. (1971). Incidental memory for location of information in text. *Journal of Verbal Learning and Verbal Behavior, 10,* 608–613.

Rubin, T. (1988). *User interface design for computer systems.* Chichester: Ellis Horwood.

Rudnicky, A. L., & Kolers, P. A. (1984). Size and case of type as stimuli in reading. *Journal of Experimental Psychology: Human Perception and Performance, 10,* 231–249.

Schwarz, E., Beldie, I. P., & Pastoor, S. A. (1983). A comparison of paging and scrolling for changing screen contents by inexperienced users. *Human Factors, 25,* 279–282.

Shepard, R. N. (1987). Toward a universal law of generalization for psychological science. *Science, 237,* 1317–1323.

Shneiderman, B. (1987). *Designing the user interface: Strategies for effective human-computer interaction.* Reading, MA: Addison-Wesley.

Silverstein, L. D. (1987). Human factors for color display systems: Concepts, methods, and research. In Durrett, H. J. (Ed.), *Color and the computer.* London: Academic Press.

Smith, S. L. (1962). Color coding and visual search. *Journal of Experimental Psychology, 64,* 434–440.

Stewart, T. F. M. (1979). Eyestrain and visual display units: a review. *Displays,* April, 25–32.

Taylor, S. E., & Rupp, B. A. (1987). Display image characteristics and visual response. In B. Knave, & P. G. Wideback (Eds.), *Work with display units 86.* Amsterdam: North-Holland.

Tombaugh, J., Lickorish, A., & Wright, P. (1987). Multi-window displays for readers of lengthy texts. *International Journal of Man-Machine Studies, 26,* 597–615.

Travis, D. S. (1990). Applying visual psychophysics to user interface design. *Behaviour & Information Technology, 9,* 425–438.

Tullis, T. S. (1988). Screen design. In M. Helander (Ed.), *Handbook of human-computer interaction.* Amsterdam: Elsevier.

van Oostendorp, H. (In press). Studying and annotating electronic text. In J. F. Rouet, & J. Levonen (Eds.), *Hypertext and cognition.* Hillsdale, NJ: Erlbaum.

Vartabedian, A. G. (1971). The effects of letter size, case, and generation method on CRT display search time. *Human Factors, 13,* 363–368.

Wilkins, A. J., & Nimmo-Smith, M. I. (1987). The clarity and comfort of printed text. *Ergonomics, 30,* 1705–1720.

Wilkinson, R. T., & Robinshaw, H. M. (1987). Proof-reading: VDU and paper text compared for speed, accuracy and fatigue. *Behaviour & Information Technology, 6,* 125–133.

Williams, D. R., MacLeod, D. I. A., & Hayhoe, M. (1981). Foveal tritanopia. *Vision Research, 21,* 1341–1356.

Williamson, N. L., Muter, P., & Kruk, R. S. (1986). Computerized presentation of text for the visually handicapped. In E. Hjelmquist, & L. G. Nilsson (Eds.), *Communication and handicap: Aspects of psychological compensation and technical aids.* Amsterdam: North-Holland.

Wright, P., & Lickorish, A. (1984). Investigating referees' requirements in an electronic medium. *Visible Language, 18,* 186–205.

Wright, P., & Lickorish, A. (1988). Colour cues as location aids in lengthy texts on screen and paper. *Behaviour & Information Technology, 7,* 11–30.

Yaginuma, Y., Yamada, H., & Nagai, H. (1990). Study of the relationship between lacrimation and blink in VDT work. *Ergonomics, 33,* 799–810.

Yankelovich, N., Meyrowitz, N., & van Dam, A. (1985). Reading and writing the electronic book. *IEEE Computer, 18,* 15–30.

9

Designing Screens for Learning

R. Scott Grabinger
Rionda Osman-Jouchoux

Division of Technology and Special Services,
University of Colorado at Denver

INTRODUCTION

Design is a series of choices that interact with each other and that reflect the theoretical underpinnings of a discipline. Designers of computer screens that present information and create interactions for learning make choices in manipulating several attributes that are common to both print and electronic media, among them, text, typography, layout, and graphics. Because screens are the direct means of communicating with the learner, the design choices determine the success or failure of instruction. The wealth of research on printed texts gives us indications about making some of these choices. That extensive research base has been supplemented by studies of the legibility and readability of information presented electronically and by research into the cognitive processes involved in reading and learning. In addition, we can take into account information on user preferences that allows us to evaluate the probable appeal of our screens to our intended audiences.

In this chapter, we begin our discussion about designing screens for instruction with a review of some of the important theoretical underpinnings that guide the design of instruction. We then review research on the legibility and readability of both print and electronic text and research into the cognitive effects of screen layouts. After examining the research, we present some design guidelines, concluding with suggestions for future investigations.

THEORETICAL UNDERPINNINGS

Learning, Cognition, and Reading

> Cognition is the activity of knowing: the acquisition, organization, and use of knowledge (Neisser, 1976, p. 1).

Computer-based applications present information via the screen, from which readers acquire, organize, and process information through interactions that lead to learning. The text and graphic elements of a screen combine to convey a specific message that will be translated into the reader's knowledge base. The goal of the designer is to arrange those text elements in appropriate combinations that create visible, recognizable, and syntactical and grammatical structures to facilitate perception, reading, and understanding.

Perception is the most basic process involved in interacting with our environment. Upon that basic process, other complex processes allow us to interact with our environment and to learn. One such complex process is reading, which Tinker and McCullough (1962) define as

> Reading involves recognition of printed or written symbols which serve as stimuli for the recall of meanings built up through past experience, and the construction of new meanings through manipulation of concepts already possessed by the reader. The resulting meanings are organized into thought processes according to the purposes adopted by the reader. Such an organization leads to modified thought and/or behavior, or else leads to new behavior which takes its place, either in personal or in social development (p. 13).

This definition of reading focuses on the memory of the learner and the situation or context within which the learner works. The reading process comprises more than one stage of memory representation (Just & Carpenter, 1987; van Dijk & Kintsch, 1983), one of short-term, verbatim memory of fragments of the screen and a second of organized semantic content. According to van Dijk and Kintsch (1983), the mental representation of the semantic content of the text, the textbase, is built of propositions. The textbase reflects the reader's organization of the text in macrostructures of the main ideas. Another mental representation proposed in the van Dijk and Kintsch (1983) theory, the situation model, defines for the reader the context of the text. The reader uses the situation model to interpret new information and relate it to existing schema. Kintsch (1989) found that coherently written texts were remembered more accurately, indicating that the learner's mental textbase was more accurate. He also noted that neither construct, the textbase, nor the situation model, is independent of the other, and that both are necessary to describe text comprehension, memory processes, and learning from text.

This cognitive description of reading is important because it defines a psychological area that may be used to guide the research and design of instructional screens. Reading requires attending to the environment, encoding and interacting with the stimulus in a meaningful manner, and linking the meanings of the stimulus with existing knowledge and prior experience. Tinker (1965) summarizes the link between perception and reading.

> The general process of perception includes stimulation, preparation for response, and the culmination in a response, the perception. The pattern in reading is along these lines. The graphic symbol is the stimulus, the meanings and interpretations (perception) are derived from the reader's past experiences, and the response relates meaning to the symbol (p. 9).

In addition, Bovy (1981) describes the implications of this relationship for instruction.

> In response to the interactive nature of attention [part of the perceptual process], which includes both features of the environment and the cognitive schema of the learner, instructional methods can activate learner attention by manipulating external features of the instructional display or by manipulating the cognitive schema of the learner (p. 208).

To sum up, both perception and reading are cognitive processes that function through an interaction between the environment and the perceiver. Therefore, instructional materials such as written text may be designed to facilitate that interaction by incorporating format features that enhance appropriate psychological processes.

INSTRUCTIONAL TEXT

Written instructional text is presented in a variety of ways, including traditional paper formats, microforms, and television or computer monitors. Whatever the presentation means, text elements, including fonts, illustrations, and graphic devices, are arranged in an empty space to communicate information and ideas to a specific audience. However, instructional text is not simply something that is passively presented. It forms the basis for an active interaction. Hartley (1978) presents the following definition of instructional text.

> . . . instructional text normally contains a wide variety of components—such as listed information, programmatically developed statements, numbered items, diagrammatic presentations, explanatory notes and pictorial features of many kinds. Furthermore, such materials are not intended for continuous reading. In an instructional setting the reader's focus of attention is constantly ranging from a place on the page to somewhere else. . . . From this point of view instructional materials are tools for use in a highly interactive and relatively unpredictable sequence of events (p. 13).

How readers approach and use instructional text, then, should be the focus for designers of instructional texts. Readers of such texts, according to Sticht (1985), are reading-to-do (using texts as a supplement to memory) or reading-to-learn (integrating text information into long-term memory). Both processes are descriptive of learning from texts, and both should be of concern in the design of instructional screens. Therefore, although reader involvement in novels is maintained with literary devices such as plot, story, characterization, theme, and dialogue, instructional texts must employ other means to maintain reader involvement and to encourage cognitive processing of content. We can examine those means through the dimensions of text design: (1) legibility, including type and typography, and (2) readability.

Legibility and Instructional Text

The instructional effectiveness of texts and screens depends on several factors, among them legibility and readability. Our focus is on the use of text format factors to make legible documents. *Format* is shape, size, type, arrangement of text elements, and all other things that contribute to the overall look and appearance of the display (Jones, 1976; Nelson, 1978). Some of the many items that affect format or appearance of screens are size of display area, shape of display area, color of background, color of foreground, type size, type style, type weight, leading, line length, columns, margins, arrangement of white space, word spaces, letter spaces, binding, contrast, reflectance value, and use of graphic devices. Legibility concerns, of course, influence the total format of the display and the ability of the reader to understand the text (Foster, 1965). The qualities of legible text, including visibility and recognizability (Reynolds, 1979), can be used by designers to facilitate retention of information and to encourage deeper processing.

Visibility qualities

Visibility refers to the perceptual detectability and discriminability of the printed character. A visible display presents symbols clearly and accurately (see Table 9-1). For example, a monitor with poor contrast between letters and background would fail the visibility test of legibility because without adequate contrast the shapes of the letters would not be discriminable from the background (see Figure 9-1). Poor contrast could be caused by poor monitor adjustment or glare from ambient lighting sources. Or, black letters on a dark background may fail visibility requirements if the symbols cannot be detected. Visibility is a prerequisite for recognizability, for without adequate visibility the reader would fail to recognize the meaning of the symbols on the display.

Research in the visibility area of legibility for both printed text and text displayed on screens has determined many typographic factors, including type sizes and contrast factors that contribute to optimal visibility. Work reported by Tinker (1963, 1965) and later updated by Rehe (1979) covers the area of visibility quite thoroughly

TABLE 9.1
Format Variables Affecting
Legibility Qualities

Visibility	Recognizability
Ambient lighting	Type style
Type size	Dot matrix size
Paper quality	Leading
Contrast	Type weight
Paper color	Word spacing
Ink color	Letter spacing
Ink quality	Symbol meaning
Monitor resolution	Line length
Reproduction quality	

These letters may be too small for a computer screen — 7 pt. Helvetica.

These letters may still be too small — 9 pt. Helvetica.

These letters may be large enough — 12 pt. Helvetica.

FIGURE 9-1. Visibility examples.

for printed text. Research pertaining to the legibility of monitors is less than 20 years old with the bulk occurring in the last decade. Most of the effort has focused on the visibility of different type styles, sizes, and contrast values (Cakir, 1980; Mills & Weldon, 1987; Snyder & Taylor, 1979; Wright & Friend, 1992). For computer screens, Mills and Weldon (1987) report that reading rates are faster for smaller type sizes, but that searching tasks are better performed with larger letters. Galitz (1993) reports that lines on computer screens should contain no more than 40–60 characters, and he recommends using two columns of text 30–35 characters wide. Lenze (1991) compared serif and sans serif type fonts in continuous text presented to subjects via a microcomputer. He found no apparent difference in reading speed or comprehension; however, his subjects preferred sans serif type. These findings for both paper and screens usually are widely practiced, since a publisher who does not produce visible materials will not remain a publisher for long.

Recognizability

Recognizability refers to the ability of a display to convey the meaning of the letters and words that are visible. A recognizable screen display presents meaningful symbols in such a way that the meaning of each symbol or combination of symbols can be identified and understood (see Figure 9-2). Recognizability interacts with the reading skill of the reader. For example, a first grader would have difficulty recognizing the meaning of all of the word symbols on this page, even though they are quite visible. Additionally, a display in Russian may be visible, but it would probably not be recognizable to most North Americans because most would not be able to recognize

Word Spacing

Thesewordsdonothaveanyspacebetweenthemmakingthemhardtorecognize.

Letter Spacing

Some of t h e s e   le t t ers are too far apart, making it
hard to read.

Line Spacing

Line spacing can effect recognizability

too. Too much space can break the mental

connection between lines.

FIGURE 9-2. Recognizability examples.

the meaning of each symbol or combination of symbols. Format
variables that affect recognizability include type style, word spacing, leading (amount of empty space between lines of text), and
letter spacing (refer to Table 9-1 and Figure 9-2). For example, a
display that used the same spacing width between words as between letters would not present readily identifiable word symbols.

The works of Rehe and Tinker set forth many widely accepted
standards for variables listed under the recognizability factor of
legibility (Rehe, 1979; Tinker, 1965). Although these same standards are assumed applicable to screen displays, the generalizability of paper standards to screen displays has not been verified.

The development of standards for visibility and symbol recognizability are steps toward readable displays. The combining of format
variables in the most legible format is the goal of the text designer.
To this end, researchers have investigated the use of content, layout, and organizational factors to facilitate reading speed and comprehension.

Readability and Instructional Text

"The quality of the content of a text is usually referred to as 'readability' and includes ease of comprehension" (Kolers, Wrolstad, &
Bouma, 1980, p. 334). Variables in this class include content factors and representation factors, layout and format factors, and organizational factors. See Table 9-2 for a summary of these factors.

TABLE 9.2
Qualities Affecting Readability

Content and Representation Factors	Layout and Format Factors	Organizational Factors
Purpose	Justification	Headings
Lexicon	Leading	Directive cues
Familiarity	Screen and text density	Spatial cues and
Vividness	White space	Text element or-
Concreteness	Line length	ganization
Similarity		
Sequencing		
Exposition		
Grammatical structure		
Complexity		
Sentence length		

Content and representation factors

Content and representation factors are related to the meaning or purpose of the writing. They include purpose, lexicon, familiarity, vividness, concreteness, similarity, sequential organization, mode of exposition, grammatical structure, sentence or clause complexity, and sentence length. However, these syntactical and semantic topics are beyond the scope of this chapter; if interested, you are referred to the vast literature on assessing readability (cf., Klare, 1974), which treats, in part, factors such as word length, word complexity, sentence length, and clause complexity.

Layout and format factors

Layout and format factors include those combinations of symbols and graphic devices that contribute to the appearance and arrangement of symbols and text elements on the page or screen. The overall effect and appearance of several format variables such as justification, screen, and text density contribute to the readability of the screen.

Justification refers to the point on the screen where a line of text begins (see Figure 9-3). Justification is an issue because computers can be set to automatically fully justify the text on a screen. The research on fully justified text tends to be mixed; however, it is generally believed that left-justified text is easier to read because it maintains the integrity of words and phrase units by keeping them intact. Galitz (1993) and Gregory and Poulton (1970) found that some readers have difficulty with fully justified text. Hartley's

Justification

In this article, the implications of constructivism for instructional design (ISD) are summarized as five principles that integrate the affective and cognitive domains of learning. Distinguishing characteristics of the two .

Left Justified

In this article, the implications for constructivism for instructional design (ISD) are summarized as five principles that integrate the affective and cognitive domains

Center Justified

In this article, the implications of constructivism for instructional design (ISD) are summarized as five principles that integrate the affective and cognitive domains of learning. Distinguishing characteristics of the two .

Right Justified

In this article, the implications of constructivism for instructional design (ISD) are summarized as five principles that integrate the affective and cognitive domains of learning.

Fully Justified

Point Size

12 Point Bold Avant Garde

12 Point Bold Bookman

12 Point Bold Boston

12 Point Bold Century Gothic

12 Point Bold Courier

12 Point Bold Futurist

12 Point Bold Geneva

12 Point Bold Helvetica

12 Point Bold New Cent. Schlbl

12 Point Bold Palatino

12 Point Bold Times

FIGURE 9-3. Typography examples.

(1987) research review led him also to conclude that left-justified text should be used on screens, particularly when line lengths are approximately 20 characters.

Screen density is the amount of empty space in relationship to text elements on the screen. The variables most often manipulated are vertical spacing, number of characters per line, line length, percent of white space, and number of lines on the screen. Text density studies have limited information presented on the screen to essential words or phrases (Morrison, Ross, & O'Dell, 1988; Ross & Morrison, 1989; Ross, Morrison, & O'Dell, 1988) and determined preferences for the proportion of text on a screen to the proportion of white space (Morrison et al., 1990). In these studies the researchers examined the effects of screens with many words compared to screens that were kept spacious with few words. Generally, they found that low-density text screens are as effective as high-text density in teaching an expository lesson. However, low-text density significantly reduces lesson completion time and users preferred low-density options over high-density versions.

Grabinger (1987, 1989, 1993) and Grabinger and Amedeo (1988) found that college students disliked texts that were crowded with type and figures and preferred texts with a balanced amount of white space and text. In cases where screens were almost, if not totally, text, students preferred double spacing. Kolers, Duchincky, and Ferguson (1981) reported that double spacing text on a computer screen reduced the number of eye fixations by 3% and decreased the total reading time by 2%.

However, as with the other typographic variable research, screen density research focuses on perception of the screen rather than on the processes of reading and studying. The results of most of this research show little, if any, consistent effect on learning. Because learning from an instructional computer screen involves the reader and complex cognitive processes, it may be more likely that changes that help the perceptual and reading processes such as organizational factors and meaning may be more valuable research material.

Organizational factors

Perception is organized and the more organized a message is the more readily it is perceived (Fleming & Levie, 1978). Frase and Schwartz (1979) suggested that it may be the organization of text elements that facilitates the reading process. Text elements include unified bodies of text, headings, illustrations, or graphic aids. The contours of the text may suggest an organization and facilitate semantic organization of the content within the reader. These ideas have led to research in the area of layout or spatial cues, such as manipulation of white space, use of headings, and indenting to reflect the structure of the information. Meyer (1976) stated that

> . . . information high in structure is better remembered and retained than low-level information. Also, the pattern of specific relations in the structure influences the recall of the information in prose (p. 199).

Thus, the learner's internal representation of the organization and structure of the text may be facilitated if the format of the text elements on the screen also represents that structure. Hartley (1980) describes this as a concern for the overall structure of the document.

Hartley goes on to state that the internal structure of the content can be represented by varying in proportion the amount of vertical space between units in the text and by indenting to convey the hierarchical nature of the subject material. Hartley (1987) pointed out that a systematic approach to spacing rules can effectively convey the structure of a piece of text whether on paper or on screen. Shebilske and Rotondo (1981) found inconsistent results in a study that used a free recall test and a multiple choice test. The free recall test showed that their "special" format improved learning and memory over the conventional formats; however, this finding was not replicated with their multiple choice test. Shebilske and Rotondo did find that their participants preferred the "special" format over the conventional format. In a newspaper study, Siskind (1979) found that newspaper readers preferred a well-done, contemporary design with more spacing cues to more traditional or poorly done designs. The use of spatial cues to separate text elements is a highly visible format factor and seems to have an effect on reader perceptions of screen text.

Headings.   Another aspect of the organization research is the use of headings to facilitate organization and retrieval tasks. Headings have also been shown to help both recall and retrieval of information, whether in statement or question forms, and whether embedded in the main body of the text or hanging in the margins (Hartley & Trueman, 1982). Holley et al. (1981) also found that students who read materials with headings learned more than students who read the same material without headings.

Directive cues.   Directive cues are format changes in the text designed to capture and focus the readers' attention on a particular portion of that text. Examples of directive cues include underlining, the use of bold and italic type, shading, or color (see Gilreath, 1993, for his proposed taxonomy of graphic cues). Perception is highly selective (Fleming & Levie, 1978), and perceptual selection reflects the fact that environmental input usually exceeds the amount of information that the perceiver can adequately handle (Kolers, Wrolstad, & Bouma, 1980). Cues facilitate the initial translation of the stimulus by providing a category difference between target and non targets, or foreground and background (Butler, 1980). Directive cues, then, work by detaching a figure from its ground for special attention or processing by the perceiver.

Most directive cue research in text is related to underlining in paper delivery systems including text books and handouts. Overall, these studies have found that underlining helps under the following conditions: first, the cues must be systematically related to expected learning outcomes (Anderson & Faust, 1967; Crouse & Idstein, 1972); second, the cues must be used sparingly to indicate only those ideas that are superordinate (Bausell & Jenkins, 1977; Garofalo, 1988; Hartley, Bartlett, & Branthwaite, 1980); and finally, the cues must not inhibit or circumvent the desired processing activities (Anderson & Faust, 1967). The skill a reader has in determining the importance of various parts of text is apparently related to maturation and overall ability. Rickards and Denner (1979) found that, for immature learners, the ability to discriminate superordinate and subordinate ideas could not be compensated for with directive cues. The use of cues, then, may help mature readers select that portion of the environment that they must first translate, then segment or organize, and finally process by relating to their own needs.

The kinds of cues used on computer displays show considerable variation. Mills and Weldon (1987) found that research with printed text has most often indicated that uppercase letters are superior for identifying single characters or individual words and that lowercase letters produce higher performance in reading continuous text (cf., Rehe, 1974; Tinker, 1955, 1963). They found consistencies with research with computer screens: for searching or recognition tasks, uppercase letters yield better performance (Mills & Weldon, 1987). Galitz (1993) also reports that uppercase letters are searched more quickly in captions and in menu choices (cf., Vartabedian, 1971; Williams, 1988).

Color as a cueing technique poses unique problem because color monitors are expensive and not universally available and high resolution color hues may vary from monitor to monitor. The colors with the most luminance are white, yellow, cyan, and green, and these colors are most useful for text on a dark background (Reynolds, 1980). Christ (1975, 1977), in an extensive review of over 40 studies that investigated the use of visual cues on visual displays, found that cueing is almost always useful in search tasks and sometimes useful in identification tasks. Christ (1977) and Tullis (1981) found that when color is not a criterial attribute (i.e., not a critical part of the definition of the concept) it does not matter whether the cues are achromatic or in a contrasting color. Recent work by Van Orden, Divita, and Shim (1993) combined luminance and flashing to highlight color- and shape-coded symbols. They found that such cueing can reduce search times. However, Fisher and Tan (1989) and Fisher et al. (1989) found that blinking, reverse video, and boxing delayed identification and location of items, although use of color to highlight did not produce delays in searching on-line.

This cueing research with screen displays supports the findings of cues in paper publications: When simple cues are related to the desired outcomes and used sparingly for important tasks they may be beneficial to performance, especially involving tasks related to identification and recognition.

Spatial cues and text element organization.   Computer-generated text sometimes lacks some of the flexibility of books and periodicals. First, only one page at a time is visible on the screen. Second, it may require time to review a previous page or preview an upcoming page. Third, the screen itself is often smaller than a single or a two-page spread in a book.

Given screen limitations, Reynolds (1980) recommends using a generous amount of white space to help organize and preserve idea units on one screen. She recommends the use of reverse print or color to emphasis important words in the text, plenty of space between paragraphs, and left-ranging headings (headings that start at the left margin rather than centered between margins). She also suggests using running heads (a group of words that are used to help readers organize their thoughts and to locate their position in the lesson) to enhance unity from one page to another (more will be said on this later in the chapter).

Line length and the number of columns on a screen affect density. Although Reynolds (1980) recommends single column text on the screen, Mourant, Lakshmanan, and Chantadisai (1981) discovered that a three-column format reduced visual fatigue. Galitz (1993) noted that the typical computer screen is too wide for comfortable reading, and he suggests that designers consider using two columns of text, each about 30–35 characters wide. Keenan (1981) also found that a line length of 40–45 characters maintained the integrity of the largest number of idea or phrase units within a sentence. On the other hand, Kolers, Duchincky, and Ferguson (1981) investigated text density (40 character and 80 character lines), spacing between words and lines (single or double), and text scrolling (static, preferred, and faster or slower than preferred). Using comprehension and eye movements to measure the effects of the different combinations of variables they recommended the use of the 80-character line and single spacing, because over a period of sustained reading the compact arrangement facilitates ocular efficiency. In studies of learner preference, Grabinger (1984, 1987, 1993) found that users prefer shorter, single-spaced lines of text.

Recommendations for Basic Typography and Spatial Factors

Much of the research described is contradictory. However, there are some general trends based on both print and computer screen research that lead to the following recommendations related to basic typography practices on the screen.

1. **Use only a few simple, familiar, and portable type styles.** A type style is a particular shape distinctive to the characters that make up the type or font. Some fonts are intended only for display, or use as titles and headings. They often set a tone for the text that follows. For example, **Avant Garde** is a modern type face useful for display purposes in screens that need to project a feeling of modernism and recency. Other fonts are more appropriate for masses of text and extended reading, including **Helvetica, Times,** and **Bookman.**

   The font family used must be portable, that is, transferable from one machine to another. Unusual fonts such as Arial, ~~Book Antigua~~, or *Monotype Corsiva* are not found on all machines; therefore, a program created with those fonts may not work properly on a computer that does not have those styles installed. For programs that will go to a wide variety of machines, use only the most common fonts. For the Macintosh, these include Times, Helvetica, New York, or Geneva, with Geneva being the most portable of the group.

   Finally, choose, at the most, two type fonts. One font family may be chosen and used for both headings and text. Or, choose one family for headings and another for the text for visual interest. However, if you find yourself using three or more styles, analyze the reasons carefully. Too many font styles destroy unity and create busy, distracting screens.

2. **Use type sizes appropriate for the audience and the amount of reading to be done. Be consistent in their use.** Type size is a matter of courtesy to the reader of the

material. Frequently, a designer chooses on a type size on the basis of trying to fit as much material as possible on the screen. Remember that the reader is going to be 18–24 in. from the screen. Any text presented on the screen must be large enough to be read by the average reader from the furthest distance. Usually a 12-point size is probably most appropriate for text, although 14 points may be appropriate for younger audiences or people reading from more than two feet from the screen. Keep in mind that point sizes are not consistent and that some 12-point type sizes are larger than others (see Figure 9-3). The size also depends, to some extent, on how much reading is expected.

Consistency, as usual, is important here. Readers pick up cues from the size of the text used. Large sizes indicate headings. Smaller sizes indicate blocks of information. If the size changes from one screen to another, the reader may become confused as to the importance or the information or the meaning of the size change. Decide on the sizes used for each heading level and for text and maintain those sizes throughout the program.

3. **Use both lower and upper case for text and extended reading.** Although all UPPERCASE words may be appropriate for cueing an important word or phrase or heading, it is easier to read words in lower case or mixed case. Uppercase letters provide fewer cues as to their uniqueness, interfering with recognizability. Now that most computers give you the options of italics and bold for emphasis, all upper case should be used sparingly. (*Special note on italics:* Depending on the font being used or the size of the type, italicized text can be difficult to read on a screen. Be sure to test it out before settling on its use.)

4. **Keep line lengths around 45 to 60 characters.** Readers prefer short lines, lines of about eight to ten words or 45 to 60 characters long. Although there is some flexibility in this recommendation, Grabinger (1984, 1987, 1993) found, in studies looking at viewer preferences, that readers prefer shorter rather than longer lines of text, especially when single-spaced. When lines are too long, the lines of text are difficult to follow completely across the screen. Another reason for keeping lines reasonably short is that lines around eight to ten words seem to permit more line breaks based on syntax and idea units.

5. **Generally, use single spacing between lines of text.** The amount of space between lines of text, leading (rhymes with *heading*), is closely related with how long the lines are. Space between the lines helps the reader maintain vertical position in the text. Readers prefer shorter lines that are single spaced. This may be because it produces shorter blocks of text that appear to be manageable chunks of information. However, as lines get longer (more than 60 characters or 10 words), double spacing may be needed. The longer the line, the harder it is to maintain position on that line, therefore more leading is needed.

6. **Left justification is adequate in most circumstances. Use full justification only when proportional spacing is available.** Which is easiest to read? Left-justified text. Fully justified text is also common, but is slightly harder to read because of the artificiality of creating line breaks based on the end of the margin rather than the syntax. Fully justified text relies on hyphenation and breaks phrases and words. In text that uses a nonproportional font, full justification often creates rivers of white space running down the screen or page. This sometimes occurs with proportional fonts as well. Generally, people use the fully justified style because of an inherent sense of neatness, thinking the page looks better if both right and left margins are equal. Although it may look neater, it is more difficult for the viewer to follow and read; so, choose left justification as often as possible.

Problems with Research into Typography Elements

As stated earlier, much of the research into the effect of typography elements on learning and reading is hardly definitive in the legibility areas of recognizability and organization. This inconclusiveness may be the result of three significant research problems. First, research into each possible combination of text format variables and their interactions is a daunting proposition. For example, a study comparing just two values for each of eight text element variables (e.g., leading, line length, directive cues, columns, and so on) yields 256 unique stimuli combinations (2^8), along with the daunting prospect of interpreting eight-way interactions. It is also unrealistic to think that any designers will limit themselves to just eight elements, each with two values on a screen;

so, research results based on highly controlled examinations of combinations of text elements have limited generalizability.

Additionally, research into text elements is often confusing and yields contradictory results. For example, consider the following titles of articles

- "Reading is slower from CRT displays than from paper: attempts to isolate a single-variable explanation" (Gould et al., 1987a).
- "Reading from CRT displays can be as fast as reading from paper" (Gould et al., 1987b).
- "Reading from screen versus paper: There is no difference" (Osborne & Holton, 1988).

These reports indicate that (a) slower reading speeds of screens may be explained by a combination of factors having to do with the image quality (Gould et al., 1987a,b) and (b) where no difference was found, studies should be extended to cover long- and short-duration reading periods. Furthermore, Osborne and Holton (1988) questioned whether identical texts would actually be presented on both paper and screen (a generalizability problem), and they suggested that a more fruitful exploration would examine the questions of whether screen presentations elicit different performance from paper presentations when both formats are presented optimally.

Second, in any particular layout, the unique contribution of each text element variable to the overall meaning of the display is likely to be quite small (Grabinger, 1989). There may be no way to ascertain to what degree a single variable contributes to the readability of a display or to the amount a reader learns. For example, paragraph indication (e.g., indented or double-spaced) is a single text element variable, which, by itself, probably has no measurable effect on learning. However, when combined with other variables to organize a display, to create chunks of ideas, or to indicate a hierarchical structure it may affect how a learner organizes and processes the text and subsequently affect learning.

Finally, a research approach that studies individual text element variables may shed light on how readers perceive and recognize those text elements, but tells little about how the reader comprehends, organizes, and processes the information represented by those elements. Determining the best ways to present elements on a page or screen begins with the processes of perception and reading. The Kolers, Duchincky, and Ferguson (1981) study attempted to combine a number of text element variables to come up with design recommendations for CRT text. A strength in their study was the use of sustained reading to gather data rather than recognition tasks. They reported evidence that suggests that recognizability of symbols becomes less important during sustained reading, probably because of the added cues provided by the additional letters and meaning in the sentences. As recognizability decreases in importance, the overall format of the page and the interaction among format variables become more important. However, they used but four variables: leading, type size, line length, and mode of presentation (i.e., video screen or paper). Some other typical variables that may be found on a page may include headings, cues, graphics, and type size. And without knowing the reader's purpose or a reader's perception of the display, it is not known whether the combinations tested are measuring ordinary performance or a special performance particular to the experimental conditions. Unless designs that reflect the perceptual structure of the reader are utilized, the results of such experiments have limited generalizability.

USING COGNITIVE PROCESSES TO GUIDE DESIGN

If activating appropriate processes is one of the goals of an effective set of screen design guidelines, then there are three basic events that a designer can try to enhance: (1) getting the learner's attention; (2) helping the learner find and organize pertinent information; and (3) integrating the information into the learner's knowledge structure. One strategy is to focus on users' perceptions of potential instructional displays and find out how they judge those displays in terms of readability and "studyability." Studyability refers to the ease with which a user can examine and learn from a screen of information. If evidence of an underlying rationale for such judgments is found, then it can be interpreted to provide information about designing screens. Grabinger (1984, 1987, 1993) and Grabinger and Amedeo (1988) found consistent rationales for the judgments expressed by viewers for model screens. Using multidimensional scaling and factor analyses techniques, these studies found that groups of viewers judged sets of model and real screens as readable or studyable using two fundamental criteria: organization and visual interest.

Organization refers to screens that appear to have a coherent arrangement of all the major elements. Organized screens have both macro and micro characteristics. In the macro area, organized screens are divided into functional areas: text, graphics, title/

status bar, and control panels. In the micro area, organized screens are structured in a way that reflects the content of the subject matter. Structured screens use directive cues for emphasis, headings as organizers, and graphic devices to separate the information into chunks and to indicate important material.

Visual interest is the second criterion. Screens that are plain, simple, unbalanced, and bare are perceived as undesirable. Visual interest refers to screens that use text elements to create an environment that invites exploration yet does not intimidate or bore the reader. A moderate degree of complexity is part of this environment, and the same factors that can help create organized screens contribute to a complex, visually interesting screen: lines, boxes, illustrations, and the placement of white space along the margins of the screen. Screens should have moderate density, appearing neither too empty or too crowded. Empty screens are viewed as boring and uninteresting. Overly crowded or complex screens are viewed as intimidating and too difficult to study.

The constructs of organization and visual interest provide some rules of thumb for arranging numerous text elements to create readable and studyable screens. Rather than focus on individual text elements, producers of computer-based instruction and hypermedia can instead focus on arranging text elements so as to create organized, structured, and visually interesting screens.

Provide a Macro Level of Organization

Generally the most useful way to operationalize this construct is to arrange the screen into functional areas. Designers should decide where status and progress information, navigation buttons, content displays, control buttons, and illustrations will be located and use graphic devices such as shading, lines, and boxes to separate one area from another. This design technique works best when consistency is also practiced. The functional areas should appear in the same locations, and the devices used to define them should be the same throughout a program and its parts.

7. **Begin macro level organization by dividing the screen into functional areas appropriate to desired tasks and consistent with the knowledge level of the users. Maintain this level of organization with only minor changes throughout the program.** The designer-defined areas of the screen represent the tasks the screen expects users to perform. Heines (1984) described the standard screen

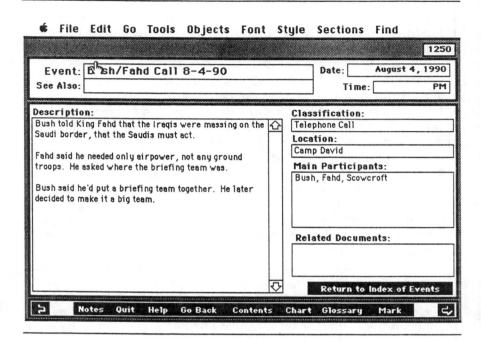

FIGURE 9-4. Functional areas.

components as orientation information, directions, student responses, error messages, and student options. In hypermedia and multimedia applications, we can add areas for information presentation and illustrations. Not every screen needs a place for each of those tasks.

For example, look at the "Events" screen for a program titled *Desert Shield* in Figure 9-4. The control buttons and options are located in two areas. Options particularly relevant to the "Events" section of *Desert Shield* are located along the bottom. That functional area is separated from the other parts of the screen by a box and shading to unify the options. Other options are located in the menu bar at the top of the screen, separated by a white ribbon. The orienting titles are in large print along the upper portion of the screen. The main information area is in the center of the screen and is composed of three fields of information. Each field is separated from the others by a box, yet all are unified by the white background that serves to tie them together.

8. **Create separate areas to indicate important status and orientation information: location, page, topic, subtopic, objective, and so on.** Because computer programs show only one page at a time, users must be continually informed as to what they are seeing and where they are within the program. With books and magazines, a user can quickly thumb back and forth through the pages. The sense of feel (e.g., mass, width, pages held between thumb and finger) of a book often indicates where readers are in the book. Unfortunately, it is simply not possible to transfer physical feeling in a computer program. Therefore, a functional area that provides users with status and orientation information, such as shown in Figure 9-4, is needed on all computer screens.

9. **Keep navigation controls (e.g., left and right arrows, section buttons) in a separate area. Throughout the program, consistently use the same area of the screen for the controls.** Options and control buttons should be located in the same functional area throughout the program. Use shading and boxes or join the buttons together to set the options and control buttons apart from the other elements on the screen and create a sense of unity.

10. **Use the bulk of the screen to present content. Separate this area from others.** Note that Figure 9-4 shows that the bulk of the screen, the central portion, is used for presenting content. That is still the most important part of the screen. Controls and titles are large enough to read and find, but small enough to help the reader focus on the central matter of the screen.

11. **Use graphic devices including boxes, shading, color, white space, and textures to organize the functional areas and set them apart from each other on the screen. When using white space, keep the bulk of the empty or white space along the exterior margins. Keep the internal margins (space between functional areas) the same width.** This is where the "art" of design comes in—the artful arrangement of graphic devices to create interesting and organized screens. Figure 9-4 shows a

variety of screen designs, including boxes, shading, and white space.

Use Structure to Create a Micro-Level of Organization

Following this macro-level organization, designers should then consider how the screen can reflect the structure of the content. Generally, users prefer screens that use headings, directive cues, and spaced paragraphs to indicate the hierarchy of the content and to break the content into studyable chunks of information. We recommend using increased spacing between paragraphs rather than traditional indentation, and by showing comparisons in side-by-side columnar arrangements.

12. **Limit screens to discrete ideas or logical units.** Use the natural separation of screens to separate ideas into meaningful units. Large ideas may need to be separated into several screens, but make them discrete and separate units. There is no need to crowd screens with several ideas. For example, when discussing the concept of recognizability we provided eight examples of recognizability factors (see Table 9-1). A computer-based presentation of this information should use at least eight screens, one for each recognizability idea and at least one additional screen to list all eight factors to provide a unified view.

13. **Use headings as organizers.** Headings of at least three levels are useful organizing points for users. Main headings providing orientation can be placed in the area of the screen that serves that task. Subheadings referring directly to the information presentation should be placed within the text. Phrasing headings, such as questions, can direct users' attention and facilitate learning.

14. **Put paragraphs into bite-sized bits of information by single spacing within the paragraph and using increased space rather than indents to separate paragraphs.** This gives readers manageable chunks of information because the information appears to be in bite-sized pieces. Unlike fiction, readers need built in pauses between each piece of information so they have a chance to reflect on what they have just read before continuing to the next unit of information.

TABLE 9.3
Hierarchical Outline

Introduction
Theoretical underpinnings
  Learning, cognition, and reading
Instructional text
  Legibility and instructional text
    Visibility qualities
    Recognizability
  Readability and instructional text
    Content and representation factors
    Layout and format factors
    Organizational factors
  Recommendations for basic typography and spatial factors
  Problems with research into typography elements
Using cognitive processes
  Provide a macro level of organization
  Use structure to create a micro level of organization
  Provide visual interest
Conclusion
  Research issues and questions
References

15. **Use indents to indicate hierarchically related subject material.** Subsume related material under their super organizing concepts. Traditional outline formats or lists with numbers, letters, and bullets should be listed under the super organizing concepts. In a hierarchical format, this suggests that one level of subheadings is an elaboration of the prior super heading. For example, examine the outline of this paper in Table 9-3.

16. **Group closely related items within a box or a common background color or shading. Use the same graphic devices, as well as white space, to separate unrelated or contrasting ideas.** Graphic devices provide a visually interesting way to link common ideas or to separate unrelated ideas. If shading is used, make sure it does not reduce the visibility of the text it surrounds.

17. **Use directive cues (i.e., bold, italic, underlining, inverse) to emphasize important terms or ideas.** Used sparingly, directive cues like color, size, bold, italic, flashing, shape, direction, brightness, underlining, uppercase, and inverse can facilitate learning by calling attention to (i.e., making more perceptible) important words or

phrases. This technique should probably be limited to one to three items per screen. Flashing, which is another technique used to draw users' attention, probably should never be used. It can be extremely distracting to users.

18. **Set up comparison–contrast situations in a side-by-side columnar arrangement.** Columnar arrangements are particularly useful for both comparisons and contrasts because it keeps in view all the items being compared.

Provide Visual Interest

Finally, designers should consider the visual interest of the screen. Viewers dislike screens that are plain or full of text without any headings, directive cues, shading, buttons, titles, or illustrations (Grabinger, 1984, 1987, 1993; Grabinger & Amedeo, 1988). It seems that a variety of well-organized text elements enrich the environment and make it more interesting to explore. Excessive complexity results when too many elements or too much information is crammed on the screen.

19. **Use accepted, general, aesthetic publication guidelines. Strive for balance, harmony, and simplicity.** Balance, harmony, and simplicity are general constructs often given to designers as the basic elements of design. All three constructs can probably be summed up in the word "moderation." Screens that display balance, harmony, and simplicity are not jammed with information, have elements distributed throughout the screen, and maintain a consistency in styles and locations from one screen to another. The following guidelines help operationalize these ideas.

20. **To help create a sense of balance, maintain consistent internal margins, and distribute the bulk of the white (empty) space around the exterior margins of the screen.** The notion of balance is a complicated concept involving both the weight of objects and the use of space. Heavily weighted objects use thick, dark lines or dark colors and shading. Lightly weighted objects use thin lines and light or no shading. *White space* is that space that contains no information, it is empty space on the screen (and could be another color depending on your

White Space and
Consistent Internal Margins

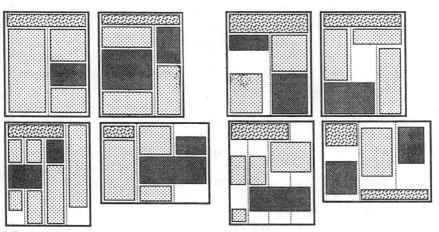

Example: White Space to Exterior
Consistent Internal Margins

Nonexample: White Space Unbalanced
Inconsistent Internal Margins

FIGURE 9-5. White space.

background color selection). The first step in creating balance is to group the text elements together on the screen and to distribute the white space around the exterior margins. Maintain consistent internal margins among the elements on the screen. Note that in Figure 9-5 the drawing labeled "consistent" has placed the largest amount of white space around the exterior margins. The text elements themselves are separated by smaller internal margins of white space, although the size of the margin between each element is the same. The drawing labeled "inconsistent" has varying sizes of internal margins. The white space distributed around the exterior is also inconsistent in size. This combination creates a disorganized, unbalanced appearance.

21. **To create a sense of harmony, use consistent design styles in objects and appropriate type styles.** Consistent design features refers to the overall style of the elements used. Examine the screen in Figure 9-4. The fields and buttons all use the rectangle style as a basic shape. Boxes around items also use the rectangle. The same type face is used for all buttons and within text fields.

Mixing those several different styles of graphics, type, sizes, or shading decreases the sense of harmony and the sense of organization.

22. **Keep screens simple. Avoid too many buttons, text fields, or graphic objects.** Designers often begin with a simple concept but add "just one more button" or "one more field" to accommodate an extra option or bit of information. Finally, by the time they are finished, the screen is cluttered with too many buttons, too much text, and too many design elements. Try for the "minimalist" look. Use as few buttons and fields as possible. Put options in the menu bar and avoid creating a button for every possible item. Don't feel obligated to fill in every piece of white space on the screen with text, graphics, or buttons. Standard options in the *Desert Shield* stack are placed in the menu bar at the top of the screen under the titles SECTIONS and FIND (see Figure 9-4).

However, the other extreme is also undesirable. Plain, simple, and bare are not liked by viewers of either model or real screen samples (Grabinger, 1993). Screens must hold some visual interest. Visual interest refers to screens that use text elements to create an environment that looks like it is worth exploring. A moderate degree of complexity is part of this environment, and the factors that can help create organized screens contribute to complex, visually interesting screens: lines, boxes, illustrations, and the placement of white space along the exterior margins of the screen. For example, the screens in Figure 9-6 are complex, yet well organized with distinct areas for buttons, illustrations, text, and titles. There is enough on the screens for visual interest, but not too much to create overwhelming complexity.

CONCLUSION

Research Issues and Questions

Good interface design requires close attention to student behavior and attitudes as well as system capabilities. The screen is the central point of the interaction between student and program, so much of interface design focuses on the screen. Although a good-looking screen requires both artistic talent and a good sense of organiza-

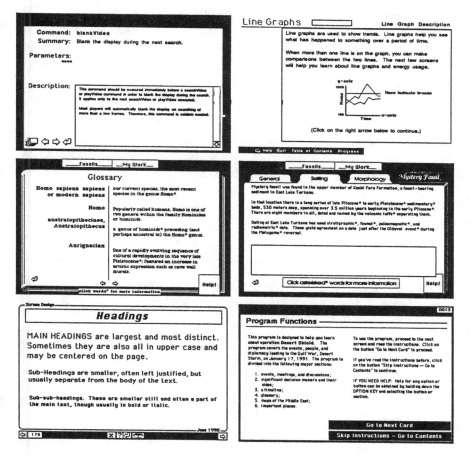

FIGURE 9-6. Screen examples.

tion, almost anyone can design attractive, functional screens by applying some common sense. Start with a design that looks useful to you and alter it to meet the needs of your program.

Evaluation and research in this field of study is problematic and needs creative solutions. Paper-and-pencil recall and essay tests may not be the best measure of how people use screen displays to construct knowledge structures, nor are they always the best way to measure problem-solving ability, creativity, or cognitive flexibility. It may be possible to compare a program with organized screens to a program with plain screens by asking learners to create an outline of the material just read to see which program facilitates the creation of an outline. Another possibility is to use semantic map-generation programs (i.e., Learning Tool, SemNet) to assess how the structure of a set of screens affects the semantic meanings generated while students study the program. In combination with essay and problem-solving activities, such an assessment could indicate whether outlines are representative of flexible, creative problem-solving skills in new contexts.

Although the concepts of organization and visual interest may seem to be common sense, common sense is not always followed by designers. In addition, knowledge of these concepts does not mean that designers will apply them in ways that create aesthetically pleasing and well-organized screens. However, the studies by Grabinger and his colleagues suggest that these constructs are important to prospective viewers and may help gain attention and build confidence in using instructional material (Keller & Burkman, 1993).

REFERENCES

Anderson, R. C., & Faust, G. W. (1967). The effects of strong formal prompts in programmed instruction. *American Education Research Journal, 4*(4), 345–352.

Bausell, R. B., & Jenkins, J. R. (1977). Effects on prose learning of frequency of adjunct cues and the difficulty of the material cued. *Journal of Reading Behavior, 9*(3), 227–232.

Bovy, R. C. (1981). Successful instructional methods: a cognitive information processing approach. *ECTJ, 29*(4), 203–217.

Butler, B. E. (1980). The category effect in visual search: Identification versus localization factors. *Canadian Journal of Psychology, 34*, 238–247.

Cakir, A. E. (1980). Human factors and VDT design. In P. Kolers, M. E. Wrolstad, & H. Bouma (Eds.), *Processing of visible language, volume 2* (pp. 481–495). New York: Plenum.

Christ, R. E. (1975). Review and analysis of color coding research for visual displays. *Human Factors, 17*, 542–570.

Christ, R. E. (1977). Four years of color research for visual displays. Proceedings of the Human Factors Society 21st Annual Meeting. San Francisco, California.

Crouse, J. H., & Idstein, P. (1972). Effects of encoding cues on prose learning. *Journal of Educational Psychology, 63*(4), 309–313.

Fisher, D. L., & Tan, K. C. (1989). Visual displays: The highlighting paradox. *Human Factors 31*(1), 17–30.

Fisher, D. L., Coury, B. G., Tengs, T. O., & Duffy, S. A. (1989). Minimizing the time to search visual displays: The role of highlighting. *Human Factors 31*(2), 167–182.

Fleming, M., & Levie, H. (1978). *Instructional message design: Principles from the behavioral sciences.* Englewood Cliffs, NJ: Educational Technology Publications.

Foster, J. J. (1965). Commentary: psychological research into legibility. *Journal of Typographic Research, 2,* 279–282.

Frase, L. T., & Schwartz, B. J. (1979). Typographical cues that facilitate comprehension. *Journal of Educational Psychology, 71,* 197–206.

Galitz, W. O. (1993). *User-interface screen design.* Boston: QED Publishing Group.

Garofalo, K. M. (1988). Typographic cues as an aid to learning from textbooks. *Visible Language 22*(2/3), 273–298.

Gilreath, C. T. (1993). Graphic cueing of text: The typographic and diagraphic dimensions. *Visible Language 27*(3), 336–361.

Gould, J. D., Alfaro, L., Barnes, V., Finn, R., Grischkowsky, N., & Minuto, A. (1987a). Reading is slower from CRT displays than from paper: Attempts to isolate a single-variable explanation. *Human Factors, 29*(3), 269–299.

Gould, J. D., Alfaro, L., Finn, R., Haupt, B., & Minuto, A. (1987b). Reading from CRT displays can be as fast as reading from paper. *Human Factors, 29*(5), 497–517.

Grabinger, R. S. (1984). CRT text design: Psychological attributes underlying the evaluation of models of CRT text displays. *Journal of Visual Verbal Languaging, 4*(1).

Grabinger, R. S. (1987, winter). Relationships among text format variables in computer-generated text. *Journal of Visual Verbal Languaging, 6*(3).

Grabinger, R. S. (1989). Reconsidering CBI screen design: Alternative to text-based designs. *Journal of Computers and Human Behavior, 5*(3), 175–183.

Grabinger, R. S. (1993). Computer screen designs: Viewer judgments. *ETRD, 41*(2), 35–73.

Grabinger, R. S., & Amedeo, D. (1988). CRT text layout: Perceptions of viewers. *Journal of Computers and Human Behavior, 4,* 189–205.

Gregory, M., & Poulton, E. (1970). Even versus uneven right-hand margins and rate of comprehension in reading. *Ergonomics, 13,* 427.

Hartley, J. (1978). *Designing instructional text.* New York: Nichols Publishing Company.

Hartley, J. (1980). Spatial cues in text. *Visible Language, 14*(1), 62+.

Hartley, J. (1987). Designing electronic text: The role of print-based research. *Educational Communications and Technology Journal, 35*(1), 3–17.

Hartley, J., & Trueman, M. (1982). Headings in text: issues and data. A paper presented to the American Educational Research Association, New York, March. (1982).

Hartley, J., Bartlett, S., & Branthwaite, A. (1980). Underlining can make a difference—sometimes. *Journal of Educational Research*, *73*(4), 218–223.

Heines, J. M. (1984). *Screen Design Strategies for Computer-Aided Instruction*. Bedford, MA: Digital Press.

Holley, C. D., Dansereau, D. F., Evans, S. H., Collins, K. W., Brooks, L., & Larson, D. (1981). Utilizing intact and embedded headings as processing aids with nonnarrative text. *Contemporary Educational Psychology*, *6*, 227–236.

Jones, G. L. (1976). *How to prepare professional design brochures*. New York: McGraw-Hill.

Just, M. A., & Carpenter, P. A. (1987). *The psychology of reading and language comprehension*. Newton, MA: Allyn and Bacon.

Keenan, S. A. (1981). Computer projections of the cognitive effects of text changes. Paper given at the annual meeting of the American Educational Research Association. Boston, Massachusetts.

Keller, J., & Burkman, E. (1993). Motivation principles. In M. Fleming & W. H. Levie, *Instructional message design: Principles from the behavioral and cognitive sciences*. Englewood Cliffs, NJ: Educational Technology Publications.

Kintsch, W. (1989). Learning from text. In L. B. Resnick (Ed.), *Knowing, learning, and instruction* (pp. 25–46). Hillsdale, NJ: Erlbaum.

Klare, G. R. (1974). Assessing readability. *Reading Research Quarterly*, *10*(1), 62–102.

Kolers, P. A., Duchincky, R. L., & Ferguson, D. C. (1981). Eye movement measurement of readability of CRT displays. *Human Factors*, *23*(5), 517–527.

Kolers, P. A., Wrolstad, M. E., & Bouma, H. (Eds.). (1980). *Processing of visible language, volume 2*. New York: Plenum.

Lenze, J. S. (1991). Serif vs. sans serif type fonts: A comparison based on reader comprehension. In D. G. Beauchamp, J. C. Baca, & R. A. Braden (Eds.), *Investigating visual literacy* (pp. 93–98). Commerce, TX: International Visual Literacy Association.

Meyer, B. J. F. (1976). The structure of prose: Effects on learning and memory and implications for educational practice. In R. C. Anderson, R. J. Spiro and W. E. Montague (Eds.), *Schooling and the acquisition of knowledge* (pp. 179–200). Hillsdale, NJ: Erlbaum.

Mills, C. B., & Weldon, L. J. (1987). Reading text from computer screens. *ACM Computing Surveys*, *19*(4), 330–358.

Morrison, G. R., Ross, S. M., & O'Dell, J. K. (1988). Text density level as a design variable in instructional displays. *ECTJ*, *36*(1), 103–115.

Morrison, G. R., Ross, S. M., Schultz, C. W., & O'Dell, J. K. (1990). Learner preferences for varying screen densities using realistic stimulus materials with single and multiple screen designs. ERIC # ED323 940. U.S. Department of Education Educational Resources Information Center.

Mourant, R. R., Lakshmanan, R., & Chantadisai, R. (1981). Visual fatigue and cathode ray tube display terminals. *Human Factors, 23*(5), 529–540.

Neisser, U. (1976). *Cognition and reality: Principles and implications of cognitive psychology.* San Francisco, CA: W. H. Freeman.

Nelson, R. P. (1978). *Publication design, second edition.* Dubuque, IA: Wm. C. Brown Co.

Osborne, D. J., & Holton, D. (1988). Reading from screen versus paper: There is no difference. *International Journal of Man-Machine Studies, 28,* 1–9.

Rehe, R. F. (1974). *Typography: How to make it more legible.* Carmel, IN: Design Research International.

Rehe, R. E. (1979). *Typography: How to make it more legible, third revised edition.* Carmel, IN: Design Research International.

Reynolds, L. (1979). Legibility studies: their relevance to present day documentation methods. *Journal of Documentation, 35*(4), 307–340.

Reynolds, L. (1980). Teletext and Viewdata—a new challenge for the designer. In J. Hartley (Ed.), *The psychology of written communication* (pp. 207–224). New York: Nichols Publishing Company.

Rickards, J. P., & Denner, P. R. (1979). Depressive effects of underlining and adjunct questions on children's recall of text. *Instructional Science, 8,* 81–90.

Ross, S. M., & Morrison, G. R. (1989). Reducing the density of text presentations using alternative control strategies and media. ERIC # ED308 836. U.S. Department of Education Educational Resources Information Center.

Ross, S. M., Morrison, G. R., & O'Dell, J. K. (1988). Obtaining more out of less text in CBI: Effects of varied text density levels as a function of learner characteristics and control strategy. *ECTJ, 36*(3), 131–142.

Shebilske, W. L., & Rotondo, J. A. (1981). Typographical and spatial cues that facilitate learning from textbooks. *Visible Language, 15*(1), 41–54.

Siskind, T. G. (1979). The effect of newspaper design on reader preferences. *Journalism Quarterly, 56,* 54–61.

Snyder, H. L., & Taylor, G. B. (1979). The sensitivity of response measures of alphanumeric legibility to variation in dot matrix display parameters. *Human Factors, 21*(4), 457–471.

Sticht, T. (1985). Understanding readers and their uses of texts. In T. Duffy, & R. Waller (Eds.), *Designing usable texts* (pp. 315–340). Orlando, FL: Academic Press.

Tinker, M. A. (1955). Prolonged reading tasks in visual research. *Journal of Applied Psychology, 39,* 444–446.

Tinker, M. A. (1963). *Legibility of print.* Ames, IA: The Iowa State University Press.

Tinker, M. A. (1965). *Bases for effective reading.* Minneapolis, MN: University of Minnesota Press.

Tinker, M. A., & McCullough, C. M. (1962). *Teaching elementary reading, second edition.* New York: Appleton-Century-Crofts.

Tullis, T. S. (1981). An evaluation of alphanumeric, graphic, and color information displays. *Human Factors, 23*(5), 541–550.

van Dijk, T. A., & Kintsch, W. (1983). *Strategies of discourse comprehension.* New York: Academic.

Van Orden, K. F., Divita, J., & Shim, M. J. (1993). Redundant use of luminance and flashing with shape and color as highlighting codes in symbolic displays. *Human Factors, 35*(2), 195–204.

Vartabedian, A. G. (1971). The effects of letter size, case and generation method on CRT display search time. *Human Factors, 13*(4), 363–368.

Williams, J. R. (1988). The effects of case and spacing on menu option search time. In Proceedings of the Human Factors Society, 32nd Annual Meeting, 341–343.

Wright, C., & Friend, L. (1992). Ergonomics for on-line searching. *Online, 16*(3), 13–27.

10

What Makes a Good Hypertext?

Cliff McKnight

Loughborough University, Loughborough, UK

INTRODUCTION

The title of this chapter suggests that it is possible to make a good hypertext in the same way that it is possible to make a good cake— take six nodes, stir in half a pound of links, pour into a graphic browser, and cook until done! Unfortunately, the chapter indeed would be "half-baked" if it attempted such a recipe. Colleagues and I have argued elsewhere that hypertext interface design is no different to the design of any on-screen information (Dillon & McKnight, 1995). Hence, although I will discuss hypertext design it should be remembered that the considerations are the same for any electronic text.

Although some might give that impression, most hypertexts are not created for the fun of it—when we assemble a body of information we usually do so for some purpose. Hypertexts are created in order for people to carry out some tasks using the information contained therein. These concepts will be discussed further in looking at some attributes of the user, information, and task that can guide the design of usable hypertext applications. It is usability (Shackel,

1991), which is the important issue in information systems design, rather than any vague concept of "good" or "user friendly."

The complexity of issues involved and the range of applications and tasks that hypertext may be used to support imply that we cannot talk of hypertext as a unified form of presentation any more than we can meaningfully describe a "typical" text. Hence, it is important to understand that when discussing hypertext we are not seeking simplistic answers to monolithic questions such as, "Is hypertext better than paper?" or "Do people learn more from hypertext systems than standard texts?"

Modern cognitive psychology and ergonomics have accumulated a substantial amount of information about humans using computers. It is not the intention of this chapter to review this work but rather to introduce readers to its basic orientation so that they might better understand the relevance to hypertext.

Information technology is now so pervasive that we are all users even if we are unaware of it—our washing machines and microwave ovens are all computer-based technology. Contemporary thinking rightly stresses that technology should be designed with users' needs in mind. As with consumer goods, in the hypertext domain it is likely that potential users will come from all walks of life and age groups. Hypertext applications exist not only in libraries, schools or offices but can also be found in museums (e.g., Poulter et al., 1993), tourist information centers (e.g., Glasgow On-line—Baird & Percival, 1989) and eventually, in the home. Thus, when we talk of hypertext and its uses, it is important that we place our discussion in context by looking at the first card in our three-card-trick and asking, "who are the target users?"

The information that users deal with when interacting with contemporary computer systems varies tremendously. With hypertext such variation is equally apparent. Hypertext systems can be used to manipulate and present lengthy texts such as journal articles (McKnight, Dillon, & Richardson, 1991), encyclopedias (Shneiderman, 1987b), computer programs (Monk et al., 1988), or English literature (Landow, 1990) to name but a few current applications. In fact, there is no reason why any information could not be presented in hypertext form—rather, the question is, looking at our second card, "what sort of information would benefit from such presentation?"

Just as users and information vary, so too do the tasks that can be performed on computers. Software is (or should be) designed with specific tasks in mind which it will support, for example, desktop publishing, database management, process control, statistical analysis, and so forth. Equally with hypertext, users will perform a variety of tasks—the third card of the trick—and consequently hypermedia must be designed accordingly. In short, when we consider users, information and tasks we draw the conclusion that different implementations of the hypertext concept will be required in different domains.

It makes little sense to talk about users, information, and tasks as if they were independent entities because clearly they are not. By definition, a user must be using something, that is, performing a task, the very act of which implies information transfer. This is the trick! The present chapter will attempt to describe the relevant issues relating to each of these elements before demonstrating how our understanding of all three is important to hypermedia. The approach is similar in some respects to the TIMS model developed by Dillon (1994) in considering the design of electronic texts.

THE USER: REMEMBER WHEN "USERS" WERE CALLED "READERS?"

Invariably, the user of a hypertext application will be reading material from a visual display unit. Thus, it is worth considering what we know about reading and its relevance to screen-displayed text. Reading is one of the most intensively studied cognitive activities, with serious investigation of it as a psychological phenomenon commencing in the last century (for a review of work at that time, see Huey, 1908). Since then, researchers have analyzed the processes involved in reading, from the level of eye-movements across the page to that of how readers comprehend visually presented material. It is not the intention of this chapter to summarize such work or present sections of it in great detail (a comprehensive review can be found in Beech & Colley, 1987). However, a brief description of the salient aspects is relevant to the present discussion.

The Psychology of Reading

Although there is some agreement about the processes involved in reading at the eye movement level, theoretical differences emerge when we come to describe letter and word recognition. It is clear that both letter and word recognition processes occur, perhaps interactively, on the basis of features such as shape, size, and context, although the relative importance attributed to any one of these factors varies. There has been some success in modeling these processes on computers (see, e.g., McClelland & Rumelhart, 1981), but a complete theoretical explanation that accounts for all the empirical observations on these phenomena has yet to be presented.

The situation is even less clear at the level of comprehension, that is, how do people form an understanding of what they read? It seems obvious that readers draw inferences from particular sentences and form representations at different levels of what is happening in the text. Various models of comprehension have been proposed to explain this. Thorndyke (1977) proposed a set of "grammar rules" by which the reader forms a structure in their mind of how the story fits together. Van Dijk and Kintsch (1983) proposed a very detailed model involving an analysis of the propositions of a text, leading to the development of a "macropropositional hierarchy" influenced by the reader's model of the situation represented in the text. Alternatively, Johnson-Laird (1983) and Garnham (1986) have proposed a "mental models" approach to text comprehension that involves the reader representing the meaning of the text as an imaginary, updatable model in their mind.

In view of the lack of agreement on the nature of comprehension, it is not surprising that measuring comprehension has also proved difficult. It is a simple enough matter to ask readers a number of questions about the text they have just read, but it is difficult to know whether memory for detail is being tested rather than comprehension. Furthermore, texts may be open to interpretation, the richness of which depends on the reader's contextual knowledge and appreciation of the author's message—all factors that make comprehension measurement a complicated issue.

It is also clear that readers acquire knowledge of how texts are structured or organized and can use these structural models to predict the likely meaning of the text (van Dijk and Kintsch, 1983) or the location of information within it. Furthermore, readers have been shown to remember spatial location of information within a text after reading it (Rothkopf, 1971).

Thus, the psychological study of reading shows us the complexity of the processes performed when reading even simple material such as isolated words and sentences. It is also clear that on matters such as comprehension, psychology has invested heavily in theoretical constructs that attempt to account for mental representation of the text but do not necessarily provide human computer scientists with useful methods for assessing readers' understanding of the material.* In the following section the potential differences between reading from paper and screen are discussed. The psychological view of reading offers an explanatory framework within which some of the findings in this area can be interpreted.

Reading from Screens

Not surprisingly, a good deal of research has addressed the potential difference between reading material from paper and reading from screen. The early literature tended to suggest that people read 20–30% slower from typical screens. Here "typical" meant a low-resolution 24-line display with white (or green) text on a black background (e.g., Gould and Grischkowsky, 1984; Muter et al., 1982; Wright and Lickorish, 1983). However, the emphasis in hypertext on easy selectability of links, multiple windows, and so forth has meant that such packages are implemented on systems with large, high-resolution screens with black characters on a white background. Under such conditions (with the addition of antialiased characters), Gould et al. (1987b) reported no significant difference in reading speed between screen and paper. The explanation for this probably lies at the image quality level: The human eye is better able to perceive and distinguish rapidly between letters and words presented on paper than they are with more typical screens; as technology improves and screen quality approaches that of paper, reading speed differences will probably cease to be an issue for the hypertext user.

In addition to speed of reading, early studies often used "accuracy" of reading as a performance measure. "Accuracy" of reading usually referred to performance in some form of proofreading task; typically, the number of errors located in an experimental text was used as a measure (Gould and Grischkowsky, 1984; Wright and Lickorish, 1983). Although it is probably true to say that few users of hypertext will be performing such routine spelling checks, many more users are likely to be searching for specific information, scanning a section of text, and so forth. For the more visually or cognitively demanding tasks such as these, a performance deficit for

---

*van Dijk and Kintsch's model is exceptional in that it also serves as a method for assessing comprehension by analyzing readers' written summaries of material. The extent to which this method is useful with lengthy texts is debatable, however.

screen-based presentation is more likely (Creed et al., 1987; Wilkinson & Robinshaw, 1987). In a study by the present author and colleagues (McKnight, Dillon, & Richardson, 1990), subjects were asked to locate answers to a set of questions in a text using either a paper version, a word processor document, or one of two hypertext versions. Results showed an accuracy effect favoring paper and the linear-format word processor version, suggesting a structural familiarity effect. Obviously, more experimental work comparing hypertext and paper on a range of texts and tasks is needed.

Users may not be aware that their speed or accuracy of performance differs between the two media. However, they are more likely to be aware of fatigue effects. Gould and Grischkowsky (1984) obtained responses to a 16-item "Feelings Questionnaire" that required subjects to rate their fatigue, levels of tension, mental stress, and so forth after several work periods on a computer and on paper. Furthermore, various visual measurements such as flicker and contrast sensitivity, visual acuity, and phoria (the vergence angle of the two eyes when the stimulus to fusion is removed), were taken at the beginning of the day and after each work period. Neither questionnaire responses nor visual measures showed a significant effect for presentation medium. These results led the authors to conclude that good-quality VDUs in themselves do not produce fatiguing effects, although the findings have been disputed by Wilkinson and Robinshaw (1987). However, to suggest as these latter authors do that Gould's equipment was "too good to show an effect" throws us back on the definition of a "typical" screen. Since typical for the hypertext user is likely to be of better quality than the average microcomputer screen, it suggests that visual fatigue may be no more of a problem than for a draughtsman facing a piece of white paper illuminated by fluorescent light. Furthermore, as screen quality improves, we would expect fatigue effects to decrease.

The effect of presentation medium on comprehension is particularly difficult to assess because, as mentioned above, there is a general lack of agreement about how comprehension can best be measured. If the validity of such methods as post-task questions or standardized reading tests is accepted, it appears that comprehension is not affected by presentation medium (see, e.g., Kak, 1981). However, such results typically involve the use of an "electronic copy" of a single paper document. The hypertext context differs significantly in terms of both document structure and size. A hypertext document is freed from the traditional structure of printed documents and is also likely to be just one member of an interrelated set of documents. The issue of comprehension takes on a new dimension in this context.

No matter what the experimental findings are, a user's preference is likely to be a determining feature in the success or failure of any technology. Several studies have reported a preference for paper over screen, although some of these may now be discounted on the grounds that they date from a time when screen technology was far below current standards (e.g., Cakir et al., 1980). Experience is likely to play a large role, but users who dislike technology are unlikely to gain sufficient experience to alter their attitude. Therefore, the onus is on developers to design good hypertext systems using high quality screens to overcome such users' reluctance to use information technology. What seems to have been overlooked as far as formal investigation is concerned is the natural flexibility of books and paper over VDUs; books are portable, cheap, apparently "natural" in our culture, personal and easy to use. The extent to which such "common sense" variables influence user preferences is not yet well understood.

Conclusion

To date, the work on reading from screens is useful in highlighting the likely problems that may be encountered by readers using hypertext. However, it must be noted that much of this work was carried out on poorer quality screens than are currently available on many hypertext systems. Furthermore, studies have tended to employ tasks that bear little resemblance to the type of activities that hypertext users perform. As technology improves, any differences resulting purely from image quality should disappear. This still leaves the questions of accuracy, comprehension, and preference open, however, and these will be considered further in the context of the text types and tasks that hypertext might be called upon to support.

THE INFORMATION: WHEN IS A BOOK
LIKE A CATALOGUE?

We live in a world where books, newspapers, comics, magazines, manuals, reports, and a whole host of other document forms are commonplace. We take such a range for granted, yet there are significant differences between these documents in terms of content, style, format, usefulness, size, and so forth. As with tasks, it is certain that hypertext will have more impact on certain types of document than others and will almost certainly create new document forms that are not feasible with paper. Hence, it would be useful to develop a framework that would facilitate the classification of texts.

At first glance, it might appear that such a classification would be relatively easy to develop. Obvious distinctions can be drawn between fiction and nonfiction, technical and nontechnical, serious and humorous, paperback and hardback and so forth, which discriminate between texts in a relatively unambiguous manner. However, such discriminations are not necessarily informative in terms of how the text is used or the readers' views of the contents—aspects that should be apparent from any typology aiming to distinguish meaningfully between texts.

The categorization of texts has received some attention from linguists and typographers (see Waller, 1987, for an excellent review). For example, de Beaugrande (1980) defines a text type as

> a distinctive configuration of relational dominances obtaining between or among elements of the surface text, the textual world, stored knowledge patterns and a situation of occurrence (p. 197).

and offers the following illustrations: descriptive, narrative, argumentative, literary, poetic, scientific, didactic, and conversational. However, de Beaugrande freely admits that these categories are not mutually exclusive and are not distinguishable on any one dimension. Waller adds that it is not at all clear where texts such as newspapers or advertisements fit in such a typology, and proposes instead an analysis of text types in terms of three kinds of underlying structure.

- topic structure, the typographic effects which display information about the author's argument, for example, headings;
- artifact structure, the features determined by the physical nature of the document, for example, page size; and
- access structure, features that serve to make the document usable, for example, lists of contents.

In a more psychological vein, van Dijk and Kintsch (1983) use the term "discourse types" to describe the semantic macrostructural regularities present in real-world texts, such as crime stories or psychological research reports. According to their theory of discourse comprehension, knowledge of such discourse types facilitates readers' predictions about the likely episodes or events in a text and thus support accurate macroproposition formation. In other words, the reader can utilize this awareness of the text's typical form or contents to aid comprehension of the material. In their view, such types are the textual equivalent of scripts or frames* and play an important role in their model of discourse comprehension. However, they stop short of providing a classification or typology themselves and it is not clear how this work can be extended to inform the design of hypertext documents.

From a less theoretical standpoint Wright (1980) describes texts in terms of their application domains.

- domestic (e.g., instructions for using appliances);
- functional (e.g., work-related manuals); and
- advanced literacy (e.g., magazines or novels).

She uses these categories to emphasize the range of texts that exist and to highlight the fact that reading research must become aware of this tremendous diversity. Research into the presentation and reading of one text may have little or no relevance to, and may even require separate theoretical and methodological standpoints from, other texts.

It is doubtful if any one classification or typology can cope adequately with the range of paper information sources that abound in the real world. In Wright's (1980) categorization, for example, the distinction between "functional" and "domestic" blurs considerably when one thinks of the number of electronic gadgets now found in the home that have associated operational and troubleshooting manuals (not least the home computer). This is not a criticism of any one classification but rather an indication that each has a limit to its range of applicability, outside of which it ceases to have relevance. Thus, one can find situations in which any typology fails to distinguish clearly between texts. We should not necessarily expect classifications designed for typographers to help developers of hypertext systems.

Some classifications aimed specifically at the hypertext domain

---

*A script (or frame) is an organized knowledge structure derived from the extraction of common elements of a range of situations. The most common example in the psychological literature is the restaurant script.

are beginning to emerge. Wright and Lickorish (1989), for example, distinguish between texts in terms of their information structure and use this to guide the design of hypertext versions. In particular, they highlight linear, modular, hierarchic, and matrix (highly symmetrical hierarchical) document structures and argue convincingly that such structures have implications for the type of linkages, visual appearance and navigation support that need to be provided by authors. Thus, the navigation support necessary for a linear structure (such as a set of instructions) might be a series of loops initiated by the reader through pointing, whereas readers of modular texts (such as an encyclopedia) will require more explicit information about where they came from and where they currently are in the information space, since the loop linkage style will not be as appropriate with such texts.

An alternative approach to text classification by Dillon and McKnight (1990) involved using a technique known as repertory grid analysis to describe readers' views of texts. Rather than devising a formal classification, this work resulted in an empirical, user-based framework for considering text types. They concluded that readers conceive of text in terms of three characteristics: how they are read, why they are read, and what sort of information they contain. By viewing text types according to these attributes, it is easy to distinguish between, say, a novel and a journal. The former is likely to be read serially (how), for leisure (why), and contain general or nontechnical information (what), whereas the latter is more likely to be studied or read more than once (how), for professional reasons (why), and contain technical information that includes graphics (what). This approach can be represented in terms of a three-dimensional "text classification space," as shown in Figure 10-1. Here, three texts are distinguished according to their relative positions on the How, Why, and What axes. The descriptors study–skim, work–personal, and general–specific may vary and are only intended as examples. Different people may employ very different terms. However, the authors argue that they are still likely to be descriptors that pertain to the attributes How, Why, and What.

According to this perspective any particular text may be classified in several ways, depending on the reader and their information needs. Not only does this mean that a text may be seen differently by two readers but also that a reader may view a text differently according to their needs at any one time. The hypertext version should thus be designed with these principles in mind, analyzing the how, why, and what questions in detail before attempting to build an electronic version of a text. The authors use the example of

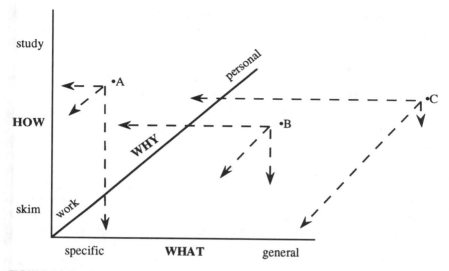

FIGURE 10-1. A three-way classification of texts based on How, Why, and What attributes.

A: Specific information, to be studied, work-related text, e.g., a relevant scientific article.

B: Less specific than A, can be read quickly, general work-related text, e.g., technical magazine.

C: Nontechnical, can be skim read, personal interest, e.g., newspaper.

a novel and suggest that, from a classification of this text type in terms of these three aspects, we would not expect a hypertext version to have much potential. However, if we consider the full range of how and why attributes that emerge as a result of analyzing novels, one can envisage an educational context where various parts of the text are analyzed and compared linguistically, thereby rendering a suitable hypertext version more useful than paper. In other words, a hypertext novel may not be suitable for reading on the train but it may be ideal for the student of English literature.

Conclusion

The classification of information types that have been proposed are based on numerous criteria: typographic and semantic macrostructures, application domain, readers' perceptions, and attributes of use. No doubt other classifications will emerge, perhaps based on altogether different criteria than any described here. Structural distinctions are likely to remain important as hypertext creates new document types based on innovative electronic structures, but distinctions based on usage patterns and readers' views always will be relevant. It is unlikely that any one classification scheme is best or suitable for all situations.

THE TASK: READING AS AN INFORMATION
MANIPULATION TASK

By "task," we usually mean the carrying out of any goal-directed activity. In the context of reading, the term includes identifying, locating, and processing relevant material. With texts this may involve looking for a book title and shelf number in a library catalogue, reading a novel, browsing a newspaper, proofreading a legal contract, or studying a mathematical theorem. In fact, if we define reading as the visual-to-cognitive processing of textual and graphical material in an information-seeking manner, and extend its traditional boundaries to include the procedures that necessarily precede contact between eye and source, such as scanning bookshelves or selecting a correct edition of a journal (i.e., gaining access to the material), then we begin to get some idea of the diversity of tasks that are performed by readers.*

At present, hypertext systems have only scratched the surface of the range of tasks they will eventually support. Indeed, hypertext applications eventually may well give rise to tasks that have not been thought of or cannot yet be effectively performed. Whatever the final outcome, it is clear that they have the potential to play a significant role in many reading scenarios.

The Diversity of Reading Tasks

It is worth considering how people use the paper medium to perform information manipulation tasks if we want to understand how hypermedia may not only support them but offer advantages to the user. Laboratory studies of reading have tended largely to concentrate on a very limited subset of tasks such as locating spelling errors on a page of text (Gould et al., 1987a), making sense of anaphoric references in sentences (Clark, 1977), or recalling episodes in short stories (Thorndyke, 1977). Although some of this work has

---

*Even in the comparatively narrow domain of experimental psychology, variations in the definition of reading exist. See for example Just and Carpenter's (1980) model of reading, which includes comprehension of the material and Crowder's (1982) definition that explicitly excludes it.

been invaluable in advancing our knowledge of the reader, it tells us very little about information usage in the real world or how to design hypertext systems for people.

People do not all interact with texts in the same fashion, and although texts may appear linear, this rarely ensures a serial style of reading. Furthermore, the same text may be read in different ways depending on the reader's task. This much is intuitively obvious from self-observation. Consider the differences between reading a newspaper and a novel. The former is likely to consist of a mixture of scanning and browsing in an unplanned fashion, reacting to interesting headlines or pictures, whereas the latter is more likely to involve serial reading of the complete text. Next, consider the differences between reading an interesting article in the newspaper and checking on a sports result or looking for the TV page. The former will involve the so-called higher level cognitive functions of comprehension, whereas the latter will be more of a recognition task. It is clear that although all these scenarios can be described as reading, they differ greatly in terms of how and why the reader interacts with the text as well as the text type under consideration. Characterizing these differences would be useful for hypertext developers because it would suggest ways in which hypertext documents should be developed in order to optimize reading performance.

Researchers as early as Huey (1908) were aware of the diversity of tasks typically performed by readers, and to this day it has remained generally accepted that this variety is worthy of consideration. For example, on the subject of electronic journals Wright (1987) drew attention to the fact that, depending on what information is being sought, readers may employ browsing, skimming, studying, cross-checking, or linear reading. However, although it is possible to compile lists of likely reading tasks and their performance characteristics, it is entirely another matter to validate them empirically.

Observing Task Performance

Schumacher and Waller (1985) make the point that reading research has tended to concentrate on outcome measures (such as speed or comprehension) rather than process ones (what the reader does with the text). Without doubt, the main obstacle to obtaining accurate process data is devising a suitable, nonintrusive observation method. Although numerous techniques for measuring eye movements during reading now exist, it is not at all clear from eye movement records what the reader was thinking or trying to do at any particular time. Furthermore, use of such equipment is rarely nonintrusive, often requiring the reader to remain immobile through the use of head restraints, bite bars, and so forth, or read the text one line at a time from a computer display—hardly equitable to normal reading conditions!

Less intrusive methods such as the use of light pens in darkened environments to highlight the portion of the text currently viewed (Whalley and Fleming, 1975), or modified reading stands with semi-silvered glass that reflect the reader's eye movements in terms of current text position to a video camera (Pugh, 1979), are examples of the creativity that researchers have displayed in order to record reading behavior. However, none of these are ideal as they alter the reading environment, sometimes drastically, and only their staunchest advocate would describe them as nonintrusive.

Verbal protocols of people interacting with texts—asking them to "think aloud"—require no elaborate equipment and can be elicited wherever a subject normally reads. In this way they are cheap, relatively naturalistic and physically nonintrusive. However, the techniques have been criticized for interfering with the normal processing involved in task performance (i.e., cognitive intrusion) and requiring the presence of an experimenter to sustain and record the verbal protocol (Nisbett & Wilson, 1977).

If we accept that a perfect method does not yet exist, it is important to understand the relative merits of those that are available. Eye movement records have significantly aided theoretical developments in modeling reading (see, e.g., Just & Carpenter, 1980), whereas use of the light pen type of technique has demonstrated its worth in identifying the effects of various typographic cues on reading behavior (see, e.g., Schumacher & Waller, 1985). Verbal protocols have been effectively used by researchers to gain information on reading strategies (see, e.g., Olshavsky, 1977). Nevertheless, such techniques rarely have been employed with the intention of assessing the likely effect of hypertext presentation on performance. More usually they have been used to test various paper document design alternatives or to shed light on reading performance in highly controlled experimental studies.

Where text is presented on computer screens it is possible to record and time the duration of displayed text, thus facilitating reasonable inference about what readers are doing.* However, as an

---

*In saying this I am assuming that the inferences are being drawn by a skilled evaluator with detailed knowledge of the task being performed by the reader. In the absence of these factors, the recorded interaction is unlikely to yield anything worthwhile.

attempt to analyze normal reading performance, this fails because there is no way of gauging the influence of the medium on performance, that is, reading electronic text cannot be directly equated to reading paper. A fuller treatment of these issues can be found in Wright (1987). Nevertheless, this method provides a simple and effective way of observing gross manipulations of text without making the person aware of the recording process.

Virtually all of the work on hypertext has employed such recording techniques to monitor user navigation and use of various commands. With the advent of cheap screen recording devices it is possible to record how the entire screen display changes throughout the course of the interaction, for later replay without resorting to video recordings. Although this is obviously useful, it does not solve the problem of how to assess the use of paper and its importance for hypertext design. Where paper and hypertext are directly compared, although process measures may be taken with the computer and/or video cameras, the final comparison often rests on outcome measures.

Evidence for Task Effects

Probably because of the difficulties outlined earlier, research has tended not to focus directly on how people read or the range of tasks they perform with texts. Instead, investigators normally test reading in circumstances where the task is specifically designed to manipulate experimental variables. Typically these have been proofreading, short story comprehension, letter or word recognition, sentence recall, and so forth. In itself this is a recognition of the variable effect of task on reading. However, there have been some studies that have sought to test task effects directly. Two are described here that illustrate the range from the single sentence to the full document level.

Aaronson and Ferres (1986) had subjects read 80 sentences one word at a time from a computer screen and perform either a recall or comprehension test item after each sentence. They observed differences in the time taken to read words in a sentence depending on the task being performed. Their results supported the hypotheses that readers tend to process and attend to the surface structure for retention tasks and the semantic structure for comprehension tasks, that is, their cognitions are altered according to the demands of the reading task.

Verbal protocol analyses combined with observation of readers' manipulations of text were used in a study by Dillon et al. (1989) to examine researchers' use of academic journals. Unlike the other studies cited, the specific intention of this work was to identify the issues that needed to be addressed in developing a hypertext database of such material. The study was reasonably successful in eliciting information on individuals' style of reading, identifying their reasons for using journals and demonstrating three reading strategies that were typically performed: rapid scan of the contents, browsing of certain relevant sections, and full serial reading of the text. The strategies matched the tasks being performed, for example, rapid scanning told the reader about the suitability of the article for his purposes, whereas browsing certain sections provided more specific information, and full serial reading was employed when the reader wanted to study the contents of the article.

Conclusion

Task demands dictate the manner in which readers manipulate information, but as yet few empirically validated performance strategies have been described. A major obstacle appears to be the lack of a suitable method for measuring such behavior. Furthermore, any task effects demonstrated with paper documents may not transfer directly to the electronic medium. Nevertheless, the sheer diversity of tasks performed with documents necessitates some consideration of the effect of task type on the manner of usage. One hypertext implementation of a document might suit some tasks but be far from optimal for others. Without appreciating the range and manner of the tasks performed with a document, the chances of designing suitable hyper versions are reduced.

UNDERSTANDING HYPERTEXT IN TERMS OF USER, TASK, AND INFORMATION INTERACTIONS

It was stated at the beginning of this chapter that questions such as, "Is hypertext better than paper?" were simplistic. The previous sections on users, tasks, and information should have given some indication of why this is the case. In the present section some of the emerging empirical data on hypertext will be discussed in the light of the interactions between these aspects.

To date, researchers and developers have, in the main, been content to discuss the apparent advantages of hypertext systems for most tasks, occasionally describing systems they have implemented and informally presenting user reactions to them (see, e.g., Marchionini & Shneiderman, 1988). Such reports are difficult to assess critically and it is easy to get carried away with the hype surrounding the new medium. If one looks at the proceedings of recent conferences on hypertext one will find that such reports are in the majority, with well-controlled experimental papers few and far between. To be fair, it is possible that this state of affairs reflects the stage of development of these systems; they seem like a good idea and they are being developed, with formal studies being seen as appropriate only at a later stage. Nevertheless, in the absence of confirmatory data, any claims for the new medium should be treated with caution.

What data have emerged need to be carefully considered in the light of the three elements discussed in the preceding since findings are often conflicting and any one study can only hope to answer a subset of the questions to be asked. The next section considers some of the experimental data in terms of comparisons that have been made between hypertext and paper, hypertext and linear electronic text, and between various implementations of one hypertext.

Hypertext Versus Paper

Perhaps the most basic comparison is between hypertext and the traditional medium of paper. Given the revolutionary form of presentation afforded by hypertext, this comparison is of considerable importance to both authors and readers, educators and learners.

In a widely reported study, Egan et al. (1989) compared students' performance on a set of tasks involving a statistics text. Students used either the standard textbook or a hypertext version displayed via SuperBook, a structured browsing system, to search for specific information in the text and write essays with the text open. Incidental learning and subjective ratings were also assessed. The authors report that

> students using SuperBook answered more search questions correctly, wrote higher quality "open-book" essays, and recalled certain incidental information better than students using conventional text (p. 205).

Students also significantly preferred the hypertext version to the paper text.

At first glance this is an impressive set of findings. It seems to lend firm support to the frequently expressed view that hypertext is better than paper in the educational setting (cf., Landow, 1990). However, a closer look at the experiment is revealing. For example, with respect to the search tasks, the questions posed were varied so that their wording mentioned terms contained in the body of the text, in the headings, in both of these, or neither. Not surprisingly, the largest advantage to hypertext was observed where the target information was only mentioned in the body of text (i.e., there were no headings referring to it). Here it is hardly surprising that the search facility of the computer out-performed humans! When the task was less biased against the paper condition, for example, searching for information to which there are headings, no significant difference was observed. Interestingly, the poorest performance of all was for SuperBook users searching for information when the question did not contain specific references to words used anywhere in the text. In the absence of suitable search parameters or look-up terms, hypertext suddenly seemed less usable. This is not a criticism of the study. To the authors' credit they describe their work in sufficient detail to allow one to assess this study fully. Furthermore, they freely admit that an earlier study using an identical methodology showed less difference between the media (paper even proving significantly better than hypertext for certain tasks!) Only on the basis of this were modifications made to SuperBook that led to the observations reported earlier.* A further series of studies comparing SuperBook not only with paper but also with a page-based display system known as PixLook and across different tasks concluded that there was no one "best" interface. Rather, particular tasks were supported to a greater or lesser extent by each interface; as the task changes, so the optimum form of interface will change (Landauer et al., 1993).

In a study by McKnight, Dillon, and Richardson (1990), subjects located information in a text on the subject of wine. This was presented in one of four conditions: paper, word processor, HyperTIES, or HyperCard. The tasks were designed in order to require a range of retrieval strategies on the part of the subject, that is, although the search facility might prove useful for some questions, it could not be employed slavishly to answer all questions. This was seen as reflecting the range of activities for which such a text would be employed in the real world.

Results showed that subjects were significantly more accurate with paper than both hypertext versions, although no effect for speed was observed. Subjects were also better able to estimate the document size with paper than with hypertexts and spent signifi-

---

*This is a classic example of how testing and redesigning a system—so-called iterative user-centered design—can lead to a more usable product. If no modifications had been carried out we might have found SuperBook being cited for very different reasons!

cantly less time in the contents and index sections of the text with the paper version. Paper and word processor versions were similar in most scores, suggesting that the familiar structure inherent in both versions supported the subjects' performance.

On the face of it, in these two studies we have two conflicting findings on the question of paper versus hypertext. However, by appreciating the users, tasks, and information types employed in these two studies we can see that they are not directly comparable in anything but a superficial manner. As evidence to support a "Yes/No" answer to the question "Is hypertext better than paper?" they are obviously limited. This is not to say that no implications can be drawn. These two experiments show that each medium has its own inherent advantages and shortcomings, for example, hyper-text is better than paper when locating specific information that is contained within the body of text but seems to offer no clear advan-tage when readers have only an approximate idea of what they are looking for. When readers access a text for the first time on a subject for which they have no specialist knowledge and cannot formulate a precise search parameter, the familiarity of paper seems to confer certain advantages.

Hypertext Versus Linear Electronic Text

As mentioned earlier in the chapter, comparisons between paper and screen reading often favor paper because of the differences in image quality between the two media. Although hypertext systems usually run on good quality screens, it is possible that image quality variables still have an influence for tasks that require fast scanning and visual detection of material. A number of studies that overcome such differences are those comparing hypertext implementations with linear, that is, nonhypertext, electronic documents on identical screens.

Monk et al. (1988) report two experimental comparisons of hy-pertext with folding and scrolling displays for examining a computer program listing. In the first study, subjects attempted 15 questions related to program comprehension. Although no effect was ob-served for number of tasks answered correctly, there was a signifi-cant difference between the hypertext and scrolling browsers in terms of the rate at which tasks were performed, with hypertext proving slower. In the second study they attempted to overcome this performance deficit by providing subjects with either a map of the structure of the program or a list of section headings. The map improved performance to levels comparable with users of the scrolling browser in the first study, but the list of titles had little effect. The authors conclude that the map is a vital component of any hypertext implementation; without it too much of the user's cognitive resources are required to navigate rather than deal with the primary task.

In another study comparing hypertext with linear electronic text, Gordon et al. (1988) asked subjects to read two articles, one in each format. Half the subjects read general interest articles with instructions for casual reading while the rest read technical articles with instructions to learn the material. Thus it can be seen that two distinct tasks and two distinct text types were employed. Performance was assessed using post-task free recall tests and question probes, whereas preference was assessed using a questionnaire.

Subjects answered significantly more questions correctly with the linear format than with the hypertext and also recalled significantly more of the general interest articles in linear format. Questionnaire data revealed a general 2:1 preference for the linear format with a 3:1 ratio expressing that this format required less mental effort than hypertext. Subjects frequently stated that they were used to the linear format and found hypertext intrusive on their train of thought. Similar to the Monk et al. study, Gordon et al. concluded that navigational decisions are more difficult with the hypertext and therefore disrupt the reader, that is, cognitive intrusion occurs. The differences between formats were greater for the general interest texts than for the technical material, suggesting possible task effects, but the authors do not discuss this in any detail. One curious aspect of this study was the use of texts on the themes "Falling in love" and "Reverse sterilization" as general interest material!

Interestingly, these studies seem to suggest that the hypertext structure places an extra burden on the reader in terms of navigation and consequently leads to poorer performance. On the face of it this is not too surprising for the users and texts employed here. The subjects were familiar with the structure of the linear documents and were only constrained by the manipulation facilities available to them with the system. With the hypertext systems, although manipulation may have been faster and more direct, the subjects needed not only to learn the new document structure but also to suppress their existing model of where information was likely to be positioned. The fact that naive users can perform equally well with hypertext versions (Monk et al.'s second study) suggests that such problems can be overcome. How performance would be altered with experience is an obvious question for further research.

Hypertext Versus Hypertext

Several studies have compared different implementations of hypertext documents to observe the effects of various organizing principles or access mechanisms on performance. This is an important area. The term hypertext does not refer to a unitary concept. When comparisons are said to be made between hypertext and paper documents they are really being made between certain implementations of hypertext and standard versions of paper texts. Each implementation consists of one designer's (or group of designers') ideas about how to build the interface between users and information. To make general claims or draw conclusions about the wider relevance of hypertext in such circumstances is problematic. However, studies comparing varying implementations can shed some light on what constitutes good hypertext.

Simpson and McKnight (1990), for example, created eight versions of a hypertext document on plants, manipulating the contents list (hierarchical or alphabetic), presence or absence of a current position indicator and presence or absence of typographic cues. Subjects (researchers and students) were required to read the text until they felt confident they had seen it all and were then required to perform 10 information location tasks before attempting to construct a map of the document structure with cards. Results showed that readers using a hierarchical contents list navigated through the text more efficiently and produced more accurate maps of its structure than readers using an alphabetic index. The current position indicator and additional typographic cues were of limited utility.

Wright and Lickorish (1990) compared two types of navigation system for two different hypertexts. The navigation systems were termed Index navigation where the reader needed to return to a separate listing to specify where to move next, and Page navigation where the reader could jump directly to other "pages" from the current display. The two texts were on houseplants and supermarket prices. Twenty-four subjects read both hypertexts, 12 per navigation system, answering multiple choice questions with the plants text and a variety of "Go To," compare and compute tasks with the supermarket text.

From their results they concluded that each navigation system had certain advantages in particular situations. For example, the paging navigation system may appear burdensome but was found to be beneficial with the houseplants text as it coupled navigation decisions with an overview of the text's structure.* However, such activity with the tasks performed on the supermarket text (where decisions about where to go were not an issue because the questions provided such information) turned out to be an extra load on working memory. As Wright and Lickorish state, "authors need to bear in mind both the structure inherent in the content material and the tasks readers will be seeking to accomplish when they are designing navigation systems for hypertext."

CONCLUSIONS

Despite the claims frequently made for hypertext, experimental comparisons reveal that it is no guarantee of better performance, whether it is measured in terms of speed, comprehension, range of material covered or problems solved. Some hypertext implementations are good, some bad. Hypertext has advantages when readers are performing certain tasks with particular texts but offers no benefit, or is in fact worse than paper, in others. This is not too surprising. We should not expect any one implementation to be superior to all paper documents. After all, the diversity of textual documentation exists in the main for a purpose, that is, to support the reader. Furthermore, as readers we all have a wealth of experience in dealing with paper texts which once learned, we apply effortlessly to our dealings with paper. Such experience, be it in the form of models of structure, rapid manipulation skills, or accurate memory for location of items in a document, is often overlooked rather than exploited by developers of hypertexts. As the technology improves, any differences based on image quality should disappear; as readers become more experienced with hypertext, initial cognitive intrusion effects should be overcome. However, there are still many other problems to be addressed before hypertext will be exploited fully. The main point to take from this chapter is that users, tasks and texts vary tremendously and only by understanding the interaction of these three aspects of document usage can we answer the question in the title—a good hypertext is one developed through user-centered, task-based design of the information resource.

---

*It may appear counterintuitive for a "paging" navigation system to improve the overview of the text's structure as opposed to Index navigation. However, in the paging condition, buttons representing the chapter titles were permanently displayed along the bottom of the screen, showing users which chapter they were currently in and allowing jumps to other chapters.

ACKNOWLEDGMENTS

This chapter draws heavily on work done with Andrew Dillon and John Richardson, former colleagues at the HUSAT Research Institute. Their unwitting contribution is gratefully acknowledged, although I'm sure they would also want me to point out that all blame must be mine!

REFERENCES

Aaronson, D., & Ferres, S. (1986). Reading strategies for children and adults: a quantitative model. *Psychological Review, 93*(1), 89–112.

Baird, P., & Percival, M. (1989). Glasgow on-line: database development using Apple's HyperCard. In R. McAleese (Ed.), *Hypertext: theory into practice.* Oxford: Intellect.

de Beaugrande, R. (1980). *Text, discourse and process.* Norwood, NJ: Ablex.

Beech, J., & Colley, A. (1987). *Cognitive approaches to reading.* Chichester: Wiley.

Cakir, A., Hart, D. J., & Stewart, T. F. M. (1980). *Visual display terminals.* Chichester: Wiley.

Clark, H. (1977). Inferences in comprehension. In D. Laberge & S. Samuels (Eds.), *Basic processes in reading: perception and comprehension.* Norwood, NJ: Ablex.

Creed, A., Dennis, I., & Newstead, S. (1987). Proof-reading on VDUs. *Behaviour and Information Technology, 6*(1), 3–13.

Crowder, R. (1982). *The psychology of reading: an introduction.* Oxford: Oxford University Press.

Dillon, A. (1994). *Designing usable electronic text.* London: Taylor and Francis.

Dillon, A., & McKnight, C. (1990). Towards a classification of text types: a repertory grid approach. *International Journal of Man-Machine Studies, 33*, 623–636.

Dillon, A., & McKnight, C. (1995). Never mind the theory, feel the data. In W. Schuler, J. Hannemann, & N. Streitz (Eds.), *Designing user interfaces for hypermedia.* Berlin: Springer.

Dillon, A., Richardson, J., & McKnight, C. (1989). The human factors of journal usage and the design of electronic text. *Interacting with Computers, 1*(2), 183–189.

Egan, D., Remde, J., Landauer, T., Lochbaum, C., & Gomez, L. (1989). Behavioral evaluation and analysis of a hypertext browser. In *Proceedings of CHI'89.* New York: Association of Computing Machinery. 205–210.

Garnham, A. (1986). *Mental models as representations of text and discourse.* Chichester: Ellis Horwood.

Gordon, S., Gustavel, J., Moore, J., & Hankey, J. (1988). The effects of hypertext on reader knowledge representation. *Proceedings of the Human Factor Society 32nd Annual Meeting*, 296–300.

Gould, J. D., & Grischkowsky, N. (1984). Doing the same work with hard copy and cathode ray tube (CRT) computer terminals. *Human Factors, 26*(3), 323–337.

Gould, J. D., Alfaro, L., Barnes, V., Finn, R., Grischkowsky, N., & Minuto, A. (1987a). Reading is slower from CRT displays than from paper: attempts to isolate a single-variable explanation. *Human Factors, 29*(3), 269–299.

Gould, J. D., Alfaro, L., Finn, R., Haupt, B., & Minuto, A. (1987b). Reading from CRT displays can be as fast as reading from paper. *Human Factors, 29*(5), 497–517.

Huey, E. B. (1908). *The psychology and pedagogy of reading*. New York: Macmillan.

Johnson-Laird, P. (1983). *Mental models*. Cambridge: Cambridge University Press.

Just, M. A., & Carpenter, P. (1980). A theory of reading: from eye movements to comprehension. *Psychological Review, 87*(4), 329–354.

Kak, A. V. (1981). Relationships between readability of printed and CRT-displayed text. *Proceedings of Human Factors Society 25th Annual Meeting*, 137–140.

Landauer, T., Egan, D., Remde, J., Lesk, M., Lochbaum, C., & Ketchum, D. (1993). Enhancing the usability of text through computer delivery and formative evaluation: the SuperBook Project. In C. McKnight, A. Dillon, & J. Richardson (Eds.) *Hypertext: a psychological perspective*. (pp. 71–136). Chichester: Ellis Horwood.

Landow, G. (1990). The rhetoric of hypermedia: a guide for authors. In D. Jonassen, & H. Mandl (Eds.). *Designing hypermedia for learning*. Heidelberg: Springer-Verlag.

Marchionini, G., & Shneiderman, B. (1988). Finding facts versus browsing knowledge in hypertext systems. *Computer,* January, 70–80.

McClelland, J., & Rumelhart, D. (1981). An interactive activation model of context effects in letter perception. Part I: An account of basic findings. *Psychological Review, 88*, 375–407.

McKnight, C., Dillon, A., & Richardson, J. (1990). A comparison of linear and hypertext formats in information retrieval. In R. McAleese, & C. Green (Eds.), *Hypertext: state of the art*. Oxford: Intellect.

McKnight, C., Dillon, A., & Richardson, J. (1991). *Hypertext in context*. Cambridge: Cambridge University Press.

Monk, A., Walsh, P., & Dix, A. (1988). A comparison of hypertext, scrolling, and folding as mechanisms for program browsing. In D. Jones, & R. Winder (Eds.), *People and computers IV*. Cambridge: Cambridge University Press.

Muter, P., Latrémouille, S. A., Treurniet, W. C., & Beam, P. (1982). Extended reading of continuous text on television screens. *Human Factors, 24*(5), 501–508.

Nisbett, R., & Wilson, T. (1977). Telling more than we can know: verbal reports on mental processes. *Psychological Review, 84*, 231–259.

Olshavsky, J. (1977). Reading as problem solving: an investigation of strategies. *Reading Research Quarterly, 4*, 654–674.

Poulter, A., Sargent, G., & Fahy, A. (1993). Hypermuse: a prototype hypermedia front-end for museum information systems. *Hypermedia, 5*(3), 165–186.

Pugh, A. (1979). Styles and strategies in adult silent reading. In P. Kolers, M. Wrolstad, & H. Bouma (Eds.). *Processing of visible language 1*. London: Plenum Press.

Rothkopf, E. Z. (1971). Incidental memory for location of information in text. *Journal of Verbal Learning and Verbal Behavior, 10*, 608–613.

Schumacher, G., & Waller, R. (1985). Testing design alternatives: a comparison of procedures. In T. Duffy and R. Waller (Eds.), *Designing usable texts*. Orlando, FL: Academic Press.

Shackel, B. (1991). Usability—context, framework, definition, design and evaluation. In B. Shackel & S. Richardson (Eds.), *Human factors for informatics usability* (pp. 21–37). Cambridge: Cambridge University Press.

Shneiderman, B. (1987b). User interface design and evaluation for an electronic encyclopedia. In G. Salvendy (Ed.), *Cognitive engineering in the design of human-computer interaction and expert systems* (pp. 207–223). Amsterdam: Elsevier.

Simpson, A., & McKnight, C. (1990). Navigation in hypertext: structural cues and mental maps. In R. McAleese, & C. Green (Eds.), *Hypertext: state of the art*. Oxford: Intellect.

Thorndyke, P. (1977). Cognitive structures in comprehension and memory of narrative discourse. *Cognitive Psychology, 9*, 77–110.

van Dijk, T. A., & Kintsch, W. (1983). *Strategies of discourse comprehension*. New York: Academic Press.

Waller, R. (1987). *The typographic contribution to language: Towards a model of typographic genres and their underlying structures*. Unpublished doctoral thesis. University of Reading, UK.

Whalley, P., & Fleming, R. (1975). An experiment with a simple recorder of reading behaviour. *Programmed Learning and Educational Technology, 12*, 120–124.

Wilkinson, R. T., & Robinshaw, H. M. (1987). Proof-reading: VDU and paper text compared for speed, accuracy and fatigue. *Behaviour and Information Technology, 6*(2), 125–133.

Wright, P. (1980). Textual literacy: an outline sketch of psychological research on reading and writing. In P. Kolers, M. Wrolstad, & H. Bouma (Eds.), *Processing of visible language 2*. London: Plenum Press.

Wright, P. (1987). Reading and writing for electronic journals. In B. Britton, & S. Glynn (Eds.), *Executive control processes in reading*. Hillsdale, NJ: Erlbaum.

Wright, P., & Lickorish, A. (1983). Proof-reading texts on screen and paper. *Behaviour and Information Technology, 2*(3), 227–235.

Wright, P., & Lickorish, A. (1989). The influence of discourse structure on display and navigation in hypertexts. In N. Williams & P. Holt (Eds.), *Computers and writing* (pp. 90–124). Oxford: Intellect.

Wright, P., & Lickorish, A. (1990). An empirical comparison of two navigation systems for two hypertexts. In R. McAleese & C. Green (Eds.), *Hypertext: state of the art* (pp. 84–93). Oxford: Intellect.

11

Task and Activity Models in Hypertext Usage

Jean-François Rouet

University of Poitiers and CNRS, France

André Tricot

University of Provence, CREPCO,
Aix en Provence, France

INTRODUCTION

A major requirement for electronic information systems is to provide effective support to the users' information processing activities. By information processing activities we mean activities in which people need to access, read, and understand information structures (e.g., texts and documents). Although early hypertext research and development efforts have focused mainly on technical aspects, such as data representation and information retrieval algorithms, system usability now has become a key issue (Wright, 1991).

Efforts to improve hypertext usability may be based on several strategies, such as domain modeling (e.g., Nanard & Nanard, 1991) or design aids (Marshall et al., 1991), which can improve the coherence and visibility of the hypertext structure and the meaning of nodes and links. Interface tools (e.g., Nielsen, 1990a) also aim at facilitating navigation and user information about the system (contents, menus, relations, and organization). However, these approaches often are limited or difficult to apply. For instance, domain modeling doesn't guarantee system usability; design aids are difficult to define (Marshall & Rogers, 1992); interface tools increase the system complexity and their efficiency is rarely evaluated.

So far, hypertext research has paid little attention to the cognitive analysis of information processing tasks. Most hypertext systems available today were primarily designed as general purpose systems, aimed at supporting users' interactions with information structures regardless of the purpose or task. Another problem is that many of the proposed systems have seldom received any empirical assessment, which makes it difficult to evaluate their effectiveness.

In this chapter we suggest that a closer analysis of information processing tasks may provide useful insights for the design of usable hypertexts. In our perspective task analysis consists in describing the different types of knowledge and skills involved in the performance of a given information processing task. In addition, task analysis involves modeling the goals and subgoals, the plan (subgoal organization), procedures (subgoal execution), strategies (conditions of execution of a group of procedures), objects, and actions. This type of approach is widespread in the area of ergonomics applied to design (Diaper, 1989; Hammouche, 1993; Johnson, 1991; Johnson & Nicolsi, 1992).

Some authors (e.g., Wright, 1990) consider that task analysis has direct implications on decisions regarding hypertext structure (e.g., linking) and design (interface). According to McKnight, Richardson, & Dillon (1988)

> In order to determine the optimum links, the author needs to anticipate the uses to which the reader will put the text. . . . If the author can foresee a range of tasks and provide "templates" to support these tasks, then the reader is more likely to interact successfully with the document (p. 339).

A serious problem, however, is that a cognitive theory of information processing tasks has yet to be proposed. It is our contention that such a theory may be partly induced from empirical studies of how real users perform those tasks, and what factors affect their performance. The purpose of this chapter is to contribute to that aim.

In the following we present different approaches to the analysis of information processing tasks, as they appear in hypertext and information retrieval literature. We have identified three types of approaches: Formal, user-centered, and integrated. Later, we focus more directly on the cognitive processes involved in using hypertext. We review empirical studies on using hypertext for two types of tasks: information search tasks and learning–exploring tasks. For each of these types of tasks we examine how presentation format affects the user's strategies and representations. Based on these findings, we propose a general framework to represent the task and activity levels involved in using hypertext. ·

TASK ANALYSIS IN HYPERTEXT RESEARCH

The tasks or activity domains for which hypertext may be useful or efficient have been subject to much debate. Bernstein (1993) defined three types of information-based activities he called information mining, manufacturing, or farming. Bernstein pointed out that these activities may call for different support environments. For example, "information mining" may be best supported by information retrieval systems, and less well supported by hypertext systems.

The issue of what information processing tasks may or may not be supported by hypertext calls for a detailed analysis of these tasks, which may be conducted from several points of views: A "system-centered" or formal point of view consists in defining formal criteria to characterize information processing tasks. A "user-centered" point of view focuses on how the user represents and performs these tasks. In this section we illustrate these two approaches in the case of information retrieval tasks, which have been most extensively studied in the literature.

Formal Approaches to Information Retrieval

From a formal point of view, the main purpose of information retrieval is to select relevant information units (recall), while ignoring irrelevant units (precision; see Salton & McGill, 1983). Research on information retrieval has focused mainly on problems such as document indexing, database structuring, search algorithms, and query languages.

In this area of research, the term "hypertext" often is used metaphorically to indicate some form of linking between database items. Database linking may be based on several techniques, such as fuzzy logic (Croft & Turtle, 1993; Frei & Stieger, 1992), neural networks (Biener, Guivarch, & Pinon, 1990; Lelu & François, 1992), or Petri nets (Stotts & Furuta, 1991).

In some systems hypertext linking was included as one of several tools (e.g., Girill & Luk, 1992). The rationale is that users may need different tools at different stages of their information retrieval activity. For instance, hypertext may be most useful in the early phases of the activity, when the user's goal is not yet completely specified.

Traditional information retrieval methods or systems have sometimes overlooked the needs of human information retrievers (Thompson & Croft, 1989). Many systems suffer from poor interface design, complex query syntax, and the need to specify target contents in advance. Using hypertext for information retrieval may alleviate these problems: The user does not have to specify target information in advance interaction with the system is made easier, and finally the user receives an immediate feedback on the relevance of his or her selections (see Agosti, 1992; van Rijsbergen & Agosti, 1992).

User-Centered Analysis of Information Search Tasks

A few authors have examined information search tasks as they may be performed by a hypertext user. For instance, Wright (1990, pp. 176–178) has defined several categories of information search activities based on characteristics of the "target," i.e., the searched information. Search target may be simple and fully known in advance, or it may be more complex and interactively specified as part of the search activity itself.

In addition, Wright pointed out the diversity of the subactivities involved in information search: reading, note taking, comparing information from several sources, and so forth. Each particular subactivity may call for specific interface tools, for instance, a note taking facility, multiple windowing, cross referencing, and footprints.

Other authors have identified situational and individual factors that may render the search task more or less difficult: expertise in the content area, reading skills, and familiarity with the system (McKnight et al., 1990). Wright (1991) indicated that memory demands of the task can be increased by some interface characteristics (e.g., a small screen). However, the cognitive cost generated by interface characteristics are not necessarily uniform across tasks.

Integrated Approaches: The Case of Cooperative Design Systems

Although most studies focus either on systems or on users, in some cases system designers have integrated cognitive or human factor considerations in their work.

Conklin and Begeman (1989) introduced gIBIS, a computerized tool aimed at supporting cooperative design. gIBIS is based on the observation that design problems involve conversations where the participants raise issues, state positions and provide pro or con arguments. In gIBIS a problem is represented as a network where nodes are issues, positions, or arguments, whereas links are typed relations between these entities. Similarly, Streitz et al. (1989) have proposed to use a rhetorical model of argumentation, along with a cognitive model of writing, as a basis for the design of SEPIA, a system to support authoring and argumentation (see also, Schuler & Smith, 1990).

These examples suggest that system design may benefit from an explicit definition of the type of activities supported. However, there are indications that even systems designed after a general task model may face usability problems. In some cases informal field tests have shown that users tend to structure information in ways unforeseen by the designer (Marshall & Rogers, 1992). In other cases, some of the proposed system's features appeared to increase the user's cognitive load. For instance, the constraint of representing one's ideas in the form of nodes and links may not be compatible with the way people go through a complex reasoning task (Conklin & Begeman, 1989).

The studies reported in this section indicate that information search tasks may be defined according to several points of view. On the one hand, what is to be done, on the other hand, what the subject actually does. What has to be done may be defined as a goal to achieve and the goal implementation in the system. What the subject actually does depends on his or her knowledge about the domain, the system and its interface, and his or her representation of what needs to be done.

Electronic information systems must comply with the specificity and limitations inherent to human information processing. In particular the way information is displayed by the system (e.g., idea networks) should be as close as possible to the representations users normally generate as part of the design process (e.g., paper and pencil sketches). However, this is just one of the many problems people may face when using information systems. Empirical studies of hypertext usage in various contexts may help build up a more comprehensive model of the actual needs of information users.

EMPIRICAL STUDIES OF HYPERTEXT USAGE: THE ROLE OF TASK REPRESENTATION AND MANAGEMENT

In his now classic review on hypertext, Conklin (1987) pointed out two potential problems hypertext users may face, disorientation and cognitive overhead. The concept of disorientation relies on an analogy of hypertext as a "semantic space" (see Dillon, McKnight, & Richardson, 1993, for a discussion of the semantic space analogy). In order to make sense of a hypertext the user must acquire a mental representation of its layout ("mental map"). Following this analogy, disorientation may be defined as not knowing where you are, where to go, or how to go there.

Cognitive overhead may be defined as an excessive burden on subjects' processes of reading and navigating the hypertext. For instance, cognitive overhead may arise when the subject cannot remember the areas of the hypertext network he or she has previously visited (see also, Wright, 1991).

Disorientation and cognitive overhead may be related to the subject's representation of the reading task and of how to manage it. Foss (1989, experiment 2) asked 10 adults to use a geographical hypertext database in order to perform a task involving the display and comparison of several cards. Foss reported two main types of problems: First, some subjects made too few comparisons and tended to lose track of their hypotheses or forget how they had come to a conclusion. This was interpreted as a "search strategy" problem, or not having a good representation of the task requirements. Second, some subjects opened too few or too many cards at the same time, or positioned the cards in a way that did not allow easy comparison. This was interpreted as a "task management" problem, or not knowing how to perform the task.

Task representation and task management are tightly interrelated. For instance, poor task management (e.g., opening too many cards) may prevent subjects from applying a good task representation (e.g., reasoning by elimination). In other terms, a coherent representation of the environment (what information is available and how to access it) is essential for effective access to the information of interest.

Given the huge diversity of text-related activities, it is difficult to consider the cognitive processes of task representation and management in general (Wright, 1991). Instead the various task domains where hypertext may be used must be considered on a case by case basis. In the next two sections we will take a closer look at two general task domains: *Information retrieval tasks* and *general learning tasks*.

Managing Information Retrieval in Hypertext

Experiments comparing hypertext and paper for information retrieval tasks have elicited two important factors which influence subjects' performance: Information search skills and strategies, and top-level structuring information.

The role of information search skills and strategies

Searching large and complex information systems requires specific cognitive skills that may not be well mastered by novice information searchers. In a study by Weyer (1982) sixteen high school students used a computerized information system ("Dynamic Book") in order to answer different types of questions about history. Weyer noted that dealing with complex questions (e.g., comparison questions) was difficult for many of his students. Moreover the students had trouble using the system's most advanced search tools (e.g., interactive cross-reference table).

McKnight, Dillon, and Richardson (1990) came to similar conclusions after asking a group of 16 adults to answer a series of questions by searching a 40-unit document presented using either print or hypertext. In the hypertext conditions the subjects spent a greater proportion of time searching the menus, and they seldom used the direct links between cards. The results suggested that the search facilities provided in hypertext may not be immediately mastered by novice users. McKnight et al. also noted that task requirements may interfere with presentation formats. For instance, subjects may be more willing to use direct links between related units if asked to summarize the document.

There is some evidence that users' performance may improve as they become familiar with the system. Gray and Shasha (1989) asked college students to answer a series of questions by searching either a printed or two computerized versions (with or without hypertext links) or a sociology chapter. The paper group answered more questions than the two computer groups, and did so faster in four out of five questions. However, in the two computer groups, search time decreased with question rank, suggesting a training effect. Finally, in the hypertext group, the effective use of direct links varied across subjects and questions, which suggests an interaction of task representation and search strategy (see also Marchionini & Shneiderman, 1988; Wang & Liebscher, 1988).

Rouet (1994) also observed an improvement of search strategies in novice hypertext users. In the first study, sixty 12- to 14-year-old students participated in four experimental sessions. At each session the subjects were asked to search the hypertext in order to answer four questions. Search effectiveness increased over experimental sessions, especially for the more complex questions. Moreover, the subjects used different search strategies as a function of question complexity, but only after some practice. Rouet suggested that practice improved students' representation of the hypertext organization and task requirements. In the second study, thirty-nine 16- to 18-year-old students searched two hierarchical hypertexts in order to answer simple, complex–explicit and complex–implicit questions. Search time decreased from first to last question in a series and also from first to second exposure to the same hypertext. Again, the selection strategy varied as a function of question characteristics: For simple questions the subjects selected mostly target hypertext units; for complex questions the subjects selected a larger proportion of superordinate or irrelevant hypertext units.

Improvement of search efficiency with training was also reported by Tombaugh, Lickorish, and Wright (1987). Tombaugh et al. asked novice computer users to read a lengthy text on screen using either a single or a multiple window format. Subjects' task was to locate the answer to 10 factual questions, after having read the whole text once. In experiment 1 subjects received minimal training and there was no advantage for multiwindow presentation. In experiment 2 subjects were trained more carefully to manipulate the pointing device and to read in multiple windows. Multiple windows resulted in significantly faster responses once subjects were familiar with the procedure.

These observations are compatible with our claim that both a task representation and a task management strategy are needed to perform hypertext search tasks. Representing the task means understanding the information needs given a task or request, for example, making a difference between a fact retrieval and a comparison question. A task management strategy relates the available information and search tool to the task representation in order to access and process the required information.

Effects of top level structure on information retrieval

Several studies have demonstrated that structured representations of the top-level structure of a hypertext (e.g., a hierarchical index) facilitate user navigation and improve search effectiveness.

Simpson & McKnight (1990) evaluated the effects of structural cues on subjects' representation a 24-unit hypertext database on house plants. They used three types of structural cues: hierarchical versus alphabetic table of contents, presence or absence of a "footprint" (marking the last opened card in the table of contents), and a typographical cue (signaling major units in capital letters). Twenty-four experienced computer users read the hypertext once and then searched the hypertext to answer 10 factual questions.

Subjects in the hierarchical condition opened the table of contents more often. They also opened a smaller number of cards both during the initial reading and question answering periods. Finally, they were able to reconstruct the organization of the hypertext more accurately. Footprints reduced the number of cards opened during initial reading but not when answering questions. The authors concluded that structural cues usually found in paper documents are also helpful in hypertext environments. However, different structural cues may be more or less efficient, depending on task demands.

The top-level structure may have a qualitative influence on subjects' content representation. Edwards & Hardman (1989) asked 27 undergraduate students to answer a series of 20 factual questions about the city of Edinburgh using a 50-card hypertext. The subjects were assigned to one of three presentation formats: hierarchical (cards were linked through embedded keywords), index (card headings were listed in an alphabetic index), or mixed (hierarchy and index). Search time decreased with from first to last question and the decrease was faster in the hierarchical format than in the two other formats, suggesting that hierarchical organization resulted in more en route learning of the content. The representations drawn by subjects after using the hypertext varied as a function of presentation format. The hierarchical presentation resulted in more hierarchical layouts. The authors suggested that hierarchical presentation may help subjects build a "cognitive map" of the hypertext.

As pointed out earlier, novice users may not readily take advantage of unfamiliar navigation tools. Mohageg (1992) asked 64 adult paid volunteers to use a hypertext geographical database to answer a series of questions. The subjects were assigned to one of four presentation formats: linear, hierarchical, network or mixed (hierarchical + network). Subjects in the hierarchical and mixed conditions needed less time to locate the answers than subjects in the network condition. Also the subjects did not use all the features of the system. For instance, in the hierarchical format, 44% of subjects failed to use the home key to return to the superordinate card. Instead they backtracked their way to the top of hierarchy.

Finally, navigation tools may be profitable only for some tasks. Wright & Lickorish (1990) observed that the effectiveness of two navigation systems (index vs. paging) varied as a function of hypertext content and task requirements. For a book-like hypertext on house plants the index mode tended to be easier to use and preferred by subjects. For a table-like hypertext and for complex questions the paging mode was more efficient. The authors concluded that different navigation systems may fit different activities.

Egan et al. (1989) found that the Superbook system was more efficient than a paper version for questions that matched words in relevant sections of the book. The system was less efficient (with respect to search time) for questions whose words did not match any word in the book. The same result was obtained in a study by Mynatt et al. (1992). Subjects using an online encyclopedia with a string search tool were more efficient at answering text-based questions than subjects using a paper version of the encyclopedia.

In the two studies the authors were careful to provide detailed explanations and training to the subjects before completing the experimental task. Pretraining may have helped the subjects plan task management strategies based on system characteristics.

The empirical evidence confirms that searching complex information systems requires adequate information processing skills. First, the subject must be able to build up a relevant task representation. For instance, when asked a question, the subject must represent the information needed to answer that question (a single fact, a relation between facts, etc.). Second, the subject must manage the task of searching that information. Hypertext environments might facilitate information search to some extent, especially when target information cannot be easily located on the basis of structural cues (e.g., headings). However, using a hypertext system requires the user to adjust his or her existing strategies to the functioning of the proposed tools, or even to create new strategies. There is consistent evidence that repeated use of a system plays an important role in this process.

Managing Learning Tasks in Hypertext

In the studies presented earlier, the phrase "information search" often was used in the sense of "locating a piece of information." However, in many cases the target information is not precisely defined in advance. The user's purpose may be to explore the system so as to acquire a representation of its content (which may in turn enable the user to define more specific targets).

The task of selecting relevant pieces of information and building up coherent study sequence may become more difficult as the task requirements or the amount of information to be studied increases. It has been suggested that hypertext may facilitate this process by allowing students to sequence the document sections according to their needs, and by providing her with different representations or "views" of complex study materials (Spiro et al., 1991). Different representation or access structures (indexes, graphical browsers, embedded links, etc.) may help the reader select and navigate relevant portions of the materials, and build up a mental representation of the high-level relationships among topics.

However, it must be pointed out that this hypothesis has received little empirical support so far (Rouet, 1992). As Charney (in press) pointed out, predefined sequences play an important role in text comprehension processes. Readers tend to consider early information as important, and they rely on referential continuity to build up high level content representations.

Thus, there are really two issues involved in learning with hypertext: One is to find out whether hypertext can effectively support text-based learning (given subjects' regular learning strategies). Another one is to find out what specific skills subjects must use or acquire in order to become efficient hypertext users.

Interactions between learning task and presentation formats

In the previous section we have illustrated the diversity of information search tasks. Similarly, learning from text can take many different forms. It is an issue to find out for what type of learning activities hypertext is best suited.

First, it appears that hypertext may support only tasks where a thorough examination of the materials is necessary. Gordon,

Gustavel, Moore, and Hankey (1988) asked 24 university students to read either general interest texts with no learning requirements ("casual reading"), or technical texts with a comprehension requirement ("technical reading"). In each group, the subjects read two texts presented in linear format, or in hierarchical hypertext format. The study period was followed by a free recall task and comprehension questions.

In the casual reading situation, linear presentation resulted in better free recall of important information (no difference was found in the technical reading situation). Linear subjects answered a slightly larger proportion of questions than hypertext subjects. The "casual reading" subjects also found the hypertext format more effortfull and preferred linear text. Gordon et al. concluded that hypertext may not be well suited for reading situations that do not explicitly aim at learning.

A problem for hypertext subjects was that they did not have a good sense of the contents of the subordinate units. Some subjects reported that they didn't know "what was behind the door," that is, what information they would get when selecting a highlighted word. Consequently, the poor effectiveness of hypertext in this study may be partly owing to interface design problems. Moreover, in this study the task and text factors were confounded, which makes it hard to find out which was responsible for the observed results.

Dee-Lucas and Larkin (1995) hypothesized that hypertext presentation may facilitate the reviewing a document after reading it once by providing direct access to the relevant sections. They compared three presentation formats of a nine-unit expository document on electricity: linear, unstructured hypertext (with an alphabetic index), and structured hypertext (with a hierarchical content map).

In the first experiment, 45 college students read the document in one of the three formats with a general reading task (i.e., to be prepared for a comprehension test). The subjects first read the document in a fixed order and then were allowed to review it. Compared to linear presentation, the two hypertext formats resulted in a larger "breadth" or recall: The subjects recalled unit titles and ideas from more text units. Furthermore, the structured hypertext condition resulted in better memory for title locations in the index.

In the second experiment, 63 college students read the same text in one of the same three conditions. However they were given a specific reading task (i.e., be prepared to summarized the document). The subjects reviewed more units than in experiment 1, and the differences between situations were greatly reduced. The authors concluded that reading for specific purposes can override the benefits or drawbacks of different presentation formats.

These empirical studies suggest that the effectiveness of hypertext depends on three types of parameters: how the learning task is defined, how the document structure is represented, how the subjects are trained.

Presentation format can influence learners' strategies

Other studies have found that subjects can adjust to some extent their reading strategies to the characteristics of the presentation format. Black et al. (1992) found that the presentation format of online definitions influenced subjects' willingness to access those definitions. Rouet (1990) found that leaving previous selections unmarked increased subjects' disorientation, as evidenced by the looping rate (i.e., accidentally revisiting previously studied nodes).

The influence of presentation format on subjects' strategies may also depend on their study skills. Students are not equally able to cope with complex information processing tasks (Lodewijks, 1982; Wagner & Sternberg, 1987). Britt, Rouet, & Perfetti (in press) observed different strategies of college students when studying a set of documents presented as hypertext. Some students tended to follow the index presentation order, whereas other students selected the documents in a different order. Likewise, only some of the students were willing to review the documents after reading them once. Thus, all the students did not take equally advantage of the opportunities offered by hypertext presentation.

Conclusions

We have pointed out that using a hypertext poses two types of task related problems: task representation problems and task management problems. Having a good task representation means knowing how to obtain the best result with minimal time and effort given tasks requirements. Efficiently managing the task means knowing how to cope with the affordances and constraints of the environment (e.g., screen size, availability of search tools).

The empirical studies conducted so far have evidenced usability problems and some studies have suggested how these problems may be solved. In several cases, poor effectiveness of hypertext could be attributed to users' lack of training. Conversely, training may allow users to master advanced tools (McKnight et al., 1990; Mohageg, 1992; Rouet, 1994; Weyer, 1982). It is likely that training improves the integration of task management and search strategy.

An advanced search strategy may take into account the qualities and limitations of the information environment (see Wright's "environmental affordances," 1993).

A constant finding across many experiments is users need for overview structure information. Structured tables of contents seem to allow the acquisition of structured representations of the hypertext, which in turn facilitates navigation. Designers should be careful in deciding how to represent structure. There are indications that many different structural cues may interfere (Edwards & Hardman, 1988; Tripp & Roby, 1990).

Wright (1991, 1993) showed that interface characteristics (how information is made accessible to the user) strongly influence users strategies for a given task.

In order to provide an analytic approach to the problem of task management in hypertext, we have distinguished two task domains: information retrieval and general learning. Although such a broad distinction is a convenient starting point, we are aware that it may not be theoretically relevant. First, there is no clearcut distinction between the two task domains. Searching for high level information may be very close to learning about a subset of the hypertext domain. Second, learning tasks may involve exploring as well as information retrieval subtasks. Recent studies have suggested that users may access a hypertext database with very different purposes and strategies in the course of a single session (de Vries, 1993).

In fact, learning defines an outcome rather than a particular type of activity. Different interactions with information structures may result in different learning outcomes. However, mere exposition to hypertext is no guarantee of effective learning, even though the hypertext structure may have been designed after expert knowledge representations (Jonassen, 1993).

Finally, the studies presented in this section have used a variety of criteria to assess user performance: navigation patterns (e.g., number of cards opened, study time), memory for hypertext content or structure, and other off-line measures. In the absence of a thorough analysis of the task requirements, it is sometimes difficult to decide if those criteria are necessary and sufficient. This points out the need for a general definition of tasks in hypertext research.

FROM TASK ANALYSIS TO ACTIVITY MODELS

In this section we propose some elements to describe task and task management in hypertext. First we propose a three-layer framework to describe the users' task and activity. Then we examine in more detail the evaluation, selection, and processing mechanisms involved in using hypertext.

A General Framework for Hypertext-Supported Tasks

In the traditional human factors perspective, a task model is often an abstract description of what should be done and the most efficient way to do it, regardless of the specific characteristics of the user. In recent years there has been an increased consideration for the users' actual representation and execution of the task, and how to take them into account in system design (Anderson, 1990; Mahling & Croft, 1993; Wright, 1993).

A comprehensive model of information usage tasks should establish a set of relations between a rational model of the task, the user's cognitive representation and the user's activity. Based on these principles, Table 11-1 presents a general categorization framework for task analysis. Three possible layers of task analysis are considered: The rational task model layer, the cognitive task model layer, and the cognitive activity layer. At each layer three main entities are defined: a goal, a set of means, and an environment.

Rational task model

A rational task model describes the most efficient way to achieve a goal in a given environment. The cost of achieving a goal may be estimated as a function of time and effort. The rational model can be formulated independently from the characteristics of a particular cognitive system (e.g., knowledge, purposes, skill, strategies). In a

TABLE 11.1
A Three-Level Analysis of Hypertext Usage

	Goal	Means	Environment
Rational task model	Formal goal definition Optimal goal structure	Rational method Optimal plan + procedures	Information database Interface
Cognitive task model	Cognitive goal representation	Actual plan Cognitive strategy	System representation (application domain, tools, interface)
Cognitive activity	Action regulation	Action execution	Currently displayed information

rational model, the *goal* is defined formally, as the desired state to be reached. The *means* consist in an optimal plan and set of actions. The *environment* consists in an information database (e.g., a hyper-text database) and an interface that allows access and navigation in the database. There may be several rational models for a given task (Simon, 1991).

Cognitive task model

The cognitive task model also consists in a representation of the goal, a representation of the environment, and possibly adequate means. The cognitive task representation plays a role in organizing (planning, monitoring) the subject's activity. It also provides criteria to evaluate and terminate the activity (Chatillon & Baldy, 1994). The cognitive goal representation is influenced by a particular sub-ject's expertise and interpretation of the task. Consequently, there may be several cognitive representations of a given rational model. For instance, prequestions or reading directions may receive differ-ent interpretations across readers. Similarly, the cognitive plan or strategy is related to, but not isomorphic to the rational method. It may vary as a function of the subject's goal representation, and can be updated as a function of incoming information (see "cognitive activity"). The *environment* of the cognitive task model is the infor-mation system as represented (i.e., learned, mastered) by the user. System representation may vary as a function of subjects' domain expertise, previous experiences, and so on.

Cognitive Activity

Cognitive activity results from the application of a cognitive task model in a particular situation. At this level the goal is represented as a regulation mechanism. The cognitive strategy results in a se-ries of actions (e.g., selecting and reading hypertext units). The envi-ronment consists of the information currently displayed and the navigation tools currently available.

The relations between the three layers are as important as the entities defined at each level. When analyzing a particular task, discrepancies may be found between the rational task model, the cognitive task representation and the user's actual activity. For in-stance, the user's actions may depart from the initial plan as a function of unexpected information or en route feedback (Hayes-Roth and Hayes-Roth, 1979).

Within this general framework, we suggest that information us-age tasks may be defined according to at least two dimensions: the specificity of the goal (which may be more or less precise) and how the goal is implemented in the system (unique or multiple implementations). The combination of these two dimensions result in four typical information usage tasks.

1. Locating: corresponds to cases where the user has to deal with an explicit request about a unique piece of information.

2. Exploring: The user doesn't have an explicit request but he or she looks for a relevant (and unique) piece of information.

3. Searching: The user has an explicit query that corresponds to a set of units in the hypertext. The set of relevant units may be grouped or distributed.

4. Aggregating: The user doesn't have a precise query but thinks that he or she may find several relevant units in the hypertext.

A particular situation is "reaggregating" where the user has previously acquired information from the hypertext and is updating his or her knowledge through a further consultation. This type of task may increase the "functionality" of knowledge by showing the user how previous knowledge can be inserted in a new context (see Spiro et al.'s concept of crisscrossing, 1991).

During a session several of these strategies may be used in turn. For instance, exploration may become aggregating if it is extended to several areas of the hypertext.

Reading Hypertext: Evaluation, Selection, and Processing

In this section we examine the relations of task representation to the activity of using a hypertext. As shown in Figure 11-1 using a hypertext may be represented as a processing cycle including three main stages: Goal evaluation, topic selection, content processing. This view is compatible with other cognitive models of computer-supported tasks (Guthrie, 1988; Norman, 1984).

Goal evaluation

As suggested earlier, the subject's task model includes a goal representation that may be modified dynamically as a function of the subject's progress in the system. Goal evaluation is the process

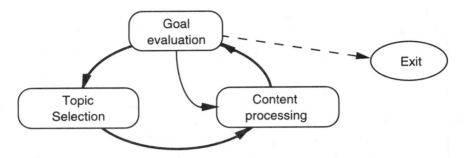

FIGURE 11-1. Global hypertext processing cycle.

by which the subject compares the current state of affairs with his or her goal representation. Goal evaluation first takes place at the very beginning of the activity: When confronted with a problem or question, the reader has first to determine whether a solution or answer can be produced, and what means should be devoted to that end. Then goal evaluation may take place each time the subject acquires information that may contribute to goal achievement.

Maintaining an active goal representation in working memory may interfere with the cognitive cost of selecting and locally processing hypertext units, because of the limited working memory capacity (Britton, Glynn, & Smith, 1985). Subjects may reduce this load by taking notes while selecting and studying documents. The issue of whether hypertext offers new means to support goal maintenance has hardly been studied so far. However, it has been showed that including a note taking facility in an electronic text environment does not result in any decrease in comprehension performance (van Oostendorp, in press). Moreover, there is evidence that providing an explicit representation of a required information search goal (e.g., a prequestion) facilitates the search process.

When searching for specific facts in a hypertext, inexperienced readers often need to reactivate their goal representation. In a series of experiments, Rouet (1991) used a prototype hypertext system to study 12- to 14-year-old students' information search strategies. The task consisted in searching a seven-unit hypertext to answer questions. The first version of the experimental system did not include any option to display the question after the search process had been initiated. This turned out to make the task very difficult for many subjects. Some subjects would typically initiate the selection process before they had a stable representation of the search goal. After a few selections, they would stop and ask the experimenter for another presentation of the question.

When question display was made available in a later version of system, it was actually used by one subject out of three on average. This percentage rose to 40% for the most complex type of questions.

Even under general study objectives, readers may need to check the problem statement while reading the hypertext. Rouet, Favart, Britt, & Perfetti (1994) used a simple hypertext system as a research tool to examine college students' learning from historical documents. College students were asked to use the system to study a series of historical controversies. Each controversy was stated in a pop-up frame that could be opened from any document page. Rouet et al. observed that on average 68% of the subjects opened the pop-up option at least once while studying the documents. Interestingly enough, question lookbacks did not occur at random locations in the study sequences. About 75% took place either at the beginning or at the end of the sequence. A possible interpretation is that subjects were monitoring their own study activity, recalling the question either to plan document selection, or to their understanding. This finding supports the hypothesis that task representation has both an organizing role and an evaluation role (see the preceding).

In the previous examples, the "goal" is a representation of the information to acquire. In other situations, the goal may be defined in terms of treatment to apply to the information. For instance, general knowledge acquisition or text summarization. In these cases goals are defined at a more abstract level, and the subject has to infer the nature of goal-relevant information. For instance, when given "general learning" directions, the subject may focus on general domain organization. In a summary task the subject may look for main points.

There is no empirical evidence that such procedural goals may be difficult to maintain in memory (e.g., that a subject may fail to remember that her task is to *summarize* the hypertext). However the influence of presentation format (e.g., linear text vs. hypertext) may vary as a function of task requirements (Dee-Lucas & Larkin, 1995).

Topic selection

Selection in hypertext is made through menus or embedded buttons. A user may have to make several selections before he or she reaches a passage of interest. In order to make selections the subject must have correct expectations about where the selectable items may lead. Not knowing where a link leads can be a serious problem when exploring a hypertext (Gordon et al., 1988). With paper documents the reader may not know where a specific information is located, but the whole document is visible and it can be manipulated with no restriction. It is a central issue to provide hypertext readers with such a sense of global visibility (Lai & Manber, 1991).

In some particular hypertext applications, knowing the destination of links is not a problem. For instance, Britt, Rouet, Georgi, & Perfetti (1994) used hypertext to present multiple history documents. The use of links was limited to connecting related documents using a "refers to" criterion, i.e., two documents were linked if one referred to the other. In this particular case the destination of links was unambiguous.

In any case, navigation requires a goal, a plan to achieve the goal, and the ability to evaluate intermediate results and to revise the plan accordingly. A correct representation of the hypertext organization (which may be partly analogous to a cognitive map; Dillon et al., 1993) is a powerful help for orientation and hence, navigation. Conversely, the analysis of subjects' navigation patterns may reflect cognitive orientation (Foss, 1989; Rouet, 1990). However, the observable part of navigation may not reflect accurately the subject's orientation. Some orientation processes may not result in explicit decisions (e.g., mentally reviewing the pages read), and some decisions may not be interpretable in terms of orientation.

Content processing

During the content processing stage the subject acquires a cognitive representation of the meaning of the selected passage. Understanding a passage of text involves a hierarchy of processing levels. At the local level, the reader has to comprehend the meaning of the text, that is, to extract its macrostructure and to integrate the content with her previous knowledge (van Dijk & Kintsch, 1983). At the global level, the reader has to evaluate whether the passage contributes to the goal, and to integrate the information with that of previously read information (i.e., the result of previous cycles, see Guthrie, 1988; Rouet, 1990). Goal evaluation may have an impact on the low level processing of a passage. For instance, the user may decide to stop reading a passage if a certain relevance threshold is not reached. Shifting between local and global levels of processing may result in some disruption of the comprehension process (Charney, in press).

In sum, when reading a hypertext, basic text processing is embedded in an elaborate cycle that includes selection of relevant passage and evaluation of goal achievement. Although such a high level management of the reading activity may be observed with conventional text, it is important to notice that in hypertext it is compulsory. There is no predefined organization that the reader might follow passively. Instead, the user has to play an active part in building up a coherent sequence of text units. This necessity of strategic control may explain the difficulties encountered by novice hypertext users.

The cycle of evaluation, selection, and processing proposed here does not account for all the specific cognitive operations that take place during hypertext usage. However, it provides a general cognitive interpretation for the concepts of task representation and task management introduced in the first part of this chapter.

GENERAL DISCUSSION AND CONCLUSIONS

In this chapter we have examined hypertext usage with an emphasis on the user's task representation and management. We have stressed the need for explicit models of information processing tasks and activities. In the studies conducted so far, task analysis was often incomplete, and there is a large heterogeneity in the authors' definition of "task." We have reviewed several approaches to the problem of analyzing information processing tasks involving hypertext. We have showed that tasks can be analyzed from the machine or the user point of view. The latter approach demonstrates that managing navigation in hypertext is a complex cognitive activity that may be responsible for some of the usability problems evidenced in the hypertext literature (disorientation, preference for traditional formats, familiarity effects, etc.).

Our task analysis suggests that these problems have to do with building task representation and task management strategies. This is only possible if users are able to identify goals, and maintain and evaluate them throughout the activity. Also, users must have at least some knowledge of the properties of the environment (e.g., top-level organization, search tools, etc.) in order to build up effective action plans.

How should hypertext be designed in order to provide effective support to information usage tasks? Although we cannot offer a general answer to this question, results from empirical studies as well as our general task analysis framework provide at least some hints.

First, information should be structured according to some categorization principle that the user can identify. The overall organization should be made explicit, if possible in a hierarchical way. However, the user should be able to visualize all the available layers at a glance. A clear, explicit top-level structure is what will allow users to make informed selections based on their goal representation.

Then the user should be able to mark, select, or extract the intermediate results of the search process. This can decrease the burden of remembering and integrating partial results from search cycles. Online notetaking facilities may contribute to that aim.

Finally, the need for training and practice should not be overlooked. It is unrealistic to expect a new, unfamiliar environment to generate immediate benefits. Instead, the users need to identify the type of information structures involved, to understand the functioning of navigation and orientation tools, and to build or adjust adequate management strategies.

Hypertext has potential for many applications in education, research, and business. However, the usability, effectiveness and desirability of hypertext applications in these areas will depend in a large part on how well system design integrates a correct model of the task as it is represented and managed by the user.

ACKNOWLEDGMENTS

The two authors contributed equally to the work presented here. We wish to thank Jocelyne Nanard for her useful comments on an earlier version of this chapter.

REFERENCES

Agosti, M. (1992). Hypertext and information retrieval. *Information Processing & Management, 29*(3), 283–285.

Anderson, J. R. (1990). *The adaptive character of thought.* Hillsdale, NJ: Erlbaum.

Bernstein, M. (1993). Enactment in information farming. *Hypertext'93 Proceedings,* Seattle. New York: ACM Press.

Biener, F., Guivarch, M., & Pinon, J.-M. (1990). Browsing in hyperdocument with the assistance of a neural network. In A. Rizk, N. Streitz, & J. André (Eds.), *Hypertext: Concepts, systems and applications.* Cambridge: Cambridge University Press.

Black, A., Wright, P., Black, D., & Norman, K. (1992). Consulting on-line dictionary information while reading. *Hypermedia, 4*(3), 145–169.

Britt, M. A., Rouet, J.-F., Georgi, M. C., & Perfetti, C. A. (1994). Learning from history texts: From causal analysis to argument models. In I. Beck, G. Leinhardt, & K. Stainton (Eds.), *Teaching and learning in history* (pp. 47–84). Hillsdale, NJ: Erlbaum.

Britt, M. A., Rouet, J.-F., & Perfetti, C. A. (in press). Using hypertext to study and reason about historical evidence. In J.-F. Rouet, J. J. Levonen, A. P. Dillon, & R. J. Spiro (Eds.), *Hypertext and cognition.* Hillsdale, NJ: Erlbaum.

Britton, B. K., Glynn, S. M., & Smith, J. W. (1985). Cognitive demands of processing expository text: A cognitive workbench model. In B. K. Britton, & J. B. Black (1985). *Understanding expository text.* Hillsdale, NJ: Erlbaum.

Charney, D. (in press). The impact of hypertext on processes of reading and writing. In S. J. Hilligoss, & C. L. Selfe (Eds.), *Literacy and computers.* New York: MLA.

Chatillon, J.-F., & Baldy, R. (1994). Performance motrice et developpement moteur, les liens au developpement cognitif. *Enfance, 2,* 299–319.

Conklin, J. (1987). Hypertext: an introduction and survey. *IEEE computer, 20*(9), 17–41.

Conklin, J., & Begeman, M. L. (1989). gIBIS: A tool for all reasons. *JASIS, 40*(3), 200–213.

Croft, W. B., & Turtle, H. R. (1993). Retrieval strategies for hypertext. *Information Processing & Management, 29*(3), 313–324.

Dee-Lucas, D., & Larkin, J. H. (1995). Learning from electronic texts: Effects of interactive overviews for information access. *Cognition & Instruction, 13*(3), 431–468.

De Vries, E. (1993). The role of case-based reasoning in architectural design: Stretching the problem space. *IJCAI'93 workshop on re-use of designs.* Chambéry (France), August 28–September 3.

Diaper, D. (1989). *Task analysis for human computer interaction.* Chichester: Ellis Horwood.

Dillon, A., McKnight, C., & Richardson, J. (1993). Space—the final chapter or why physical representations are not semantic intentions. In C. McKnight, A. Dillon, & J. Richardson (Eds.), *Hypertext: A psychological perspective.* Chichester: Ellis Horwood.

Edwards, D. M., & Hardman, L. (1989). "Lost in hyperspace": cognitive mapping and navigation in a hypertext environment. In R. Mc Aleese (Ed.), *Hypertext: Theory into practice.* Oxford: Intellect Ltd.

Egan, D. E., Remde, J. R., Gomez, L. M., Landauer, T. K., Eberhardt, J., & Lochbaum, C. C. (1989). Formative design-evaluation of SuperBook. *ACM Transactions on Information Systems, 7*(1), 30–57.

Foss, C. L. (1989). Detecting lost users: Empirical studies on browsing hypertext. *Rapport de recherche INRIA no 972.* Sophia-Antipolis.

Frei, H. P., & Stieger, D. (1992). Making use of hypertext links when retrieving information. In D. Lucarella, J. Nanard, M. Nanard, & P. Paolini (Eds.), *ECHT'92, Proceedings of the 4th ACM Conference on Hypertext.* New York: ACM Press.

Girill, T. R., & Luk, C. H. (1992). Hierarchical search support for hypertext on-line documentation. *International Journal of Man-Machine Studies, 36,* 571–585.

Gordon, S., Gustavel, J., Moore, J., & Hankey, J. (1988). The effect of hypertext on reader knowledge representation. *Proceedings of the 32nd Annual Meeting of the Human Factors Society*, Santa Monica, CA: Human Factors Society.

Gray, S. H., & Shasha, D. (1989). To link or not to link? Empirical guidance for the design of nonlinear text systems. *Behavior Research, Methods, Instruments and Computers, 21*, 326–333.

Guthrie, J. T. (1988). Locating information in documents: examination of a cognitive model. *Reading Research Quarterly, 23*(2), 178–199.

Hammouche, H. (1993). *De la modélisation des tâches à la spécification d'interfaces utilisateur.* INRIA Research Report # 1959, Rocquencourt, France.

Hayes-Roth, F., & Hayes-Roth, B. (1979). A cognitive model of planning. *Cognitive Science, 3*, 275–310.

Jonassen, D. H. (1993). Effects of semantically structured hypertext knowledge bases on users' knowledge structures. In C. McKnight, A. Dillon, & J. Richardson (Eds.), *Hypertext: a psychological perspective* (pp. 153–168). Chichester: Ellis Horwood.

Johnson, P. (1991). User interaction: a framework to relate tasks, users, and design. In H. J. Bullinger (Ed.), *HCI'91*. Stuttgart: Elsevier.

Johnson, P., & Nicolsi, E. (1992). Task-based user interface development tools. In D. Diaper (Ed.), *HCI-Interact'90* (pp. 383–387). Amsterdam: Elsevier.

Lai, P., & Manber, U. (1991). Flying through hypertext. *Hypertext'91 Proceedings, San Antonio.* New York: ACM Press.

Lelu, A., & François, C. (1992). Hypertext paradigm in the field of information retrieval: a neural approach. In D. Lucarella, J. Nanard, M. Nanard, & P. Paolini (Eds.), *ECHT'92, Proceedings of the 4th ACM Conference on Hypertext.* New York: ACM Press.

Lodewijks, H. (1982). Self-regulated versus teacher-provided sequencing of information in learning from text. In A. Flammer & W. Kintsch (Eds.), *Discourse processing* (pp. 509–520). Amsterdam: North-Holland.

Mahling, D. E., & Croft, W. B. (1993). Acquisition and support of goal-based tasks. *Knowledge Acquisition, 5*, 37–77.

Marchionini, G., & Shneiderman, B. (1988). Finding fact versus browsing knowledge in hypertext systems. *IEEE Computer, 20*, 70–80.

Marshall, C. C., Halasz, F. G., Roger, R. A., & Jansen, W. C. (1991). Aquanet: a hypertext tool to hold your knowledge in place. *Hypertext'91 Proceedings, San Antonio.* New York: ACM Press.

Marshall, C. C., & Rogers, R. A. (1992). Two years before the mist: experience with Aquanet. In D. Lucarella, J. Nanard, M. Nanard, & P. Paolini (Eds.), *ECHT'92, Proceedings of the 4th ACM Conference on Hypertext.* New York: ACM Press.

McKnight, C., Dillon, A., & Richardson, J. (1990). A comparison of linear and hypertext formats in information retrieval. In R. McAleese, & C. Green (Eds.), *Hypertext: state of the art* (pp. 10–19). Oxford: Intellect.

McKnight, C., Richardson, J., & Dillon, A. (1988). The construction of hypertext documents and databases. *The Electronic Library, 6*(5), 338–342.

Mohageg, M. H. (1992). The influence of hypertext linking structures on the efficiency of information retrieval. *Human Factors, 34*(3), 351–367.

Mynatt, B. T., Leventhal, L. M., Instone, K., Farhat, J., & Rohlman, D. S. (1992). Hypertext or book: Which is better for answering questions? *Proceedings of CHI'92* (pp. 19–25). New York: ACM Press.

Nanard, J., & Nanard, M. (1991). Using structured types to incorporate knowledge in hypertext. *Hypertext'91 proceedings.* New York: ACM Press.

Nielsen, J. (1990a). *Hypertext and hypermedia.* Boston, MA: Academic Press.

Norman, D. A. (1984). Stages and levels in man-machine interaction. *International Journal of Man-Machine Studies, 21*(4), 365–375.

Rouet, J.-F. (1990). Interactive text processing in inexperienced (hyper-) readers. In A. Rizk, N. Streitz, & J. André (Eds.), *Hypertext: Concepts, systems and applications, Proceedings of the European Conference on Hypertext.* Cambridge, UK: Cambridge University Press.

Rouet, J.-F. (1991). *Compréhension de textes didactiques par des lecteurs inexpérimentés dans des situations d'interaction sujet-ordinateur* (comprehension of computer-presented text by inexperienced readers). Unpublished doctoral dissertation, University of Poitiers (France), Department of Psychology.

Rouet, J.-F. (1992). Cognitive processing of hyperdocuments: when does nonlinearity help? In D. Lucarella, J. Nanard, M. Nanard, & P. Paolini (Eds.), *ECHT'92, Proceedings of the 4th ACM Conference on Hypertext, Milano.* New York: ACM Press.

Rouet, J.-F. (1994). Question answering and learning with hypertext. In R. Lewis, & P. Mendelsohn (Eds.), *Proceedings of IFIP WG3.3 workshop: Lessons from learning* (pp. 39–52). Amsterdam: North-Holland.

Rouet, J.-F., Favart, M., Britt, M. A., & Perfetti, C. A. (1994). *Representation and use of multiple documents by novice and expert history students.* Paper submitted for publication.

Salton, G., & McGill, M. J. (1983). *Introduction to modern information retrieval.* New York: McGraw-Hill.

Schuler, W., & Smith, J. (1990). Author's Argumentation Assistant (AAA): A hypertext-based authoring tool for argumentative texts. In A. Rizk, N. Streitz, & J. André (Eds.), *Hypertext: Concepts, systems and applications, Proceedings of the European Conference on Hypertext, Versailles.* Cambridge: Cambridge University Press.

Simon, H. A. (1991). Cognitive architectures and rational analysis: comment. In K. van Lehn (Ed.), *Architectures for intelligence.* Hillsdale, NJ: Erlbaum.

Simpson, A., & McKnight, C. (1990). Navigation in hypertext: Structural cues and mental maps. In R. McAleese, & C. Green (Eds.), *Hypertext: state of the art* (pp. 74–83). Oxford, UK: Intellect.

Spiro, R. J., Feltovitch, P. J., Jacobson, M. J., & Coulson, R. J. (1991). Cognitive flexibility, constructivism and hypertext: Random access instruction for advanced knowledge acquisition in ill-structured domains. *Educational Technology, 31*(5), 24–33.

Stotts, P. D., & Furuta, R. (1991). Dynamic adaptation of hypertext structure. *Hypertext'91 proceedings.* New York: ACM Press.

Streitz, N. A., Hannemann, J., & Thüring, M. (1989). From ideas and arguments to hyperdocuments: travelling through activity spaces. *Hypertext'89 proceedings.* New York: ACM Press.

Thompson, R. H., & Croft, W. B. (1989). Support for browsing in an intelligent text retrieval system. *International Journal of Man-Machine Studies, 30,* 639–668.

Tombaugh, J., Lickorish, A., & Wright, P. (1987). Multi-window displays for readers of lengthy texts. *International Journal of Man-machine Studies, 26,* 597–615.

Tripp, S. D., & Roby, W. (1990). Orientation and disorientation in a hypertext lexicon. *Journal of Computer-based Instruction, 17*(4), 120–124.

van Dijk, T. A. (1980). *Macrostructures.* Hillsdale, NJ: Erlbaum.

van Dijk, T. A., & Kintsch, W. (1983). *Strategies of discourse comprehension.* Hillsdale, NJ: Erlbaum.

van Oostendorp, H. (in press). Studying and annotating electronic text. In J.-F. Rouet, J. J. Levonen, A. P. Dillon, & R. J. Spiro (Eds.), *Hypertext and cognition.* Hillsdale, NJ: Erlbaum.

van Rijsbergen, K., & Agosti, M. (1992). Editorial—The context of information retrieval. *The Computer Journal, 35*(3), 193.

Wagner, R. K., & Sternberg, R. J. (1987). Executive control in reading comprehension. In B. K. Britton, & S. M. Glynn (Eds.), *Executive control processes in reading* (pp. 1–22). Hillsdale, NJ: Erlbaum.

Wang, X. H., & Liebscher, P. (1988). Information seeking in hypertext. Effects of physical format and search strategy. *Proceedings of the ASIS annual meeting, 25,* 200–204.

Weyer, S. A. (1982). The design of a dynamic book for information search. *International Journal of Man-Machine Studies, 17,* 87–107.

Wright, P. (1990). Hypertext as an interface for learners: some human factors issues. In D. H. Jonassen, & H. Mandl (Eds.), *Designing hypermedia for learning, Proceedings of the NATO advanced research workshop.* Heidelberg: Springer Verlag.

Wright, P. (1991). Cognitive overheads and prostheses: some issues in evaluating hypertexts. *Hypertext'91 proceedings.* New York: ACM Press.

Wright, P. (1993). To jump or not to jump: Strategy selection while reading electronic texts. In C. McKnight, A. Dillon, & J. Richardson (Eds.), *Hypertext: a psychological perspective* (pp. 137–152). Chichester: Ellis Horwood.

Wright, P., & Lickorish, A. (1990). An empirical comparison of two navigation systems for two hypertexts. In R. McAleese & C. Green (Eds.), *Hypertext: state of the art.* Oxford: Intellect.

12

Lessons Learned from Redesigning Hypertext User Interfaces

Keith Instone
Barbee Teasley
Laura Leventhal

Bowling Green State University,
Bowling Green, OH

INTRODUCTION

Designing effective and usable hypertext systems is difficult. One way to help designers create better hypermedia systems is to use the process of iterative design and redesign. This chapter describes several hypermedia user interfaces that were iteratively designed and presents some of the lessons learned from these processes. Emphasis is on empirical evaluations of these redesigns and how the empirical evidence was fed back into the design process.

HYPERTEXT USABILITY

Although increased attention is being paid to the usability of all types of software, designing usable hypertext presents a special challenge. Hypertext, simply defined, is text presented on a computer in such a way that certain portions of the text or materials are active (i.e., hyper), and can be used to access related text (called nodes) via a connection (link) between the two elements. In its more elaborate forms, hypertext can include graphics, sounds, pictures, animation, or videos, portions of which may be hyper. Thus, the information in a hypertext can be accessed in numerous ways, including sequential or nonsequential orders. This is in contrast to more traditional media, such as textbooks, which are most typically designed to be used linearly. Developing a good hypertext interface is challenging, since the hypertext exploration is by nature somewhat freeform and the varieties and richness of information is likely to be extensive. The twin goals of hypertext authors are to enable and empower users to access the information in ways that are creative, useful, and possibly unique to them, although not creating a navigation quagmire.

In the early days of hypertext, developing a system that simply "worked" was a great accomplishment, largely because of the tremendous problems of organizing the information and providing navigation. For example, others have pointed out that data and presentation in hypertext are tightly coupled (Baird, 1990; Shneiderman et al., 1991). If the underlying document structure is meaningless or garbled, then even the best interface cannot create usability. Design guidelines have been proposed that recognize the importance of document structure and suggest that design begin with the semantic classification of underlying objects, and move on through identifying the metaphor, all user interaction states, error conditions, and finally the screen layout (Balasubramanian & Turoff, 1995).

Now, however, we are ready to demand more in terms of usability from hypertext than just a well-structured system. As Eason has pointed out, there are at least three tightly interrelated aspects of software usability: the system itself, the task the user is attempting to perform, and characteristics of the user (Eason, 1984). One can simply not assess usability of any software by looking only at the software. Consider, for example, a study done by Nielsen that compared 92 different benchmark measurements of usability in hypertext (Nielsen, 1989). Using meta-analysis, he found that only 17 of the factors analyzed had relatively large effects. Among the top 10 effects, five were related to individual differences, and two were related to task factors. Only three were directly related to the system. Thus, reviews of hypertext systems that focus on number of nodes, number or configuration of links, or the presence of clever features are not adequate.

What are some approaches that can be used to understanding what factors and combination of factors impact hypertext usability? Broadly, we see three primary approaches being used. First, there are empirical and laboratory studies of specific usability issues and tools. These are the sorts of studies summarized in meta-analyses (Nielsen, 1989; Chen & Rada, submitted). For example, Hammond and Allinson looked at the effect of the user's task (guided tour, exploratory, or directed task) on their choice of navigation mechanism (Hammond & Allinson, 1989). Others have compared learning of information that was presented in textual form, caption form, or hypertext form, off of a screen (Instone et al., 1993a). The strategy of focusing evaluation on a feature or small number of features is an effective approach to developing design guidelines. It also provides useful insights into users' cognitive processes.

A second approach is to compare entire hypertext systems with each other or against a standard, such as a paper book. Examples include comparisons of: SuperBook to paper books (Egan et al., 1989); TIES, HyperCard, word processor, and paper (McKnight et al., 1990); and Emacs-Info, Guide, HyperTies, and MaxiBook (Rada & Murphy, 1992). This second approach is useful because it explores the interplay of many factors and how they affect various measures of usability while using a fully functional hypertext document. (For an extensive review of work using both of these approaches, see Nielsen, 1993a.)

The third approach to understanding usability is to examine cases in which a hypertext system has been redesigned to improve usability. This approach provides insights not only into critical design features, but also into the activities that can be used fruitfully in the redesign process. Furthermore, such cases provide insights into which kinds of changes have the greatest payoff and which have lesser payoff.

When redesign is undertaken, developers are employing the technique of *iterative design.* Iterative design has been used successfully as a software engineering approach, and can be readily incorporated into usability engineering (Nielsen, 1993c). Basically, iterative design involves the creation of an initial version of the product (a user interface, in the case of usability engineering), followed by evaluation of the product. The initial design might be a storyboard description, a functioning prototype or a version 0 of the software (an actual implementation). In any case, based on the tests and evaluation of the product, a new version is produced and tested. Particularly when the redesigned software is being evaluated for usability, the early versions may be created without worrying about efficiency and optimization constraints. The goal of iterative design is to identify problems early enough that they can be solved fairly early in the design process.

In some cases, the new design may not solve the noted usability problems. In other cases, the new design may introduce new problems. Regardless of the source of the problem, redesign decisions need to be made on the basis of cost versus benefit. Although some problems, such a menu wording, might be changed easily, other problems may require a lot more work. The severity of the problem needs to be taken into account in deciding whether its remedy is worth the cost. Typically, the redesign process is controlled in the sense that each iteration of the design is justified by expected improvements in usability. The evaluation process need not always involve actual users, but can be done through heuristic analysis done with usability experts or expert users (Nielsen & Mack, 1994). (See Waterworth & Chignell, 1989, for an alternative taxonomy of approaches to understanding usability in hypertext.)

Beside being an effective technique for designing hypertext systems, we believe that the lessons learned from redesign provide a third source of insights and understanding in hypertext. Although the lessons clearly are more anecdotal than empirical, they can also provide clues and guidelines of general characteristics or usable and unusable systems.

In this chapter, we have pulled together a number of cases where redesign has been used in enhancing the usability of hypertext systems, and the reasoning and historical data behind the redesign have been documented. In all cases, the design of the document structure, taxonomy of links, and content of nodes are not issues. Our goal in bringing these studies together is to identify the kind of lessons that really are learnable from redesign as well as some insights into the circumstances where redesign is effective. First we will describe each of the cases, then we will discuss the overall "lessons learned" from these redesign case studies.

CASE 1: COMPUTER SCIENCES ELECTRONIC MAGAZINE

The Computer Sciences Electronic Magazine (CSEM) is an interactive multimedia application (Koons et al., 1992) containing articles about IBM Research Lab projects in Computer Science, designed for use by IBM employees. As an electronic magazine, its contents include text, video, and still pictures and uses metaphors from print, video, and computing. Standard magazine terminology such as *cover, article,* and *sidebar* are used. The project has some features in common with information kiosks, although as a magazine, it tends to focus on a more restricted audience, incorporates more text, and involves longer interactions.

The original design of CSEM was based on assumptions from previous applications. Thus, the first design incorporated features that were designed to satisfy both active users, who like to take charge of navigating, and passive users, who wish to view the magazine with minimal interactions. The document structure included a cover, articles (which were subdivided into topics), and departments. Early designs were testing in laboratory and field situations, using IBM employees and, more informally, conference attendees. The general findings were that the system was difficult to use when it broke from the magazine or VCR metaphors.

The redesigned CSEM looked more like a magazine, acted more like a VCR, and had a simpler graphic design. For example, a table of contents, index, glossary, and page numbers were added to make it more like a magazine. The standard buttons from a VCR, such as play, reverse, and fast forward, were added to control the video segments. To simplify the screens, larger buttons and fonts were used and fewer choices were provided on each page.

CASE 2: CHI '89 INFOBOOTH

The CHI '89 InfoBooth was an interactive electronic information kiosk used at the CHI '89 conference. The InfoBooth was used to provide information about the conference program, the host city, and the attendees (Salomon, 1990a). A visually oriented, iterative methodology was used to design the InfoBooth (Salomon, 1990b). The design process had three distinct phases: initial design specification, storytelling prototype, and functional prototype. Rather than creating written specifications, visual prototypes were prominently used.

The initial design specification involved a series of rough screen drawings to demonstrate possible functionality and screen organization. Next, "slide shows" (screen designs with limited functionality) were presented to people outside the project, to get feedback about their expectations from different portions of the screen. The third stage involved adding some of the underlying functionality, having subjects perform specific tasks, and then interviewing them. The types of problems that were revealed when testing functional

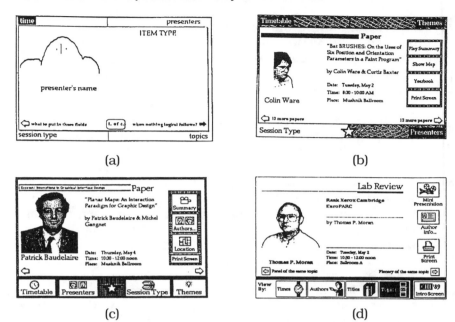

FIGURE 12-1. Four versions of the "presentation information" screen. (a) the initial design specification phase. (b) the storytelling prototype phase. (c) the functional prototype phase. (d) the final design.

prototypes involved ways of drawing the user's attention to useful tools, and proper labeling or icons for tools and features (see Figure 12-1).

One problem uncovered in the functional prototyping stage was the "Yearbook Navigation Problem." The Yearbook component of the InfoBooth had pictures of many of the attendees, along with addresses, hotel information, and links to presentations, if any, by each person. To access the information, there was an alphabetic array of buttons that, when clicked, took the user to the first person for a particular letter. There was also an Index button above the alphabet array that, alternatively, provided a list of people for the chosen letter. Clicking on a name in the Index display for a letter took you directly to that person. When viewing a particular person, whether reached via the alphabet array directly, or via an Index list, the user could go to the next or previous person (alphabetically).

For the functional prototype version, the alphabetic buttons looked like tabs and the Index button stood out. Users did not have trouble navigating within the Yearbook. But in the final version,

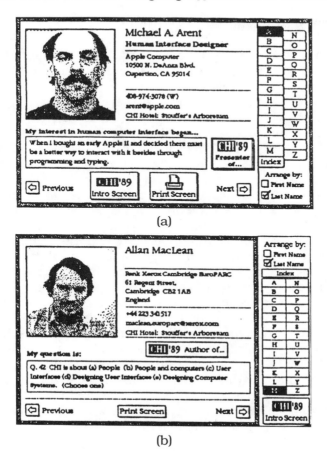

(a)

(b)

FIGURE 12-2. Two versions of the Yearbook screen. In the functional prototype version (a), the Index tab stands out. In the final version (b), the Index button was much harder to find.

which was redesigned to fix other problems, the alphabetic buttons no longer looked like tabs and the Index button did not stand out (see Figure 12-2). Trace data from users at the conference, as well as results from a questionnaire, showed that users had trouble finding the Index button and expected to get an index for a letter (instead of the first person under that letter) when selecting a letter from the alphabet array.

This example shows that "visual changes need to be retested" (Salomon, 1990b).

CHI InfoBooth Revisited

A follow-up study was done to explore issues related to the "missing" index button in the Attendee Yearbook component (Leventhal et al., 1994a). This study was designed to look at how changing functionality and interaction sequencing can affect usability, without changing any visual aspects.

In the original InfoBooth design, clicking on a letter from the Alphabet palette on the Cover Card took the user to the first Person card for that letter. The same effect occurred even if a Person already was displayed. If the user did discover the Index button and click it, they would be placed in the Index Mode. When in the Index Mode, the index listing of about 20 people for the selected letter appeared. Selecting a different letter from the Alphabet palette then took the user to another Index card. We call this a "mixed" search mode because sometimes clicking on a letter on the Alphabet palette would result in transition to an Index card (if the system was in the Index Mode) and other times (if the Index button had not been pressed) the user would transition to a Person card.

Two new navigation methods were programmed into the existing InfoBooth for the purposes of the study (see Figure 12-3). The second method was called the "Person" method, because a click on the Alphabet palette always would take the user to the first person in that letter. The third method was called the "Index" method, because an Index card always appeared. Note that these last two conditions are modeless, as regards the Index button and its effect on the operation of the Alphabet palette.

For the study, each user was asked to answer 10 questions. The questions varied in difficulty and types of answers required. Thirty subjects, selected to be similar in computer familiarity to CHI attendees, used the Yearbook to answer the 10 questions. Each got one of the three navigation methods (a between-subjects design) and the subjects within a group received a different, random ordering of the questions. The accuracy of the answers, time to answer the questions, and the number of cards visited were recorded.

The results showed no significant difference among the three navigation methods on accuracy or time (see Table 12-1). However, for the 20 subjects not in the Index method group, the data were examined to see how well they did at finding and using the Index button (the Index button was deleted in the Index mode, since it was not needed). Nine of these 20 subjects did find the Index button. The mean times before and after finding the Index button were analyzed for these subjects, and a significant difference was found (see Table

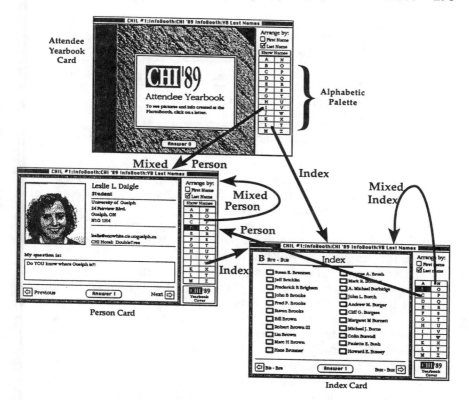

FIGURE 12-3. A state-transition diagram of the three navigation modes in the fol-low-up InfoBooth experiment. The key difference between the modes is where the user went when selecting a letter from the Alphabetic Palette. In Index mode, users always went to an Index Card. In Person Mode, users always went to a person card (and had to click on the "Show Names" button to get to an Index Card). In Mixed Mode (used in the original InfoBooth), users would jump to another Index Card when already looking at an Index Card; otherwise, users went to the first Person Card for that letter.

TABLE 12.1
Time and Number of Cards Visited
for Each of the Three Navigation Modes*

	Time (seconds)	Cards Visited
Person	101.3	22.2
Mixed	122.8	24.6
Index	91.3	5.8

*Time was not significant; cards visited was.

TABLE 12.2
Numbers Showing the Effect of Finding the "Index"
Button, for the Person and Mixed Mode Groups*

	Time (seconds)	Cards Visited
Before finding Index	111.6	27.2
After finding Index	47.1	4.8

*The Index mode group did not have an Index button. Both before and after differences are highly significant.

12-2). This finding points out how crucial gaining access to the Indexes is. We speculate that this finding is due to users' typical preference for and better performance with hierarchical organizations, compared to alternative topologies in hypertext (Leventhal et al., 1994b; Simpson & McKnight, 1990).

For the number of cards visited, there was an overall significant difference among methods (see Table 12-1). Planned comparisons showed that the difference between the Mixed and Person methods was not significant. However, the Mixed and Person methods combined were significantly higher than the Index group scores. Parallel to the results based on time, subjects in the Person and Mixed groups showed improved performance and visited significantly fewer cards after they found the Index button. These findings point out the detrimental effect of having a moded activity that is not clearly signaled to the user. The Index method, which was not moded, resulted in overall better performance than either of the other, moded, methods. However, if and when the users in the moded groups discovered and started correctly using the index mode, performance did improve.

Although the original redesigns of InfoBooth focused on the visual layout of the interface, this follow-up study focused on redesigning the navigation style. Visually, all three methods used in this study were the same. The study showed, however, the pitfalls of using a moded style of navigation, particularly when the mechanism for changing the mode was not prominent to the users, nor was the change in mode signaled to the user by anything other than a change in functionality (there were no visual cues that the mode had changed). In addition, the original version erred in making the hierarchical (indexed) mode of navigation the secondary mode, and a linear mode the default. This is a problem because hierarchical navigation appears to be understood easily and utilized by users of hypertext. Although linear navigation is also understandable, it can be frustrating and inefficient.

CASE 3: GLASGOW ONLINE

Glasgow Online is an information kiosk for tourists, and thus represents a hypertext system designed for the general public. Early, incomplete, versions were subjected to usability testing and these observations led to refinements of the design (Hardman, 1989).

One change made to Glasgow Online's user interface is shown in Figure 12-4. The ARRANGE BY button of Figure 12-4a is really the heading for the three buttons next to it. Early Glasgow Online users were confused because it looked like an ordinary button that you could click on. Figure 12-5b shows how ARRANGE BY was made to look different, and how it was used to group the other buttons together.

Early Glasgow Online users also had some difficulty understanding the purpose of the EXIT button. It was changed to CONTENT and moved to the left. The NEXT buttons that were in that corner of the screen were removed because they duplicated functionality and led to confusion among the users.

Another problem with having an inactive area of the screen look like a button was fixed in Figure 12-5. The TRAVEL DESTINATIONS heading was no longer shaded so that users would recognize it more as a heading and not as a hot spot. Figure 12-5 also shows the change to make on-screen help more visible by placing it in double rectangles. Finally, the RAIL button was highlighted, to follow the conventions to indicate which section the user is in (much like why the A tab is highlighted in Figure 12-5). This helps the user understand where they are within the hypertext document.

Overall, the ongoing evaluation of Glasgow Online as it was being developed resulted in numerous changes to the interface. Hardman points out that the structure of the information in the hypertext was hierarchical and correctly designed to support the readers' tasks. However, the presentation of the information was critical to the users' success. This was especially true in this instance of an information kiosk, where users receive no training prior to using the system and yet need to be instantly successful. She also points out that many of the problems were observed for only a small portion of the users, yet they were serious problems nonetheless. If even 10 percent of users are hindered by a feature of a design, that is still 10

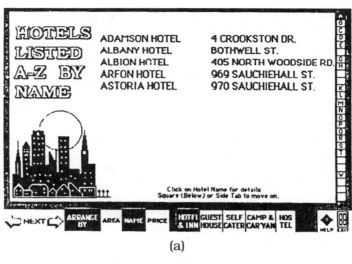

(a)

(b)

FIGURE 12-4. Two versions of the HOTEL AND INNS screen from Glasgow Online. The changes made in (b) focused on the buttons at the bottom. The EXIT button on the lower right became the CONTENTS button on the lower left. The appearance of the ARRANGE BY menu title was changed so that it did not look like a button anymore.

percent that have an unsatisfactory experience with the hypertext. Perhaps in a system designed for prolonged use, this would be acceptable, and users could readily learn to deal with the problem. But for an information kiosk, such rates are unacceptable.

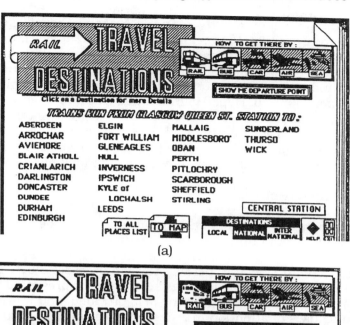

(a)

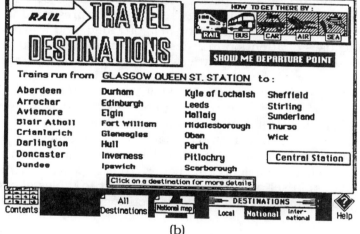

(b)

FIGURE 12-5. Original (a) and redesigned (b) screens listing possible destinations from Queen Street Station, from Glasgow Online. The buttons at the bottom were changed much like in Figure 12-4. Here, however, the layout of the information was also altered to make it easier to find the screen title and the help, among other things.

CASE 4: HYPERHOLMES I AND II

HyperHolmes is an example of a hypertext system that was evaluated differently than the preceding examples during the redesign process. Instead of doing standard usability testing to find problems and pinpoint strengths of the design, actual controlled experiments were done (Instone et al., 1993b). HyperHolmes I, the original version of the system, was compared with the book version of the information (Leventhal et al., 1993). Based on the results of this study and observation of users, the system was redesigned, creating HyperHolmes II. HyperHolmes II was also subjected to the same experimental procedure, in order to empirically verify that the new interface was in fact an improvement. By controlling the redesign process a bit more, we were able to draw more specific conclusions and were able to make design recommendations more confidently.

About HyperHolmes

HyperHolmes is a hypertext encyclopedia about the fictional character, Sherlock Holmes. It contains entries about the various characters, places, and themes from the Holmes' detective stories by Sir Arthur Conan Doyle. Hypertext navigation is done by clicking on capitalized words embedded in the entries, or presented in one of the overviews. A search mechanism is provided, and was one of the main focuses of attention in redesigning the system. HyperHolmes specifically includes text entries, map entries, overview and summary cards, and a starting node, called the "Holme card."

Version I provided a way to look both at a list of other nodes that point to the current screen (incoming links) and at a list of the outgoing links (hot spots), whereas version II provided only the first function. In both versions, an alphabet slide bar shows the relative position of the current node within the entire document and can be used to navigate to neighboring nodes. To help provide hierarchical organization, a set of overview cards, similar to tables of contents, were provided, with each overview focusing on a particular topic, such as London or personal facts about Holmes. Detailed maps of London and other geographical entities are provided and have clearly marked "hot spots" that take the reader to other parts of the hypertext.

A snapshot of HyperHolmes I is shown in Figure 12-6. This figure shows how the system might look after the user had performed a search and asked to see a list of incoming links. The search window has moved to the back, whereas the incoming links list lays on top of the main window, which presents an entry about Craniology. Perhaps the most dominant feature is the overlapping windows. Contrast this figure with Figure 12-7, which shows the redesigned version, HyperHolmes II. The main HyperHolmes window was expanded and the overlapping windows were replaced with tiled ones. This change allows the user to have the search tool with its list of

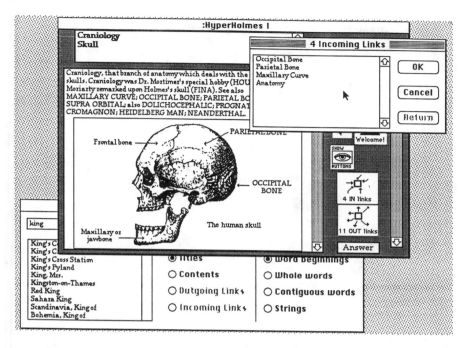

FIGURE 12-6. HyperHolmes I has separate windows for the searching and following incoming and outgoing links.

hits and the incoming link list constantly present on the screen. Thus, the user was automatically given the list of incoming links, and did not have to remember the meaning of the tool icon or make the effort to activate the function. Furthermore, users were constantly reminded of the search tool by its presence in the lower right corner. The Outgoing Links interface was removed and the search criteria were simplified. A new, global button was added to take user directly to the Overview Menu card, thus circumventing the need to go first to the Holme card, and then to the overviews. The information about Holmes on the left was left unchanged in size and content. The alphabetic slide bar was rotated and moved to the lower left side to better simulate the left-to-right action associated with page turning.

About the Experiments

The task used to evaluate both versions of HyperHolmes and to compare HyperHolmes to the paper version of the encyclopedia involved giving subjects a series of questions to answer. Questions

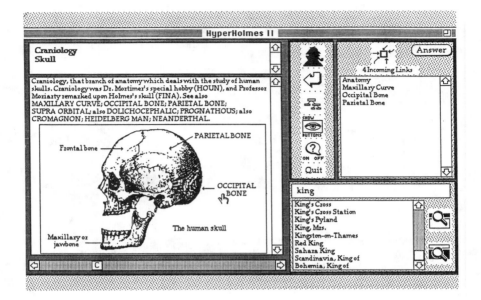

FIGURE 12-7. HyperHolmes II uses only one main window, with searching moved to the bottom right corner, incoming links moved to the upper right, and outgoing links removed. Other changes include removing some search choices and adding an Overviews button.

varied in the type and amount of information needed to answer them. For example, some questions could be found easily by searching through the node titles for a key word taken from the question. Other questions involved finding a relevant graphic (map) and following a link to some text for additional information. Both accuracy and speed in answering the questions were assessed.

The results showed that both speed and accuracy were significantly better for HyperHolmes II than HyperHolmes I (see Table 12-3), and much better than for the book (paper) form. Hyper-

TABLE 12.3
Overall Results from Testing HyperHolmes I
and II, and in Comparison to the Book Form*

	Accuracy	Speed (seconds)
HyperHolmes I	1.38	236
HyperHolmes II	1.73	178
Book	1.23	201

*Accuracy scores ranged from zero to two.

Holmes II users also were more efficient in their navigation patterns (e.g., visited fewer nodes to answer the same questions) and significantly fewer reported that they became "lost" while using the system. Thus, it appears that the redesigned HyperHolmes indeed was better. These results suggest that the complexity of a system, and hence the cognitive effort needed to use it, can be reduced by eliminating overlapping windows, reducing the number of tools available, or by simplifying the hierarchical structure of the document.

CASE 4: SUPERBOOK

SuperBook is another example of a hypertext system that was tested empirically repeatedly during its many iterations (Egan et al., 1989, 1991; Landauer et al., 1993). SuperBook is a text browser, which means it supports rapid searching and browsing of machine-readable text. It is not exactly a hypertext system, since it is not intended for an author to create links and nodes. From a user's point of view, however, it acts like a hypertext system, because pieces of text are (dynamically) linked to other parts of the document.

There are four main windows of SuperBook. The title window has buttons across the top representing tools. The dynamic Table of Contents window is on the left. The right window contains the formatted text (content) of the document. The lower window is the search mechanism.

A frequently used way to find information in SuperBook is to first enter in a search term or terms. The user is given feedback on the number of paragraphs containing hits and the results of the search are posted to the table of contents, with numbers next to each section to indicate the number of hits by chapter, section, and subheading. Clicking on an asterisk next to a heading causes it to be expanded, showing the subsections and the hits for each of them. Selecting a heading causes that portion of the text to be displayed in the right window. Bold text is used to emphasize the words that match the search criteria. Users can also browse with SuperBook by exploring the table of contents, or by opening up the entire book in the content windows and scrolling.

Version 0 of SuperBook was evaluated empirically and compared for performance using a paper version of the same information. The results suggested improvements that could be made to the user interface. From the usage data, it became clear that the most effective strategy was to start with a search term, look through the table of contents based on the resulting hits, and then select a page to view. Thus, for Version 1, this process was streamlined and visually emphasized. In addition, text was highlighted better in Version 1. Along with a basic system improvement in search speed, Version 1 users out-performed Version 0 users.

In the next iteration the system had the constraint of having to work on a smaller, personal computer-sized screen. In order to avoid having a degradation of usability for this new version owing to the smaller screen, it was carefully redesigned. This version was named MiteyBook and added the features of automatic posting of search hits to the table of contents, and automatic loading of the text page to the next section containing a hit. The windows were laid out to encourage a search strategy involving a word look-up, followed by use of the table of contents, followed by examination of the text page containing the first hit. Evaluation of MiteyBook use showed even better performance than the first two versions.

WHAT CAN REDESIGN TEACH US ABOUT HYPERTEXT USABILITY?

The preceding sections have described how iterative design was used in the development of several different hypertext systems. In all cases, feedback and data gathered from users of early versions of the hypertexts were used to guide redesign of the system. We believe that these studies provide a wealth of insights into what to do and what not to do when designing hypertexts, and hence provide insights about hypertext usability. The before-and-after comparisons provide at least suggestive evidence, if not actual empirical, statistically tested support, for a variety of design guidelines. For example, Hardman illustrates guidelines that summarize her findings from Glasgow Online (Hardman, 1989). These include

- Menu headings should be visually distinct from menu items.
- Information should be arranged to support intended usage of hypertext.
- Readers should be able to tell which screen items are buttons.
- Readers often return to the main contents screen for reorientation.

As we have pointed out, redesign can help pinpoint issues and concerns for hypertext usability, much like empirical studies of features and wholesale comparisons of alternative media. Redesign is costly, however, in terms of both development resources and time. One important question is whether redesign as an approach is an efficient way of learning about hypertext usability. In the studies that we summarized, the developers had opportunities to learn about usability in the specific context of their systems. How successful were the redesign efforts that we reported on? In addition, what are the cost–benefit tradeoffs of evaluation and redesign compared to the increase in usability that results? Several of these case studies illustrate more precisely the extent of improvement that can be garnered through redesign efforts. Table 12-4 shows the percent of improvement in various usability metrics that were obtained in experimental studies that compared earlier and later versions of the designs. These numbers are comparable to the 38 percent improvement per iteration reported by Nielsen (1993b) and the 12 percent by Bailey (1993).

Unfortunately, in the case of the Computer Science Electronic Magazine and Glasgow Online, no hard data is provided that allows us to determine the actual extent of improvement in overall usability obtained by redesigning.

The redesigned interfaces also give better performance with respect to the baseline of paper. Figure 12-8 shows the relative (to paper versions of the documents) improvements of the redesigned HyperHolmes and SuperBook interfaces. Notice that in terms of speed, early versions were actually slower than paper, but the improved user interfaces were faster than the benchmark.

We conclude, then, that redesign, as well as empirical studies or media comparisons, can provide valuable information about hypertext usability. Particularly when redesigned hypertext systems lead to improvements in usage patterns, the changes of the redesign point to specific hypertext features that may influence usability.

We further conclude that redesign, although powerful, is never easy. There are no automated formulas to guarantee that redesigns

TABLE 12.4
Percent Improvement in Usability Metrics
Obtained through Redesign

	Speed	Accuracy
InfoBooth Mixed vs. Index	35	—
HyperHolmes I vs. II	25	25
SuperBook 0 vs. 2	46	9

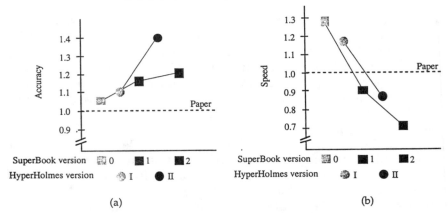

FIGURE 12-8. Results of evaluating successive versions of SuperBook and Hyper-Holmes. All scores are standardized with respect to performance with the paper versions of the documents. In (a), accuracy in answering questions is shown. In (b), the time taken to answer the questions is shown.

will be improvements over the originals. As the studies that we reviewed suggest, redesigned hypertext systems often are substantially different from the original designs. From our abstracted studies, we suggest that redesign is most successful after the original design has been evaluated, either through usability testing or inspections. Designers and experimenters who plan to use a redesign approach must plan to allocate resources for this type of evaluation of the original hypertext. With high quality evaluative feedback, improved redesigns are not likely to just be lucky guesses and are likely to really reveal important factors in hypertext usability.

REFERENCES

Bailey, G. (1993). Iterative methodology and designer training in human-computer interaction. *INTERCHI '93*, 198–205.

Baird, P. (1990). Hypertext—towards the single intellectual market. In J. Nielsen (Ed.), *Designing user interfaces for international use*. Amsterdam: Elsevier.

Balasubramanian, V., & Turoff, M. (1995). A systematic approach to user interface design for hypertext systems. *28th Hawaii International Conference on System Sciences* (IEEE Press).

Chen, C., & Rada, R. (submitted). Interacting with hypertext: a meta-analysis on usability studies. *Human-Computer Interaction*.

Eason, K. D. (1984). Towards the experimental study of usability. *Behaviour & Information Technology*, 3(2), 133–143.

Egan, D. E., Lesk, M. E., Ketchum, R. D., Lochbaum, C. C., Remde, J. R., Littman, M., & Landauer, T. K. (1991). Hypertext for the electronic Library? CORE sample results. *Hypertext '91 proceedings*, 299–312.

Egan, D. E., Remde, J. R., Gomez, L. M., Landauer, T. K., Eberhardt, J., & Lochbaum, C. C. (1989). Formative design-evaluation of SuperBook. *ACM Transactions on Information Systems, 7*(1), 30–57.

Hammond, N., & Allinson, L. (1989). Extending hypertext for learning: an investigation of access and guidance tools. In *People and computers V.* (pp. 293–304). Cambridge: Cambridge University Press.

Hardman, L. (1989). Evaluating the usability of the Glasgow online hypertext. *Hypermedia, 1*(1), 34–63.

Instone, K., Brown, E., Leventhal, L., & Teasley, B. (1993a). The challenge of effectively integrating graphics into hypertext. In L. Bass, J. Gornostaev, & C. Unger (Eds.), *Human-computer interaction: third international conference, EWHCI '93* (pp. 290–297). Berlin: Springer-Verlag.

Instone, K., Teasley, B. M., & Leventhal, L. M. (1993b). Empirically-based re-design of a hypertext encyclopedia. *INTERCHI '93 proceedings,* 500–506.

Koons, W. R., O'Dell, A. M., Frishberg, N. J., & Laff, M. R. (1992). The computer sciences electronic magazine: translating from paper to multimedia. *CHI '92 proceedings*, 11–18.

Landauer, T., Egan, D., Remde, J., Lesk, M., Lochbaum, C., & Ketchum, D. (1993). Enhancing the usability of text through computer delivery and formative evaluation: the SuperBook project. In C. McKnight, A. Dillon, & J. Richardson (Eds.), *Hypertext: a psychological perspective* (pp. 71–136). New York: Ellis Horwood.

Leventhal, L., Instone, K., & Teasley, B. (1994a). Hypertext-based kiosk systems: seven challenges and an empirical study. *Proceedings of the 1994 East-West International Conference on Human-Computer Interaction* (pp. 226–237). Berlin: Springer-Verlag.

Leventhal, L., Teasley, B., Instone, K., & Farhat, J. (1994b). Age-related differences in the use of hypertext: experiment and design guidelines. *Hypermedia, 6*(1), 19–34.

Leventhal, L. M., Teasley, B. M., Instone, K., Rohlman, D. S., & Farhat, J. (1993). Sleuthing in HyperHolmes: an evaluation of using hypertext vs. a book to answer questions. *Behaviour & Information Technology, 12*(3), 149–164.

McKnight, C., Dillon, A., & Richardson, J. (1990). A comparison of linear and hypertext formats in information retrieval. In R. McAleese, & C. Green (Eds.), *Hypertext: state of the art* (pp. 10–19). Oxford: Intellect.

Nielsen, J. (1989). The matters that really matter for hypertext usability. *Hypertext '89 proceedings*, 239–267.

Nielsen, J. (1993a). *Hypertext and hypermedia.* Boston: Academic Press.

Nielsen, J. (1993b). Iterative user-interface design. *IEEE Computer, 26*(11), 32–41.

Nielsen, J. (1993c). *Usability engineering.* Boston: Academic Press.

Nielsen, J., & Mack, R. L. (1994). *Usability inspection methods.* New York: Wiley.

Rada, R., & Murphy, C. (1992). Searching versus browsing in hypertext. *Hypermedia, 4*(1), 1–30.

Salomon, G. (1990a). Designing casual-use hypertext: the CHI '89 Info-Booth. *CHI '90 proceedings,* 451–458.

Salomon, G. (1990b). How the look affects the feel: visual design and the creation of an information kiosk. *Human factors society 34th annual meeting,* 277–281.

Shneiderman, B., Kreitzberg, C., & Berk, E. (1991). Editing to structure a reader's experience. In E. Berk, & J. Devlin (Eds.), *Hypertext/hypermedia handbook* (pp. 143–164). New York: Intertext.

Simpson, A., & McKnight, C. (1990). Navigation in hypertext: structural cues and mental maps. In R. McAleese, & C. Green (Eds.), *Hypertext: state of the art* (pp. 73–83). Norwood, NJ: Ablex.

Waterworth, J. A., & Chignell, M. H. (1989). A manifesto for hypermedia usability research. *Hypermedia, 1*(3), 205–234.

13

Technology, Representation, and Cognition: The Prefiguring of Knowledge in Cognitive Flexibility Hypertexts

Punyashloke Mishra

University of Illinois at Urbana-Champaign

Rand J. Spiro

University of Illinois at Urbana-Champaign

Paul J. Feltovich

Southern Illinois University School of Medicine

INTRODUCTION

It is now widely accepted that technology is not neutral with regard to its effects on cognition. By this we do not imply merely that different technologies have differing strengths or weaknesses as they relate to thought processes but, rather that different technologies (or media) engender different mind-sets or ways of thinking. Relatedly, many of the characteristics that promote these ways of thinking are *inherent* in the nature of the media and, thus, invisible to the users of these media. In this chapter we shall briefly look at the manner in which different media and representational techniques influence both the processes and the outcomes of cognition. We shall then focus on computer based hypertexts (specifically hypertexts based on Cognitive Flexibility Theory; Spiro, Coulson, Feltovich, & Anderson, 1988/1994) and the kinds of epistemic orientations and conceptual structures that this new theoretical-technological nexus supports: How does that hypertext technology *prefigure* the kinds of cognitive activity that will occur in its users (Feltovich, Spiro, & Coulson, 1989)?

TECHNOLOGY AND COGNITION

The effects of particular technologies on cognition, knowledge, and society at large often are subtle and complexly woven (see, e.g., Salomon, 1979). Strict cause–effect relationships may not be apparent. Moreover, these effects often are not immediately appreciated but, rather, show their influence on far longer time scales—decades or maybe even hundreds of years.

A fruitful way of thinking about the manner in which media influence cognition is that different media *prefigure* cognitive processes and the development of cognitive structures in different ways. In its original usage in the theory of history (White, 1973), a "prefigurative scheme" meant a set of implicit cognitive biases that determine the "ground rules," so to speak, of cognitive processing and analysis (e.g., what kinds of data are important, how they should be evaluated, how arguments should be structured, etc.). White's idea of prefiguration was that it is precognitive and precritical. He argued that prefiguration not only helped delimit the borders of a domain, but also helped determine how concepts will be used to identify the objects in the domain and the nature of the relationships between those objects. All of these attributes are applicable to our use of the term. The important point, again, is that quite often these prefigurative schemes are invisible to the people employing them, but still affect their thinking in essential ways (much like the way the lenses of eyeglasses affect vision without their long-time users being aware at most times that they are looking through them).

PREFIGURING IN WRITING AND PRINT

The idea that the *nature* of media (i.e., not just its contents, not just what it "says," but rather its structure, how it works, what it *does*) influences people's thinking in basic ways is not a new one. Every new technology—from the process of writing to the telephone, from the invention of the camera to the digital computer—has had its share of supporters, who see in it the possible emancipation of humankind, and also its share of detractors, who see in it the death of much of the good that has existed. An ancient argument of this kind can be found in Plato's dialogue, *Phaedrus,* in which Socrates (actually Plato speaking through Socrates) makes the argument that writing (and books) would destroy thought. The crux of the argument is that books merely make statements; they do not argue back. Socrates claimed that this passivity would undermine reflective thought—the ability to think deeply about things, to question and examine every assertion. The crucial concern for Socrates was not *what* people would write, but rather, the effects of the print medium itself, on the fundamental nature of thinking. The technology of writing (and print that followed it) changed our view of the world. Writing today is so ubiquitous, so much a part of our world, that it is difficult, if not impossible, to imagine a solely oral culture. Knowledge in such cultures would be more fluid; it could change radically with every retelling. This would be in radical contradistinction to the notion of immutable, absolute, ever-available authority that is associated with certain texts in print culture.

The invention of movable type and printing in the fifteenth century was responsible for creating an intellectual revolution that impacts us even today. In contrast to Socrates, who focused on what was lost through the process of *writing* (specifically its effect on argument and dialogue), others have proposed that it was the advent of the printing press that made a wide variety of intellectual options possible (Bolter, 1990; Eisenstein, 1980; McLuhan, 1962, 1964; Ong, 1982; Provenzo, Jr., 1986). Indeed, the invention of printing was followed by a series of dramatic changes in all aspects of social, cultural, political, and scientific life in Europe and, from there, the rest of the world. For example, it solidified the notion of ownership of ideas and the convention that arguments could be decided by invoking the appropriate text (although it is notable how greatly these basic assumptions have been undermined recently; e.g., Feltovich, Spiro, Coulson, & Myers-Kelson, 1995).

Most of the significant effects of the invention and spread of print can be traced to certain specific properties of print media: In particular, print created objects that were *mobile, immutable, presentable, and readable;* and these properties led to fundamental changes in human cognition (Latour, 1990). These properties ensured (or seemed to ensure) that discussions could be carried beyond the conversational arena, that ideas could be transported without change in their essential nature, and that they could be universally and *consistently* understood (at least by those who knew the conventions) in a way that more mutable, "unreliable" oral retellings could not. The crucial argument here is that initially it was the medium, this new fixed object, that was immutable. Then the idea of immutability passed on from the medium to the message, with attendant implications of accuracy, fixedness, and truthfulness. Thus, print, by its very nature, prefigured the manner in which discourse could be, and was, structured. As Delany and Landow have stated

> The written text is the stable record of thought, and to achieve this stability the text had to be based on a physical medium: clay, papyrus, or paper; tablet, scroll or book. But the text is more than just the shadow or trace of a thought already shaped; in a literate culture, the textual structures that have evolved over the centuries *determine* thought almost as powerfully as the primal structure that shapes all expression, language. So long as the text was married to a physical medium, readers and writers took for granted three crucial attributes: that the text was *linear, bounded, and fixed.* Generations of scholars and authors internalized these qualities as rules of thought, and they had pervasive social consequences (Delany & Landow, 1991, p. 3).

COMPUTER-BASED HYPERTEXT AND COGNITION

Hypertext systems, both as knowledge access and storage systems, and as learning environments, have been attracting considerable attention recently (e.g., Landow, 1992; Spiro & Jehng, 1990). The term *hypertext* refers to computer based information systems that are characterized by their mutability: They can be "restructured" along different dimensions, for different purposes, at different times. As such, they are distinguished from other media by the extent to which they engender *nonlinear* and *multidimensional* explorations of their content. Hypertext has the ability to produce large, complex, richly connected, and cross-referenced bodies of information in a number of different forms (text, graphics, audio, video as well as other kinds of data). Often, the term "hypermedia" has been used to refer to systems containing multiple media representations. That term has been used interchangeably with "hyper-text." We prefer the latter term, which conveys the sense of *text* as any object of study that affords rich interpretation (as it is used, for example, in poststructuralist theory; e.g., Barthes, 1970).

Just as every new technology imposes its own constraints on the communication process (as well as providing new opportunities), hypertext systems do so as well. Our concern here is not so much the content of these systems, but rather how their *form* influences the cognitive structures and processes of those who use them. In contrast to the linear, bounded, and fixed nature of printed text, computer-based hypertexts are nonlinear, unbounded, and dynamic. For example, they make possible fluid and nearly unlimited juxtaposition and linkage of elements, without regard to the physical location of the elements (in contrast to conventional text). We will now begin to address the cognitive consequences of these characteristics of hypertext, especially as they bear on two issues: (1) the use of hypertext to promote learning; and (2) the design of hypertext to optimize flexibility and knowledge usability in learning.

LEARNING THEORY AND EDUCATIONAL GOALS IN THE CONTEXT OF HYPERTEXT: COGNITIVE FLEXIBILITY AND ADVANCED KNOWLEDGE ACQUISITION

The raw capabilities of hypertext, for example, the ability to provide links to different information nodes, are not sufficient to insure that they will be effective as learning and teaching devices. Two main problems have been identified with the design of hypertext learning systems (e.g., Spiro, Feltovich, Jacobson, & Coulson, 1991a; Spiro & Jehng, 1990): (a) the lack of a sound theoretical framework to guide the enterprise—too much hypertext development has been technology-driven rather than theory-driven; and (b) the neglect of what cognitive science and educational psychology have to say about learning. If computer-based systems will inevitably change the way in which students think, the new media technologies have to be structured so that these changes will be beneficial. For this to happen, designers should have guiding principles about what kinds of cognitive change are desirable and how using the systems will effect those changes in students. In this chapter we will consider the following learning outcomes to be desirable ones: Students should be able to go beyond merely memorizing facts to the formation of a deeper understanding of important but complex knowledge, and they should develop an ability to use that knowledge in new situations (i.e., knowledge transfer). To accomplish these goals, learners should cultivate multifaceted and flexible knowledge representations that can be used in many kinds of situations and contexts. These learning goals have been referred to as being those of "*advanced knowledge acquisition*"—learning beyond the "introductory" stage for some subject matter (Spiro et al., 1988/1994).

A step toward formulating a theory of advanced knowledge acquisition has been taken by the developers of *Cognitive Flexibility Theory* (Feltovich et al., 1989; Spiro et al., 1988/1994; Spiro, Feltovich, Coulson, & Anderson, 1989; Spiro, Feltovich, Jacobson, & Coulson, 1991a,b; Spiro & Jehng, 1990; Spiro, Vispoel, Schmitz, Samarapungavan, & Boerger, 1987). They have argued that effective learning in complex and ill-structured domains cannot be achieved by utilizing or building rigid, single-purpose schemas. Inflexibly prepackaged knowledge structures are useful for situations that match those in which learning took place. However, in most domains that require application of knowledge to naturally occurring situations, inflexible, precompiled knowledge structures are a hindrance. Just as one can never cross the same river twice, quite often when one approaches a new situation in a complex knowledge domain a new set of "intellectual tools" have to be assembled for the particular situation at hand. Flexible cognitive representations enhance the transfer of knowledge to contexts different from those that had been involved originally in the teaching of the material. Such representations increase the likelihood that knowledge *ensembles* can be *constructed* as required. Rigid schemas often are artificially induced generalizations from individual cases, whereas what is needed instead is to determine patterns in the way general principles work across different cases and situations. Spiro et al. (1987) offer the metaphor of "criss-crossing a landscape" from many different directions as a way of learning about complex domains (see also, Wittgenstein, 1953).

> The best way to come to understand a given landscape is to explore it from many directions, to traverse it first this way and then that (preferably with a guide to highlight significant features). Our instructional system for presenting a complexly ill-structured "topical landscape" is analogous to physical landscape exploration, with different routes of traversing study-sites (cases) that are each analyzed from a number of thematic perspectives.
>
> The notion of "criss-crossing" from case to case in many directions, with many thematic dimensions serving as routes of traversal, is central to our theory. The treatment of an irregular and complex topic

cannot be forced in any single direction without curtailing the potential for transfer. If the topic can be applied in many different ways, none of which follows in a rule-bound manner from the others, then limiting oneself in acquisition to, say, a single point of view or a single system of classification, will produce a relatively *closed* system instead of one that is open to context-dependent variability. By criss-crossing the complex topical landscape, the twin goals of highlighting multi-facetedness and establishing multiple connections are attained. . . . *Information that will need to be used in a lot of different ways needs to be taught in lots of different ways* [italics in original; Spiro et al., 1987, pp. 187–188].

In today's complex world, such flexible approaches to knowledge acquisition and application are essential. Our claim is that to achieve these kinds of goals, certain fundamental ways of thinking must be changed. We argue that hypertexts based on Cognitive Flexibility Theory not only change the kinds of specific knowledge structures built for a topic, but also change the *kind* of thinking people do (in ways that will be illustrated throughout the next section). These changes in the manner of thought do not result from telling learners what they should do, but rather from the way the hypertexts are designed and built—the theory of cognition is designed *into* the medium and the requirements for its use.*

In the next section we shall discuss some of the specific theoretical tenets of hypertext systems modeled on the principles of Cognitive Flexibility Theory. We will describe the manner in which such systems *prefigure* the shape of knowledge and cognitive processes, and thereby enhance the ability of learners to flexibly assemble situationally appropriate knowledge "complexes" from a variety of knowledge sources.

---

*A possible misunderstanding of our approach is that we take ill-structured subject matter and impose order on it through its inclusion in our hypertext systems. This is not the case. As will become evident later in this chapter, the characteristics of knowledge domain complexity and ill-structuredness are not only retained in the hypertexts, they are given special *prominence*. So, the knowledge domain (landscape) remains ill-structured; hypertexts based on Cognitive Flexibility Theory are structured to be vehicles for helping learners grow into being able to handle this kind of complexity in a sophisticated way. (Of course, local regions of greater orderliness can also be detected within the larger complexity that is provided. Also, for domains that are more well-structured as a whole—and there are far fewer of these than one might imagine—traditional media might perhaps be more efficient in promoting knowledge acquisition.)

PREFIGURATION IN HYPERTEXTS BASED
ON COGNITIVE FLEXIBILITY THEORY

There are a large number of ways in which Cognitive Flexibility Theory (CFT) structures hypertexts differently from other hypertext systems. Some of the significant attributes of the CFT hypertext approach, with particular emphasis on the manner in which they prefigure the kinds of knowledge structures and processes created by students, are described in the following. (The discussion will be at a general level, concerned with theoretical issues. For specific details on CFT hypertexts see, e.g., Spiro & Jehng, 1990; Spiro et al., 1988/1994.)*

Multiplicity

Hypertexts developed in accord with CFT have at their core the idea that learning and knowledge acquisition are better achieved when students develop *multiple representations* and interpretations of the domain under consideration. Unitary explanations, though simpler to teach and learn, often misrepresent crucial facets of complex, ill-structured domains (Feltovich et al., 1989; Zook & DiVesta, 1991).

---

*Prototype hypertexts based on CFT have been developed in a variety of domains, ranging from high school biology to military strategy; film criticism to cardiovascular medicine. In general, they all share certain features. Screens present options for various kinds of explorations. The options always include a case-by-case reading or a theme-based traversal across cases. For example, in the domain "twentieth century social and cultural history," one might choose to read a case about the automobile, or one about aspects of modern art. Or one could request a display of just those parts of the various cases that illustrate one of the multiple conceptual themes for the domain (or some combination of them). So, considering a possible multi-thematic traversal, it might become interesting for a student at some stage of learning and in some educational setting (all of the uses of the hypertexts are intended to be situated in some meaningful task context, e.g., answering an essay question or solving a problem), to see how the theme of "fragmentation in modern society" intersects with the theme of "rapid change," across cases that have an economic emphasis. After the student selects these options with a few clicks of a mouse button, the hypertext would then re-edit its text and image base to show just those cases and case segments that were pertinent to all of the three selected perspectives. In essence, the highly multidimensional thematic space is used to construct diverse criss-crossings of the topic—multiple text organizations of the same content material that each serve their own unique instructional purposes in illuminating different views of the domain's multifacetedness. Again, this is just the most skeletal of overviews of a highly complex approach to hypertext design that has many theory-based features—the interested reader will find ample detail in the cited papers.)

Multiple representations, however, expose people to the contextual and situational differences in how these representations should be used and can emend the deficiencies of single representations (Spiro et al., 1989). Computer based hypertexts can harness a variety of media sources such as video, photographs, graphs, and diagrams, thus allowing the computer to take on the strengths (and differing symbol manipulations capabilities) of different media. Combining text with graphics and video can lead to an experience that combines the analytic/reflective modes of thinking with the spatial and temporal modes. However, CFT hypertexts go beyond such straightforward multimedia capabilities. CFT hypertexts promote the use of multiple *conceptual* knowledge representations, such as multiple analogies, multiple themes, multiple points of view, and multiple lines of argument (e.g., Spiro et al., 1989). The multiplicity of representational schemes prevents the easy adoption of single and monolithic explanations.

Summary: prefiguration of multiplicity (the limitations of single representations and the importance of multiple representations)

Providing learners with the possibility of adopting multiple representations (conceptual and modal) and structuring the content matter such that it they can form multiple interconnections prefigures the technology-content-learner triad in certain specific ways. Students who have used this kind of system will be more skeptical of unitary, and "all-purpose" generalizations. They will realize that relying on a single *conceptual* viewpoint (argument, analogy, organizational logic) is incomplete and merely leads to a partial understanding of the domain. Moreover, using multiple media and representational formats should open learners to different ways of learning—rather than restricting them to the analytic/reflective mode so emphasized by the linear print media.

Complexity

A variety of misconceptions or biases in learning and understanding of complex subject matter that students bring to the classroom have been identified (e.g., Feltovich, Spiro, & Coulson, 1993; Feltovich et al., 1989; Spiro et al., 1988/1994, 1989). These authors have argued that these misconceptions develop in part because of simplifications that are imposed on complex and irregular subject matter at early stages of learning. These simplifications, although intended to ease and aid understanding, actually hinder the acquisition of advanced understandings and prevent the development of flexible cognitive structures that will help students apply the knowledge in new situations (Feltovich et al., 1989; Spiro et al., 1988/1994, 1989). Most previous learning theories have advocated incrementally increasing the complexity of the subject matter with increasing student experience. However, often this does not work out as intended: Students often become fixated with the simplistic models or overly reduce the more accurate, more sophisticated models in the direction of the simplifications (e.g., Feltovich et al., 1989). In contrast, CFT proposes the idea of confronting the student at the very beginning of instruction with selected, small-scale cases — bite-sized chunks of complexity as it were (Spiro & Jehng, 1990). These "mini-cases" are chosen to be illustrative of the features of complexity or irregularity of the domain to be learned at large (e.g., they illustrate the importance of multiple rather than single representations), yet they are "small" enough not to overload the student's cognitive processing capabilities—they are cognitively manageable staging grounds for the introduction of complexity. This *"new incrementalism"* of CFT emphasizes the spiral-like development of knowledge by the gradual increase of the number and size of specific cases and the ideas that link across them, thus progressively bringing out the "contours" of the complex topical landscape. (This contrasts with the "old incrementalist" sequencing logic of beginning with simple presentations that lack the most important features of complexity and thus induce epistemic expectations in learners that leave them unprepared for later, more in-depth treatments of the content.)

Summary: prefiguration of complexity

The introduction of complexity at the initial stages of the instructional process (albeit in manageable chunks) guards students from being seduced by or seeking inappropriately simplistic interpretations and understandings in complex and ill-structured knowledge domains. Students are exposed to the limitations of "first-pass understandings" and are made more aware of such things as the existence of exceptions to "rules" and the deceptiveness of superficial similarities.

Context-dependency

CFT hypertext systems are based on the idea of developing abstract concepts through the exploration of their application in the direct context of different case examples, so that the need for tailoring of abstractions to their contexts of application is highlighted. It is the nature of complex and ill-structured domains that abstractions, rules, principles, and the like, do not retain absolute, context-independent meaning. Rather, their meaning is highly content-sensitive and must be tailored to the particulars of situations. CFT hypertext systems enable learners to explore instantiations of concepts across numerous different case contexts, experiencing the nuances of change in conceptual meaning that occur. Information no longer remains an abstract, decontextualized static "thing-out-there," but is seen to be embedded within a context. Facts do not remain self-evident, isolated bits of information, but rather, are "constructed" by their perceived relationship to other facts and by their usefulness in understanding cases. The meaning of facts and concepts will shift as the criteria for associating them with other facts and concepts in interpreting cases change. Thus, the meaning of concepts, ideas, and facts become contingent on the nature of the questions being asked, the nature of relationships being investigated, and so on.

Summary: prefiguration of context-dependency

CFT hypertexts emphasize critical thinking skills in students. Critical thinking relies, among other things, on relating things to one another—determining relationships among different topics and ideas. However, determining these relationships is not a matter of "connecting anything with anything else." What is needed is a rationale to seek and find these connections, to put forth tentative hypotheses, and to seek further information to build on them or to reject them. CFT hypertext (with its framework of cases and broad thematic, conceptual descriptions) structures the interaction with the student along exactly these lines. By emphasizing the creation of knowledge by studying the variable interplay between cases and broad thematic ideas, CFT hypertexts emphasize to students the limitations of strictly abstracted, "top down," overly conceptually driven processing. They become more involved in teasing out the meanings of concepts as they are applied to specific cases, rather than trying to generate a simple rule or abstracted meaning that explains everything. They begin to pay more attention to *tailoring* their understandings to the given situation to which their knowledge is to be applied, rather than seeing cases/examples as mere instances of some universally applicable abstract idea that they are to grasp. Concepts become less deterministic, working differently in different situations and contexts, rather than being rigid constructs that can dictate some "right answer." The learning of a concept is achieved not in a way that is like reading a dictionary definition but, rather, by seeing it used in a variety of contexts and settings, ("Conceptual Variability and "Openness" in Conceptual Structures"). CFT hypertexts, by supporting the linkage and tailoring of concepts to practice (actual case examples), enhance the development of context-sensitive, adaptable knowledge structures.

Interconnectedness

By utilizing a large variety of exploration routes across the many cases and conceptual themes in a CFT hypertext, learners develop a sense that there are many ways to traverse some body of knowledge but *no single path* that is sufficient for achieving understanding. This is because CFT hypertexts undermine the standard, rigid classification of concepts and ideas that is exemplified in the organization of chapters of textbooks. Such a classification inappropriately conveys the idea that knowledge can be compartmentalized in discrete and predetermined (and usually hierarchical and nested) knowledge structures. In contrast, in a CFT hypertext the relationships and organizations among topics are multiple and evolving. Tendencies toward strict hierarchical and compartmentalized structuring are subverted in favor of structuring that emphasizes the overlapping, entangled, "web-like" nature of knowledge, with a multiplicity of possible connections among cases and concepts, and fluid systems of classification (Feltovich, Coulson, Spiro, & Dawson-Saunders, 1992).

Summary: prefiguration of interconnectedness (noncompartmentalization and multiple interconnectedness in knowledge organization).

Built into CFT hypertexts is an emphasis on the web-like nature of knowledge, reflecting the "messiness" of the world of knowledge use and avoiding the essentially false distinctions often drawn between subject areas. Concepts have differently configured applications across different cases and are not split apart into separate "chapters." Classifications of objects and situations change in different circumstances. Thus, irregularity in classification within complex, ill-structured domains is highlighted and the need for situation-based reclassification of knowledge elements is made salient and modeled. What becomes important is *intertextuality*—the ability of "texts" (including graphics, movies, etc.), and their component parts, to refer to each other in complex ways, supporting, ignoring, or denying the meanings of other texts according to context. By emphasizing the "fuzziness" that exists in the manner in which concepts and other abstractions are applicable, learners become attuned to seeking "family resemblance" forms of meaning (Wittgenstein, 1953), rather than a single, highly specified understanding that is applied universally, and multiple, flexible processes of classification rather than strict processes of compartmentalized classification.

Inexhaustibility of Understanding

CFT hypertexts make it clear that cases, concepts, and ideas can, at different times, be harnessed to support different concerns and points of view. Thus the beginning learner is "primed" to appreciate the subtle nuances of differences in "truth" across different cases, under different conceptual interpretations, according to different objectives, and so on. In this regard, CFT promotes the *"revisiting"* of cases and thematic explorations (as well as thematic commentaries) as circumstances or the learner's knowledge and appreciation change. It must be emphasized that revisiting is not the same as repeating (Spiro et al., 1991a). Simple repeating is boring (and not greatly beneficial to learning), whereas revisiting contains the excitement of seeing the same thing with a new and different set of "lenses," for example, recently acquired experiences or new points of view. Revisiting is important not only to bring out the multifacetedness of cases (that is hard to grasp on any single reading, in any single context), but also to bring out the manner in which different cases and thematic interpretations "change" with changes in experience or perspective. (This realization is facilitated in CFT hypertexts by the use of "context-sensitive selective highlighting" of relevant portions of the learning material: Depending on the recent context of hypertext exploration by the learner, different elements of the material currently under view are graphically accentuated.)

Summary: prefiguration of the inexhaustibility
of understanding

Users of CFT hypertexts realize that learning does not mean merely adding something new to what existed before; it means changing the way we think about the things we "knew" before that are connected to it. Learning does not just build on what is already known, it affects what was previously encountered in intricate and fascinating ways. This process of revisiting earlier sites of learning from the perspective of new contexts and purposes elicits a mind-set of knowledge questioning and renewal. There is always more that can be learned, seen, and appreciated in any rich case of knowledge application and understanding, and this is accomplished by adopting a new attitude to the *revisiting* of material; the required attitude is that a revisitation is more of a "new view" than a repetition.

"Openness" in Conceptual Structures

CFT hypertexts provide a set of organizing principles within which to structure the learner's engagement with the given domain, but these are loose guides rather than closed, highly denotative structures (Spiro et al., 1991b; Spiro & Jehng, 1990). Conceptual themes are provided for the student, but the way the hypertext is used makes it repeatedly clear (e.g., through theme-search options) that their meaning changes in important ways across different contexts of application (across different cases). The student realizes that, rather than a common core of meaning across the various uses of the concepts, those uses are linked only by overlapping patterns of family resemblance (Wittgenstein, 1953)—the conceptual structures are nothing more than rough starting point for thought, subject to processes of interpretation and tailoring to the specific details of the case at hand. The structure of the hypertext, without prestored links, yet allowing for a set of broadly gauged themes or ideas for guidance in criss-crossing, allows students to recognize the unique and individual nature of individual cases even while seeing them as being the results of the dynamic interplay of conceptual themes and case particulars. This militates against the temptation to try to build universally applicable, rigid knowledge structures, while allowing learners to become actively engaged in the more fluid, context-dependent production of meaning. So, something *is* provided to subjects, a seemingly unconstructive practice; however, what is provided are open structures to help one start in one's construction of new knowledge, rather than closed structures that restrict constructive activity. (Also, the student is free to go beyond the presented information, to develop further cases, principles, and conceptual themes.)

Summary: prefiguration of "openness"
in conceptual structures

CFT hypertexts put students in charge of the task of their own meaning-making, but also give them a *compliant* guiding framework within which to work (Spiro et al., 1991b). Knowledge in complex and ill-structured domains is difficult to "hand down" or precodify. CFT hypertexts are designed to make students less dependent on explicit transmission of knowledge from an authority (either in the form of a teacher or a textbook). However, CFT hypertexts do not leave students "out in the cold." They show students the contributions that can be made by expert knowledge and how experts can be used as consultants (within the CFT hypertext itself) in understanding problems or situations. Thus, learners see that it is neither the case that knowledge is a fixed and given thing, nor that there is no role at all for being guided by conceptual structures. Rather, one *constructs* knowledge based *partly* on *open* and *flexibly adaptive* knowledge structures that are provided as *starting points* for the students.

Adaptive Flexibility

The main aim of CFT hypertexts is to help students acquire flexible cognitive skills that can take multiple, interrelated concepts and *apply* them to new, diverse, and largely unexpected circumstances (rather than confining students to the simpler capabilities of recalling how something was taught and then applying it in roughly the same way). This is of great importance in advanced learning situations that require complex and interdependent conceptual applications that differ in the particulars of application from context to context. It is this stress on the achievement of knowledge *transfer* rather than knowledge retention, on the development of situation-specific knowledge assembly rather than generic schema retrieval, that is the most essential goal for learners as they work with CFT hypertexts. Knowledge cannot be applied indiscriminately to new situations but must be assembled for application, with guidance from prior experience, from various acquired conceptual and case sources, and from the case at hand.*

---

*Although we do not consider the findings to be definitive yet, early studies have provided a preliminary indication that the "criss-crossing" instructional approach based on Cognitive Flexibility Theory leads to improved transfer of knowledge to new situations. Reflecting a similar pattern found in other experiments are the results of Jacobson & Spiro (1995). In that study, subjects were randomly assigned either to an experimental condition that used hypertext that permitted a nonlinear, theme-based traversal of cases in the domain of "science, technology, and society," or they were assigned to control conditions that required more linear reading of the *same* content that the experimental condition read (also presented

Summary: prefiguration of adaptive flexibility

In a sense, this emphasis on transfer of knowledge lies at the core of Cognitive Flexibility Theory. By focusing on the building of certain kinds of flexible cognitive structures and processes, CFT aims at instilling a certain philosophy of learning and education. This philosophy aims at making understanding interesting and fun for students without forsaking the inherent challenges in understanding difficult concepts and ideas. It aims to create more open-minded and flexible students, students who are independent, adaptive, original thinkers. These students are not likely to accept broad generalizations easily, are likely to be skeptical about issues, and likely to be sensitized to the contingency and context-dependency of ideas. They should respect expertise but not be overawed by it. They should be ready to tackle new situations, bringing to them not rigid preconceptions, but rather, rich, complex understandings selectively constructed for the present situation from previous encounters with associated cases and relevant concepts.

CONCLUDING REMARKS

Various themes of Cognitive Flexibility Theory and associated principles of hypertext design have been presented in the context of a set of goals of advanced knowledge acquisition in complex domains. The point of this chapter is that these goals can be accomplished partly through having the identified "learning values" (e.g., the importance of multiple representations; context-dependency; inexhaustibility of understanding) *prefigured* in the structure of the technological medium itself—the learner not only discovers specific

---

on the computer). Subjects in the control condition had a higher mean on tests of factual memory for the presented material. Apparently, a single, orderly scaffolding for material facilitates reproductive memory. However, the experimental condition, which effectively employed multiple organizations of the same material (i.e., the kind of "criss-crossing" of a topic's conceptual landscape that is at the core of Cognitive Flexibility Theory), scored significantly higher than the controls on a test that required *application* of the presented material to a new situation (a problem-solving essay involving a totally new case). The nonlinear and multidimensional approach seems to produce the intended transfer of instructed knowledge to new situations. (Again, we believe further empirical research is required to definitively demonstrate this conclusion across a range of contexts.)

things about some subject matter when using the hypertext medium (that are, of course, themselves structured to support the cognitive goals of CFT), but also assimilates fundamental presuppositions about the nature of knowing, coming to know, and using what one knows. At a general level, it is hoped that the prefigurative influences built into these hypertexts will help to replace habits of mind that might be simplistic, rigid, and passively receptive to authority, with views of the learning enterprise that acknowledge complexity, are more flexible, and that privilege the constructive processes of the learner.

ACKNOWLEDGMENTS

This research was supported in part by the National Science Foundation under Grant No. RED-9253157. The US government has certain rights in this material. Any opinions, findings, and conclusions or recommendations expressed are those of the authors and do not necessarily reflect the views of the funding agencies.

We would like to acknowledge Dr. Richard Coulson and Dr. Michael Jacobson for helpful discussions on some of the topics of this chapter. A special debt of gratitude is owed to Dr. Herre van Oostendorp and the other editors of this volume for their insightful and helpful reactions to an earlier draft.

REFERENCES

Barthes, R. (1970). *S/Z*. New York: Hill & Wang.

Bolter, J. D. (1990). *Writing space: The computer in the history of literacy.* Hillsdale, NJ: Erlbaum.

Delany, P., & Landow, G. P. (Eds.) (1991). *Hypermedia and literary studies.* Cambridge, MA: MIT Press.

Eisenstein, E. L. (1980). *The printing press as an agent of change: Communications and cultural transformations in early-modern Europe.* Cambridge: Cambridge University Press.

Feltovich, P. J., Coulson, R. L., Spiro, R. J., & Dawson-Saunders, B. K. (1992). Knowledge application and transfer for complex tasks in ill-structured domains: Implications for instruction and testing in biomedicine. In D. Evans & V. Patel (Eds.), *Advanced models of cognition for medical training and practice* (pp. 213–244). Berlin: Springer-Verlag.

Feltovich, P. J., Spiro, R. J., & Coulson, R. L. (1989). The nature of conceptual understanding in biomedicine: The deep structure of complex ideas and the development of misconceptions. In D. Evans & V. Patel

(Eds.), *The cognitive sciences in medicine* (pp. 113–172). Cambridge, MA: MIT Press.

Feltovich, P. J., Spiro, R. J., & Coulson, R. L. (1993). Learning, teaching and testing for complex conceptual understanding. In N. Frederiksen, R. Mislevy, & I. Bejar (Eds.), *Test theory for a new generation of tests* (pp. 181–217). Hillsdale, NJ: Erlbaum.

Feltovich, P. J., Spiro, R. J., Coulson, R. L., & Myers-Kelson, A. (1995). The reductive bias and the crisis of text (in the law). *Journal of Contemporary Legal Issues, 6*(1), 187–212.

Jacobson, M. J., & Spiro, R. J. (1995). Hypertext learning environments, cognitive flexibility, and the transfer of complex knowledge: An empirical investigation. *Journal of Educational Computing Research, 12*(4), 301–303.

Landow, G. P. (1992). *Hypertext: The convergence of contemporary critical theory and technology.* Baltimore, MD: Johns Hopkins Press.

Latour, B. (1990). Drawing things together. In M. Lynch, & S. Woolgar (Eds.), *Representation in scientific practice.* Cambridge, MA: MIT Press.

McLuhan, M. (1962). *The Gutenberg galaxy: The making of typographic man.* Toronto: University of Toronto Press.

McLuhan, M. (1964). *Understanding media.* New York: The New American Library.

Ong, W. J. (1982). *Orality and literacy: The technologizing of the word.* London: Methuen.

Provenzo, E. F. (1986). *Beyond the Gutenberg galaxy: Microcomputers and the emergence of post-typographic culture.* New York: Teachers College Press.

Salomon, G. (1979). *Interaction of media, cognition and learning.* San Francisco: Jossey-Bass.

Spiro, R. J., Coulson, R. L., Feltovich, P. J., & Anderson, D. K. (1988). Cognitive flexibility theory: Advanced knowledge acquisition in ill-structured domains. In *Proceedings of the 10th Annual Conference of the Cognitive Science Society* (pp. 375–383). Hillsdale, NJ: Erlbaum. Also appeared in R. B. Ruddel, M. R. Ruddell, & H. Singer (Eds.) (1994). *Theoretical models and processes of reading* (pp. 602–615). Newark, DE: International Reading Association.

Spiro, R. J., Feltovich, P. J., Coulson, R. L., & Anderson, D. (1989). Multiple analogies for complex concepts: Antidotes for analogy-induced misconception in advanced knowledge acquisition. In S. Vosniadou, & A. Ortony (Eds.), *Similarity and analogical reasoning* (pp. 498–531). Cambridge, MA: Cambridge University Press.

Spiro, R. J., Feltovich, P. J., Jacobson, M. J., & Coulson, R. L. (1991a). Cognitive flexibility, constructivism, and hypertext: Random access instruction for advanced knowledge acquisition in ill-structured domains. *Educational Technology (special Issue on Constructivism), 11*(5), 24–33.

Spiro, R. J., Feltovich, P. J., Jacobson, M. J., & Coulson, R. L. (1991b). Knowledge representation, content specification, and the development of skill in situation-specific knowledge assembly: Some constructivist issues as they relate to cognitive flexibility theory and hypertext. *Educational Technology, 31*, 22–26.

Spiro, R. J., & Jehng, J. C. (1990). Cognitive flexibility and hypertext: Theory and technology for the nonlinear and multidimensional traversal of complex subject matter. In D. Nix & R. J. Spiro (Eds.), *Cognition, education, and multimedia: Explorations in high technology* (pp. 163–205). Hillsdale, NJ: Erlbaum.

Spiro, R. J., Vispoel, W. L., Schmitz, J., Samarapungavan, A., & Boerger, A. (1987). Knowledge acquisition for application: Cognitive flexibility and transfer in complex content domains. In B. C. Britton, & S. Glynn (Eds.), *Executive control processes*. Hillsdale, NJ: Erlbaum.

White, H. (1973). *Metahistory*. Baltimore, MD: Johns Hopkins University Press.

Wittgenstein, L. (1953). *Philosophical investigations*. New York: Macmillan.

Zook, K. B., & F. J. DiVesta (1991). Instructional analogies and conceptual misrepresentations. *Journal of Educational Psychology, 83*, 246–252.

Author Index

A

Aaronson, D., 227, *235*
Abelson, R. P., 47, *73*
Abowd, G., 125, *135*
Adams, R. B., 59, *75*
Afflerbach, P. P., 82, *95*
Agosti, M., 242, *260*, *264*
Akin, O., 122, *135*
Alexander, P. A., 45, 50, 51, 56, 58, 59,
    69, 71, 82, 85, 88, *95, 95, 96*
Alfaro, L., 105, 110, *118,* 165, *176,*
    197, *209,* 217, 224, 236
Allen, J., 66, *69*
Allinson, L., 15, 20, *38,* 267, *285*
Amedeo, D., 190, 198, 204, *209*
Anderson, D. K., 288, 292, 294, 295,
    296
Anderson, J. R., 253, *260*
Anderson, K. T., 56, *70*
Anderson, R. A., 82, *95*
Anderson, R. C., 192, *208*
Anderson, R. E., 47, 66, 67, *69*
Anderson, T. H., 13, *35,* 81, 82, *95*
Anderson-Inman, L., 18, 22, *35*
Anstis, S. M., 169, *175*
Applebee, A. N., 61, *71*
Armbruster, B. B., 13, *35,* 48, *69,* 81,
    82, *95*
Ash, D., 7, 23, 26

B

Bader, G., 56, *70*
Baecker, R. M., 157, *157*
Bailey, G., 283, *284*
Bailey, R. W., 166, 173, *175*
Baird, P., 214, *235,* 266, *284*
Baird, W., 82, *97*
Baker, L., 20, *35*
Balasubramanian, V., 266, *284*
Balathy, E., 45, 49

Baldy, R., 254, *261*
Banks, W. P., 168, *177*
Barnes, V., 105, *118,* 165, *176,* 197,
    209, 224, *236*
Barron, B., 8, 20, 34, *35*
Barthes, R., 291, *303*
Bartlett, F. C., 10, *35*
Bartlett, S., 192, *209*
Baskin, A. D., 20, 21, *41*
Bauer, D., 167, *175*
Bausell, R. B., 192, *208*
Beale, R., 125, *135*
Beam, P., 163, 168, *178,* 217, 236
Beaton, R. J., 167, *178*
Beck, I. L., 12, 15, *35*
Becker, H. J., 26, 66, *70*
Beech, J., 215, *235*
Beeman, W. O., 56, *70*
Begeman, M. L., 243, *261*
Beishutzen, J., 18, *35*
Beldie, I. P., 169, *175, 179*
Bereiter, C., 7, 9, 16, 21, 23, 24, *35,*
    36, 40, 45, 50, 51, *73,* 94, *97*
Bergqvist, U., 167, *178*
Berk. E., 266, *286*
Bernstein, M., 56, *70,* 241, *260*
Bertram, B., 82, *96*
Bever, T. G., 163, *175*
Bielaczyc, K., 21, *35*
Biener, F., 243, *260*
Black. A., 251, *260*
Black, D., 251, *260*
Blackburn, B., *175*
Blanchard, J., 45, *70*
Bock, G., 125, 127, *135*
Boerger, A., 13, 16, 27, *40,* 292, 293,
    305
Bolter, J. D., 44, 45, *70,* 289, *303*
Borkowski, J. C., 58, *70*
Bouma, H., 187, 191, *210*

Bournique, R., 174, *176*
Bovy, R. C., 183, *208*
Braithwaite, A., 192, *209*
Bransford, J. D., 8, 12, 15, 20, 34, *35*, *37*, 51, *70*
Brassard, A., 125, 127, *135*
Brett, C., 8, 23, 24, *40*
Brewer, W., 108, *117*
Bridwell-Bowles, L., 61, 66, *73*
Britt, M. A., 19, 20, *36*, 251, 257, 258, *260*, *261*, *263*
Britton, B. K., 16, *38*, 137, *157*, 256, *261*
Brooks, L., 191, *210*
Brown, A. L., 7, 8, 12, 13, 20, 21, 23, 26, *35*, *36*, 56, *70*
Brown, E., 267, *285*
Brown, J. S., 47, *70*, 90, *96*
Brown, R., 56, *71*, 88, *96*
Bruce, B., *97*
Buchanan, J., 66, *69*
Burkman, E., 208, *210*
Burtis, P. J., 8, 16, 21, 23, 24, *36*, *40*
Burwell, R., 163, *175*
Bush, V., 18, *36*
Butler, B. E., 192, *208*
Buttigieg, M. A., 172, *178*

C

Cakir, A., 186, *208*, 219, *235*
Calhoun, C., 8, 23, 24, *40*
Campbell, R., 103, *117*
Campione, J. C., 7, 20, 21, 23, 26, *36*
Card, S. K., 138, *157*
Carey, L., 137, *158*
Carpenter, P. A., 11, *38*, 104, 109, *118*, 182, *210*, 224, 226, 236
Carr, M., 58, *70*
Carroll, J. M., 103, *117*, 153, *157*
Carver, R. P., 175, *176*
Case, R., 21, *36*
Cavonius, C. R., 167, *175*
Chan, C. K. K., 16, 21, *36*
Chan, K., 172, *176*
Chantadisai, R., 193, *210*
Chapanis, A., 102, *118*
Charney, D., 249, 258, *261*
Chatillon, J.-F., 254, *261*
Chen, C., 167, *284*
Chen, D., 18, 22, *35*
Chen, H., 172, *176*

Chi, M. T. H., 16, 21, *36*
Chignell, M. H., 274, 286
Chiu, M., 21, *36*
Christ, R. E., 192, *208*
Clarinina, R. B., 83, *96*
Clark, H., 224, *235*
Clark, H. M., 48, *73*
Cockburn, A., 127, 130, 132, *135*
Cognition and Technology Group at Vanderbilt, 8, 12, *36*
Cole, M., 48, *72*
Coleman, E. B., 174, *176*
Colley, A., 215, *235*
Collins, A., 20, *36*, 47, 66, *70*, 90, *96*
Collins, K. W., 191, *210*
Conklin, J., 243, 244, *261*
Cook, L. K., 15, *39*
Coté, N., 8, 12, 13, 16, 21, 27, 34, *37*, *38*, *40*
Coulson, R. L., 45, 54, 74, 249, 255, *264*, 288, 289, 291, 292, 294, 295, 296, 298, 299, 300, 301, *303*, *304*, *305*
Coury, B. G., 193, *208*
Creed, A., 168, *176*, 218, *235*
Croft, W. B., 242, 253, *261*, *262*, *264*
Crouse, J. H., 192, *208*
Crowder, R., 224, 225
Cunningham, D., 105, *118*
Czaja, S. J., 173, *176*

D

Daniels, H. A., 61, *70*
Danner, F. W., 59, *71*
Dansereau. D.F., 191, *210*
Dawson-Saunders, B. K., 298, *303*
Day, J. D., 20, *36*
de Beaugrande, R., 220, *235*
de Bruijn, D., 48, *70*, 138, *158*, 168, *176*
Dee-Lucas, D., 20, *38*, 250, 257, *261*
DeForest, M., 12, *39*
Delany, P., 290, *303*
deLeeuw, N., 16, 21, *36*
de Mul, S., 1–6, 48, *70*, 138, *158*, 168, *176*
Denner, P. R., 192, *211*
Dennis, I., 168, *176*, 218, *235*
De Vries, E., 252, *261*
Diaper, D., 240, *261*
Dillon, A., 4, 5, *6*, 48, 58, 60, *70*, 99, 100, 101, 103, 106, 107, 109,

112, *118*, 163, 165, 168, *176*, *178*, 213, 214, 218, 222, 227, 230, *235*, 236, 240, 242, 244, 245, 251, 258, *261*, *262*, *263*, 267, *285*
Dipinto, V. M., 50, *74*
DiVesta, F. J., 294, 295
Divita, J., 193, *212*
Dix, A. J., 15, 20, *39*, 125, *135*, 214, 231, 236
Draper, S. W., 122, *136*
Duchincky, R. L., 162, 163, 169, *177*, 190, 193, 197, *210*
Duffy, S. A., 193, *208*
Duffy, T. M., 18, *37*, 105, *118*
Duguid, P., 90, *96*
Dunn, S. C., 48, *73*
Duran, R. P., 15, 19, *37*
Dyck, J. L., 15, *39*
Dyer, H., 103–118

E

Eason, K. D., 5, 6, 101, *118*, 266, *284*
Eberhardt, J., 162, *176*, 248, *261*, 267, 281, *285*
Edelsky, C., 66, *69*
Edwards, D. M., 247, 252, *261*
Egan, D. E., 100, *118*, 162, 168, 173, 174, *176*, 229, 230, *235*, 236, 248, *261*, 267, 281, *285*
Eisenberg, P., 48, 57, *73*
Eisenstein, E. L., 289, *303*
El-Hindi, A., 58, *71*
Englelbart, D. C., 18, *37*
Erickson, T., 22, *37*, 170, *176*
Evans, S. H., 191, *210*

F

Fahy, A., 214, *237*
Farhat, J., 248, *263*, 274, 278,*285*
Faust, G. W., 192, *208*
Favart, M., 257, *263*
Feldman, S. C., 80, 81, 86, *96*
Feltovich, P. J., 5, 45, 54, *74*, 249, 255, *264*, 287, 288, 290, 291, 292, 293, 294, 295, 296, 297, 298, 299, 300, 301, 302, *303*, *304*, *305*
Ferguson, D. C., 162, 163, 169, *177*, 190, 193, 197, *210*
Ferraro, F. R., 172, *177*

Ferrera, R. A., 20, 21, *36*
Ferres, S., 227, *235*
Finlay, J., 125, *135*
Finn, R., 105, 110, *118*, 165, *176*, 197, *209*, 217, 224, 236
Fish, M. C., 80, 81, 86, *96*
Fisher, D. L., 170, *176*, 193, *208*
Flavell, R., 166, 167, *177*
Fleming, M., 190, 191, *209*
Fleming, R., 226, *237*
Fletcher, C. R., 16, *38*
Flower, L. S., 4, *6*, 137, *158*
Foertsch, M. A., 61, *71*
Foley, P., 162, *177*
Foltz, P. W., 8, 11, 18, *37*
Foss, C. L., 244, 258, *261*
Foster, J. J., 185, *209*
François, C., 242, *262*
Franklin, S. P., 18, *38*
Frase, L. T., 190, *209*
Frei, H. P., 244, 258, *261*
Freivalds, A., 168, *177*
Frenckner, K., 163, 165, 170, 172, *176*
Friend, L., 186, *212*
Frishberg, N. J., 268, *285*
Furuta, R., 242, *264*

G

Gal, I., 59, *75*
Galitz, W. O., 186, 188, 192, 193, *209*
Gall, J. E., 5, *6*
Gallo, M. J., 49, *72*
Garner, R., 56, 59, *71*, 77, 78, 82, 83, 85, 86, 87, 88, 89, 95, *96*
Garnham, A., 110, *118*, 216, *235*
Garofalo, K. M., 192, *209*
Garrison, S., 20, 34, *35*
Gay, G., 56, *74*, 89, *96*
Georgi, M. C., 19, 20, *36*, 258, *260*
Gillingham, M. G., 3, 56, 59, *71*, 77, 78, 82, 83, 86, 87, 88, 95, *96*
Gilman, B. R., 48, *73*
Gilreath, C. T., 191, *209*
Girill, T. R., 242, *261*
Glavanov, D., 9, *40*, 224
Gleitman, L. R., 11, *37*
Glenn, C. F., 10, 13, *41*
Globerson, T., 77, *97*
Glynn, S. M., 137, *157*, 256, *261*

Goetz, E. T., 43, *71*
Goffman, E., 127, *135*
Goldman, S. R., 7, 8, 9, 10, 11, 12, 13,
    14, 15, 16, 17, 18, 19, 20, 21,
    22, 23, 24, 25, 26, 27, 28, 29,
    30, 31, 32, 33, 34, *35, 37, 38,*
    40, 41, 83, 97
Gomez, L. M., 162, 174, *176,* 229, *235,*
    248, *261,* 267, 281, *285*
Goodson, B., 66, *71*
Gordon, A., 7, 23, 26
Gordon, S., 18, *38,* 232, 236, 250, 257,
    262
Gould, J. D., 105, 110, *118,* 163, 165,
    169, *176, 177,* 197, *209,* 217,
    218, 224, 236
Grabinger, R. S., 4, 181, 182, 183,
    184, 185, 186, 187, 188, 189,
    190, 191, 192, 193, 194, 195,
    196, 197, 198, 199, 200, 201,
    202, 203, 204, 205, 206, 207,
    208, *209*
Graesser, A. C., 18, *38*
Grant, K. R., 130, *135*
Graves, D. H., 23, *38*
Gray, S. H., 59, *71,* 245, *262*
Greene, E., 10, *38*
Gregory, M., 188, *209*
Griffin, P., 48, *72*
Grischkowsky, N., 105, *118,* 163, 165,
    169, *176, 177,* 197, *209,* 217,
    218, 224, 236
Grosz-Ngate, M., 89, *96*
Guivarch, M., 243, *260*
Gustavel, J., 18, *38,* 232, 236, 250,
    257, *262*
Guterman, E., 77, *97*
Guthrie, J. T., 19, *38,* 58, *69,* 77, 82,
    83, 86, 87, 88, 95, *96, 97,* 255,
    258, *262*

H

Haas, C., 137, 138, 156, *158*
Hadley, M., 67, *73*
Halasz, F. G., 156, *158,* 240, *262*
Hammond, N., 15, 20, *38,* 267, *285*
Hammouche, H., 240, *262*
Hankey, J., 18, *38,* 232, 236, 250, 257,
    262
Hannafin, M. J., 5, *6*
Hanneman, J., 243, *264*

Hansen, J., 137, 138, *158*
Hardman, L., 247, 252, *261,* 275, 282,
    285
Hare, V. C., 82, 85, 95, *96*
Harpster, J. L., 168, *177*
Hart, D. J., 219, *235*
Hartley, J., 184, 191, 192, *209*
Harwood, K., 162, *177*
Hasselbring, Ted, 34
Haugh, D., 172, *177*
Haupt, B., 110, *118,* 197, *209,* 217,
    236
Hayes, J. R., 4, *6,* 137, *158*
Hayes-Roth, F., 254, *262*
Hayhoe, M., 166, *179*
Heider, F., 10, *38*
Heines, J. M., 199, *210*
Hidi, S., 59, *71,* 82, *97*
Hiebert, E. H., 59, *71*
Hillinger, M. L., 44, 49, 52, *71, 72*
Hiltz, S.R., 122, *135*
Hittleman, D. R., 43, *71*
Hjalmarsson, A., 122, *135*
Hofer, E., 20, 21, *41*
Hollan, J. D., 126, *135,* 155, *158*
Holley, C. D., 191, *210*
Holton, D., 197, *211*
Horney, L., 18, 22, *35*
Horning, A. S., 82, 83, *97*
Huey, E. B., 103, *118,* 161, 167, 169,
    177, 215, 225, 236
Huola, J. F., 171, *177*
Hurvich, L. M., 162, 166, *177*
Hutchins, E. L., 126, *135,* 155, *158*

I

Idstein, P., 192, *208*
Instone, K., 248, *263,* 265, 266, 267,
    268, 270, 271, 272, 273, 274,
    275, 276, 277, 278, 279, 280,
    281, 282, 283, 284, *285*
Irwin, J., 82, 86, *97*

J

Jackson, M. D., 162, *177*
Jacobson, M. J., 50, *71,* 249, 255, *264,*
    291, 292, 299, 300, 301, *304,*
    305
Jameson, D., 162, 166, *177*
James S. McDonnell Foundation, 27n

Jandreau, S., 163, *175*
Jansen, W. C., 240, *262*
Jehng, J. C., 12, 13, 15, 16, 17, 20, *40*, 45, *74*, 290, 291, 292, 294, 296
Jenkins, J. R., 192, *208*
Jetton, T. L., 45, 50, 51, 56, 59, *69, 71*, 82, *95*
Johnson, D. D., *97*
Johnson, M. K., 15, *35*, 51, *70*
Johnson, N. J., 10, *39*
Johnson, P., 240, *262*
Johnson-Laird, P. N., 16, *38*, 216, 236
Johnston, P. H., 59, *71*
Jonassen, D. H., 88, *97*, 252, *262*
Jones, G. L., 184, *210*
Jones, S., 125, 127, *135*
Jones, W. P., 171, *177*
Jungeblut, A., 61, *71*
Juola, J. F., 171, 172, *177*
Just, M. A., 11, *38*, 104, 109, *118*, 182, *210*, 224, 226, 236

K
Kak, A. V., 218, 236
Kang, T. J., 172, *177, 178*
Kantor, R., 20, 34, *35*
Kaplan, R., 163, *175*
Kaufer, D. S., 137, *158*
Kay, Alan, 19
Keenan, L. N., 138, *157*
Keenan, S. A., 193, *210*
Keller, J., 208, *210*
Kellogg, W. A., 153, *157*
Kerr, E. B., 122, *135*
Ketchum, R. D., 100, *118*, 230, 236, 281, *285*
Kiesler, S., 122, 127, *136*
Kim, I., 174, *176*
Kim, Y. H., 43, *71*
Kintsch, E., 15, 16, *38, 39*
Kintsch, W., 10, 12, 15, 16, *38, 39*, 47, 75, 80, *98*, 107, 110, *119*, 182, 183, *210, 212*, 216, 220, *237*, 258, *264*
Kinzer, C. K., 49, *72*
Kirsch, I., 61, *71*
Klare, G. R., 188, *210*
Kline, P., 104, *118*
Knuth, R. A., 18, *37*, 105, *118*
Kolers, P. A., 162, 163, 169, 170, *177*, *178*, 187, 190, 191, 193, 197, *210*
Koons, W. R., 268, *285*
Kozminsky, E., 12, *38*
Krap, A., 82, *97*
Kreitzberg, C., 266, 286
Kruk, R. S., 171, 172, *178, 179*
Kruk, R. S., 165, 168, 169, *177*
Kulikowich, J. M., 45, 50, 51, 56, 58, 59, *69, 71*, 82, 88, *95, 96*

L
Laar, D. V., 166, 167, *177*
Lachman, R., 77, 80, 81, 86, 87, 88, 89, 94, 95, *97*
Laff, M. R., 268, *285*
Lai, K. Y., 130, *135*
Lai, P., 258, *262*
Lakshmanan, R., 193, *210*
Lamon, Mary, 34
Landauer, T. K., 100, 104, *118*, 162, 173, *176, 177*, 229, 230, *235*, 236, 248, *261*, 267, 281, *285*
Landow, G. P., 214, 229, 236, 290, *303, 304*
Langer, J. A., 10, 16, *38*, 61, *71*
Lansdale, M. W., 168, *177*
Lansman, M., 137, *158*
Larkin, J. H., 20, *38*, 56, *70*, 250, 257, *261*
Larkin, K. M., 47, *70*
Larson, D., 191, *210*
Lashley, K. S., 9, *39*
Latour, B., 290, *304*
Latrémouille, S. A., 163, 168, *178*, 217, 236
LaVancher, C., 21, *36*
Lave, J., 90, *97*
Lelu, A., 242, *262*
Lenze, J. S., 186, *210*
Lesk, M., 100, *118*, 230, 236, 281, *285*
Leu, D. J. Jr., 43, 44, 45, 46, 47, 48, 49, 50, 51, 52, 53, 54, 55, 56, 57, 58, 59, 60, 61, 62, 63, 64, 65, 66, 67, 68, 69, *71, 72*
Leventhal, L., 5, 248, *263*, 265, 266, 267, 268, 269, 270, 271, 272, 273, 274, 275, 276, 277, 278, 279, 280, 281, 282, 283, 284, *285*

Levie, H., 190, 191, *209*
Lewin, L., 18, 22, *35*
Lickorish, A., 163, 169, 170, *179*, 217, 222, *237*, *238*, 246, 248, *264*
Liebhaber, M., 172, *177*
Liebowitz, H. W., 168, *177*
Liebscher, P., 246, *264*
Lin, X. D., 7, 20, 21, *39*
Lin, Xiadong, 34
Lochbaum, C. C., 100, *118*, 162, *176*, 229, 230, *235*, 236, 248, *261*, 267, 281, *285*
Lodewijks, H., 251, *262*
Lorch, R. F. Jr., 13, 15, *39*, 86, *97*
Lovelace, E. A., 139, *158*
Luk, C. H., 242, *261*
Lunn, R., 168, *177*
Lutz, J. A., 138, *158*

M

Macdonald, C., 132, *136*
MacDonald, M. C., 26, *39*
Macintosh Human Interface Guidelines, 141, *158*
Mack, R. L., 153, *157*, 268, 286
Mackay, W., 128, *135*
MacLeod, D. I. A., 166, *179*
Mahling, D. E., 253, *262*
Malone, T. W., 130, *135*
Manber, U., 258, *262*
Mandel, T. S., 12, *38*
Mandler, J. M., 10, 12, *39*
Mannes, S. M., 16, *38*, *39*
Marchionini, G., 5, *6*, 44, *72*, 228, 236, 246, *262*
Marmolin, H., 128–135
Marshall, C. C., 240, 243, *262*
Martindale, M. J., 78, 89, *97*
Martinez, M. E., 66, *72*
Matthews, T. D., 20, 21, *41*
Maurutto, P., 164, 165, 173, *178*
Mawby, K., 157, *157*
May, F. B., 43, *72*
Mayer, R. E., 15, *39*
Mazur, J., 56, *74*
McClard, A. P., 56, *70*
McClelland, J. L., 162, *177*, 216, 236
McCullough, C. M., 182, *211*
(James S.) McDonnell Foundation, 27n
McGill, M. J., 241, *263*

McGrath, D., 48, *72*
McKeown, M. G., 12, 15, *35*
McKnight, C., 5, *6*, 101, *118*, 168, *176*, 213, 214, 215, 216, 217, 218, 219, 220, 221, 222, 223, 224, 225, 226, 227, 228, 229, 230, 231, 232, 233, 234, *235*, 236, *237*, 240, 242, 244, 245, 247, 251, 258, *261*, *262*, *263*, 267, 274, *285*, 286
McLean, R. S., 7, 23, *40*, 94, *97*
McLuhan, M., 289, *304*
McNamara, D. S., 15, 16, *39*
McNamara, T., 171, *177*
McQuillan, P., 56, *70*
Mead, N. A., 66, *72*
Mead, R., 173, *178*
Merrill, D. M., 20, *39*
Meyer, B. J. F., 13, 15, *39*, 48, *72*, 190, *210*
Meyrowitz, N., 162, *180*
Miller, R. M., 59, *73*
Mills, C. B., 165, 168, *177*, 186, 192, *210*
Minuto, A., 105, 110, *118*, 165, *176*, 197, *209*, 217, 224, 236
Mishra, Punyashloke, 287–303
Mohageg, M. H., 248, 251, *263*
Monk, A. F., 15, 20, *39*, 214, 231, 236
Moore, J., 18, *38*, 232, 236, 250, 257, *262*
Moran, T. P., 156, *158*
Morris, A., 103–118, 174, *178*
Morris, J., 20, 34, *35*
Morrison, G. R., 190, *210*, *211*
Morrison, R. E., 169, *178*
Mourant, R. R., 193, *210*
Mulis, I. V. S., 61, *71*
Murch, G. M., 167, *178*
Muresan, Pavel, 175
Murphy, C., 267, 286
Murray, D., 124, *136*
Murray, J., 15, *37*
Muter, P., 4, 161, 162, 163, 164, 165, 166, 167, 168, 169, 170, 171, 172, 173, 174, 175, *177*, *178*, *179*, 217, 236
Muth, K. D., 82, *97*
Myers, J., 61, *72*
Myers-Kelson, A., 289, *304*
Mynatt, B. T., 248, *263*

N

Nagai, H., 162, *180*
Nakagawa, K., 7, 23, 26
Nanard, J., 240, *263*
Nanard, M., 240, *263*
Nas, G. L. J., 169, *178*
Nastos, D., 157, *157*
Nathan, M. J., 16, *38*
Nathan, R., 62, *72*
National Commission on Excellence in
    Education, 61, *72*
Neisser, U., 182, *211*
Nelder, J. A., 173, *178*
Nelson, R. P., 184, *211*
Nelson, T., 18, *39*
Nes, F. L. van, 167, 170, *178*
Neuwirth, C. M., 137, *158*
Newman, D., 48, 66, 67, *72*
Newstead, S., 168, *176*, 218, *235*
Nezworski, T., 12, *41*
Nicolisi, E., 240, *262*
Nielsen, J., 110, *118*, 240, *263*, 266,
    267, 268, 283, *285*, 286
Nimmo-Smith, M. I., 168, *179*
Nisbett, R., 226, *237*
Norman, D. A., 103, *118*, 122, 126,
    135, *136*, 155, *158*, 255, *263*
Norman, K., 251, *260*
Norton, G., 66, *69*
Nylen, P., 167, *178*

O

Oakhill, J., 82, *98*
O'Dell, A. M., 268, *285*
O'Dell, J. K., 190, *210*, *211*
Oestreicher, L., 122, *135*
Olshavsky, J., 226, *237*
Ong, W. J., 289, *304*
Osborne, D. J., 197, *211*
Osman-Jouchoux, Rionda, 4, 181–208

P

Palme, J., 127, *136*
Paris, S. G., 56, 57, 58, 59, *72*, *75*
Pastoor, S. A., 169, *175*, *179*
Pawlak, V., 167, *178*
Pearson, P. D., 47, *69*, *97*
Pearson, D., 44, *74*
Pellgrino, J. W., 8, 20, 34, *35*, *37*
Percival, M., 214, *235*

Perfetti, C. A., 19, 20, *36*, 251, 257,
    258, *260*, *261*, *263*
Perlmutter, N. J., 26, *39*
Pickle, J. M., 49, 67, *73*
Pinon, J.-M., 243, *260*
Pirolli, P., 21, *35*, *39*
Pliskin, N., 128, *136*
Posner, J., 157, *157*
Poulter, A., 214, *237*
Poulton, E., 188, *209*
Prince, G., 18, *39*
Provenzo, E. F., 289, *304*
Prown, A. L., 20, 21, *36*
Puchnicky, R. L., 162, 163, 169, *177*
Pugh, A., 226, *237*

R

Rada, R., 167, 267, *284*, 286
Radl, G. W., 167, *178*
Rao, D., 122, *135*
Rao, R., 130, *135*
Ravitch, D., 61, *72*
Rayner, K., 11, *39*, 169, *178*
Recker, M. M., 21, *39*
Rehe, R. F., 185, 187, 192, *211*
Reichman, K., 25, *40*
Reinking, D., 3, 43–69, 44, 61, 66, 67,
    72, *73*, 77, 81, *97*
Reis, R., 82, 85, 95, *96*
Reisel, J. F., 168, *178*
Rellinger, E., 58, *70*
Remde, J. R., 100, *118*, 162, *176*, 229,
    230, *235*, 236, 248, *261*, 267,
    281, *285*
Renninger, K. A., 82, *97*
Reynolds, L., 185, 192, 193, *211*
Rich, E., 168, *178*
Richardson, J., 5, *6*, 101, *118*, 168,
    176, 214, 218, 227, 230, *235*,
    236, 240, 242, 244, 245, 251,
    258, *261*, *262*, *263*, 267,
    285
Rickards, J. P., 192, *211*
Rigney, J. W., 20, *40*
Robert, J. M., 138, *157*
Robinshow, H. M., 163, *179*, 218, *237*
Roby, W., 252, *264*
Rogers, R. A., 240, 243, *262*
Rogoff, B., 90, *97*
Rohlman, D. S., 248, *263*, 278, *285*
Rosenblitt, D., 130, *135*

Ross, S. M., 190, *210, 211*
Rothen, W., 20, 21, *41*
Rothkopf, E. Z., 139, *158*, 169, *178,* 226, *237*
Rotondo, J. A., 191, *211*
Rouet, J.-F., 19, 20, *36,* 239, 240, 241, 242, 243, 244, 245, 246, 247, 248, 249, 250, 251, 252, 253, 254, 255, 256, 257, 258, 259, *260, 261, 263*
Rozin, P., 11, *37*
Rubin, A., 82, *96, 97*
Rubin, T., 165, 167, *178*
Rudnicky, A. L., 170, *178*
Rumelhart, D., 43, *73,* 216, 236
Rumerlhart, D. E., 10, *40,* 43, 73, 216, 236
Rupp, B. A., 167, *179*
Rutherford, M., 7, 23, 26
Ryan, E. R., 59, *73*

S

Sachs, J. S., 9, 10, *40*
Salomon, G., 22, *37,* 77, *97,* 170, *176,* 269, 271, 286, 288, *304*
Salton, G., 241, *263*
Samarapungavan, A., 13, 16, 27, *40,* 292, 293, *305*
Samuels, S. J., 48, 57, *73,* 86, *98*
Sargent, G., 214, *237*
Satov, O., 175
Saul, E. U., 9, 11, 12, 13, 15, 16, 21, 27, 34, *37, 40,* 83, *97*
Sawyer, R., 77, 82, 83, 86, 87, 88, 95, *96*
SCANS (The Secretary's Commission on Achieving Necessary Skills), 61, 67, *74*
Scardamalia, M., 7, 9, 16, 21, 23, 24, 34, *35, 36, 40,* 45, 50, 51, *73,* 94, *97,* 224
Schackel, B., 101, *118,* 213, *237*
Schaefermeyer, M. J., 123, *136*
Schank, R. C., 44, 47, *73*
Schare, B. L., 48, *73*
Schick, J. E., 59, *73*
Schiefele, U., 58, *73*
Schmitz, J., 13, 16, 27, *40,* 292, 293, *305*
Schneiderman, B., 18, *40,* 125, *136,* 168, *178*

Schnotz, W., 8, 19, 20, *40*
Schon, D. A., 23.*40*
Schreiner, R., 77, 81, *97*
Schriver, K., 137, *158*
Schuler, W., 243, *263*
Schultz, C. W., 190, *210*
Schultze, S. K., 58, *69*
Schumacher, G., 216, *237*
Schwartz, B. J., 190, *209*
Schwartz, D., 20, 34, *35*
Schwarz, E., 169, *175, 179*
(The) Secretary's Commission on Achieving Necessary Skills (SCANS), 61, 67, *74*
Seidenberg, M. S., 26, *39*
Sereno, S. C., 11, *39*
Severinson Eklundh, K., 121, 122, 123, 124, 125, 126, 127, 128, 129, 130, 131, 132, 133, 134, 135, *136,* 137–157, 138, 149, 153, *158, 159*
Sewell, E. H. Jr., 123, *136*
Shanahan, T., 44, 60, 61, 62, *73, 74*
Sharples, M., 137, 157, *159*
Shasha, D., 245, *262*
Shebilske, W. L., 191, *211*
Sheingold, K., 67, *73*
Shepard, R. N., 173, *179*
Shields, M., 56, *70*
Shim, M. J., 193, *212*
Shneiderman, B., 5, *6,* 165, 166, 170, *179,* 214, 228, 236, *237,* 246, *262,* 266, 286
Short, E.J., 59, *73*
Shulman, G. L., 168, *177*
Signer, B. R., 50, *74*
Silverstein, L. D., 166, *179*
Simon, H. A., 254, *263*
Simpson, A., 233, *237,* 247, *263,* 274, 286
Siskind, T. G., 191, *211*
Sjöholm, C., 138, *159*
Slater, W., 82, 85, 95, *96*
Slotta, J. D., 16, *36*
Smith, J., 243, *263*
Smith, J. B., 137, *158*
Smith, J. W., 256, *261*
Smith, L., 59, *75*
Smith, S. L., 167, *179*
Smith Lea, N., 8, 23, 24, *40*
Smith, T., 82, 85, 95, *96*

Snyder, H. L., 186, *211*
Soled, S. W., 48, *73*
Songer, N. B., 15, 16, *39*
Southall, S. D., 139, *158*
Spiro, R. J., 5, 12, 13, 15, 16, 17, 20,
  27, *40*, 45, 50, 54, *71*, *74*, 249,
  255, *264*, 287–303, 288, 291,
  292, 294, 295, 296, 298, 299,
  300, 301, *303*, *304*, *305*
Spratt, J. A., 59, *75*
Sproull, L., 122, 127, *136*
SRI, Inc., 67, *74*
Stark, H. A., 15, *41*
Stein, N. L., 10, 11, 12, 13, *41*
Steinberg, E. R., 20, 21, *41*, 77, 78, *98*
Sternberg, R. J., 251, *264*
Stewart, T. F. M., 164, *179*, 219, *235*
Sticht, T., 184, *211*
Stieger, D., 244, 258, *261*
Stotsky, S., 60, *74*
Stotts, P. D., 242, *264*
Stoutjesdijk, E., 18, *35*
Stratman, J., 137, *158*
Streitz, N. A., 243, *264*
Suchman, L., 107, 112, *119*
Sundblad, Y., 128–135
Swallow, J., 7, 23, *40*, 94, *97*

T

Tan, K. C., 170, *176*
Tannen, D., 25, 26, *41*
Tao, L., 49, *73*
Taylor, B. M., 86, *98*
Taylor, G. B., 186, *211*
Taylor, S. E., 167, *179*
Teasley, B., 265, 266, 267, 268, 269,
  270, 271, 272, 273, 274, 275,
  276, 277, 278, 279, 280, 281,
  282, 283, 284, *285*
Temple, C., 62, *72*
Tengs, T. O., 193, *208*
Tennyson, R. D., 20, 21, *41*
Thimbleby, H., 127, 130, 132, *135*
Thompson, R. H., 242, *264*
Thorndike, E. L., 58, *74*
Thorndyke, P., 216, 224, *237*
Thuring, M., 243, *264*
Tierney, R. J., 44, 60, 61, *74*
Tiessen, E., 27, *41*
Tinker, M. A., 183, 185, 187, 192, *211*
Tobias, S., 80, *98*

Tombaugh, J., 169, *179*, 246, *264*
Trabasso, T., 11, 13, *41*, 48, *74*
Trast, S., 172, *177*
Travis, D. S., 166, *179*
Treu, S., 174, *176*
Treurniet, W. C., 163, 168, *178*, 217,
  236
Tricot, A., 5, 239–260
Trigg, R. H., 156, *158*
Tripp, S. D., 252, *264*
Trueman, M., 191, *209*
Trumbull, D., 56, *74*
Tullis, T. S., 166, *179*, 192, *212*
Turner, J. C., 56, 57, 58, *72*
Turner, S. V., 50, *74*
Turoff, M., 122, *135*, 266, *284*
Turtle, H. R., 242, *261*
Tyler, S., 51, *74*

U

U.S. Congress Office of Technology Assessment, 51, *74*

V

van Dam, A., 162, *180*
van den Broek, P. W., 11, 13, *41*
van der Berg, S., 48, *75*
Vanderbilt University Cognition and
  Technology Group, 8, 12, *36*
van Dijk, T. A., 8, 12, 16, *38*, *41*, *42*,
  47, *75*, 80, *98*, 107, 110, *119*,
  182, 183, *212*, 216, 220, *237*,
  258, *264*
Van Dyke Parmak, H., 45, 56, *75*
van Nes, F. L., 167, 170, *178*
van Oostendorp, H., 1–6, 8, 16, 34, *42*,
  48, *70*, 138, *158*, 168, 170, 175,
  176, *179*, 256, *264*
van Orden, K. F., 193, *212*
van Rijsbergen, K., 242, *264*
van Waes, L., 138, *159*
Varma, S., 12, 13, 34, *37*, *38*
Varnhagen, C. K., 13, *38*
Vartabian, A. G., 170, *179*, 192,
  212
Vispoel, W. L., 13, 16, 27, *40*, 292,
  293, *305*
Voss, J. F., 14, *42*, 51, *74*
Vye, N. J., 12, 20, 34, *35*
Vygotsky, L., 23, *42*

W

Wade, S. E., 59, *75*
Waern, Y., 122, *135*
Wagner, D. A., 59, *75*
Wagner, R. K., 251, *264*
Waller, R., 216, 220, *237*
Walsh, P., 15, 20, *39*, 214, 231, 236
Wang, X. H., 246, *264*
Ward, D., 27, *41*
Ward, N. J., 171, *177*
Wasik, B. A., 56, 57, 58, *72*
Waterworth, J. A., 274, 286
Watt, J. H., 48, *75*
Waynant, P., 82, *96*
Weber, I., 137, *158*
Weldon, L. J., 165, 168, *177*, 186, 192, *210*
Weyer, S. A., 245, 251, *264*
Whalley, P., 226, *237*
White, H., 288, *305*
White, S. H., 56, *71*
Whitehead, A. N., 8, *42*
Wilkins, A. J., 168, *179*
Wilkins, H., 124, *136*
Wilkinson, R. T., 163, *179*, 218, *237*
Williams, D. R., 166, *179*
Williams, J. R., 192, *212*
Williamson, N. L., 171, *179*

Willingham, Mark. G., 77–95
Wilson, T., 226, *237*
Winograd, P. N., 59, 71, *75*
Witte, R., 59, *75*
Wittgenstein, L., 292, 299, 300, *305*
Woodruff, E., 7, 23, *40*, 94, *97*
Wright, C., 186, *212*
Wright, P., 163, 169, 170, *179*, 217, 221, 222, 225, 227, *237*, *238*, 239, 240, 242, 244, 245, 246, 248, 251, 252, 253, *260*, *264*
Wrolstad, M.E., 187, 191, *210*

X

Xiadong, Lin, 34

Y

Yaginuma, Y., 162, *180*
Yamada, H., 162, *180*
Yankelovich, N., 162, *180*
Yuill, N., 82, *98*

Z

Zack, M. H., 126, 129, *136*
Zaenen, A., 163, *175*
Zanting, A., 18, *35*
Zech, L., 20, 34, *35*
Zook, K. B., 294, 295

Subject Index

A

Access structures, 171, 220. *See also* Navigation
  CHI Infobooth, 269–270–275
  hierarchical format, 203, 247–252
  of hypertext, 247–252
"Accuracy" of reading, 217–218
Achievement, locus of control in, 59
Activity models, 252–260
  cognitive activity, 254–255
  cognitive task model, 254
  rational task model, 253–254
  reading hypertext, 255–259
    content processing, 258–259
    goal evaluation, 255–257
    topic selection, 257–258
Adaptive flexibility in cognitive flexibility, 301–302
Adults
  search skills, 245
  task strategies, 88–89, 227–228
Advanced learning
  cognitive flexibility theory in, 291–293
    adaptive flexibility, 301–302
    complexity, 295–296
    context-dependency, 296–298
    goals, 294–303
    inexhaustibility of understanding, 299–300
    interconnectedness, 298–299
    multiplicity, 294–295
    openness in conceptual structures, 300–301
  connecting reading and writing, 60–61
  hypertext in, 17, 50–51
  linear text, 12, 15
  printed media, 50–51

Age
  hypertext advantages and, 17
  type of research and, 50
Aggregating in information use, 255
Air Force service personnel, 52–55
Algorithms, 173
Alphabetical structure, 247, 250
Alternating in e-mail, 129
Annotation, 170
  in hypertext environment, 22
  in paper model for computer-based writing, 156
Argumentative task in *Paper* software, 149–150
Artifact structure, 220
Assessment
  in Computer Supported Intentional Learning Environment, 28–31
  of hypertext usability, 266–267
  of reading performance in hypermedia, 3, 8, 22
  of screen design, 207–208
  of strategic knowledge, 57–58
  of usability, 101–102
Automaticity theory, 48

B

Background information. *See* Prior knowledge
Balance in screen design, 204
Books. *See* Paper media
Boys, in communication, 65
Browsing, 228
Bush, Vannevar, 18

C

Case of characters, 170, 192, 195
Causal mechanisms, 13, 17
Character size, 163, 169, 194–195

CHI'89 InfoBooth, 269–275
Cloze, 82–84, *85*
Cognition. *See* Comprehension; Learning strategies
Cognitive activity, 254–255
Cognitive flexibility theory, 50–51, 287–303
  adaptive flexibility, 301–302
  in advanced learning, 291–303
  complexity, 295–296
  context-dependency, 296–298
  hypertext and cognition, 290–291
  inexhaustibility of understanding, 299–300
  interconnectedness, 298–299
  multiplicity, 294–295
  openness in conceptual structures, 300–301
Cognitive overhead, 244
Cognitive science
  in electronic text processing, 2
  in hypertext design, 102–105
Cognitive task model, 254
Collaborative learning
  Computer Supported Intentional Learning Environment, 23–33
    grade school science project, 27–33
    instructional emphasis, 24
    technology, 23
    in undergraduate class, 24–27
  hypertext in
    Lego design, 89–90
    preservice teacher program, 90–93
    science report, 93–94
College students
  comprehension of electronic information, 49
  Computer Supported Intentional Learning Environment, 24–27
  prior knowledge in interactive process, 52–55
  search skills, 245–245, 250–251, 257
  task strategy resources, 87
  type of research on, 50
Color blindness, 165
Color in text presentation, 165–167, 192–193
Columnar arrangements, 186, 193, 204
Communal database system, 23–33
  grade school science project, 27–33

instructional emphasis, 24
  technology, 23
  in undergraduate class, 24–27
Communication
  e-mail, 4, 121–133
    basic properties, 123
    in breaking barriers, 65
    connecting reading and writing, 61–65
    dialogue perspective, 122–125
    interface of dialogue, 125–133
    perspectives on use, 122
    trace process, 33
    rich vs. lean, 126–127
Complexity in cognitive flexibility, 295–296
Complex knowledge. *See* Advanced learning
Comprehension
  cognitive ergonomics and computer science perspective, 2
  cognitive science perspective, 2
  in hypertext environment
    applicability of linear strategies, 16–17, 26, 78–79
    assessment, 8, 18–19
    communal database, 26–27, 32–33
    Computer Supported Intentional Learning Environment, 23–33
    skills required, 19–23
    structure, 17–18, 78–79
    task in, 227–228
  during interactive processes
    prior knowledge, 51–55
    strategic knowledge, 56–58
  interest and, 58, 60
  models, 7–8, 9–17, 80, 182–183, 216–217
  outcomes vs. process, 47–51
  paper vs. electronic media, 163–165, 217–219
  readability, 187–194
  resources for in electronic text, 3, 77–95
    context strategy, 89–94
    requirements of readers, 78–79
    task strategy, 86–89
    text, 79–86
  screen characteristics, 186
  structure of information vs. process, 12

Computer-based writing, paper model, 137–157
  advantages of paper media, 139–140
  direct manipulativeness, 154–155
  evaluation of, 147–151
  functionality and interface, 140–141
  numbering pages, 147
  orientation and navigation, 144–145
  overview of text, 145–147, 152–154
  Paper program, 140–157
  planning, reviewing, and cooperation, 155–157
  spatial position of text, 152
  writer's perspective of text, 137–139
  writing and editing process, 141–144
Computer science, in electronic text processing, 2
Computer Sciences Electronic Magazine, 268–269, 283
Computers in classroom, 65–68
Computer-supported collaborative work, 128
Computer Supported Intentional Learning Environment (CSILE), 23–33
  grade school science project, 27–33
  instructional emphasis, 24
  technology, 23
  in undergraduate class, 24–27
COM system, 124, 127–128, 131, 133
Conceptual structures in cognitive flexibility, 300-301
Considerateness of text, 78
Content monitoring, 28–31
Content processing in hypertext reading, 258–259
Context
  in cognitive flexibility, 296–298
  in electronic mail, 131–133
  in reading, 108, 258–259
  in writing, 137–139, 140
Context strategy resources, 3, 78–79, 89–94
Continuous text, reading, 4, 161–175
  dynamic text presentation, 171–172
  electronic vs. paper, 161–162, 163–165
  independent variables, 165–171
  individual differences, 173–174
  interactions of variables, 172–173
  measures of, 162

  typography in, 163
  visual fatigue, 162
Conversation
  vs. e-mail, 124–125
  rich medium, 126–127
  trace process, 33
Cooperation, in computer-based writing, 155–157
Criss-crossing in cognitive flexibility, 292–293, 301
Critical thinking skill. *See* Advanced learning
Cross-connection process, 12–13
CSILE. *See* Computer Supported Intentional Learning Environment
Cues
  in hypertext, 20, 78–79, 247–252
  miscue research, 47, 49
  in screen design, 191–194, 203–204
  spatial arrangement of text, 139
  in text comprehension, 12–13, 15
Customization, of e-mail, 125–126

D

Database linking, 242
Databases
  Computer Supported Intentional Learning Environment, 23–33
  grade school science project, 27–33
  instructional emphasis, 24
  technology, 23
  in undergraduate class, 24–27
  development by learner, 22
  skills required for learning, 19
Descriptive text organization, 13–14
Desert Shield software, 200, 206
Design
  Task, Information, Manipulation, and Standard Reading framework in, 115–117
  theory and, 103–106
  user-centered, 101–103
Dialogue, in e-mail, 4, 122–125
  interface aspects, 126–133
Directive cues, 191–193, 203–204
Directness, in e-mail, 126
Discourse types, 220–221
Disorientation, 244
Distance between reader and material, 169

Domain modeling, 240
Dynamic text presentation, 171–172

E
Economic issues, 67
Editing
  HyperReport software, 93
  Paper software, 141–144, 155–157
  screen size in, 138
Educational psychology, in hypertext
    design, 103–104
Electronic bulletin boards, 62–65
Electronic games, 59–60
Electronic journals, 225, 227–228
Electronic mail, 4, 121–133
  basic properties, 123
  connecting reading and writing, 61–
    65
  dialogue perspective, 122–125
  interface, 125–126
    discourse context, 131–133
  grasp of current situation, 127–128
    interactivity and turn-taking, 128–
    130
    lack of feedback, 131
  as lean medium, 126–127
  perspectives on use, 122
  speed of communication, 123–124
  templates for discourse types, 130
Electronic text. *See also* Computer-
    based writing; Hypertext
  vs. paper, 100
  "accuracy of reading," 217–218
  advantages of electronic, 162
  comprehension, 229–231
  fatigue effects, 218
  reading speed and comprehension,
    163–165, 191, 197, 217–
    219
  user preferences, 22, 219
  reading continuous text, 4, 161–175
    dynamic text presentation, 171–
    172
    electronic vs. paper, 161–162,
    163–165
    independent variables, 165–171
    individual differences, 173–174
    interactions of variables, 172–173
    measures of, 162
    typography in, 163
    visual fatigue, 162

resources for comprehension in, 3,
    77–95
  context strategy, 89–94
  requirements of readers, 78–79
  task strategy, 86–89
  text, 79–86
screen design, 4, 181–208
  legibility, 184–187
  organization, 198–204
  readability, 187–194
  reader involvement, 184
  research issues, 206–208
  theoretical basis, 182–183
  typography and spatial factors,
    194–198
  visual interest, 204–206
Task, Information, Manipulation, and
    Standard Reading framework
  components, 106–112
  as theory for design, 115–117
  verbal protocols, 112–115
Electro-Text, 22
Elementary school students. *See* Grade
    school students
E-mail. *See* Electronic mail
Encyclopedia, 248
Endangered species, 27–33
Engine systems, 52–55
Enumeration terms, 20
Envisionments, 16–17
Eudora mail system, 133
Evaluation. *See* Assessment
Exceptional students, electronic com-
    munication, 65
Exploring in information use, 255
Expository text characteristics, 78
External locus of control, 59
External supports
  ineffectiveness, 20–21
  prior knowledge in interactive pro-
    cess, 54
Eye movements, 225–226

F
Factual knowledge, 51
Far transfer performance, 21
Fatigue effects, 162, 218
Feelings Questionnaire, 218
Flashing, 193
Flexibility in cognitive flexibility, 301–
    302

Flicker, 167
Footprints, 247
Format, 184–185, 188–190, 247–252
Formative experiments, 67
Frame, 221–224
Full serial reading, 228

G

g1BIS, 243
Gender, in communication, 65
Girls, in communication, 65
Glasgow Online, 275–277, 283
Global context
   in content processing, 258–259
   in reading, 108
   in writing, 137–139, 140
Goal evaluation in hypertext reading,
   255–257
Grade school students
   collaborative learning, *92*, 93–94
   Computer Supported Intentional
      Learning Environment, 27–33
   connecting reading and writing, 62–
      65
   reading achievement level and on-
      screen choices, 49–50
   task strategy resources, 87–88
   type of research on, 50
Graphical signals
   in comprehension, 15
   in hypertext, 20, 247
Graphics. *See also* Typography
   nonlinearity of, 9
   in screen design, 201–202, 203,
      204–206

H

Harmony in screen design, 204, 205–
   206
Headings, 191, 202, 282
Hierarchical format, 203, 247–252,
   274
Highlighting, 170
High school students
   cloze and maze, 83–84
   search skills, 245–246
   text resources and vocabulary, 80
   type of research on, 50
Human information usage. *See* Users
HyperHolmes I and II, 277–281, 283–
   284

HyperReport, *92*, 93–94
Hypertext. *See also* Electronic text
   assessment of learning, 3
   classification, 221–224
   cognitive flexibility theory, 287–303
      adaptive flexibility, 301–302
      in advanced learning, 291–303
      complexity, 295–296
      context-dependency, 296–298
      inexhaustibility of understanding,
         299–300
      interconnectedness, 298–299
      multiplicity, 294–295
      openness in conceptual structures,
         300–301
      prefiguration, 287–290, 294–303
   coining of term, 18
   comprehension, vs. linear electronic,
      229–231
   assessment, 8, 18–19
   cognitive ergonomics and computer
      science perspective, 2
   cognitive science perspective, 2
   in Computer Supported Intentional
      Learning Environment, 23–
      33
   learner role in, 7–8
   linear text implications, 16–17
   organizational cues in, 15
   paper comparison, 217–219, 218–
      219
   skills required, 19–23
   structural cues, 15
   structure of environment in, 17–
      18
   defined, 266, 291
   design aspects, 4–5, 213–235
      CHI'89 InfoBooth, 269–275
      *Computer Sciences Electronic Maga-
         zine*, 268–269
      Glasgow Online, 275–277
      HyperHolmes I and II, 277–281
      information classification, 214–
         215, 219–224
      interactions, 228–235
      iterative design and redesign, 5,
         267–284
      SuperBook, 281–282
      tasks, 213–215, 224–228
      usability, 214–219, 265–268
  graphics, 9

human information usage, 3–4, 99–117
   in artifact design, 101–103
   paper vs. electronic text, 100–101
   theory and design, 103–106
   user-control vs. system control, 52–55
integrating into classroom, 65–68
interactive model of reading and, 43–69
   applicability, 43–69
   connecting reading and writing, 60–65
   interest and motivation and, 58–60
   prior knowledge and, 51–55
   processes vs. learning outcomes, 47–51
   strategic knowledge and, 56–58
   teachers and technology, 65–68
learning strategies, 3
origin, 18
search and retrieval skills, 229–231
task models, 5, 239–260
   activity models, 252–259
   analysis, 241–244
   cognitive theory in, 239–241
   representation and management, 244–252
   trace process, 33
Hyphenation, 169

I

IBM, 268–269
Inconsiderate electronic text, 88–89
Incrementalism in cognitive flexibility, 296
Indentation, 169, 203
Indexes, 247, 250
Individual differences. *See also* Users
   accommodating, 174
   age, 173–174
   in human-computer interaction, 173
Individual interest, 59–60
Inexhaustibility of understanding in cognitive flexibility, 299–300
Inferential processes, 48, 82–84, *85*
Informational text, 13–15
Information classification
   application domains, 221
   discourse types, 220–221

hypertext, 221–224
   in hypertext design, 5, 214–215, 219–224
   interaction with user and task, 228–234
   text type by structure, 220
Information science, in hypertext design, 103–104
Inserted questions, 49
Instantiated schema, 108
Instructional learning systems, 82–83
Instructional text, defined, 184
Integration
   of e-mail, 125–126
   of technology into classroom, 65–68
Interactive model in electronic environment
   e-mail, 128–131
Interactive model in electronic learning environment, 43–69
   applicability, 43–69
   connecting reading and writing, 60–65
   interest and motivation and, 58–60
   prior knowledge and, 51–55
   processes vs. learning outcomes, 47–51
   strategic knowledge and, 56–58
   Task, Information, Manipulation, and Standard (TIMS) Reading framework, 106
   teachers and technology, 65–68
   in usability, 101
Interconnectedness in cognitive flexibility, 298–299
Interest
   in interactive processes, 58–60
   situational vs. individual, 59–60
Interface. *See also* Users
   in Computer Supported Intentional Learning Environment, 27, 31–33
   in electronic text processing, 2
   in e-mail, 122, 125–126 `
      dialogue, 126–133
   in paper model for computer-based writing, 140–141, 150–151
   in reducing strategic knowledge needs, 56
Interface tools, 240
Interline spacing, 168, 196
Internal locus of control, 59

Intertextuality in cognitive flexibility, 298–299
Iterative design and redesign, 5, 267–284
  CHI'89 InfoBooth, 269–275
  Computer Sciences Electronic Magazine, 268–269
  Glasgow Online, 275–277
  HyperHolmes I and II, 277–281
  SuperBook, 281–282
  usability in, 267–268, 282–284

J

Journals
  e-mail communication, 62–65
  reading tasks and, 225, 227–228
Justification, 188–189, 196

K

Key words, 32
Kintsch and van Dijk model, 80, 216–217
Knowledge
  during interactive processes
    prior knowledge, 51–55
    strategic knowledge, 56–58
  interest and, 58, 60

L

Language, linearity, 9
Language learners, 10
Language studies, 24–27
Learners. See Users
Learning strategies
  cognitive and computer science perspectives, 2
  linear ve. nonlinear, 3
  presentation format in hypertext, 249–252
Legibility
  format, 184–185
  recognizability, 186–187
  visibility, 185–186
Lego design, 89–90
Letter recognition, 215–216
Light pens, 226
Limited attention models, 57
Linear text
  comprehension, 9–17
    assessment, 8
    vs. hypertext, 231–232

implications for hypertext, 16–17, 26
  linguistic vs. nonlinguistic input, 9
  organization of information, 10–15
  representation and task influences, 15–16
in hypertext environment, 222, 248, 250
prior knowledge and effectiveness, 52–55
reading continuous text, 4, 161–175
  dynamic text presentation, 171–172
  electronic vs. paper, 161–162, 163–165
  independent variables, 165–171
  individual differences, 173–174
  interactions of variables, 172–173
  measures of, 162
  typography in, 163
  visual fatigue, 162
Line length, 193–194, 195
Linguistic signals
  in comprehension, 15
  in hypertext, 20
Links, 240, 242, 266
Literacy, 61
Local context
  in content processing, 258–259
  in writing, 137–139, 140
Locating in information use, 255
Locus of control, 59

M

MacReader, 83, 84–85
Macropropositions, 80–81
Macrostructure, 80–81, 87
Mainstreaming, 65
Management, task, 244–252
Manipulation skills, in TIMS, 108–109
Margins, 204–205
Math teachers, 66
Maze, 82–84, 85
Meaning relationships, 9
Mental models, 3, 16–17, 47
  in assessment, 8
  in TIMS, 107–108
Mental representations, 47
  in assessment, 8
  goals and task requirements in, 16

in hypertext environment, 16–17, 243–244, 247–252
in reading, 182–183
in TIMS, 107–108
types of, 15–16
Meta-analysis, 266–267
Metacognitive processes, 20
Metamemory, 21
Microstructure, 80–81, 87
Middle school students
  cloze and maze, 83–84
  search skills, 246, 247, 256
Miscue research, 47, 49
Motivational factors, in interactive processes, 58–60
Multiplicity in cognitive flexibility, 294–295
Multiwindow display, 169, 245, 246

N

Navigation
  CHI Infobooth, 272–275
  in e-mail, 125–126
  HyperHolmes, 278
  hypertext, 56, 233–234, 248, 258
  information structure and, 222
  Paper, 144–145, 155
  in screen design, 201
Nelson, T., 18
Network structure, 248
Newspapers, 191
Nodes, 266
Non-Western cultures, 10
Notetaking, 170
  in hypertext environment, 22
  in paper model for computer-based writing, 156

O

Online databases. *See* Databases
Online encyclopedia, 248
On-screen choices, reading achievement level and, 49–50
Oral tradition, 10
Orientation
  in screen design, 201
  in writing, 139–140, 144–145, 152
Outcome-based research, 47–51
Overview. *See* Text overview

P

Paging, 169. See also *Paper* software
Paper media. *See also* Linear text
  application of models to electronic text, 2
  complex knowledge measures, 50–51
  vs. electronic, 100
    "accuracy of reading," 217–218
    advantages and disadvantages, 162, 219
    fatigue effects, 218
    reading speed and comprehension, 163–165, 191, 197, 217–219
    recall, 50
    user preferences, 22, 219
  factual knowledge measures, 50–51
  manipulation skills, 108–109
  prefiguration in, 289–290
  reader interaction with, 43–45
  search and retrieval skills, 229–231
  task in reading, 224–225
  underlining, 192
  as writing model, 137–157
    advantages of paper media, 139–140
    Paper program, 140–157
    writing model and writer's perspective of text, 137–139
Paper program
  blank areas, 150–151
  closing pages of document, 151
  direct manipulativeness, 154–155
  evaluation of, 147–151
  functionality and interface, 140–141
  numbering pages, 147
  orientation and navigation, 140, 144–145, 155
  overview of text, 139, 145–147, 152–154
  page breaks, 150
  planning, reviewing, and cooperation, 155–157
  spatial position of text, 152
  writing and editing process, 141–144
Paragraphs, 202
Perceptual issues
  reading of continuous text, 4, 161–175
    dynamic text presentation, 171–172
    electronic vs. paper, 161–162, 163–165

independent variables, 165–171
individual differences, 173–174
interactions of variables, 172–173
measures of, 162
typography in, 163
visual fatigue, 162
screen characteristics, 4, 181–208, 282
legibility, 184–187
organization, 198–204
readability, 187–194
reader involvement, 184
research issues, 206–208
theoretical basis, 182–183
typography and spatial factors, 194–198
visual interest, 204–206
writing environment, 137–140
Phaedrus (Plato), 289
Phylogenetic tree, 31, *32*
Pixel attributes, 167–168
Planning, in computer-based writing, 155–157
Plato, 289
Polarity in text presentation, 163, 167
Prefiguration
cognitive flexibility theory in, 294–303
adaptive flexibility, 301–302
complexity, 295–296
context-dependency, 296–298
inexhaustibility of understanding, 299–300
interconnectedness, 298–299
multiplicity, 294–295
openness in conceptual structures, 300–301
terminology, 288
in writing and print, 289–290
Presentation format, 184–185, 188–190, 247–252
Print media. *See* Paper media
Prior knowledge, 78
during interactive processes, 51–55
interest and, 58, 60
text resources, 86
Problem resolution organization, 14–15
Problem solving in writing, 137–138
Procedural scripts, 47
Procedural text, 13

Processes
in comprehension, 216
in reading, 215–216
Processing
in hypertext reading, 258–259
relative time spent on resources, 80–81
Proofreading, 156–157, 217–218
Proportional spacing, 169, 196
Protocols, verbal, 112–115, 226, 227–228

Q
Quoting, in electronic mail, 132–133

R
Rapid scanning, 228
Rapid serial visual presentation, 171–172
Rational task model, 253–254
Readability, 187–194
content and representation factors, 188
layout and format factors, 188–190
organizational factors, 190–194
qualities affecting, 187, 188t
text resources, 81–82
Readability formulas, 81–82
Reader response journals, 62–65
Readers. *See* Users
Reading
cognitive and computer science perspectives, 2
comprehension models and measurement, 216–217
of continuous text, 4, 161–175
access devices, 171
case, 170
dynamic text presentation, 171–172
electronic vs. paper, 161–162, 163–165
independent variables in, 165–171
individual differences, 173–174
interactions of variables, 172–173
measures of, 162
visual fatigue, 162
defined, 224
disciplines providing theories, 103–104

human information usage, 3–4, 99–
117
   in artifact design, 101–103
   paper vs. electronic text, 100–101
   theory and design, 103–106
in hypertext environment
   activity model, 255–259
   annotations, 21–22
   applicability of linear strategies,
      26, 78–79
   assessment, 8, 18–19
   Computer Supported Intentional
      Learning Environment, 23–
      33
   vs. paper, 217–219
   skills required, 19–23
   structure in, 17–18, 78–79
interactive model in electronic learn-
      ing environment, 3, 43–69
   applicability, 43–69
   connecting reading and writing,
      60–65
   interest and motivation and, 58–60
   prior knowledge and, 51–55
   processes vs. learning outcomes,
      47–51
   strategic knowledge and, 56–58
   teachers and technology, 65–68
in linear environment, 7–8
   models of, 9–17
processes involved, 215–216
resources for comprehension in hy-
      pertext, 3, 77–95
   context strategy, 89–94
   requirements of readers, 78–79
   task strategy, 86–89
   text, 79–86
screen characteristics, 4, 181–
      208
   legibility, 184–187
   organization, 198–204
   readability, 187–194
   reader involvement, 184
   research issues, 206–208
   theoretical basis, 182–183
   typography and spatial factors,
      194–198
   visual interest, 204–206
Task, Information, Manipulation, and
      Standard Reading framework
   components, 106–112

   as theory for design, 115–117
   verbal protocols, 112–115
   task in, 224–228
Reading achievement level, 49–50
Reading speed
   paper vs. electronic media, 163–165,
      197, 217
   screen characteristics, 186
Recall, 8, 19, 50, 191, 227
Recognizability, 186–187, 197–198
Redesign. *See* Iterative design and re-
   design
Reflective activity, 21
Repertory grid analysis, 222–223
Reporting task, in *Paper* evaluation,
   149–150
Representation, task, 244–245
Representation models. *See* Mental
   representations
Resolution, 168
Responsive text, 44
Retrieval skills. *See* Search and re-
   trieval
Revisions. *See* Editing
Revisiting in cognitive flexibility, 299–
   300
Rote memorization, 16
Rumelhart, D., 43–44
Running heads, 193

S
Sans serif type, 186
Scaffolding knowledge, 21, 28
Scanning, 228
Schema theoretic research, 47
Schools
   computers in classroom, 66
   funds spent on technology, 67
Science, collaborative learning, 27–33,
   92, 93–94
Science teachers, 66
Screen characteristics
   color, 165–167
   designing for instruction, 4, 181–
      208, 282
   legibility, 184–187
   organization, 198–204
   readability, 187–194
   reader involvement, 184
   research issues, 206–208
   theoretical basis, 182–183

typography and spatial factors, 194–198
visual interest, 204–206
flicker, 167
reading of continuous text and
case, 170
color, 165–167
distance between reader and material, 169
flicker, 167
highlighting, 170
hyphenation, 169
indentation, 169
interline spacing, 168
multiple windows, 169, 245–246
pixel attributes, 167–168
polarity, 167
proportional spacing, 169
resolution, 168
screen size, 168
scrolling vs. paging, 169
typography, 169
typography in, 163
visual fatigue, 162
words per screen, 168
in writing and editing, 138
Screen density, 168, 189–190
Script, 221–224
Scrolling vs. paging, 169
Search and retrieval, 19, 229–231, 241–260
task analysis
activity models, 252–260
cognitive activity, 254–255
formal approaches, 241–242
integrated approaches, 243–244
ognitive task model, 254
presentation format and, 249–251
rational task model, 253–254
representation and management244–252
structure and, 247–249
user-centered, 242–243
Searching and retrieval
in Computer Supported Intentional Learning Environment, 32
Seeding the database, 28, 31
Sentence construction, 28–31
SEPIA, 243
Serif type, 186
Signals. See Cues

Simplicity in screen design, 204
Single spacing, 193–194
Situational interest, 59–60
Situation representation, 16–17, 47, 183
Social reading context, 90–93
Socrates, 289
Software. See specific programs
Software design, classroom context as basis, 65–68
Spacing in text presentation, 168, 169, 189–190, 194–198, 201–202, 204–206
Spatial cues, 193–194
Spatial orientation, 139–140, 144–145, 152, 201
Spelling, 28–31
Spoken communication. See Conversation
Standard reading processor, 109–112
Strategic knowledge
during interactive processes, 56–58
interest and, 58
macro- vs. micro-, 56–58
Strategy resources, 3, 78–79, 86–94
Structure
in comprehension, 10–15, 17–18, 78–79
of e-mail, 125–126
in expository text, 78
of hypertext
classification, 222
cognitive flexibility theory, 293
in retrieval, 247–252
Kintsch and van Dijk model of comprehension and vocabulary, 80–81
in readability, 82
in screen design, 190–194, 198–204
spatial arrangement of text, 139
in Task, Information, Manipulation, and Standard Reading framework, 108
text resources, 85–86
in text type, 220
Students
Computer Supported Intentional Learning Environment, 26–27
locus of control, 59
Studyability, 198

SuperBook, 229–230, 248, 281–282,
283–284
System control, prior knowledge and
effectiveness, 52–55

T
Table of contents, 247
Task
in comprehension, 15–16
defined, 224
e-mail and, 122
in hypertext design, 5, 213–214,
239–260
activity models, 252–259
analysis, 241–244
cognitive theory in, 239–241
diversity of reading tasks, 224–225
effects of, 227–228
interaction with user and information type, 228–234
representation and management,
244–252
research methods, 225–227
Information, Manipulation, and Standard (TIMS) Reading framework, 3–4
assumptions of human information
usage, 105
components, 106–112
as theory for design, 115–117
verbal protocols, 112–115
in *Paper* software evaluation, 149–
150
screen design and, 197–198
in text classification, 222–223
Task strategy resources, 3, 78–79, 86–
89
Teachers
collaborative learning in preservice
program, 90–93
connecting reading and writing, 61
technology and, 65–68
Teaching methods and technology, 66–
67
Temporal mechanisms, 13, 17
Textbase, 16, 80, 183
Text browser, 281
Text overview
logical, 153
in *Paper* software, 145–147, 152–154
physical, 153

in writing, 139–140
Text resources, 3, 79–86
cloze and maze, 82–84, *85*
low-frequency vocabulary, 79–81
prior knowledge, 86
readability, 81–82
structure, 85–86
Text structure. *See* Structure
Text type
access structure in, 220
artifact structure in, 220
defined, 220
topic structure in, 220
Text worlds, 16–17
Theory and design, 103–106
Times Square format, 172
TIMS. *See* Task, Information, Manipulation, and Standard Reading
framework
Topic selection in hypertext reading,
257–258
Topic structure, 220
Top-tagging, in Computer Supported
Intentional Learning Environment, 32
Trace process, 33
Training
in search skills, 245–247
in strategic knowledge, 57–58
Transmission model of learning, 11–12
True learning, 16
Typography, 163, 169, 186, 194–198
case, 195
interline spacing, 196
justification, 196
line lengths, 195
problems with research, 196–198
type size, 194–195
type styles, 194

U
Underlining, 192
University students. *See* College stu-
dents
Unix mail system, 125, 133
Usability. *See* Users
Usenet, 132–133
Users, 3–4, 99–117. *See also* Interface
in artifact design, 101–103
control of system and prior knowl-
edge, 52–55

in electronic text processing, 2
e-mail, 125–126
in hypertext design, 5, 214–215
    assessing usability, 265–268
    electronic media vs. paper, 217–
        219
    interaction with information classi-
        fication and task, 228–234
    iterative design and redesign, 267–
        268, 282–283
    preferences in, 219
    reading processes, 215–217
individual differences
    accommodating, 174
    age, 173–174
    in human-computer interaction, 173
    in usability, 266
individual interest, 59–60
instructional text and, 184
interaction with text, 43–45
paper vs. electronic text, 100–101
search task analysis, 242–244
Task, Information, Manipulation, and
        Standard Reading framework
    assumptions, 105–106
    components, 106–112
    as theory for design, 115–117
    verbal protocols, 112–115
in text classification, 222–223
text comprehension, linear models,
        11–12
theory and design in usability, 103–
        106

V

van Dijk and Kintsch model, 80, 216–
        217
Verbal protocols, 112–115, 226, 227–
        228
Visibility qualities, 185–186
Visual fatigue, 162, 218
Visual interest in screen design, 199,
        204–206, *207*
Visual navigation, 125–126
Vocabulary, 17
    task strategy resources, 87–88
    text resources, 79–81

W

Western cultures, 10
White space, 204–205
Windows in text presentation, 169,
        245–246
Wine making, 112–115
Word processors. *See* Computer-based
        writing
Word recognition, 215–216
Words per screen, 168
Work situations, 89–90, 124–125
Writing
    connecting with reading
        benefits, 60–62
        in electronic environment, 62–65
    in hypertext environment
        annotations, 21–22
        applicability of linear strategies, 26
    hypertext vs. paper in research, 229–
        231
    paper model for computer-based,
        137–157
        advantages of paper media, 139–
            140
        direct manipulativeness, 154–155
        evaluation of, 147–151
        functionality and interface, 140–
            141
        numbering pages, 147
        orientation and navigation, 144–
            145
        overview of text, 145–147, 152–
            154
        Paper program, 140–157
        planning, reviewing, and coopera-
            tion, 155–157
        spatial position of text, 152
        writer's perspective of text, 137–
            139
        writing and editing process, 141–
            144
    prefiguration in, 289–290
    surface text cues, 12–13